BEST BACKCOUNTRY SKIING IN THE NORTHEAST

SECOND EDITION

**50 CLASSIC SKI AND SNOWBOARD TOURS
IN NEW ENGLAND AND NEW YORK**

David Goodman

Appalachian Mountain Club Books
Boston, Massachusetts

AMC is a nonprofit organization, and sales of AMC Books fund our mission of protecting the Northeast outdoors. If you appreciate our efforts and would like to become a member or make a donation to AMC, visit outdoors.org, call 800-372-1758, or contact us at Appalachian Mountain Club, 10 City Square, Boston, MA 02129.

outdoors.org/books-maps

Distributed by National Book Network.

Front cover photograph of skier Alex Leich in Tuckerman Ravine © Jamie Walter
Back cover photograph of skier Andrew Drummond skiing Katahdin © Jamie Walter
Interior photographs by David Goodman except where noted
Cartography by Larry Garland © Appalachian Mountain Club
Locator map (pages iv–v) by Ken Dumas © Appalachian Mountain Club
Interior design by Eric Edstam
Cover design by Jon Lavalley

ISBN 978-1-62842-124-8

Library of Congress Control Number: 2020946049

The paper used in this publication meets the minimum requirements of the American National Standard for Information Sciences-Permanence of Paper for Printed Library Materials, ANSI Z39.48-1984. ∞

Outdoor recreation activities by their very nature are potentially hazardous. This book is not a substitute for good personal judgment and training in outdoor skills. Due to changes in conditions, use of the information in this book is at the sole risk of the user. The author and the Appalachian Mountain Club assume no liability for accidents happening to, or injuries sustained by, readers who engage in the activities described in this book.

Interior pages and cover are printed on responsibly harvested paper stock certified by The Forest Stewardship Council®, an independent auditor of responsible forestry practices. Printed in the United States of America, using vegetable-based inks.

FSC
www.fsc.org
MIX
Paper from responsible sources
FSC® C005010

5 4 3 2   20 21 22 23 24

To Sue
Who I will follow anywhere

LOCATOR MAP

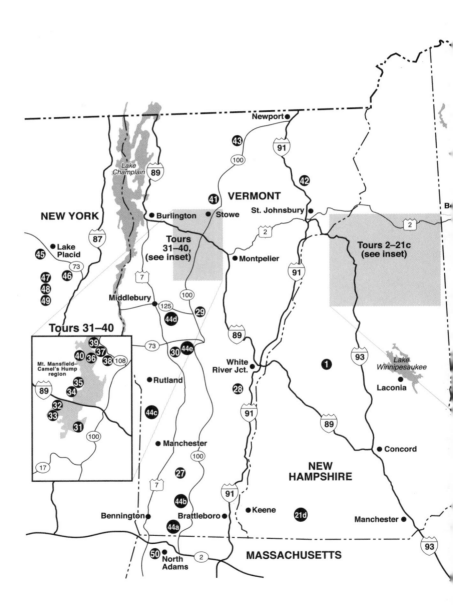

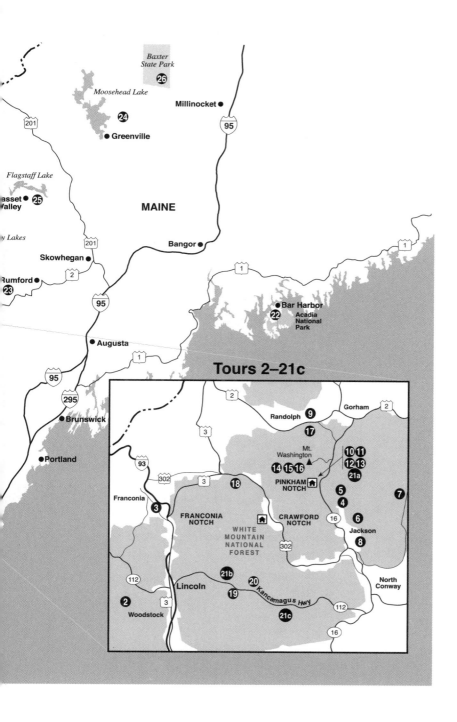

Tours 2–21c

MAINE

Baxter State Park 26

Moosehead Lake

Millinocket ●

95

24

● Greenville

Flagstaff Lake

asset ● 25
alley

y Lakes

Skowhegan ●

Rumford ● 23

Bangor ●

● Bar Harbor
22
Acadia
National
Park

● Augusta

● Brunswick

● Portland

Randolph 9

Gorham 2

● 17

Mt. Washington ▲
14 15 16
PINKHAM NOTCH

10 11
12 13
21a

5
4

7

Franconia

3

FRANCONIA NOTCH

18

CRAWFORD NOTCH

16

6

Jackson

8

WHITE MOUNTAIN NATIONAL FOREST

302

North Conway

112

Lincoln

21b

20 Kancamagus Hwy

19

112

2 3

Woodstock

21c

16

93

302

LEGEND

Federal Land
State Land
Municipal Land
Private Conservation Land
Easement

————— Ski Tour
- - - - Alternate Route
– – Gully, Glade, or Snowfield
————— Connecting Trail
 Backcountry Area

On route	Off route	
🏠	🏠	Lodge, Cabin, or Hut
🛆	🛆	Campground
⊏	⊏	Shelter
◿	◿	Tentsite
P	P	Parking
Ⓐ	Ⓐ	Appalachian Trail

△ Four Thousand Footer

▲ Peak or summit

Ⓔ Emergency Cache

➘ Gate

TABLE OF CONTENTS

Locator map iv
Author's Note: An Invitation to the Revolution xi
Preface: The Backstory xiii
Acknowledgments. xv
The Backcountry World xvii
    The Northeastern Renaissance xvii
    Tour Ratings xxiv
    Ski Equipment. xxvi
    Mountaineering Skills xxx
    Avalanche Awareness xxxiii

SECTION 1
NEW HAMPSHIRE
❶ Mount Cardigan. 1
❷ Mount Moosilauke 7
❸ Cannon Mountain. 14
❹ Black Mountain Ski Trail 19
❺ Wildcat Valley Trail. 23
❻ Doublehead Ski Trail. 28

Granite Backcountry Alliance Glade Zones 32
❼ Baldface Mountain 33
❽ Maple Villa 36
❾ Crescent Ridge 39

Mount Washington and the Presidential Range 43
❿ Tuckerman Ravine: A Guide for Skiers and Riders 44
⓫ Avalanche Brook Ski Trail 67
⓬ Gulf of Slides 71
⓭ John Sherburne Ski Trail. 76
⓮ Great Gulf. 80
⓯ Oakes Gulf and Monroe Brook 87
⓰ Burt and Ammonoosuc Ravines. 92
⓱ King Ravine 98

18 Zealand Falls Hut Tours 103
19 Greeley Ponds. 108
20 Sawyer Pond 111
21 Recommended Ski Tours in New Hampshire 114

SECTION 2
MAINE
22 Acadia National Park 123
23 Rumford Whitecap and Black Mountain 130
24 Lodge-To-Lodge Skiing in the 100-Mile Wilderness 134
25 Maine Huts & Trails 141
26 Katahdin and Baxter State Park. 146

SECTION 3
VERMONT
27 Stratton Pond 159
28 Mount Ascutney 164

RASTA Backcountry Zones 167
29 Braintree Mountain Forest 169
30 Brandon Gap 173

Camel's Hump 177
31 Monroe Trail. 178
32 Honey Hollow Trail. 182
33 Bald Hill 186

Bolton Backcountry 189
34 Woodward Mountain Trail. 192
35 Bolton–Trapp Trail 198

Mount Mansfield Region 205
36 Teardrop Trail. 206
37 Bruce Trail 211
38 Skytop Trail. 218
39 Steeple Trail 223
40 Nebraska Notch and Dewey Mountain 228
41 Sterling Valley. 233
42 Willoughby State Forest 237
43 Big Jay 242
44 Recommended Ski Tours in Vermont. 247

SECTION 4
NEW YORK

The Adirondacks: A Ski History 257
45 Jackrabbit Trail...263
46 Johns Brook Valley Hut Skiing.......................................268
47 Wright Peak Ski Trail 273
48 Avalanche Pass and Lake Colden 279
49 Mount Marcy 284

SECTION 5
MASSACHUSETTS

50 Thunderbolt Ski Trail, Mount Greylock..............................291

Postscript: Saving Winter...299
Leave No Trace 301
Index...305
About the Author 311
AMC Books Updates 312

AUTHOR'S NOTE

AN INVITATION TO THE REVOLUTION

Welcome to the backcountry skiing revolution.

In the first edition of this guidebook, published in the late 1980s under the title *Classic Backcountry Skiing*, I wrote about a backcountry skiing renaissance. I chronicled the growing interest in reviving 1930s-era ski trails and the evolution of equipment and technique that allowed skiers to travel to high and wild places.

That renaissance grew into a thriving and boisterous subculture that pushed the boundaries of skiing away from resorts into untracked frontiers. Telemark skiers led the initial charge, but snowboarders and alpine skiers eventually followed. I use the term *skiing* throughout this book to refer to all these ways of sliding on snow.

Interest in backcountry skiing has now exploded. With innovative alpine touring gear and splitboards, anyone who can ski can backcountry ski.

From this passion for traveling in wild places, a movement has taken root. Backcountry skiers, traditionally secretive and solitary, have banded together to do something that has not been done since the 1930s: team up with conservationists and local communities to develop and protect new backcountry ski terrain. Hundreds of people from near and far come together for festive work weekends to create what they will later ski.

Backcountry skiers are working together to both save their habitat and blaze new ground. Community-supported skiing—like community-supported agriculture (CSA), but for skiing—has spread from Vermont to New Hampshire to Maine and beyond. Backcountry skiing has emerged from the shadows to become part of the fabric of rural areas.

What began as a renaissance became a movement, and is now a revolution that has changed the face of skiing.

This revolution is about much more than skiing; it's about community. When we build trails, we build connections. With the land and with other people.

Backcountry skiers are completing a circle. When the Civilian Conservation Corps traveled to struggling rural towns in the wake of the Great Depression, it didn't merely create ski trails. It restored hope. It built a foundation for a better future.

When I first wrote a backcountry skiing guidebook for New England in the 1980s, I paid tribute to this generous effort by a previous generation to share the beauty and joy of wild places. I hoped that a new generation would pick up the torch that had been lit by these pioneers. And I wanted to bring people together.

Community is the antidote to isolation and conflict. It is how social change happens, how we tackle climate change and save winter. It is how we build peace. Community is the seed from which all good things grow.

Consider this book an invitation. Come for the skiing. Stay for the community. Build a brighter future. Join the revolution.

— D.G.

PREFACE

THE BACKSTORY

Three decades ago, I embarked on a journey across the Northeast and through history to write a backcountry skiing guidebook. As I write this thirtieth-anniversary edition, I thought I would share how that winding journey came about.

In 1987, I received a call (no email back then) from the Appalachian Mountain Club (AMC) asking me if I would write a book about backcountry skiing in New England.

I was a budding journalist, ski bum, political activist, and climber and had never written a book. The invitation seemed incredible: somebody wanted to hire me to sniff out and write about the best powder skiing? Sure, I gamely replied.

I spent a winter living out of my 1974 Dodge Dart, skiing my brains out all over New England with my friends. At that time, I was working as a mountaineering instructor for the Hurricane Island Outward Bound School in Maine, which provided me with a large pool of marginally employed comrades who were always up for insane adventures. I provided plenty of those.

My editors foolishly left it to my discretion how to approach the subject. I decided to combine my passion for history with my love for high and wild places by writing a historical guidebook about skiing in the highest mountains of New England. In the 1980s, only a handful of intrepid telemarkers were skiing in the great ranges of the Northeast. But I had heard stories about how skiers had been crisscrossing the high peaks of New England since the 1920s. I wanted to find out where these skiers had gone and hear their tales. Perhaps, I speculated, the seeds they planted could blossom again.

I sought out and interviewed many of the people who designed, cut, and skied trails in the 1930s and 1940s. As they told me about this rich era of ski exploration, a forgotten subculture came back to life. I set off in search of their creations. It was like hunting for buried treasure. I felt a thrill every time I found and skied one of the historic trails, as if I were reconnecting part of New England's past with its present. Thus was born *Classic Backcountry Skiing: A Guide to the Best Ski Tours in New England*, which AMC published in 1988.

Classic Backcountry Skiing included 33 ski tours in all six New England states. I figured 100 skiers would buy it, and I would know 95 of them. To my amazement, the book had a wide audience. I often saw tattered, loose-leaf copies (the pages fell out due to defective binding) on car dashboards at trailheads all around New England. The book won two national awards, and *Backcountry Magazine* dubbed it "the Eastern backcountry bible." *Classic Backcountry Skiing* came out just as interest in backcountry skiing in the Northeast was growing. People were looking for an alternative to the increasingly industrialized downhill ski scene. They found it right in their own backyards.

A decade later, it was time for an update. I expanded my coverage of backcountry skiing into the Adirondacks, one of my favorite mountain ranges. *Backcountry Skiing Adventures: Classic Ski and Snowboard Tours in Maine and New Hampshire* came out in 1999, followed two years later by a second volume that covered Vermont and New York. I included snowboarding in an effort to help point the way for riders seeking freedom and looking for wilder snow, just as backcountry skiers were doing in the 1980s. A twentieth-anniversary edition followed in 2010, *Best Backcountry Skiing in the Northeast: 50 Classic Ski Tours in New England and New York.*

Since that first edition, I have had great company in life and on the trails: my kids, Jasper and Ariel, and my wonderful wife and fellow adventurer, Sue Minter. I also have been busy pursuing my passion for investigative journalism and writing books about people and movements that are changing the world. That's my excuse for taking several years to research and write a ski book that it took me a year to do in the late 1980s.

This book has significantly changed over the years. Trails have been rerouted and renamed, and some have vanished. Tours that were once great to ski have deteriorated to the point that I no longer feel they qualify as "classics" (apologies if you discovered this the hard way). Other old trails—such as the Thunderbolt, once a faint shadow—have been given new life. While the first edition included just two hut-based ski tours, the current edition includes five, including two wonderful hut-to-hut routes in Maine.

Venturing into the wilds often involves misadventures, and researching this book had its share of them. There was the time my partner broke a ski halfway through a 20-mile traverse of the Pemigewasset Wilderness; the snowshoers I encountered in New Hampshire who were clinging to life high up in a tree, terrified of a moose calf on the trail; the easy ski tour in the Northeast Kingdom of Vermont that ended in getting lost and hitchhiking 20 miles back to my car in the dark; and the ski patrollers in Vermont who threatened to arrest me for emerging onto a ski area from the Long Trail. Luckily, petty tyrants are no match for backcountry skiers; glade skiing turns out to be an enjoyable way to elude the sheriff.

I have been elated, humbled, and humored by these beautiful mountains during the decades that I have been lost and found while skiing here. I hope that this book inspires your own adventures. It doesn't matter where you go, only that you go. May these snowy summits entice you to venture out in the rarefied mountain air, embrace you with powder, and feed your soul, as they have done for me.

ACKNOWLEDGMENTS

The best ski tours are the ones enjoyed with friends. I am grateful to many people who joined me on the trail, and hope it was more pleasure than misery. The conversation made every adventure fun, whether the skiing was heavenly or hateful. Thanks to my partners during the research for this edition: Steve Amstutz, Alec Brecher, Lindsay Deslauriers, Adam Deslauriers, John and Sue Dillon, Dan Elliot, Jonathan and Kate Goldberg, Barry Goodman, Elaine Gordon, Rick Jenkinson, Patrick Kane, Jim Lyall, Belle McDougall, Bill Minter, Brad Moskowitz, Daniel Moss, Skip Repetto, Sharon Sisler, Kirk Siegel, Lee Spiller, Caroline Weaver, Jon Williams, Eriks Ziedins, and Ed Ziedins. To all of you, I say thanks for coming along and sorry if I stole first tracks.

Special thanks to the pioneers of the community-supported skiing movement for sharing their passion, knowledge, and favorite ski lines with me: Zac Freeman and Angus McCusker of the Rochester/Randolph Area Sports Trails Alliance and Tyler Ray of Granite Backcountry Alliance. You are channeling the best of the past and creating the future of skiing.

I'm deeply grateful to the people who know more than me and generously shared their expertise to help ensure the accuracy of what I write (whatever I got wrong is on me, not them). Thanks to Jeff Leich of the New England Ski Museum, Frank Carus of the Mount Washington Avalanche Center, Andrew Drummond of Ski the Whites, Josh Wilson of the Barkeater Trails Alliance, Eben Sypitkowski of Baxter State Park, Ben Leoni of Ski the East, Jason Flynn of Acadia National Park, Blair Mahar of Thunderbolt Ski Runners, Jake Risch and Dan Houde of Friends of Tuckerman Ravine, and Mike Snyder, Vermont's Commissioner of Forest, Parks, and Recreation.

Steep and deep thanks to some of New England's best ski photographers, who generously contributed images for stoke and inspiration: Jerimy Arnold, Lincoln Benedict, Arnaud Côté Boisvert, Kyle Crichton, Andrew Drummond, Cait Fitzgerald, Corey Fitzgerald, Paul Lohnes, W. Neil Fisher, David Metsky, Brian Mohr, and Jamie Walter. Thanks also to DPS Skis for its support during my research.

My gratitude to Tim Mudie, AMC senior book editor, who has offered wise counsel and shepherded this book from start to finish. Thanks also to Larry Garland, AMC's ace cartographer, and Abigail Coyle, AMC's senior book production manager, who made this assortment of words and images look beautiful.

My deepest thanks goes to my amazing kids, Ariel and Jasper Goodman. They have joined me on these trails and been my reason to return. May you blaze many of your own joyful journeys into the world.

This book is dedicated to my wife, Sue Minter. Many moons and mountains ago, she encouraged me to travel far and high and tell stories about it. She has been on this journey with me from the beginning, and she is the wind beneath my wings in the grandest adventure of all—life.

THE BACKCOUNTRY WORLD

THE NORTHEASTERN RENAISSANCE

Every time skiers glide from a trailhead and vanish into a winter wilderness, we feel like explorers setting off for the New World. Laying first tracks into the snow, we sense that we are the first visitors to these wild places.

But if the snow could speak, it would tell another story. It would simply welcome us back. For we are merely traveling in the tracks of skiers who plied these routes for decades and then mysteriously vanished.

Backcountry skiing is not a new sport in the Northeast. It is actually a revival of a sport that enjoyed its heyday in the 1930s, then fell into a long period of dormancy until recently.

The first skiers in New England were Scandinavian loggers and railroad builders in the mid-1800s who formed the first ski club in the United States in Berlin, New Hampshire, in 1882. It was later named the Fridtjof Nansen Ski Club, after the famous Norwegian Arctic explorer who skied across Greenland in 1888. Skis began appearing in Hanover, New Hampshire, and in North Adams, Massachusetts, by the turn of the twentieth century, and the popularity of the sport slowly began to pick up. Mountain skiing began attracting interest soon after people gained basic proficiency with the unwieldy new mode of travel. The first ski ascent and descent of Mount Marcy in the Adirondacks was accomplished in 1911, Mount Washington was skied in 1913, and Mount Mansfield in Vermont was first skied in 1914. Around the same time, interest in ski racing began to rise among students at Dartmouth College in New Hampshire. The first official downhill race in the country was held on New Hampshire's Mount Moosilauke in 1927.

Skiers of this early era participated in every aspect of the sport. They might be proficient at ski jumping, downhill, slalom, and cross-country skiing, sometimes called *langlauf* ("long-run") skiing. Skiers used the same skis for everything, so no distinction was made between cross-country and downhill skiing, other than where people chose to ski. It was all simply skiing. In the 1920s, ski bindings consisted of a toe bar with a leather heel strap, much like today's cable bindings. Skis were long, heavy hickory boards without metal edges, and boots were leather with a box-shaped toe.

Throughout the 1920s, skiers looking for downhill skiing opportunities in New England sought out narrow summer hiking trails, logging roads, and streambeds. This was not easy terrain to ski, and skiers soon began searching for more open slopes. Katharine Peckett, the daughter of an affluent New Hampshire inn owner, decided after returning from a vacation in Switzerland to clear a small hill near her father's inn near Franconia. She opened the first resort-based ski school in the United States in 1929. Around this same time, skiers began making forays into Tuckerman Ravine on Mount Washington. Although ski touring through the woods was still an enjoyable pastime, skiers increasingly were drawn to the thrill of a good downhill run. Skiers began traveling far and wide in search of mountains that offered the best downhill skiing.

By the 1930s, skiing had captured the imagination of New Englanders. In 1931, the first "snow trains" left North Station in Boston, headed for New Hampshire, and snow trains to Vermont began rolling out of New York City that same year. Within its first year of operation, the Boston & Maine snow train transported 8,371 passengers to New Hampshire; more than 10,000 skiers boarded the train the following year.

Equipment evolved to keep pace with the rising interest in downhill skiing. Skis with metal edges appeared, and steel cable bindings were introduced. These bindings offered the option of latching down the heel cable for skiing on steeper terrain.

The CCC: How the Great Depression Launched Skiing

A major catalyst for ski activity in the Northeast came about as a direct result of the Great Depression. President Franklin Roosevelt created the Civilian Conservation Corps (CCC) in March 1933 to provide work for unemployed men. One of the most popular New Deal programs, it had the dual purpose of addressing national conservation needs and providing jobs. During its nine years of existence, the CCC mobilized 3 million men, who worked throughout the United States on reforestation, trail construction, land erosion control, fire control, and construction of dams, bridges, roads, and buildings. The CCC left an enduring national legacy: it built an estimated 800 parks, planted nearly 3 billion trees, constructed scenic byways such as the Blue Ridge Parkway, and became a model for the modern service corps movement.

The CCC will be remembered best by New England skiers for the numerous ski trails that it built. Vermont was the greatest beneficiary in this regard, since the state's CCC contingent was under the supervision of State Forester Perry Merrill, an avid skier. Under Merrill's direction, the CCC cut some of the most famous ski runs in the East. Among the trails that still endure are the Nose Dive, Teardrop, Bruce, Ski Meister, Perry Merrill, and (Charlie) Lord trails on Mount Mansfield. In New Hampshire, the CCC's contributions include the Richard Taft Trail on Cannon Mountain, the Alexandria Trail on Mount Cardigan, Gulf of Slides Trail near Mount

Skiers climbing and descending the Taft Trail on Cannon Mountain in the 1930s. *Photo by Winston Pote, courtesy of the New England Ski Museum*

Washington, and the Wildcat Trail on the north side of Wildcat Mountain. Many other CCC contributions to skiing in New England are cited throughout this book.

Charlie Lord was the master designer of the CCC trails on Mount Mansfield. Lord, who died in 1997 at age 95, once explained to me his formula for creating the high-quality runs for which the CCC became famous: "The only guide we had was we tried to make them interesting for ourselves. We were a selfish bunch, you know. The trails were made for a fairly good skier—not experts, but we tried to pick a route that would challenge us." Very few of the CCC men were skiers, since skiing was even then a sport of the middle and upper classes. "But," said Lord, "some of them were quite enthused about skiing" and enjoyed coming out to watch the big ski races that took place on their trails.

The construction of the CCC ski trails initiated a new era of down-mountain skiing. This was the term used to describe downhill skiing in the backcountry. Down-mountain trails—also called "walk-up" trails because skiers had to hike up them in order to ski down—defined the character of skiing in the early 1930s. On some of the longer trails, such as the Bruce Trail on Mount Mansfield, hiking up and skiing down just once took a full day.

A few select trails were challenging enough to merit classification as Class A race trails. Class A trails had to have a vertical drop of 2,000 feet in approximately 1 to 1.5 miles, with at least one section having a gradient of 30 to 35 degrees. The Class A trails of the Northeast included the Nose Dive on Mount Mansfield, Taft Trail on Cannon, the Wildcat Trail on Wildcat Mountain, Thunderbolt on Mount Greylock,

Swiss ski expert Peter Gabriel comes to an elegant and timely stop above the Great Gulf, circa 1940. *Photo by Winston Pote, courtesy of the New England Ski Museum*

and Whiteface Trail on Whiteface Mountain. These were trails on which a racer could receive a coveted rating based on his or her time. "A" racers were the fastest, while "B" and "C" racers were close behind.

Ski technique was evolving from the telemark turn and snowplow to styles more suited to racing. The better coaches were advocating Christiania and stem turns, which marked the beginning of the parallel skiing technique, and people quickly abandoned the graceful telemark in favor of the faster parallel turn.

The popularity of the CCC trails changed the direction of skiing. Exploring the mountains on skis was taking a back seat to skiing established down-mountain trails. These wide ski trails were simply a joy to ski. They were a welcome relief from negotiating the narrow hiking trails.

Abner Coleman confessed in the Appalachian Mountain Club journal, *Appalachia*, in 1936:

> The direction of the movement in Vermont is following the widespread preference for downhill running. To some extent this delightful obsession is unfortunate, if only because it leaves a lot of ideal terrain to the mercy of snowshoers.
>
> The winter countryside is but little used even by those who live in it. The stampede, rather, both of natives and visitors, has been toward the localities providing down-mountain runs.

The heyday of the down-mountain trails was brief. In 1934, the first rope tow was introduced at a ski hill in Woodstock, Vermont. Within seven years, J-bars, T-bars, and chairlifts sprang up on almost every major ski mountain in New England. In 1938, an aerial tramway was erected on Cannon Mountain in New Hampshire. The CCC trails often became the nucleus of the new downhill ski areas, as was the case with the Nose Dive at Stowe in Vermont, Taft Trail at Cannon Mountain Ski Area, and Wildcat Trail at the Wildcat Ski Area. Those trails that were not crowned with a chairlift were often abandoned, to be reclaimed by the forest. This was the fate of a number of trails, including the now-defunct original Chin Clip on Mount Mansfield and Katzensteig Trail on Wildcat Mountain.

But many of the down-mountain trails survived. Some, such as the Snapper Trail on Mount Moosilauke, were preserved as hiking trails, and others, such as the Teardrop and Bruce trails on Mount Mansfield, Thunderbolt on Mount Greylock, and Tucker Brook Trail on Cannon Mountain, were maintained by dedicated local skiers. These volunteers often cleared the trails in defiance of new state and federal regulations that forbade skiing on trails not considered "safe" for the new breed of lift-served skiers. The renegade backcountry skiers were determined to preserve the experience of skiing wild snow away from the crowded ski resorts.

Fraser Noble, one of the down-mountain skiing holdouts who maintained the Pine Hill Trail on Wachusett Mountain in Massachusetts, eloquently captured the spirit of backcountry skiing, then and now. He told me:

> It's hard to convey to people who haven't done any walking for skiing what the experience is about. It's quite different than just buying an impersonal lift ticket and skiing the mountain from the top. You work hard for the run and get far more exercise than you do when just downhill skiing. The scenery is also an important part of it. These trails were not just a slash down a mountain. They had a lot of interesting natural rolls and turns in them. Also, when you walk up, you have time to have long chats with people you're skiing with. That's part of the whole ski experience, too.

The advent of lift-served skiing was the death knell for backcountry skiing—or at least prompted a period of suspended animation. Those who once flocked to the mountains of the North Country to explore new ski routes were now schussing the downhill slopes of Vermont and New Hampshire. Skiers of the era recall how the number of people skiing in the backcountry around places like Mount Mansfield dropped from about 40 on a typical weekend in the early 1930s to a half dozen by the mid-1940s.

Ski equipment evolved in ways that reflected the new interest in downhill skiing and deepened the split between downhill and ski touring. Rigid boots and bindings that locked down the heel made it impossible to ski uphill or on flat terrain. Similarly, the sport of cross-country (a.k.a. Nordic) skiing evolved its own specialized equipment. By the 1950s, Nordic gear was typified by lightweight, skinny racing skis designed for use only on groomed and tracked ski trails. Downhill and cross-country skiing parted ways, and the radically different equipment made it impossible to bridge the divide. This division continued to grow until the late 1970s.

People who cross-country skied in the backcountry during the 1950s and 1960s were a relatively small and hardy bunch. Joe Pete Wilson, who skied in Vermont and the Adirondacks and was a member of the 1960 U.S. Olympic biathlon team, recalled being asked about cross-country skiing when he worked at a ski resort in the mid-1960s. People's curiosity was piqued by the high school and college students they had seen cross-country skiing. He gave a few lessons and answered people's questions.

A cross-country skiing revival was brewing at colleges such as Dartmouth, whose ski team and coach, Al Merrill, were nationally renowned. Students noticed that Merrill and a few of his friends "would go out 'touring' after hours," recounted David Hooke in *Reaching That Peak*, a history of the Dartmouth Outing Club (DOC). In 1964, Merrill "was persuaded to give the DOC 'several pointers on ski touring.'" By January 1965, ski touring 'was fast becoming the winter's most popular sport.'" In March 1965, a DOC newsletter stated:

> [DOC] managed a surprising number of ski touring trips this winter despite the often filthy snow conditions. Large numbers of men, most of whom traveled on hand-hewn skis garnished with makeshift bindings, glided through weather as diverse as red klister and blue stick. It's a good feeling when your ski sticks on the kick and slides on the glide—an occasional bright eye, raised brow and incredulous mouth numbly muttering, "Christ, it works!!!"

A turning point in the revival of cross-country skiing was the sudden availability of inexpensive skis. In the mid-1960s, the first fiberglass downhill skis came on the market. People quickly traded in their old wooden downhill skis, which were easily converted into cross-country skis with a little shaving and narrowing to lighten them. Hooke reported that at Dartmouth, "It is understandable, given the spirit of the times, why touring would have had such appeal: not only was there now a whole lot of obsolete downhill equipment, but converting it and using it would be a great way to get away from 'it all'—meaning lift lines, crowds, and the other trappings of the 'new' Alpine skiing of the day."

The 1970s saw the growth of ski-touring centers. By the late 1970s, another small-scale revival began brewing within the world of cross-country skiing. A small group of mountaineers-turned-skiers, cross-country ski instructors, and alpine skiers who had grown bored with the lift-served ski scene wanted to add some adventure to their skiing. In an effort to combine mountain climbing with skiing, they began experimenting with using downhill skiing techniques on cross-country skis. Cross-country skiers began parallel skiing and even revived the defunct telemark turn. Experimentation and brainstorming were at a high pitch among skiers around Stowe and Killington, Vermont. The audacious Ski to Die Club was born in the Adirondacks. The publication in 1978 of Steve Barnett's classic book, *Cross-Country Downhill*, generated further excitement about the potential for Nordic skiing to access wild places.

The renewed interest in backcountry skiing generated an evolution in equipment. The lightweight skis and boots of ski tourers and racers were inadequate for the rigors of backcountry skiing. Karhu and Fischer, both with U.S. headquarters in New England at the time, were two of the earliest companies to respond to the demand from telemarkers and mountain skiers for a heavy-duty ski. The metal-edged Fischer Europa 77 went on sale in the early 1970s, and the Fischer Europa 99 and Karhu XCD-GT were introduced in 1978, becoming instant classics. Backcountry skiers now had gear to go anywhere.

By the 1990s, telemark (a.k.a. freeheel) skiers were borrowing technique and equipment from their alpine brethren and heading into the high mountains. The backcountry skiing revival was in full swing. Skiers fled the increasingly homogenized and expensive scene at ski areas in search of a wilderness experience.

Snowboarders (a.k.a. riders) joined in the quest for untamed territory. In 1977, Jake Burton began making his first snowboards in his Londonderry, Vermont, workshop. He convinced Stratton Mountain to allow his innovation on its ski slopes, and the rest is history: snowboarding boomed, its popularity driven by a new generation of snow sliders. Snowboards evolved into splitboards, a snowboard that splits in two to become skis for uphill travel and locks together as a single plank for the downhill. Riders are now a regular presence on backcountry trails.

Alpine touring (AT) gear has changed the backcountry game. AT skis and boots have become lighter, more comfortable, and higher performing. Now anyone who can downhill ski can backcountry ski. The telemark ski scene has faded as skiers have snapped up AT gear in droves and headed for the untracked hills. The increasing number of people has given rise to a movement of community-supported skiing, as groups such as Granite Backcountry Alliance in New Hampshire and the Rochester/Randolph Area Sports Trails Alliance in Vermont are crafting new backcountry ski terrain for the first time since the days of the CCC.

Skiing has come full circle since the 1930s. Skiers and riders have thrown open the door to a vast mountain landscape that they are exploring with newfound passion.

The quest for adventure and a love of the mountains has an uncanny way of transcending the barriers of time to bring together everyone who feels its pull.

TOUR RATINGS

The tours in this book were chosen because they are "classics." Classic tours in the Northeast have a special character. The mountain ranges in this region are unlike any others in the United States. Though the peaks may be smaller, they include many of the features that skiers seek out in the great ranges.

Several qualities are necessary for a tour to be considered a classic.

- **History.** Many of the tours in this book are historically significant, having formed the hub of down-mountain skiing activity nearly a century ago. Numerous trails were built by the Civilian Conservation Corps (CCC) in the 1930s. They represent an important part of the culture and history of the Northeast, as well as some of the best skiing to be found anywhere. The popularity and the enduring quality of these ski tours today are a testament to the trailblazers, who had a keen eye for choosing elegant and exciting routes.

- **Aesthetics.** A classic ski tour should highlight scenery that captures the spirit of the northeastern mountains and forests. What this area lacks in jagged skylines and vast open bowls, it makes up for in picturesque birch forests and accessible mountain summits. A classic tour may travel the full range of terrain, or it may showcase one aspect of the Northeast's special landscape.

- **Quality.** Classic tours showcase high-quality ski terrain. Quality means variety: the best tours hold your interest because they call on a full range of techniques. A classic tour might include gliding on the flats, skinning up a mountain, and skiing or riding down an exciting powder run.

In short, a classic tour has it all.

Difficulty

The ski tours in this book are intended for experienced skiers and riders who are comfortable on a variety of terrain. Most classic tours in this book feature good downhill skiing. None of the tours is intended for novice skiers. Each ski tour is rated *moderate, more difficult, most difficult,* or *ski mountaineering.*

- **Moderate.** The terrain is mostly flat with gentle hills. A snowplow or step turn is sufficient for skiing downhill. These tours are generally not suitable for snowboards.

- **More difficult.** The terrain includes extended, steeper uphill and downhill sections. Proficiency at turning on steeper terrain—using parallel, telemark, snowplow, kick turns, or other techniques—is necessary. **More difficult+** denotes trails that are on the steeper and more challenging end of this rating spectrum.

- **Most difficult.** The terrain includes continuous downhill skiing and riding on steeper trails, glades, or open slopes. The ability to link turns, sometimes quickly, is necessary.

- **Ski mountaineering.** The terrain is steep and exposed, and there may be consequences for falling. These tours require mountaineering judgment and avalanche awareness to assess the safety of the snow and ski conditions.

All of these difficulty ratings approximately describe the skills needed to ski the terrain in typical Eastern conditions: variable powder on a solid base that may be broken up by another skier's tracks. However, *conditions are everything*. A tour that is considered moderate in fresh powder can be ferocious in breakable crust. An easy ski tour can challenge the best skiers if conditions are difficult. You must know your ability to ski in various conditions and know when the conditions exceed your abilities. There is no shame in deciding to walk down a steep, narrow chute that you are not comfortable skiing; it actually takes considerable experience to know your limits.

This is a regional rating system. The rating of each tour is relative to the difficulty of other tours in the Northeast.

Backcountry Snowboarding

The steeper tours in this book—those rated *more difficult*, *most difficult*, and *ski mountaineering*—are suitable for snowboarding. Snowshoes or splitboards with climbing skins are essential for the climb. Please help promote world peace: *do not walk in the skin track,* which ruins it for other skiers and riders.

Backcountry riding in Maple Villa, Intervale, New Hampshire. *Photo by Cait Fitzgerald*

If you use snowshoes, ensure that the snowshoe bindings fit your snowboard boots, and poles are helpful for negotiating flatter sections. Enjoy the ride.

Slope Steepness

The steepness of some routes is described in terms of the angle of the slope. Skiers and climbers tend to overestimate slope angles (e.g., a 40- to 50-degree headwall may feel vertical). The most accurate way to determine the steepness of a slope is with an inclinometer, or slope meter. Better compasses have built-in inclinometers, and there are a variety of inexpensive handheld slope meters as well as phone apps that measure slope angle. Proficiency in estimating slope angles is especially important when assessing avalanche hazard, where the difference between a 20-degree slope and 35-degree slope is critical (see "Avalanche Awareness" on page xxxiii for more on this subject).

In general, 20-degree slopes are considered advanced-intermediate downhill terrain, such as the Sherburne Ski Trail on Mount Washington. Slopes of 30 degrees are advanced downhill terrain, such as the middle and lower sections of Hillman's Highway on Mount Washington. Forty-degree slopes are the realm of expert skiers. It takes experience and skill to be comfortable on slopes of this steepness, especially if the grade is sustained. An example of the latter is the top of the Tuckerman Ravine headwall, just below the Lip.

A Word about Snowmobiles

Occasionally, these ski tours intersect or coincide for a short distance with snowmobile trails. There is often antagonism between skiers and snowmobilers, and I am afraid that skiers bear some blame for whatever bad feelings exist. Skiers do not own the mountains. Snowmobilers have as much right to enjoy the outdoors on their designated trails as skiers do on ski routes. Furthermore, skiers often depend on the kindness of snowmobilers if an evacuation becomes necessary. I have seen snowmobilers provide help during emergencies, often at great inconvenience to themselves.

Skiers should declare peace. A friendly smile or wave to snowmobilers when on shared trails goes far toward restoring mutual respect and civility to these encounters in the mountains. It will also keep you from getting run over.

SKI EQUIPMENT

In the 1930s, there was only one type of ski. You couldn't go wrong: you used the same ski for cross-country, ski jumping, and downhill skiing. Today, you must choose your niche:

- **Cross-country:** Skis primarily for groomed trails or light backcountry terrain that does not involve significant downhill. Skis do not have metal edges.
- **Nordic backcountry:** Rugged cross-country skis for moderate touring where downhill control is not the priority. The skis are wider, have a full or partial

metal edge, may be waxless or waxable, and are often paired with a heavy-duty cross-country binding intended for off-trail skiing.

- **Telemark:** Alpine-style skis with a pronounced sidecut and a full metal edge, geared toward control and turning on steep terrain. They are paired with plastic telemark boots and a stiff, powerful freeheel binding.
- **Alpine touring (AT):** Also known as *randonée*, ski mountaineering, or skimo, this gear consists of alpine skis and boots with bindings that hinge at the toe for climbing but lock down the heel for the descent.
- **Splitboards:** Snowboards that split down the long axis of the board to become skis for the ascent, then fasten together to become a snowboard for the descent.

Following are general guidelines about what to look for in equipment. Gear changes rapidly, so the best resource is a ski shop that specializes in backcountry gear. For recommendations on the latest ski models and equipment, consult gear reviews in magazines such as *Backcountry* (backcountrymagazine.com) and online forums.

No single ski and boot combination does everything well. Buy equipment for the kind of terrain that you most enjoy skiing. Lightweight gear is the choice for moderate touring, and heavier equipment is best for more challenging terrain and conditions. The more skiing you do, the more equipment options you will need. Skiing is most enjoyable when you have the right tool for the job.

If you ski only occasionally, consider renting backcountry ski gear. This enables you to use the latest and most appropriate equipment for where you will be skiing. It also allows you to "try before you buy." Backcountry ski equipment can be rented in popular mountain towns such as North Conway, Lake Placid, and Stowe, as well as at some ski areas.

Boots

Good backcountry boots are the most important investment you will make. You will be in your ski boots for most of the day. Comfort is king in boot selection: if your feet are comfortable, you will be happy. If your feet hurt, no amount of pretty scenery will arrest your misery. Boots also make a critical difference in your ability to control your skis. Big skis require big boots to drive them. Make sure your equipment is well matched and that your boots match the binding system (see below).

Telemark boots will be either a 75-mm "duckbill" style toe or the New Telemark Norm (NTN). AT skiers should look for boots with tech inserts—holes on the sides of the toe and in the heel—that work with the latest generation of tech bindings (see below). Any boot designed for touring and downhill turns also should have both a ski mode and a tour or walk mode.

Skis

Ski tours rated as *moderate* in this book are best enjoyed on cross-country or Nordic backcountry gear: typically waxless or waxable skis with metal edges and backcountry boots. A good backcountry touring ski should be wide enough so it is stable in ungroomed snow and have a sidecut to facilitate turning.

The tours that are rated *more difficult* feature a good mix of uphill and downhill skiing. These tours are best skied on telemark or AT skis or on splitboards.

Tours rated *most difficult* feature more challenging downhill skiing and riding. You will enjoy these tours most on wide, heavy-duty, metal-edged telemark or AT skis or splitboards.

Backcountry skis that are shorter and wider are easier to maneuver on tight Eastern trails and woods. Wider skis offer a more stable platform for skiing crud, powder, and heavy snow, whereas a stiffer, narrower ski provides more control in steep, firm conditions.

Bindings

* **Alpine Touring: Lightweight tech bindings that mate with boots with tech fittings have revolutionized backcountry skiing.** Many are featherweight, releasable, and work well going both uphill and downhill. These are the most popular for backcountry touring. There are heavier options that offer more power and control for skiing downhill. While all AT bindings have a release mechanism, some have limited adjustability in their release tension, and only a few (generally the heavier options) are certified to the DIN standards used in alpine bindings.
* **Telemark: Heavy-duty cable bindings or the New Telemark Norm (NTN) are the best choice for telemark skiers to use in the backcountry.** Free-pivot bindings that have a tour mode—where there is no tension from the binding or boot—are a welcome energy saver over the course of a long tour. The lightweight backcountry boot-binding systems made by Salomon and Rottefella (NNN-BC) are fine for moderate touring on rolling terrain, but they do not offer adequate control on descents.

Poles

Adjustable poles are a good choice for backcountry skiing. These poles can collapse or extend, depending on the demands of the terrain. Two-section poles are simpler and less likely to collapse unexpectedly than three-section poles.

Climbing Skins

The use of climbing skins is essential on most ski tours in this book rated *more difficult* and *most difficult*. Tours rated *moderate* can generally be completed with only ski wax or waxless cross-country or backcountry skis. Climbing skins—made of fabric and covered with directional hairs or "nap"—attach to the base of the ski or splitboard. These hairs mat down when gliding forward but grip the snow when going uphill, preventing the ski from sliding backward. Skins can be made of nylon, mohair, or a combination of both. Generally, mohair skins have better glide whereas nylon have better grip, but both work well for skiing in the Northeast.

Your skins should be trimmed to your skis or splitboard and cover the bases from edge to edge. Skins that are even slightly too narrow will slip on steep terrain. If you have multiple pairs of skis of different lengths and widths, you will need multiple pairs of skins. A tail hook is a nice feature, too. Kicker skins—which cover only about half the ski length—work well on moderate terrain.

Skins require care. They should be dried out after each use, folded back together, and stored in a dry place.

Packs

Look for a solidly constructed day pack that is designed to carry skis or snowboards. Jury-rigged ski attachments can be a constant aggravation. A good ski pack should have a capacity of 25 to 35 liters. A sternum strap is crucial to stabilize the load when skiing downhill, and a well-padded waist belt makes all the difference in comfort. Look for packs with space for an avalanche shovel and probes. Cheap packs fall apart. Invest in a good pack, and it will last for years.

Odds and Ends

- **Ski helmet.** For skiing steeper terrain.
- **Eye protection is essential for skiing through trees or on trails.** Ski goggles are best, but sunglasses or sport shades will also do the job.
- **Crampons and ice ax** are useful for climbing into or out of very steep terrain (such as those rated *ski mountaineering*), especially in Great Gulf, King Ravine, on Katahdin, and for many routes in Tuckerman Ravine. Aluminum crampons that weigh less than a pound per pair and superlight aluminum alloy ice axes are ideal for skiers. Be sure the crampons fit your ski boots.
- **Headlamp.** *Of course* you will return before dark. Except when you don't.

Backcountry Repair

Your equipment *will* break. Backcountry skiing is abusive. Skis break, bindings rip out, poles pretzel, and packs detonate (trust me—it's all happened to me). You can count on each of these mishaps to occur at the worst moment.

Backcountry skiers should be equipped to perform functional field repairs. Following are useful items needed for a repair kit.

- **Screwdriver.** Bring a palm-size ratcheting driver with multiple bits (available in ski shops and some hardware store) and be sure one bit fits your binding screws.
- **Hose clamps.** Useful for quickly repairing broken poles and skis. Have some small enough to fit around a pole, and large enough to fit around overlapping broken ski ends.

- **Ski straps.** Voilé-style ski straps are indispensable for makeshift repairs, including fastening boot to skis and skins to skis. Keep a few in your pack.
- **Aluminum flashing.** Can be used to splint a broken or bent pole or ski. For a pole, wrap a section around the break and hold it in place with hose clamps. Skis can be similarly splinted.
- **Screws.** Carry extra binding screws and a few oversized screws in case a binding hole becomes stripped.
- **Spare pole basket.**
- **Lighter and ski scraper.** It's not repair gear, but you need it.
- **Nylon cord.** For binding and pack repair.
- **Multitool.** The models that include pliers, screwdrivers, wire cutters, and a knife are best.
- **Extra binding.** Telemarkers should consider keeping an extra three-pin binding in the bottom of your pack. AT skiers should have extra binding parts as well. At 0 degrees with night approaching, you'll appreciate not having to improvise.
- **Extra tip loop and tail clip.** For skin repairs.
- **Gorilla tape.** Unlike duct tape, Gorilla tape works. Wrap a wad around a pencil, ski pole, or water bottle. And keep a roll in your car to replenish your supply. It's always useful for something.

MOUNTAINEERING SKILLS

Good skiing skills will get you down the mountain. Good mountaineering skills will get you out of the mountains.

Every backcountry skier should be proficient with the skills summarized here. I strongly encourage skiers to take courses, seek mentors, and read up on wilderness skills, first aid, and especially avalanche safety.

Navigation

Trails can be especially difficult to follow in winter. Blazes on summer hiking trails are often obscured by snow or are difficult to see, particularly during snowstorms. Whiteouts, which are especially disorienting on exposed mountaintops, are not uncommon. It is essential, therefore, that skiers be proficient with backcountry navigation.

- **Map and compass.** Maps are the single most important items for navigation. Ideally, if you are following a map closely, the compass rarely comes out. Carry a waterproof topographic map of the area in which you are traveling and know how to read it.

  The best way to stay oriented with a map is to check it frequently, especially when you arrive at obvious landmarks. *Keep the map accessible at all times.* If you have to dig for it in your pack, you won't bother checking it until it is too late.

- **GPS.** Phone-based Global Positioning System (GPS) apps have become standard backcountry navigation tools. They can pinpoint where you are and where you're going. Maps for many ski tours now exist only on apps. But phones can malfunction and go dead. Carry a spare phone battery or a portable charger and cord, along with a hard copy map.

First Aid

Prevention is the key to avoiding winter emergencies. Recognizing danger signs and being alert to the condition of members of your party are critical. Medical emergencies in winter are a different ballgame than in summer. I've seen problems progress from minor to life threatening in a frighteningly short time.

All backcountry skiers should have some training in first aid, preferably in wilderness first aid. Carry a basic first-aid kit that includes blister repair materials (such as 2nd Skin or Compeed), alcohol swabs, ibuprofen, SAM splint or wire mesh splint, gauze pads, and tape.

Hypothermia and frostbite are the two most common problems in winter. Cold-weather injuries are social diseases; they can generally be avoided if all members of a party are carefully watching out for each other. Following are practical prevention tips. Consult a good wilderness first-aid resource for details on treatment.

Hypothermia is a condition in which the temperature of the body core drops below its normal level of 98.6 degrees Fahrenheit. Signs of early stages of hypothermia include shivering, blue lips and fingernails, poor decision making, confusion, slurred speech, clumsiness, and lack of fine motor coordination.

The basic ways to prevent hypothermia are:

- Eat and drink throughout the day in winter. Have snack foods accessible, and snack often. Food is fuel.
- Don't wear cotton.
- Shed layers of clothing *before* you begin sweating, and add layers before arriving at exposed summits.
- "If your feet are cold, put on a hat." As much as 75 percent of the body's total heat production can be lost through the head and neck.
- Check in with your partners. "Feeling tired? Cold? Fingers and toes warm?" Talk throughout the day, and respond accordingly: rest, add or shed clothing, eat.
- Be alert for poor decision making (e.g., when your partners are not zipping their jackets or wearing hats when they should be). This is a red flag for hypothermia.

Frostbite occurs when body tissue freezes. It can affect any part of the body, but parts that protrude are especially susceptible. Ears, nose, fingers, and toes must be closely monitored in cold weather.

There are two main types of frostbite. *Superficial frostbite* is indicated by patches of gray or yellowish skin that may be hard or waxy to the touch, although underlying tissue is still soft. The affected area feels numb, tingly, or very cold. *Deep frostbite* occurs when a body part (usually hands or feet) is fully frozen, including both skin and underlying tissue. The affected part feels numb and wooden, and it is difficult for the victim to move it.

Prevention is crucial with frostbite. If someone complains of numbness or tingling in the extremities, *stop and deal with it*. Waiting until a more convenient time can result in permanent damage.

Preventing frostbite is a group effort. When skiing on very cold days or on an exposed mountain, partners should continually check each other for white splotches on the face, ears, cheeks, and nose. Other pointers to help prevent frostbite:

- Avoid tight boots. They are a prime cause of frostbitten toes.
- Mittens are warmer than gloves. Bring spare dry hand gear.
- Consider carrying hand warmers (though do not add direct heat to frostbitten skin).
- Carry a wind- and waterproof parka with a hood (hoods are invaluable for staying warm and keeping the elements out).
- Avoid summiting at times of extreme cold combined with high wind.
- Constantly wiggle cold toes and fingers. Keep moving.
- If someone is frostbitten, he or she may also be hypothermic. Look for signs of both and treat accordingly.
- Superficial frostbite is best treated by skin-to-skin contact—no rubbing!

Winter Camping

Knowing how to comfortably spend a night outdoors in winter opens up new possibilities for backcountry travelers. Multiday ski tours can be planned to visit the most remote wilderness. It is also important to know how to spend a night outside safely in winter in case you are unexpectedly caught out after dark. Familiarize yourself with the skills and gear to stay warm in the woods. Build snow shelters for fun (kids love to help) so that you know how to hunker down in an emergency.

The Backcountry Attitude

One thing I can always count on when I slide off into the mountains: things will not go as I planned. The snow will be heinous. A binding will break. We will get lost. The headlamp won't work. A water bottle will leak.

Following are some thoughts on the backcountry attitude that will see you through.

Mountaineering judgment. Mountaineers need a greater margin of safety in winter than in summer. An unplanned night out in the snow without adequate equipment can have serious consequences.

Good judgment in the mountains involves considering multiple variables. Assess each individual in your party (Are they experienced skiers? Are they fit? How long will it take them?). Reassess each person's condition when making decisions (What time is it? Is everybody warm? Does anybody look exhausted?). Size up the objective hazards you will encounter (How exposed is the route? Is there significant avalanche danger? What is the weather forecast? What are the snow conditions?). Be honest, be humble, and revise your plans accordingly.

Anticipation is critical in the mountains. The more you prepare for the unlikely, the greater your margin of safety. If you play close to your limit, be prepared for the consequences when things don't go the way you had planned.

Self-reliance. Being self-reliant in the mountains is a basic ethic of mountaineers. Having the ability to be self-reliant requires proficiency in first aid and mountaineering skills. Do not count on being bailed out by someone else if an accident occurs. Traveling with this attitude should influence your choice of route, equipment, and skiing companions.

Relying on cell phones in the backcountry is perhaps the best example of how people substitute gadgets for common sense. Bring a cell phone to use GPS navigation apps and to make an emergency phone call. But anticipate that it may not work. Batteries die and reception is poor or nonexistent in the mountains.

Instead of relying on a phone, take a wilderness first-aid class. Or a mountaineering course. Or an avalanche workshop. Instead of the false security of thinking that you can call 911 from the mountains, take comfort in knowing that you probably don't need to call for help. You can make good decisions, prevent trouble, and take care of yourself. That's the time-honored ethic of mountaineering. And it is your best insurance for being safe and happy in the mountains.

Humility. The mountain always wins. Have high hopes and low expectations. I usually have a goal when I head out—bagging a summit, completing a traverse, descending a beautiful run. Then Mother Nature, Father Time, and Lady Luck join in. Anything can and will happen. Roll with it. Improvise. Scale back. Be humble. Redefine success. Spending a day in the mountains with friends is wonderful. If I achieve what I set out to do, if there's good snow, if the sun is shining—those are the bonuses and surprises that keep me coming back.

Sense of humor. When you ski in absurd places in absurd conditions, you need to be able to laugh—at yourself, at your friends, at your predicament. Appreciating the absurd is essential for skiing in the East. If you don't laugh, you will cry. So bring your skis, your pack, your plans, and especially your sense of humor. Now go. Let it rip. And laugh.

AVALANCHE AWARENESS

Avalanches pose a serious danger to backcountry skiers. The Mount Washington Avalanche Center estimates that there are hundreds of avalanches in the Northeast each winter, with dozens of avalanche cycles per year just on the east side of Mount Washington; fortunately, very few of these involve people. Although the western

A sign at Hermit Lake Shelters (HoJo's) informing skiers of the daily avalanche hazard in Tuckerman Ravine.

United States may have more ski touring terrain that is prone to avalanche, the Northeast has its share. And an avalanche in the Northeast can be as deadly as an avalanche in Colorado.

Since 1954, fifteen people have been killed in avalanches in the Presidential Range of the White Mountains, notably in Tuckerman Ravine and Gulf of Slides. In addition, there have been avalanche fatalities in the Adirondacks and on Katahdin.

The danger of avalanches is greatest on slopes of 30 to 45 degrees, whether in the trees or on an open slope. Avalanche danger is also about what's around you. If you are on a low-angle slope with a steep gully above you, you might be at risk. If you are skiing a relatively small slope or gully, trees or streambeds below you can spell trouble. The force of an avalanche pushing a human body through the trees will have traumatic effects. These areas are known as "terrain traps" and should be carefully considered. Avalanche debris accumulates in these areas and can render even a small avalanche deadly.

Avalanche hazard is at its peak during a snowstorm and in the first 24 hours afterward. In addition, the ravines around Mount Washington are extremely prone to wind loading. A foot or more of snow can blow into Tuckerman Ravine even without a snowstorm. Wind-loaded slopes and gullies can be unstable despite low avalanche danger elsewhere. A new cornice at the top of a slope or a smooth,

bulging "pillow" mid-slope often indicates wind loading; avoid these slopes for several days until they settle.

The ski routes described in this book that are most prone to avalanche are Katahdin and all the ravines and gulfs of the White Mountains—Tuckerman, King, Burt, and Ammonoosuc ravines, Oakes Gulf, Gulf of Slides, and Great Gulf. In addition, any ravines, gullies, brooks (including Monroe Brook), slides, or steep, open slopes that you might be skiing can avalanche when the necessary combination of conditions exists.

If you ski on steep, open terrain, especially around Mount Washington, the Adirondacks, or Katahdin, you should carry standard avalanche safety equipment. This includes a collapsible avalanche shovel, avalanche transceiver (a.k.a. beacon), and a probe. Many skiers also use airbag packs to help prevent burial. Take one of the many avalanche safety classes taught in the Northeast and know how to use this equipment. The Mount Washington Avalanche Center website (mountwashingtonavalanchecenter.org) maintains a list of avalanche awareness courses taught in the Northeast.

The key to traveling in avalanche-prone terrain is prevention. Records show that 90 percent of avalanche victims trigger the avalanche themselves. *When in doubt, back off.* It simply is not worth the risk of sliding onto a suspect slope. Just because someone else skied a slope does not prove that it is stable. Passing up a tempting powder run takes considerable experience and wisdom. And don't be fooled by firm snow, which causes many hard-slab avalanches on Mount Washington.

Whenever you plan to ski in and around avalanche terrain, gather as much data as you can. If you are skiing in the White Mountains, check the daily advisory issued by the Mount Washington Avalanche Center. Find out how much snow or rain has fallen where you plan to go and where the wind blew. When skiing, observe the terrain and look for obvious signs of instability such as recent avalanche activity, avalanche debris, shooting cracks in the top layers of snow, "whumphing" sounds from a settling or collapsing snowpack, stiff wind slabs, and layers of cohesive snow on top of weaker snow and/or crusts that might provide a sliding surface. Feel the snow with your ski poles, under your skis, and with your gloved hand. Dig a snow pit if you know how to interpret the results. Basic avalanche training teaches you what to look for and what to do if you or someone you are skiing with is caught in a slide.

The more you develop an interest in backcountry skiing, the more you need to know about avalanches. This is especially true if you plan to ski in the western United States and elsewhere. Take a course and encourage your ski partners to join you.

Previous page: An avalanche class analyzing snow stability in Tuckerman Ravine. *Photo by Cait Fitzgerald*

1 NEW HAMPSHIRE

1 MOUNT CARDIGAN

The Alexandria and the Duke's ski trails are classic down-mountain runs that descend the east side of the Firescrew-Mount Cardigan summit ridge to the Appalachian Mountain Club's historic Cardigan Lodge. The Kimball Ski Trail descends through lower-elevation forest. The bald summits of Cardigan and Firescrew offer spectacular views.

Distance: 3.2 miles, AMC Cardigan Lodge to top of Duke's Ski Trail, round trip; 5 miles, AMC Cardigan Lodge to Mount Cardigan summit, ascending via Holt-Clark and Clark trails, descending on the Alexandria and Kimball ski trails, round trip
Elevation: *Start/Finish*: 1,392 feet, AMC Cardigan Lodge; *Highest point*: 3,149 feet, Mount Cardigan summit; *Vertical drop*: 1,750 feet
Maps: *Southern New Hampshire Trail Map 3: Mount Cardigan* (AMC) shows hiking trails but not ski trails
Difficulty: Most difficult, Alexandria Trail; More difficult, Duke's Trail and Kimball Trail
Gear: AT, telemark, snowboard
Additional Information: For reservations at AMC Cardigan Lodge and information on Cardigan ski clinics: Appalachian Mountain Club, 603-466-2727, outdoors.org

HOW TO GET THERE

AMC Cardigan Lodge is located at 774 Shem Valley Road, Alexandria, NH 03222. From the south, take I-93 north to New Hampton (Exit 23). Follow NH 104 west approximately 6 miles to Bristol. From Bristol, take Route 3A north toward Plymouth for 2.1 miles. At the blinking light with a white stone church on the far left corner, turn left onto West Shore Road. Proceed 2.9 miles before turning left onto North Road, and drive about a mile to the town of Alexandria; then after 0.2 miles turn

MOUNT CARDIGAN

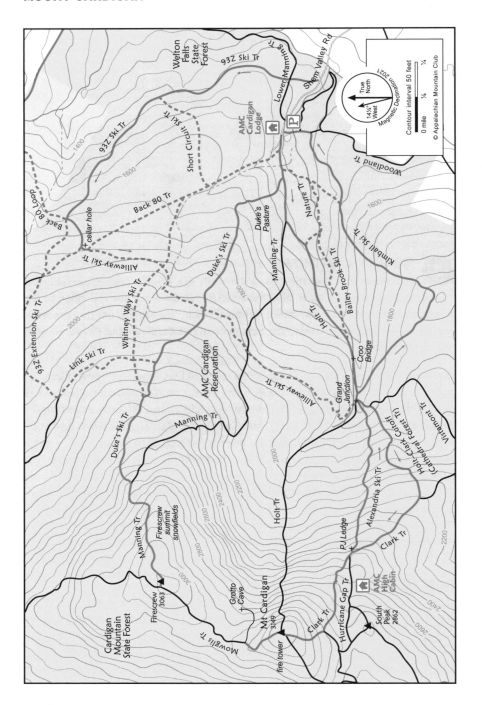

right onto Washburn Road, then bear right onto Mount Cardigan Road. Follow Mount Cardigan Road for 3.6 miles. Stay left at the intersection with Brook Road and follow Shem Valley Road 1.5 miles to Cardigan Lodge (*GPS coordinates*: 43° 38.970′ N, 71° 52.664′ W). Brown AMC signs point the way at key intersections. Shem Valley Road is plowed in winter but is notoriously difficult driving. Drive slowly and carry a shovel and tow cable in case of mishaps.

HISTORY

The ski trails on Mount Cardigan and neighboring Firescrew are among the most historic runs in New England. Mount Cardigan—"Old Baldy" to the locals—was the center of activity for the Appalachian Mountain Club's skiers after the club purchased 600 acres and a barn on the east side of the mountain in 1934. The club's interest was inspired by the fact that Cardigan, at 3,149 feet, is the second-highest peak in southern New Hampshire (3,165-foot Mount Monadnock is the highest in the region) and about 100 miles from Boston. Today, Mount Cardigan is the crown jewel of a 1,200-acre reservation owned by AMC.

The "Appies," as AMC members were called, quickly set about developing the slopes of Cardigan and Firescrew for downhill skiing. The first ski trail cut by AMC volunteers was the Duke's Trail on Firescrew. Firescrew got its name from the spiraling plume of fire seen for miles when the mountain burned in 1855. The Duke's Trail was named for Duke Dimitri von Leuchtenberg, a man of Russian nobility who fled his native country during the Russian Revolution and settled in Bavaria. In the 1930s, the duke was invited by Katharine Peckett to teach skiing at Pecketts-on-Sugar Hill, the first ski resort in the United States, located near Franconia, New Hampshire. He also directed work projects for the Civilian Conservation Corps (CCC) in central New Hampshire. When a group of Appies brought the duke to Mount Cardigan in 1933, he motioned "with a graceful sweep of his arm" to the pasturelands at the foot of the mountain and declared it an ideal place to teach beginning skiers. He then continued walking up the mountain and blazing what became the Duke's Trail, which volunteers dutifully cut in the summer of 1934. True to the duke's prediction, Duke's Pasture—the slopes just west of the current lodge off the Manning Trail—is still used as a site for AMC ski clinics.

In the winter of 1934, AMC hired Charles Proctor to teach skiing. A former Dartmouth skier and a member of the U.S. Olympic ski team, Proctor was responsible for the design of numerous ski trails in New Hampshire. In 1935, the state of New Hampshire hired Proctor to lay out the Alexandria Ski Trail (named for the nearby town) for expert skiers. The CCC was brought in to provide labor for the job, and the down-mountain trail was first skied that winter.

The Kimball Ski Trail was another popular run lower on the mountain that was intended for intermediate skiers. It was also cut during the summer of 1934. The trail was named for Helen F. Kimball, a Boston philanthropist who provided funds for AMC's purchase of the Cardigan Ski Reservation, as the site was then known.

News spread quickly about the skiing on Cardigan. By 1938, the crowds flocking to Cardigan were straining the capacity of the small AMC lodge. A new lodge was built in 1939, which is still in use. The hutmaster even ran a rope tow up Duke's Pasture to accommodate all the people. Skier traffic on Mount Cardigan dropped off significantly after World War II, a casualty of the lift-served skiing opportunities that blossomed throughout the White Mountains.

With the revival of backcountry skiing that began in the 1980s, skier traffic on Mount Cardigan has once again picked up, and the venerable ski lodge, which underwent a major renovation in 2005, is filled most winter weekends. AMC Cardigan Lodge, with bunks for 60 people, currently offers full-service lodging on weekends and self-service lodging midweek. Skiers preferring a backcountry experience can stay 2 miles up the mountain at AMC High Cabin, a rustic self-service facility with bunks for twelve. The simple cabin, which was built in 1931 and renovated in 2004, has a woodstove and composting toilet. One drawback is that you must carry up your own firewood. All lodging reservations may be made with AMC (see above). Information about local conditions may be obtained on the AMC website (outdoors.org) or by contacting the Cardigan Lodge manager (603-744-8011).

THE TOUR

The well-maintained trails on Mount Cardigan remain exciting, high-quality ski tours. Skiers can ascend and descend via the same ski trail or undertake a 5.5-mile grand tour of Cardigan: ski up either the Duke's or the Alexandria trail, cross the Firescrew–Mount Cardigan ridge on the Mowglis Trail, and descend on the opposite ski trail. The Duke's Trail is about 1.25 miles long and is easier than the Alexandria Trail.

Leaving Cardigan Lodge on the Manning Trail, the slopes of Duke's Pasture appear shortly on the right. The Duke's Trail has no trail sign, but it is the obvious ski trail that leaves from the top of the pasture. When skiing up the Duke's Trail, you can find the remains of the old rope-tow engine at the top of the pasture; the rusting car chassis from which the engine was taken is on the right.

The Duke's Trail is about 15 feet wide with a moderate 20-degree pitch. It is framed by beautiful old hardwoods. The trail has gentle S-turns near the top that hold your interest on the descent. The top of the Duke's Trail ends at a junction with the Manning Trail on open snowfields that lie just beneath the bald cone of Firescrew. Views of the heart of the White Mountains unfold to the north as you weave turns through the widely spaced stunted spruce and fir trees that dot the summit snowfields. Many skiers opt to end their tour at the top of the snowfields, retracing their tracks down the Duke's Ski Trail; however, the panoramic views make the final ascent to the Firescrew summit on the Manning Trail (climbing due east into the forest from the summit snowfields, following the yellow blazes) worth it. The descent of the Duke's Trail features long traverses at a moderate angle with plenty of room for turns. The steepest pitch is the section just above Duke's Pasture at the bottom of the trail.

Skiing the summit snowfields of Firescrew with the Mount Cardigan summit in the background. *Photo by Paul Lohnes*

For skiers seeking a steeper, more sustained run with lots of turns, the Alexandria Ski Trail beckons. To reach the bottom of the Alexandria Ski Trail, follow the Holt Trail 0.8 miles from Cardigan Lodge, cross a bridge over Bailey Brook, and arrive at the three-way trail intersection known as Grand Junction. A large trail sign shows the way. The Alexandria Ski Trail continues straight ahead. However, the preferred skinning route from Grand Junction is via the Cathedral Forest and the Clark trails, which intersect the top of the Alexandria Trail just below PJ Ledge. PJ Ledge is certain to stop you: its huge views of the cliffy flanks of Firescrew are breathtaking.

From PJ Ledge, continue up the Clark Trail to where it breaks out of the trees onto the rocky summit cone. No tour of Cardigan is complete without ascending its dramatic alpine summit. A rime-encrusted fire tower crowns the peak. On a clear day, there are commanding views of Mount Monadnock to the south; Ascutney, Killington, and Camel's Hump to the west; Mounts Moosilauke and Washington and the Franconia Ridge to the north; and Lake Winnipesaukee to the southeast.

In good snow conditions, the summit is flanked by skiable snowfields; during periods of lower snow, the summit cone is not skiable and may require Microspikes or similar traction devices to ascend.

Descending from the summit, the short upper section of the Clark Trail is only about 8 feet wide and is tricky to negotiate. The reward is the Alexandria Ski Trail. It opens to about 25 feet in width and drops 800 vertical feet in 0.75 miles. The trail ranges in steepness from 20 to 25 degrees.

The Alexandria Ski Trail showcases the creativity and craftsmanship characteristic of the best CCC ski trails. It was designed by a skier for skiers. It constantly bends and turns like a restless snake and often has a sporting double fall line. The trail is wide enough to link continuous turns. All of which explains why the Alexandria endures as one of the best down-mountain ski trails in the East.

The final prize on a descent of Cardigan is the Kimball Ski Trail, which is blazed but not signed and is often overlooked. After descending the Alexandria Trail, ski back through Grand Junction. Continue about 100 yards on the Holt Trail, then turn right on an unsigned but obvious trail with blue blazes. After a gradual 15-minute climb, the trail arrives at a clearing on a knoll. The Kimball Trail continues on the left. The mile-long trail is about 15 feet wide and descends gently through a softwood forest. The dark green canopy of the forest gives this trail a warm, deep-woods ambience. The trail ends at AMC Cardigan Lodge.

The slopes of Mount Cardigan continue to offer excellent skiing even after nearly a century. As you swoosh down the Alexandria Ski Trail, picture the person ahead of you on 10-pound hickory skis with cable bindings, bearing down the hill and reveling in the discovery of this "new" sport called skiing. The fine ski trails of Mount Cardigan provide definitive proof that floating through deep snow down the side of a mountain with spectacular views of the New England countryside is a timeless thrill.

OTHER OPTIONS

In addition to these down-mountain classics, novice skiers will enjoy a number of other historic cross-country ski trails on Cardigan. A popular, rolling 5-mile tour heads out on 93Z trail, loops back on the Allieway, and finishes on the Kimball Ski Trail. For those who want to practice their telemark or backcountry ski technique, the gentle slopes of Duke's Pasture near the lodge are a time-honored place to hone your skills.

2 MOUNT MOOSILAUKE

Mount Moosilauke is a historic ski mountain capped by a summit featuring expansive views of the White Mountains. The Moosilauke summit cone is also flanked by large skiable snowfields. The most popular descent is the Carriage Road, which offers a moderate route up and down one of New Hampshire's most scenic mountains.

Distance: 10.2 miles, Carriage Road bottom to Mount Moosilauke summit, round trip; 10 miles, Ravine Lodge Road winter trailhead to Mount Moosilauke summit, ascending and descending via Gorge Brook Trail/Snapper Trail/Carriage Road
Elevation: *Start/Finish*: 2,080 feet, Ravine Lodge Road; 1,720 feet, Carriage Road bottom; *Highest point*: 4,800 feet, Mount Moosilauke summit; *Vertical drop*: 2,720–3,080 feet, depending on starting point
Maps: *White Mountain National Forest Map & Guide* (AMC), *White Mountains* (Map Adventures), *White Mountain National Forest West* (Trails Illustrated)
Difficulty: More difficult
Gear: AT, telemark, snowboard

HOW TO GET THERE

To Ravine Lodge Road trailhead: From I-93, take the North Woodstock exit (Exit 32) to NH 112. Go west on NH 112 for 2.5 miles, then west on NH 118 for another 6.8 miles. Ravine Lodge Road is on the north side of NH 118. Turn onto Ravine Lodge Road and drive 0.7 miles north until you reach a gate and parking area (*GPS coordinates*: 43° 59.001′ N, 71° 49.513′ W).

To Carriage Road trailhead: To ski the full length of the Carriage Road from the bottom, continue west past Ravine Lodge Road for 3.2 miles on NH 118 (from the west, it is 2.5 miles north of the NH 25 junction). Turn right at a small bridge onto Breezy Point Road (there is a brown sign for Moosilauke Carriage Road here). After 1.6 miles, the road dead-ends at the Carriage Road. Take care not to block the road or driveways when parking (*GPS coordinates*: 43° 58.024′ N, 71° 49.995′ W).

HISTORY

The history of skiing on Mount Moosilauke is intimately tied to the history of the Dartmouth Outing Club (DOC). The DOC began purchasing tracts of land on Moosilauke in 1920 and now owns more than 4,500 acres on the mountain. DOC skiers were a major force in New England ski history, partly because of their activities on Moosilauke. They were assisted by the legendary German ski coach Otto Schniebs, whom they hired in 1930. Schniebs advised the Dartmouth skiers to abandon their stiff, upright skiing style and adopt the technique pioneered by Hannes Schneider at his renowned Arlberg ski school in Austria. This "called for a low crouch, an up-and-down motion, skis apart in the stem position, and use of

MOUNT MOOSILAUKE

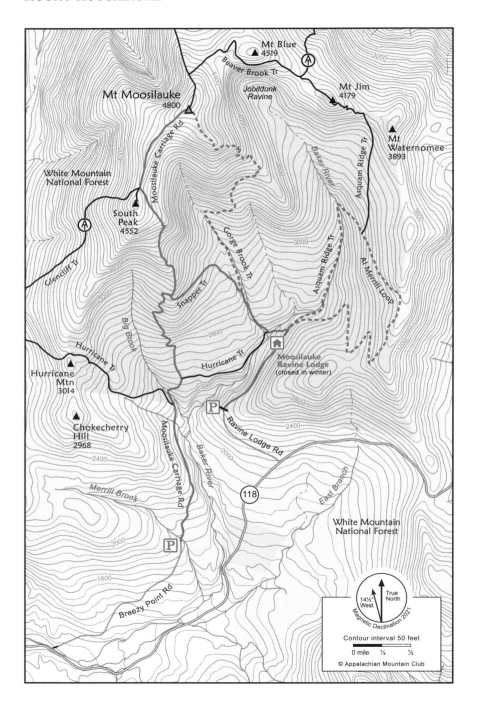

Mt Blue
▲ 4519

Beaver Brook Tr

Mt Moosilauke
4800

Jobildunk
Ravine

Mt Jim
4179

White Mountain
National Forest

Mt
Waternomee
3893

South
Peak
4552

Moosilauke Carriage Rd

Baker River

Asquam Ridge Tr

Glencliff Tr

Corge Brook Tr

Asquam Ridge Tr

Al Merrill Loop

Snapper Tr

Big Brook

Hurricane Tr

Hurricane Tr

Moosilauke
Ravine Lodge
(closed in winter)

Hurricane
Mtn
3014

P

Chokecherry
Hill
2968

Moosilauke Carriage Rd

Baker River

Ravine Lodge Rd

118

East Branch

White Mountain
National Forest

Merrill Brook

P

Breezy Point Rd

True
North

14½°
West

Magnetic Declination 2021

Contour interval 50 feet

0 mile   ¼   ½

© Appalachian Mountain Club

poles. The graceful telemark went into eclipse," wrote ski historian Allen Adler in his book, *New England & Thereabouts: A Ski Tracing*.

A popular anecdote about Schniebs comes from a talk he gave in Boston. As described in the *American Ski Annual*, Schniebs was posed a difficult question:

> "Otto," asked a bright-eyed young lady who had the look of one haunted by a deep problem, "what would you do if you were coming down a steep narrow trail a little too fast and there were stumps and trees and ice and things all around?"
>
> "Vell," [Schniebs replied], "either take the damned skis off und valk, or shtem—shtem like hell!"

Together, the DOC and Mount Moosilauke are credited with a number of notable skiing firsts. The first organized downhill race in the United States took place on the Mount Moosilauke Carriage Road in April 1927. Called the Moosilauke Down Mountain Race, it had about fifteen entrants. The race started at the junction of the Carriage Road and Glencliff Trail; Charles Proctor won with a time of 21 minutes. (Proctor went on to design many notable ski trails, including the Alexandria Trail on Mount Cardigan, and the Gulf of Slides and Sherburne trails around Mount Washington.) Moosilauke also hosted the first invitational club ski races in 1931. In March 1933, the Carriage Road was the site of the first U.S. National Downhill Championship Race. DOC skier Henry Woods won the race in 8 minutes, with classmate Harry Hillman (of Hillman's Highway fame in Tuckerman Ravine) coming in a close second.

Al Sise raced in that first championship. He recounted to me, "Nobody ever thought about course preparation back then. There were big drifts on the trail, and I flew off one of those and landed on something soft. It turned out to be the guy who started in front of me!" The fallen competitors promptly shared a nip from a brandy flask and charged down the mountain.

Sise explained that in other races "the guy who fell the least number of times—say, less than twelve—won on the Carriage Road races. As Alex Bright used to say, 'If you didn't fall, it was a sure sign you weren't skiing fast enough!'"

Just before the 1933 national championship on Moosilauke, an inaugural race was held on the Richard Taft Trail on Cannon Mountain. Compared with the narrow Carriage Road's many switchbacks, the Taft Trail was wide open and steeper. "Those who correctly interpreted this development knew that the future of downhill racing lay on that kind of trail and that the Carriage Road was obsolete," wrote David Hooke in his comprehensive DOC history, *Reaching That Peak*. Dartmouth skiers were a proud and competitive bunch, and they were determined to have a trail that kept them and their mountain at the forefront of skiing. This led Coach Schniebs to design Hell's Highway, the most famous—and feared—ski trail to grace the side of Mount Moosilauke.

Hell's Highway was cut by Dartmouth students in the summer of 1933. It started just below South Peak, descending the steep west side of Gorge Brook Ravine to the bottom, where it followed what is now Gorge Brook Trail to the Ravine Lodge. The result was a trail that was described in a 1939 guidebook to skiing in the East as "the steepest and most difficult trail in New England, requiring expert technique." The upper part of the trail dropped 900 feet in a half-mile, including the famous 38-degree section known as the Rock Garden.

The steepness of Hell's Highway was to be its undoing. The devastating 1938 hurricane that nearly leveled New England caused a landslide on the Rock Garden; the sections of exposed bedrock that remained never again held snow. The trail quickly disappeared into ski lore. The general vicinity of Hell's Highway can be seen today from Gorge Brook Trail; the prominent treeless slide paths that rake the west walls of Gorge Brook Ravine lie just right (north) of the fabled ski route as you look up.

The loss of Hell's Highway prompted the DOC to search for new ski terrain. The result was the construction of the Dipper and Snapper ski trails in 1939, of which only the latter still exists. "Snapper" was the nickname of Ed Wells, a well-known DOC skier who was involved in designing the trail. It referred to the terse "zingers" that the otherwise reticent Wells would contribute during the nightly trail crew bull sessions. The Snapper Trail was primarily a recreational trail, although a few races were held on it.

By the 1980s, the skiing on Mount Moosilauke had become marginal. Both the Snapper and the Carriage Road had grown in, to the point where there was barely room to make turns. A descent of the Carriage Road typically involved a thigh-burning, 3-mile snowplow down an icy chute. More than one backcountry skier broke equipment or found religion on this run.

A new generation of Dartmouth skiers has restored the luster to Mount Moosilauke. Starting in 1989, the DOC took on the ambitious task of rebuilding and redesigning trails on the mountain, in part to make them skiable again. With the aid of a federal transportation grant, chain saw-wielding volunteers and a bulldozer were let loose on the mountain. The result: the Snapper Trail and the Carriage Road are once again fine ski tours.

Moosilauke is a skiing classic both for its rich ski history and for its dramatic landscape. Skiing up its exposed summit ridge provides an exciting alpine experience. Skiers frequently enjoy a mild climb, only to battle a raging wind once they break out of the trees in the final push for the summit. Otto Schniebs discovered this the hard way. It is said that Schniebs was lured to the United States by the promise of fine skiing. Upon being brought to Mount Moosilauke, he was appalled by the pathetically small size of the mountain compared to his native Alps. His attitude changed when he hiked the mountain and was forced to crawl on his hands and knees along the summit ridge because of the ferocious weather. This story is instructive: use good judgment when determining how and whether to attempt the summit in poor conditions. Those climbing to the top may need to skirt the summit cone to one side to avoid catching the full force of the weather.

The summit of Mount Moosilauke is its most dramatic feature. A long, wind-swept, treeless ridge caps the mountain. From the top, there are panoramic views of successive ridges of New Hampshire's White Mountains to the east and Vermont's Green Mountains to the west. The view of the massive snowy flanks of Mount Washington is especially impressive from this vantage point. The gentle snowfields that run north of the summit offer picturesque skiing. As you make turns, you have the sensation of floating over all New England. Be warned that summit snow conditions can be tricky. You may be skiing on top of windblown crust one minute, bouncing over firm sastrugi (the fragile, rippled snow patterns that are formed by the wind) the next, and end up in feathery powder as you traverse a protected pocket where snow has eddied.

THE TOUR

The best skiing on Mount Moosilauke is on the Carriage Road. In a previous edition, I recommended skiing Gorge Brook Trail, but it is now too narrow to enjoyably descend and is best skied only as an optional ascent route.

The Moosilauke grand tour begins on Ravine Lodge Road (trailhead directions earlier). From the parking lot at the second gate on Ravine Lodge Road, it is a 1-mile ski to the Ravine Lodge. Just before the lodge, take the left fork, which leads directly

Skiing the summit snowfields of Mount Moosilauke against the spectacular backdrop of the Franconia Range. *Photo by David Metsky*

to the hiking trails that you will ski (the right fork leads to the Ravine Lodge and the trailhead for Al Merrill Loop).

The historic Ravine Lodge, owned by Dartmouth College, strikes an impressive pose. Its enormous windows peer directly out at Mount Moosilauke. The original Ravine Lodge was built in 1937 and was intended as a ski lodge. The enormous log structure fell into disrepair and was torn down in 2016. The new Ravine Lodge opened in 2017 and is a masterpiece of timber framing. The lodge is open to the public for lodging and dining from April to November.

From the Ravine Lodge, it is 3.6 miles to the summit whether you ascend on Gorge Brook Trail or via the Snapper Trail to the Carriage Road. Do not take the Hurricane Trail to the Carriage Road; the trail is obscure and indirect. Trail signs at the Ravine Lodge direct you to the hiking trails, which lead to the right as you face the mountain. Drop down and cross the Baker River and turn left immediately. Bear right at the Hurricane Trail junction and quickly climb a short steep rise, which is where you don climbing skins. After 0.6 miles, you reach the junction with Snapper Trail. I prefer skiing to the summit via the Snapper/Carriage Road since it travels along the summit ridge for about a mile, affording great views. If the weather is bad, ascending via the Gorge Brook Trail offers more protection from the elements.

The Carriage Road is the classic route of ascent and descent on Mount Moosilauke. It has a relatively gentle grade and gets progressively wider as it descends. However, there are a few other factors to consider, one being the southeast-facing Carriage Road receives a good deal of sun. On warm spring afternoons, the sun-baked snow on the Carriage Road can be arduous to descend.

In 1991, the Snapper Trail was completely relocated from its original site to its current location. The Snapper is 1.1 miles long, climbing 900 feet from Gorge Brook to the Carriage Road. The trail climbs gradually through a beautiful birch forest, getting steeper as it nears the Carriage Road. Coming down, the Snapper is now a long descending traverse. Watch out for drainage ditches that cross the trail, and beware of the final short, steep drop to the Gorge Brook Trail junction.

The Carriage Road is now about 15 feet wide, with an average grade on the upper section of 13 degrees. Skiers descending the Carriage Road can now swoop several miles of leisurely turns. On the ascent, don't forget to turn around and take in the sweeping views.

For those who want to ski the Carriage Road from the bottom, the trail begins at the site of the former Breezy Point Hotel at the end of Breezy Point Road (see earlier directions on page 7). The Carriage Road is an obvious, wide path that begins where the plowed road ends. The trail ascends moderately for the first 1.5 miles, then begins climbing more steeply.

The series of switchbacks on the Carriage Road just below the Snapper Trail junction were the source of a humorous event that took place during the U.S. National Downhill Championship Race in 1933. Some of the bolder skiers realized that they could save time by cutting through the woods and eliminating the broad turns at the bottom. The brothers Leonard and Hollis Phillips, fresh from training at the Hannes Schneider ski school in Austria, were determined to win the race. They had their father stand at the opening of the cutoff path that they had blazed when they climbed up; he held a long branch in front of the detour so other skiers could not use it. When his sons came by, he swiftly stepped aside, allowing them to fly through the trees and save time. Despite these efforts, neither brother won the race.

The Carriage Road is not particularly scenic at lower elevations, where it passes through second-growth hardwood forests. The path intersects with the Snapper 3 miles from the Breezy Point trailhead, where it is another 2.1 miles to the summit. Just before the Glencliff Trail junction, the Carriage Road narrows to about 8 feet. This is what much of the road felt like until it was widened. The upper mile of the Carriage Road is part of the Appalachian Trail (AT), offering an opportunity to ski a section of this legendary 2,193-mile path that extends from Georgia to Maine. The AT follows a pronounced ridge above treeline, offering excellent views in all directions. This section should not be attempted in poor or deteriorating weather conditions because there is no quick exit from the ridge.

The Moosilauke summit has a variety of notable historical ruins. In addition to several plaques, there are rock walls that form the outline of a building. These are the remains of the Tip Top House, a summit hotel that burned down in October 1942. Looking down to the southeast, a concrete foundation remains where a summit shelter once stood; it was removed in 1979.

On the descent, the final half-mile from the Snapper Trail junction to the Ravine Lodge demands quick turns or a good snowplow through a final chute.

Moosilauke is a big mountain tour. Skiing to the summit and back is a 10-mile day. Plan to spend at least six hours on your skis, leaving the trailhead no later than 10 A.M. To fully appreciate what this grand and historic mountain offers, ski it on a clear day. And don't forget your camera for the glorious pictures you can take of skiing on the summit. Your photos will allow you to enjoy this ski tour all year round.

OTHER OPTIONS

The Al Merrill Loop is a 5-mile circuit that leaves from the Ravine Lodge. The loop follows old roads and is suitable for beginner backcountry skiers. It offers excellent views of Mount Moosilauke. A trail map is posted on a trailhead kiosk just above the Ravine Lodge.

③ CANNON MOUNTAIN

The Tucker Brook Trail is a 1930s-era down-mountain classic that descends the undeveloped western side of Cannon Mountain. The most popular trail access is from the Cannon Mountain Ski Area.

Distance: 3.6 miles, top of Cannon Mountain lifts to Tucker Brook Road
Elevation: *Start/Highest point*: 4,020 feet (top of Cannon Mountain lifts); 3,520 feet (top of Tucker Brook Trail); *Finish*: 1,200 feet; *Vertical drop*: 2,820 feet
Maps: *White Mountain National Forest Map & Guide* (AMC), *White Mountains* (Map Adventures), White Mountain National Forest Franconia West (Trails Illustrated). These maps show the terrain but not the Tucker Brook Trail.
Difficulty: Most difficult
Gear: AT, telemark, snowboard
Fee: Cannon Mountain Ski Area permits uphill skiing on designated trails for a reduced fee. You may also purchase a Cannon lift ticket to ride the chairlift or tramway to gain access to the Tucker Brook Trail from the top. Cannon does not sell single-ride lift tickets to skiers.

HOW TO GET THERE

The top of the Tucker Brook Trail is reached from the Cannon Mountain Ski Area Aerial Tramway or the Cannonball Express Quad chairlift (trail directions follow). You must shuttle a car to the finish. The easiest and closest place from which to shuttle your car is the Peabody Slopes base area, Exit 34C off I-93 (*GPS coordinates*: 44° 10.683′ N, 71° 42.077′ W). From the Peabody Slopes parking lot, turn left (north) onto NH 18 and drive past Mittersill Alpine Village. Turn left onto Kerr Road, then bear left at a stop sign onto Wells Road. After 1.4 miles, Tucker Brook Road enters from the left and Wells Road turns sharply right. Turn left onto Tucker Brook Road and follow it 0.4 miles until it dead-ends; this is where the Tucker Brook Trail finishes. Parking for several cars is available at the end of Tucker Brook Road. If this trailhead parking lot is full, you must park on Wells Road. No parking is allowed along Tucker Brook Road; cars have been towed from here.

HISTORY

In the early 1930s, skiers in the Franconia/Sugar Hill area looked longingly at the steep flanks of Cannon Mountain. Their sense of awe was understandable: Cannon is one of the most imposing mountains in the East. On the other side of the mountain, the southeastern face drops precipitously into a mile-wide cliff that has long challenged rock and ice climbers.

The first Cannon skiers placed their hopes for developing ski trails on the western side of the mountain, where they believed the snow fell deepest and held longest. Led by Katharine Peckett, who founded the nation's first ski school in Sugar Hill and raised money to cut ski trails, local skiers banded together in the early 1930s.

CANNON MOUNTAIN

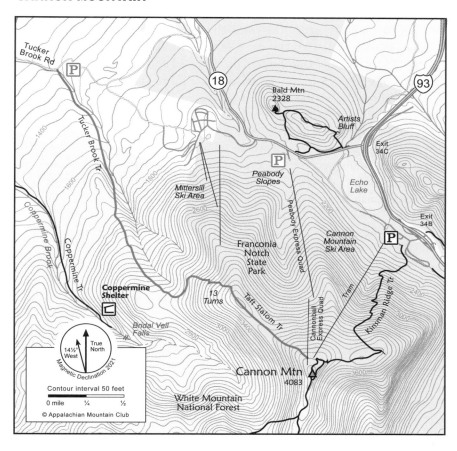

Peckett enlisted ski instructor and Russian nobleman Duke Dimitri von Leuchten-berg to design the Richard Taft Trail to the summit of Cannon (the Duke's Trail on Cardigan Mountain would later be named for him). Locals began building the Taft Trail, and the Civilian Conservation Corps (CCC) completed it in the summer of 1933. The CCC went on to cut the Tucker Brook Trail and Coppermine Trail down the western flanks of Cannon Mountain.

The Coppermine and Tucker Brook trails were audacious propositions in their day. From the summit of Cannon Mountain, these trails descended nearly 3,000 vertical feet in just under 4 miles. True to predictions, the trails boasted reliable stashes of powder and were loaded with sharp turns to challenge and interest skiers. The most famous part of Tucker Brook was the 13 Turns—the rapid-fire switch-backs at the top of the run. The Tucker Brook and Coppermine trails had everything going for them except one: they were located on the wrong side of the mountain.

The Richard Taft Trail on the north face of Cannon was an instant hit with the Boston-area ski clubs. This steep and wide Class A race trail set a new standard for down-mountain descents. The Taft Trail was quickly followed by other trails, including Hardscrabble, Cannon, and Ravine. When the state of New Hampshire was deciding in the late 1930s where to site the aerial tramway and the ski area, the obvious choice was to focus on the north face of the mountain, with the Taft and its sister trails as the nucleus of the new ski resort. The tramway from Franconia Notch to the summit of Cannon Mountain—the first aerial tramway in the United States and a remarkable feat of engineering—opened in June 1938 on the northeast face. The Tucker Brook and Coppermine trails were swiftly forgotten.

One of the trailblazers on Cannon was Sel Hannah, a former Dartmouth ski team member who went on to become an Olympic skier and a pioneering ski area designer. Hannah, who died in 1991, told me that the location of the tramway and the ski area "seemed ludicrous to me because of the wind in Franconia Notch, and because of what a rough mountain it is." Hannah had lobbied unsuccessfully to locate the ski area on the protected western slopes around the Tucker Brook and Coppermine trails. He was philosophical about losing the debate. "In the end, Cannon was good to me," said the man who later founded Sno-Engineering, the international ski-area consulting firm. "I spent my whole life trying to fix the damn mountain."

The Tucker Brook Trail retained a small loyal following of local skiers over the years. People maintained the trail in summer and skied it in winter. The enduring attraction of the Tucker Brook Trail, as Hannah noted, was that "it was very fun, it didn't get too much traffic, and it was like old-fashioned skiing: powder snow, no packing, no grooming."

Many things have changed on Cannon since those early days. The Coppermine Trail, which used to branch off from the Tucker Brook Trail, is now a hiking path that ends at Bridal Veil Falls. Mittersill Ski Area, which used to connect with Cannon via the Richard Taft Trail, went broke and was abandoned in 1984. For decades, its empty trails and rusting lift towers were an ungroomed powder haunt for Cannon locals. Most of the Richard Taft Trail was lost when Mittersill closed. In 2010, the state of New Hampshire and Cannon Mountain acquired the lands that include the upper part of Mittersill and installed a new chairlift on the abandoned terrain. The venerable Taft Trail and Mittersill have risen from the snowpack to thrill skiers again.

THE TOUR

The Tucker Brook Trail lives on as an unpatrolled backcountry ski trail that is informally maintained by local skiers. Its upper section incorporates the start of the Richard Taft Trail, and its lower section passes through the cross-country ski trail network of the Franconia Inn. The run is frequented by the die-hard community of powder seekers who come in search of the untamed ski experience of days gone by.

Skiing the snow-plastered Tucker Brook Trail on Cannon Mountain.

A word of common-sense caution: Although the most popular access to this trail is via the lifts and trails of the Cannon Mountain Ski Area, *the Tucker Brook Trail is not maintained or patrolled by the ski area*. This is a backcountry ski trail located in the White Mountain National Forest. Ski here with the attitude and preparation appropriate for any backcountry tour. In the event of a mishap, you are on your own for rescue.

There are two ways to access Tucker Brook: skinning up from the bottom of the trail or from the Cannon Mountain Ski Area. To ski it from Cannon, you first must shuttle your car. The easiest and closest place to arrange this is at the Peabody Slopes base area. Your best bet for finding a kind local who might help with the shuttle is to ask someone in the parking lot or to try inside at the ski area bar. Dropping a car and returning to Cannon takes about 20 minutes.

To access Tucker Brook from Cannon, you can purchase a reduced-rate uphill skiing ticket and ski up the designated skinning trails. Or you can purchase a lift ticket and ride the lift to the summit of Cannon Mountain (check cannonmt.com for ticket deals). The summit can be reached via the Cannon Mountain Ski Area Aerial Tramway or by taking the Peabody Express Quad and Cannonball Express Quad chairlifts. If you purchase a lift ticket you should take some runs and savor the ski history of this mountain. Check out some of the original ski runs by starting on Taft Slalom and dropping into Upper and Middle Hardscrabble. The steep serpentine course will give you new respect for your elders.

For more ski lore, visit the New England Ski Museum (603-823-7177, newenglandskimuseum.org), located next to the tramway base station, which has wonderful exhibits about New England skiing. The tramway itself was a skiing milestone. The original 1938 tramway was replaced in 1980 with the current 70-passenger tramway. The cable car travels more than a mile, rising 2,022 vertical feet.

When you have had enough of the hardpack, prepare to delve into some powder. From the top of the tramway or the Cannonball Express Quad chairlift, ski down the Taft Slalom. At the bottom of a long straightaway, keep your speed up and go straight, passing a Cannon Mountain Ski Area boundary sign. This was the route of the original Richard Taft Trail. When you come to a stop, take off your skis and boot up a short distance on a wide, well-traveled path; you likely will be joined by other skiers and snowboarders. The trail brings you to the top of a small knoll (according to some maps this is 3,650-foot Mount Mittersill; the knoll is unnamed on other maps), from which you have fine views to the south of the wild Kinsman Ridge and the Cannon Balls, a series of three mountain peaks. Continue down the main trail from this knoll. This trail leads to the Mittersill trails, which connect back to the Cannon base area.

To find the Tucker Brook Trail, begin slowly skiing down from the top of the Mount Mittersill knoll. The Tucker Brook Trail departs on the left at a large ski area boundary sign that informs you that you are leaving the patrolled terrain of Cannon. The trail begins as a 10-foot-wide path through tight fir trees. This quickly gives way to a ski trail that steadily widens as you descend. The top of the Tucker Brook Trail is no place for cruising—you immediately plunge into the legendary 13 Turns (count them—they're all there). With a pitch of 28 degrees, double fall-line traverses, and rapid direction changes, you will be either on your toes or on your butt. It is a fun, energetic opening act. Don't blow all your energy at the top, because you have many turns yet to come.

The 13 Turns plunges 600 vertical feet in a half-mile. The trail then contours south at 2,800 feet around the head of a deep, unnamed brook drainage (the Tucker Brook Trail never actually comes close to Tucker Brook, which flows next to NH 18). The trail then bends to the right and heads northeast alongside the brook for the rest of its length. The Tucker Brook Trail changes character dramatically in its lower section. In the next 2.2 miles, the trail widens to about 25 feet and the grade eases back to 20 to 24 degrees. There is room here for wide, sweeping turns. The woods alongside the trail offer plenty of opportunity to find your own hidden powder troves.

The final mile of the trail passes through the Franconia Inn cross-country ski trail network. Blue trail signs appear and side trails depart on the left. Stay to the right, and you will come out at the end of Tucker Hill Road, where you parked or arranged for a pickup.

The Tucker Brook Trail is well traveled by the full spectrum of snow sliders, from alpine skiers to telemarkers to snowboarders. I have skied it when the 13 Turns were covered by moguls and other times when it has been buried in powder. Thanks to its relatively easy access and its great terrain, you will be lucky—or will have risen very early—to claim first tracks. When you reach the bottom, you will fully appreciate why this trail has lured so many for so long.

④ BLACK MOUNTAIN SKI TRAIL

The Black Mountain Ski Trail is a 1930s-era trail that climbs to just below the summit of Black Mountain in Jackson. The wide trail features a historic cabin and fun, twisting downhill skiing with plenty of room to make turns.

Distance: 2.6 miles, Melloon Road trailhead to Black Mountain Cabin, round trip
Elevation: *Start/Finish*: 1,250 feet; *Highest point*: 2,450 feet; *Vertical drop*: 1,200 feet
Map: *White Mountain Winter Recreation Map & Guide* (AMC), *White Mountain National Forest Map & Guide* (AMC), *White Mountains* (Map Adventures), *White Mountain National Forest East* (Trails Illustrated), *Jackson Ski Touring Foundation Trail Map* (download at jacksonxc.org)
Difficulty: More difficult
Gear: AT, snowboard, telemark
Additional Information: Black Mountain Cabin reservations, White Mountain National Forest, 1-877-444-6777, recreation.gov

HOW TO GET THERE

From the town of Jackson, follow Carter Notch Road for 3.6 miles. Turn right on Melloon Road at a brown sign for Black Mountain Ski Trail, cross a small bridge, and park in the large plowed trailhead parking lot on the left (*GPS coordinates*: 44° 11.718′ N, 71° 11.565′ W).

HISTORY

The Black Mountain Ski Trail was cut by the Civilian Conservation Corps (CCC) in the 1930s. It is one of the many gems that the CCC sprinkled throughout the New England mountains. The ski trail is crowned by a CCC-built cabin at the top, a beautifully restored log structure with interesting details including curved ends and a stone chimney. The cabin, which sleeps eight people, was renovated in 1992.

The Black Mountain Ski Trail showcases the artisanship of the CCC trail builders. It dodges, weaves, twists, and turns with the mountain, holding your interest on both the ascent and descent. The trail is maintained by the White Mountain National Forest.

For a small peak, Black Mountain (elevation 2,757 feet) has long captured the imagination of skiers. The Black Mountain Ski Area, located on the south side of the mountain for which it is named, opened in 1935 and is the oldest ski resort in New Hampshire. The Black Mountain Ski Trail climbs the west side of the mountain and is not associated with the ski area.

THE TOUR

The Black Mountain Ski Trail climbs at a pleasant grade. The trail is more relaxed than the Doublehead Ski Trail (tour 6). The Black Mountain Ski Trail faces west and is bathed in afternoon sun. You ascend through a forest of birches and fir trees. "The trail may be used by all classes of skiers," declared a 1939 skiing guidebook.

BLACK MOUNTAIN SKI TRAIL

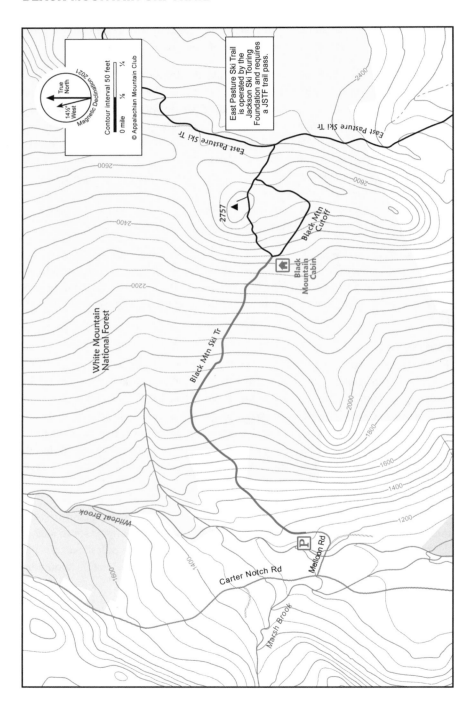

East Pasture Ski Trail is operated by the Jackson Ski Touring Foundation and requires a JSTF trail pass.

Contour interval 50 feet

True North

14½° West

Magnetic Declination 2021

0 mile   ¼   ½   ¾

© Appalachian Mountain Club

East Pasture Ski Tr

East Pasture Ski Tr

2757

Black Mtn Cutoff

Black Mountain Cabin

2600

2400

2200

White Mountain National Forest

Black Mtn Ski Tr

2000

1800

1600

1400

1200

Wildcat Brook

1400

1600

Mellon Rd

Carter Notch Rd

Marsh Brook

At 1.3 miles, the ski trail reaches the Black Mountain Cabin. Several trails depart from the Black Mountain Cabin. One trail heads off to the north (left) and reaches the summit of Black Mountain in 0.4 miles. This is a narrow hiking trail that is not well suited for skiing. Another trail departs to the south (right) and connects with East Pasture Trail, which is maintained for skiing by the Jackson Ski Touring Foundation (JSTF). This trail heads down into Jackson village. A JSTF trail pass (available at the JSTF office in Jackson) is required to ski East Pasture Trail.

For the best skiing, turn around and descend the fine trail you've just climbed. Numerous turns are packed into this 1.3-mile descent, but the trail never gets too pushy. I felt as if I was following an animal downhill as it bounded playfully back and forth in its quest for lower ground. It is remarkable to consider that this trail, cut nearly a century ago, has endured to thrill new generations of skiers.

Previous page: Charging down the historical Black Mountain Ski Trail.

⑤ WILDCAT VALLEY TRAIL

This is a thrilling, scenic ski tour from the top of Wildcat Mountain to the town of Jackson.

Distance: 5 miles, Wildcat Ski Area to Prospect Farm/Carter Notch Road; 8 miles, Wildcat Ski Area to NH 16/Dana Place Inn; 10.2 miles, Wildcat to Jackson
Elevation: *Start/Highest point*: 4,060 feet, top of Wildcat Ski Area; *Finish*: 1,800 feet, Prospect Farm; 1,000 feet, Dana Place Inn; 755 feet, Jackson; *Vertical drop*: 2,300–3,300 feet
Maps: *White Mountain Winter Recreation Map & Guide* (AMC), *White Mountains* (Map Adventures), *White Mountain National Forest East* (Trails Illustrated), *Jackson Ski Touring Foundation Trail Map* (download at jacksonxc.org)
Difficulty: More difficult
Gear: Nordic backcountry/telemark
Fee: This is a fee trail of the Jackson Ski Touring Foundation. A trail pass must be purchased at the Jackson Ski Touring Foundation office in Jackson (located in the center of town on NH 16A), and a single-ride lift ticket for the Wildcat Express Quad or uphill skiing ticket can be purchased at the Wildcat Ski Area.
Additional Information: Jackson Ski Touring Foundation, 603-383-9355, jacksonxc.org

HOW TO GET THERE

This tour requires a car shuttle. Leave a car in Jackson at the Prospect Farm parking lot at the end of Carter Notch Road, 5.3 miles from Jackson Ski Touring Foundation office. This is the most popular ending point (*GPS coordinates*: 44° 12.621′ N, 71° 11.709′ W).

You may also leave a car in Jackson at the Rocky Branch trailhead parking lot on NH 16 (*GPS coordinates*: 44° 12.288′ N, 71° 14.438′ W), at the Dana Place Inn on NH 16, or at the Jackson Ski Touring Foundation (JSTF) office (*GPS coordinates*: 44° 08.815′ N, 71° 11.067′ W) on the town green in Jackson. See "Other Options" on page 27 regarding each of these alternatives, and check with the JSTF regarding the status of parking at the Dana Place Inn.

To get to the Wildcat Ski Area from Jackson, drive 11 miles north on NH 16 to the Wildcat Ski Area parking lot (*GPS coordinates*: 44° 15.885′ N, 71° 14.416′ W). Either skin up (check uphill skiing policy at skiwildcat.com) or take the Wildcat Express Quad to the summit of the mountain and ski straight ahead to a signboard displaying the names of the peaks. The Wildcat Valley Trail begins to the right of this sign.

If you cannot leave a car in Jackson, inquire with the JSTF in the morning about arranging a taxi shuttle back to the Wildcat Ski Area in the afternoon. The upper Wildcat Valley Trail closes at 2 P.M.

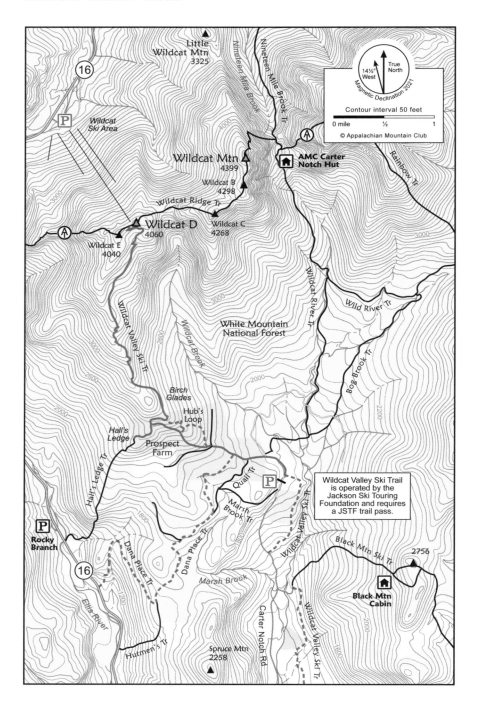

Little Wildcat Mtn 3325

16

Nineteen Mile Brook

Nineteen Mile Brook Tr

Wildcat Ski Area

True North

14½° West

Magnetic Declination 2021

Contour interval 50 feet

0 mile ½ 1

© Appalachian Mountain Club

Wildcat Mtn 4399

AMC Carter Notch Hut

Wildcat B 4298

Wildcat Ridge Tr

Rainbow Tr

Wildcat D 4060

Wildcat C 4268

Wildcat E 4040

Wildcat River Tr

Wild River Tr

Wildcat Valley Ski Tr

Wildcat Brook

White Mountain National Forest

Bog Brook Tr

Birch Glades

Hub's Loop

Hall's Ledge

Prospect Farm

Quail Tr

P

Wildcat Valley Ski Trail is operated by the Jackson Ski Touring Foundation and requires a JSTF trail pass.

Hall's Ledge Tr

Marsh Brook Tr

Wildcat Valley Ski Tr

Black Mtn Ski Tr

2756

P

Rocky Branch

Dana Place Tr

Dana Place Tr

Black Mtn Cabin

16

Marsh Brook

Ellis River

Carter Notch Rd

Wildcat Valley Ski Tr

Hutmen's Tr

Spruce Mtn 2258

Nature's art gallery: the breathtaking view of Mount Washington from the Wildcat Valley Trail.

HISTORY

The Wildcat Valley Trail (WVT) has long been one of the more popular back-country ski trails in New England. Cut in 1972 by volunteers from the Jackson Ski Touring Foundation, the run was meant to be the adrenaline-pumping jewel in the network of trails that links the town of Jackson with the surrounding White Mountains. A half-century later, the goal of the original trail crews is still achieved every time a skier drops off the summit of Wildcat Mountain to begin the 3,000-foot descent to Jackson.

The Wildcat Valley Trail offers a unique New England skiing experience. The ski tour travels the full range of the local mountain environment. Beginning at treeline between the windswept D and E peaks of Wildcat Mountain where the Appalachian Trail travels, the WVT quickly drops into thick spruce groves that are so familiar in the White Mountains. During the time that it takes to ski the trail, skiers will pass through old farm pastures, traverse stands of mountain birch, and follow old logging roads. Although it is not a pure wilderness tour, it makes up for what it reveals of human settlement by providing a glimpse of past decades of New England culture.

This trail has venerable ancestry. One of the most popular down-mountain ski trails cut by the Civilian Conservation Corps in the 1930s was the Wildcat Trail, a Class A race trail on the northwest side of Wildcat Mountain. The trail boasted a vertical drop of 2,000 feet in 1.5 miles, with grades as steep as 33 degrees. The original Wildcat Trail eventually formed the hub of the trail network of the Wildcat Ski Area, and much of that same route can still be skied today with chairlift access. Following the loss of the Wildcat Trail to the downhill ski area, it took some twenty years before Wildcat Mountain once again became home to a trail for backcountry skiers looking for challenging down-mountain skiing.

The Jackson Ski Touring Foundation is a treasured institution. Founded in 1972, it is a community-based not-for-profit organization that maintains more than 150 kilometers of cross-country ski trails, utilizing the land of more than 80 local land-owners. "We're in the business of doing public good," explained founding JSTF Executive Director Thom Perkins. He noted that a "substantial number" of Jackson residents are members of the nonprofit foundation. "We're part of the culture of the village." And JSTF has done much to shape that culture: Jackson is now one of the premier cross-country ski destinations in the East. JSTF trails also link to a number of backcountry ski trails in the White Mountain National Forest, including the Black Mountain, Doublehead, and Avalanche Brook ski trails, which are described in other chapters. If you are spending a weekend in Jackson, consider spending a day in the backcountry and another day on lightweight skis flying around the world-class cross-country ski trails in the village.

THE TOUR

This ski tour begins at the Wildcat Mountain Ski Area. You can reach the start by taking the Wildcat Express Quad to the top of the mountain (a single-ride lift ticket is available at Wildcat). Or you can purchase an uphill skiing ticket and ski up the mountain.

The WVT begins just beyond the top of the Wildcat Express Quad. As you ski off the lift you will see a signboard showing the names of the surrounding peaks. Stop to take in the sights, especially the views of the snow-plastered summit of Mount Washington. To the right of the signboard is a sign marking the start of the WVT. This sign warns skiers about the difficult nature of the trail. Heed these words: despite the popularity of this route, it is a demanding undertaking that is not suitable for novice skiers. Rescue is difficult, and the skiing can be treacherous in icy or crusty conditions. This trail entrance closes at 2 P.M.

The first 50 feet of the WVT is exposed to summit weather and can be wind-blown and icy, but the trail immediately enters the forest. The excitement begins quickly as the WVT snaps back on itself with a series of hairpin turns. This is an old-school Nordic downhill trail, taking long traverses rather than steep fall lines. The trail alternates downhill running with flat and rolling terrain. This variation is why Nordic backcountry or telemark equipment is the most appropriate gear for this tour; AT skiers and splitboarders will not appreciate the numerous transitions.

After about 2 miles, the WVT emerges from the forest into the open pastures of Prospect Farm. There is a beautiful 6-acre birch glade here that JSTF trail crews have improved for skiing. This sun-dappled glade beckons you to make turns. Take your time and relish weaving through the birches. Shortly after the glade, watch for a sign marking the boundary of the White Mountain National Forest and another sign for the Wildcat Valley Trail (marked as Trail 46 on signs and JSTF maps). Follow arrows to the village. You are now entering the JSTF Prospect Farm trails, a beautiful network of regularly groomed, well-graded old logging roads. The WVT soon intersects the trail to Hall's Ledge (denoted on maps as "scenic overlook"), which is a half-mile down a spur trail. This is a mandatory view! A large clearing with a picnic table offers views of the mountains surrounding Jackson, including Spruce, Kearsarge, Moat, Black, and Iron mountains. A bit farther up the spur trail are views of Mount Washington and its dramatic ravines. Stop, snack, and savor this grand panorama.

From Hall's Ledge, the WVT opens into a wide well-graded ski trail that descends for more than a mile on a long, straight run through Prospect Farm. Pass several trail junctions, taking care to follow signs for Trail 46/Wildcat Valley Trail.

The most popular way to ski the WVT is to continue descending through Prospect Farm and finish at a parking lot at the end of Carter Notch Road. When you roll into Jackson, you can take advantage of the WVT's most pleasant feature: the opportunity to end the route on the doorstep of one of the area's several eating and drinking establishments.

OTHER OPTIONS

From the junction with Dana Place Trail or Quail Trail, turn right and continue about 4 miles to the Dana Place Inn via Dana Place Trail (Trail 9). The Rocky Branch trailhead and parking lot is also 0.8 miles away. This variation makes it easier to hitchhike back to Wildcat on NH 16, but it adds considerable mileage through flat terrain.

I do not recommend skiing the WVT another 5 miles past Prospect Farm into downtown Jackson. It requires some road walking and is a trudge on backcountry ski equipment. If you choose to do it, be sure to have a JSTF trail pass and map, as the WVT intersects with numerous cross-country ski trails en route to the village.

6 DOUBLEHEAD SKI TRAIL

The Doublehead Ski Trail is a 1930s-era down-mountain trail full of exciting twists and turns. It starts at the summit of North Doublehead.

Distance: 3.2 miles, Dundee Road to North Doublehead summit, round trip
Elevation: *Start/Finish*: 1,570 feet, Dundee Road; *Highest point*: 3,051 feet, North Doublehead summit; *Vertical drop*: 1,481 feet
Maps: *White Mountain Winter Recreation Map & Guide* (AMC), *White Mountains* (Map Adventures), *White Mountain National Forest East* (Trails Illustrated), *Jackson Ski Touring Foundation Trail Map* (download at jacksonxc.org)
Difficulty: More difficult
Gear: AT, telemark, snowboard
Additional Information: Doublehead Cabin reservations, White Mountain National Forest, 1-877-444-6777, recreation.gov

HOW TO GET THERE

From the covered bridge in Jackson, take NH 16B, and turn right on Black Mountain Road. Pass the Black Mountain Ski Area and bear right onto Dundee Road. Just past Doublehead Drive, the parking area and sign for the Doublehead Ski Trail is on the left (*GPS coordinates*: 44° 09.682′ N, 71° 09.055′ W). The Doublehead Ski Trail begins at the parking lot.

HISTORY

A tour on the Doublehead Ski Trail is a perfect way to sample the talent and artistry of the master trail builders of the Civilian Conservation Corps (CCC). The CCC built the Doublehead Ski Trail in 1934 to meet the growing appetite for skiing in the Mount Washington Valley. Snow trains delivered skiers to the nearby town of Glen, and there was a desire for ski terrain in Jackson to accommodate the visitors. Ski trails were duly cut on Black Mountain, Bear Mountain, and North Doublehead. The latter trail retains the classic character of other CCC creations: swooping turns, double fall lines, and a fast descent. This is a well-preserved jewel from an earlier era of skiing.

An early and enthusiastic assessment of the CCC's efforts appeared in the December 1934 issue of *Appalachia*: "The lower mile is comparatively moderate in grade, but the upper part is steep enough to be interesting for even the best runners."

The bottom section of the Doublehead Ski Trail was rerouted in 2017 to start and end at the parking area on Dundee Road, which was built to accommodate increased skier traffic. Volunteers with Granite Backcountry Alliance help maintain the trail.

DOUBLEHEAD SKI TRAIL

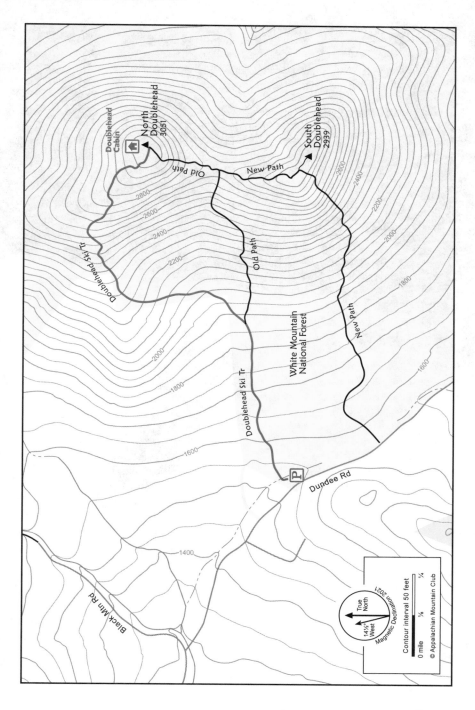

THE TOUR

From the parking lot, climb 1.6 miles to the North Doublehead summit. The summit has trees, but it offers a nice view over the town of Jackson to the west. The summit is also home to the Doublehead Cabin. Many CCC trails had a cabin at the top, providing shelter for skiers and winter hikers. The Doublehead Cabin was built in 1932 and is a fine example of backcountry craftsmanship. Its beauty is in the details—from the ship's prows over the gables to the stone chimney that crowns the cabin. The cabin, which sleeps eight people, is managed by the U.S. Forest Service (reservation info above).

The spacious Doublehead Ski Trail is a delight. The trail ranges from 15 to 25 feet wide, with a pitch of about 20 degrees. It has a sporting double fall line for most of the descent. The trail avoids the steep, ledgy summit slopes of the mountain by detouring to the northeast from the North Doublehead summit. After this moderate entry, the trail swings back southwest and steepens. There is plenty of room for turns and there are lots of them. Like the best CCC trails, it swoops, plunges, and rolls, holding your interest all the way up and down the mountain. You will enjoy returning to this trail again and again to experience it in all conditions. And you can expect the snow to vary widely—the middle section of the trail has southern exposure and can be affected by the sun, while the lower parts of the trail stay cold and dry.

The Doublehead Ski Trail can be enjoyed by skiers of many abilities. Experts will revel in the continual descent. There are enough turns to keep you on your toes, but the trail is also forgiving enough to be fun for less experienced skiers. It is also wide enough for snowplows and bailouts if needed.

Doublehead has several other hiking trails, notably New Path up South Doublehead and Old Path, which ascends the col between the twin summits. Both of these trails are too narrow and steep for skiing, and climbing either of them requires a strenuous boot-up. Skiers should stick to skiing uphill and downhill on the trail built especially for them nearly a century ago. This timeless masterpiece springs back to life with each new blanket of snow.

Previous page: Skiing the twists and turns of the Doublehead Ski Trail.

GRANITE BACKCOUNTRY ALLIANCE GLADE ZONES

Granite Backcountry Alliance (GBA) formed in 2016 to help launch "a movement of human-powered activities that is the basis for an emerging outdoor economy." It took its inspiration from the movement in Vermont led by the Rochester/Randolph Area Sports Trails Alliance (RASTA), which formed in 2013 and pioneered a first-in-the-nation partnership with the U.S. Forest Service to create and manage backcountry ski zones.

GBA grabbed the baton of the backcountry skiing movement and took off at a sprint. In its first few years, it spearheaded community projects that have resulted in numerous new glade zones throughout New Hampshire and western Maine.

"It's no secret that glading has been going on for a long time in New England," says Tyler Ray, GBA's founder. By working with landowners and land managers, many of whom are skiers themselves, glading has gone from rogue to respectable. "It's aboveboard and people are doing it collectively and there's an excitement to that," says Ray.

Today, a GBA work weekend draws hundreds of people to the mountains of New Hampshire and western Maine to cut and craft what they will soon ski. People come for the community and stay for the skiing. Rural mountain communities are finding that backcountry recreation can be part of their future viability.

GIMBY—Glade in My Backyard—has become GBA's clarion call. "Every community should be so blessed to have a glade zone in town," says Ray.

The popularity of glade zones has led Granite Backcountry Alliance to ask skiers to give back in a few ways:

- Be a good neighbor: park and drive responsibly in neighborhoods
- Practice Leave No Trace principles: pack it in, pack it out
- Be part of the action: join glading parties in the fall

Note: The GBA backcountry zones featured in this book are just a sampling of what is evolving in the mountains. These zones are works in progress. For updated maps and information on backcountry zones consult granitebackcountryalliance.org.

⑦ BALDFACE MOUNTAIN

The alpine, treeless summit of South Baldface Mountain offers skiing set against a vast White Mountain panorama. The Baldface Glades, cut by volunteers of Granite Backcountry Alliance, provide nearly 3,000 vertical feet of alpine and glade skiing for a thrilling tour.

Distance: 4 miles, NH 113 to Baldface Knob; 4.7 miles, NH 113 to South Baldface summit, 8.8 miles, round trip
Elevation: *Start/Finish*: 500 feet, NH 113; *Highest point*: 3,029 feet, Baldface Knob; 3,576 feet, South Baldface Mountain; *Vertical drop*: 2,500–3,000 feet, depending on high point
Maps: *White Mountain National Forest Map & Guide* (AMC), *White Mountains* (Map Adventures), *White Mountain National Forest East* (Trails Illustrated). Maps showing glade zones can be downloaded from granitebackcountryalliance.org.
Difficulty: Most difficult
Gear: AT, telemark, snowboard
Additional Information: Granite Backcountry Alliance, granitebackcountryalliance.org

HOW TO GET THERE

The parking lot for the Baldface Circle trailhead is located on NH 113 on the Maine–New Hampshire line, 2223 Main Road, Chatham, NH 03813 (*GPS coordinates*: 44° 14.855′ N, 71° 00.853′ W), about a 40-minute drive from North Conway.

THE TOUR

The 4-mile-long treeless white expanse that is capped by South and North Baldface mountains has long lured a small cadre of White Mountain skiers to its high-alpine setting. Thanks to the volunteers of Granite Backcountry Alliance (GBA), which received permission from the White Mountain National Forest to cut glades on the east side of South Baldface in 2018, Baldface is quickly becoming a classic White Mountain ski and snowboard tour.

Baldface owes both its treeless summit and its name to a fire that swept the top of the mountain in 1903. Those white slopes are a beacon that lures skiers upward. From the parking lot on NH 113 in North Chatham, New Hampshire, the Baldface Circle Trail departs across the road about 60 yards north of the parking lot. Ski on a flat, winding trail for 0.9 miles before turning sharply left onto the Slippery Brook Trail. This hiking trail, which is blazed yellow and also sports blue plastic GBA markers, is the ascent route. Climb steadily for 2.6 miles until you reach an intersection with the Baldface Knob Trail, where you turn right. For those who wish to forgo the summit and prefer to ski lower-angle glades, blue GBA markers on your right indicate the entrance to glades shortly after the Baldface Knob Trail junction. If you want to continue up to the treeless alpine zone, follow the trail as it

BALDFACE MOUNTAIN

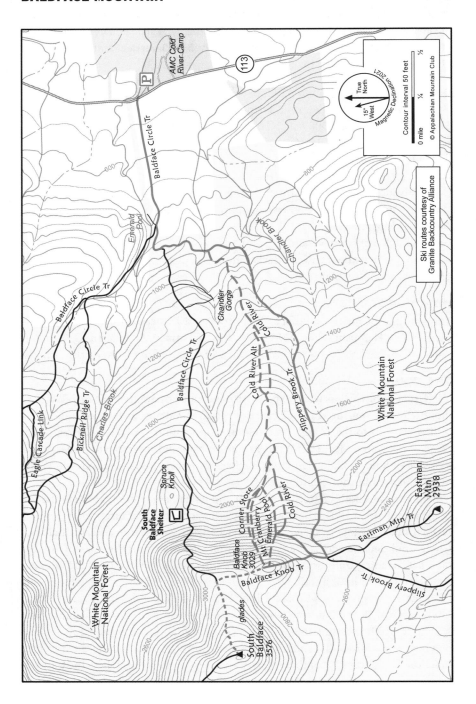

twists and climbs steeply for about a half-mile (many people boot up this section) until finally emerging from the trees onto Baldface Knob.

A breathtaking White Mountain vista erupts all around you on Baldface Knob (3,029 feet). Wildcat Mountain and the Carter–Moriah Ridge frame the skyline. Beneath you, the Wild River Wilderness forms an uninterrupted dark green carpet. The bright white summit of Mount Washington resembles a searchlight illuminating the surrounding peaks.

From Baldface Knob, the South Baldface summit (3,576 feet) is just a half-mile away. On a clear day, the scenery on the climb and descent of South Baldface makes this a worthwhile side trip. The skiing on the summit is on moderate angle slopes, but this alpine zone is exposed to the full force of the weather. If conditions are not favorable, it is best to limit your skiing to below treeline, where there is plenty to explore.

The best ski action lies below Baldface Knob. The glades directly below the knob, including Corner Store and Emerald Pool, plunge downhill steeply, weaving through the trees. After some running traverses, you enter the long, continuous Cold River Glades. You can weave turns of all styles here, threading around the trees. The final 1.5 miles provide fast and fun Eastern trail skiing on the Baldface Circle Trail, which leads back to the parking lot.

South Baldface is a full-day tour that showcases the best of White Mountain skiing, from alpine to glades to trail skiing. This is a tour on which skiers and riders can have it all.

Enjoying the powder and panorama on Baldface. *Photo by Jamie Walter*

⑧ MAPLE VILLA

A modern revival of a CCC-era trail, the Maple Villa glade zone features exciting glade skiing, great views, and easy access.

Distance: 4 miles, parking lot to east zone, round trip
Elevation: *Start/Finish*: 600 feet; *Highest point*: 2,200 feet; *Vertical drop*: 1,600 feet
Maps: Download map at granitebackcountryalliance.org
Difficulty: More difficult+
Gear: AT, telemark, snowboard
Additional Information: Granite Backcountry Alliance, granitebackcountryalliance.org

HOW TO GET THERE
From NH 16A in Intervale, turn onto East Branch Road. The Maple Villa parking lot (70 East Branch Road, Intervale, NH 03845) is on the right in 0.3 miles (*GPS coordinates*: 44° 06.087′ N, 71° 08.615′ W).

HISTORY
Like a phoenix rising out of the New Hampshire mountains, Maple Villa has come back to life. The Maple Villa Trail was constructed in 1933 by the Civilian Conservation Corps, with assistance from some of the leading skiers and trail designers of that era, including Charlie Proctor and John Carleton, both Olympians. The original trail was 2.5 miles long and dropped 2,000 vertical feet from the summit of Bartlett Mountain (2,640 feet) to NH 16 in Intervale. The trail was built to tap into "the growing popularity of [Joe] Dodge's [AMC Pinkham Notch] camp and the earlier Boston snow trains," according to a 1937 description.

Ski areas blossomed around North Conway at this time. Among them was the Intervale Ski Area, which opened in the mid-1930s and abutted the Maple Villa Trail. As the newly developed ski areas rose in popularity, however, the earn-your-turns Maple Villa Trail faded into obscurity. The small Intervale Ski Area was abandoned around 1976.

In 2018, volunteers with Granite Backcountry Alliance (GBA) made the historic Maple Villa Trail the centerpiece of one of its first glade zones. This sprawling zone is near bustling North Conway and takes advantage of the area's ski history, world-class views, and, of course, excellent skiing. This helps explain why Maple Villa is now one of the busiest GBA zones. Skiers can come for lunch laps or to spend the day—an outing of any length here is worthwhile.

THE TOUR
From the Maple Villa parking lot (which is located on land owned by the Upper Saco Valley Land Trust, a GBA partner), the skin track follows the old Maple Villa Trail, crossing several bridges. You soon have the option of taking one of three skin tracks that access three distinct sections (as of this writing). The east zone is

MAPLE VILLA

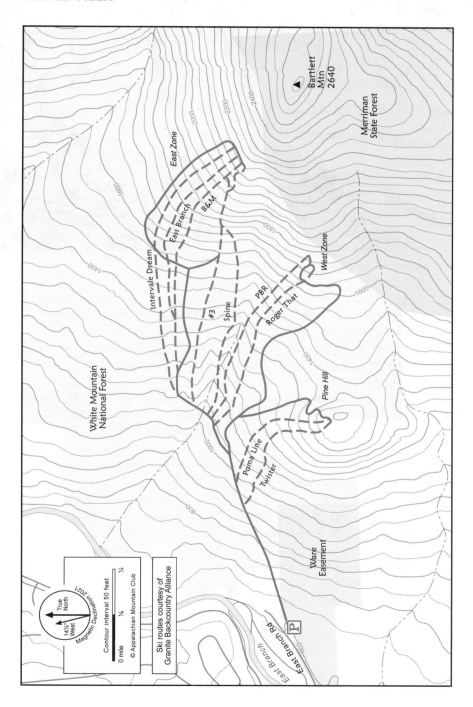

Weaving through the glades of Maple Villa. *Photo by Jamie Walter*

the farthest from the parking lot and consists of a variety of medium to steeper ski lines that are all about 800 vertical feet long; skiers often lap these lines. The west zone is accessed by staying on the Maple Villa Trail and sports several lines with a more moderate pitch. The Pine Hill zone has the steepest and shortest lines and is closest to the parking lot.

Skiing to the east zone affords a glimpse of all the skiable terrain. Rick Jenkinson, the GBA glade chief who helped design and cut the Maple Villa glades, explains that the trails were named to evoke history, geography, and a sense of humor. As you follow the skin track and cross a bridge onto a plateau, you look up to see the bottom of the west zone runs, including PBR, named for Fred Pabst Jr. of Pabst Brewing fame, founder of the Intervale Ski Area.

From the top of the east zone, the runs include Intervale Dream (owners of the Intervale Ski Area dreamed of expanding here before their ski area went bust), East Branch (the river at the base of the zone), and B&M (the railroad of the snow trains).

As you descend the Maple Villa glades, stop and take in the spectacular landscape. To the north, the bright white summit of Mount Washington beckons. To the east, Mount Carrigain appears as a broad mountainous throne.

The Maple Villa glades have a drop-and-roll rhythm, with short, steep pitches alternating with lower-angle slopes. All the zones funnel into the Maple Villa Trail, a fun pipeline that leads back to the parking lot.

Maple Villa is a social place. This is a backcountry ski area crafted by and for the community and much loved by it. Ski it, and you will understand why.

9 CRESCENT RIDGE

Distance: 4 miles, round trip
Elevation: *Start/Finish*: 2,000 feet; *Highest point*: 3,000 feet; *Vertical drop*: 1,000 feet
Maps: Download map at granitebackcountryalliance.org
Difficulty: More difficult+
Gear: AT, telemark, snowboard
Additional Information: Granite Backcountry Alliance, granitebackcountryalliance.org

HOW TO GET THERE

From US 2 in Randolph, turn onto Randolph Hill Road. Drive 2 miles, turning right on Town Hill Road and left on Mount Crescent Trail. The road ends at Crescent Ridge Trail parking lot (*GPS coordinates*: 44° 23.512′ N, 71° 17.173′ W).

THE TOUR

Crescent Ridge sits opposite one of the most majestic landscapes in the East. The ski zone is located in the 10,000-acre Randolph Community Forest, the largest town forest in New Hampshire, and stares directly at Mount Adams, Mount Madison, and King Ravine. The views alone make the skiing memorable. So too does the bountiful snow and excellent terrain.

Snowboarding powder on Crescent Ridge. *Photo by Cait Fitzgerald*

CRESCENT RIDGE

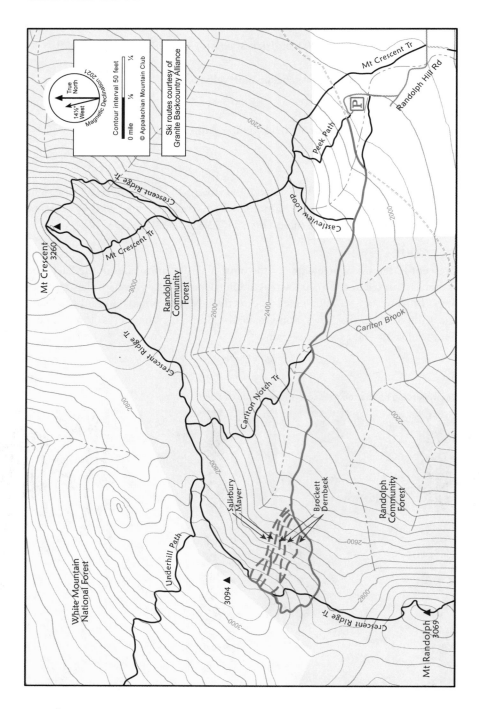

Crescent Ridge powder skiing. *Photo by Cait Fitzgerald*

Crescent Ridge, cut in 2017, was the first glading project undertaken by Granite Backcountry Alliance (GBA). "We needed a significant project to showcase our concept before we tackled bigger projects," explains GBA Granite Chief Tyler T. Ray. "Crescent Ridge allowed people to see what we were promoting in real time. It really put us on the map."

Crescent Ridge is a 2-mile-long ridgeline that connects Mount Crescent (3,260 feet) and Randolph Mountain (3,069 feet). A section of this ridge now has been transformed into a powder-packed glade accessible to all skiers. It is one of GBA's most popular zones. "It's special because it has significant snowfall and amazing views," says Ray.

From the parking lot on Randolph Hill Road, ski past a kiosk for the Randolph Community Forest and follow a snowmobile trail. Note GBA's blue plastic trail markers on the trees and be alert for snowmobiles. In 0.25 miles, turn right on Carlton Notch Trail. After 0.6 miles, Carlton Notch Trail branches to the right; stay left on the Crescent Ridge skin track, keeping an eye out for GBA blazes. The trail soon emerges into a large clearing, part of a wildlife management area. From here, there is a breathtaking panorama of the Northern Presidential Range. You are staring directly into King Ravine, the deep and forbidding bowl beneath Mount Adams. This is a rare vantage point from which to behold New Hampshire's grandest mountainscape.

The trail climbs at a steeper grade for another 0.75 miles until finally reaching Crescent Ridge. Turn right (north) and ski along the ridge, surveying the offerings below. A variety of cut lines drop down, many of them named for citizens of Randolph who helped make the glade zone a reality.

The descent weaves through a spacious forest. There is plenty of room to find fresh powder, even days after a storm. Skiers of many abilities will enjoy threading through the trees. The main glade runs are about 500 vertical feet in length. Most skiers take several laps, sampling different glades each time. The descent back to the car is an enjoyable turn-filled run that drops 1,000 vertical feet in 2 miles.

Crescent Ridge is a playful zone in a majestic landscape with something for every skier or rider.

MOUNT WASHINGTON AND THE PRESIDENTIAL RANGE

Mount Washington (elevation 6,288 feet) is the crown jewel of the White Mountains—the highest point in the Northeast and the third-highest mountain in the East. Standing watch over New England, Mount Washington has long been a magnet for winter explorers. Ice climbers, snowshoers, cross-country skiers, snowboarders, and alpine skiers all share the trails on this mountain as they make their way to their respective destinations. Much of the rich ski history of this region is presented in the section on Tuckerman Ravine.

The Presidential Range radiates north and south from Mount Washington and comprises more than a dozen of the highest peaks of the White Mountains, including Mounts Madison, Adams, Jefferson, Clay, Monroe, Franklin, and Eisenhower. Great ravines and gulfs are cut into the sides of these mountains, all of which beckon skiers. The climate above timberline in the Presidential Range, which occurs between 4,500 and 5,000 feet, is similar to northern Labrador. The alpine flora and fauna here are typically found only in extreme conditions that exist hundreds of miles farther north.

All of the ski tours described in this section are located in the Presidential Range of the White Mountains. These tours offer sweeping views of surrounding peaks and valleys. Some of the routes, such as Tuckerman Ravine and Gulf of Slides, are unique for New England. They offer wide, open-bowl skiing above timberline, much like skiing in the larger mountain ranges of the western United States. Mount Washington and the Presidential Range are also unusual for their distinctly alpine topography. The gullies of Oakes Gulf, Great Gulf, King Ravine, Burt Ravine, Ammonoosuc Ravine, and Tuckerman Ravine are classic, elegant high-mountain passageways.

The tours described in this section are only a small sampling of the terrain offered in the White Mountains. Vast wilderness skiing opportunities exist in this region. Skiing the classic routes described in this section should inspire winter explorers to strike out in search of other remote but equally rewarding tours.

10 TUCKERMAN RAVINE: A GUIDE FOR SKIERS AND RIDERS

Tuckerman Ravine is the most famous center of backcountry skiing in the East. There are a variety of very steep and extreme ski routes in and around the ravine and on Mount Washington.

Distance: 2.4 miles from Pinkham Notch Visitor Center to Hermit Lake Shelters; 3.1 miles from Pinkham Notch Visitor Center to floor of Tuckerman Ravine; 4.2 miles from Pinkham Notch Visitor Center to Mount Washington summit, one way

Elevation: *Start/Finish*: 2,020 feet, Pinkham Notch Visitor Center; *Highest point*: 4,400 feet (Tuckerman Ravine floor), 6,288 feet (Mount Washington summit); *Vertical drop*: 4,268 feet, Mount Washington summit to Pinkham Notch

Maps: *White Mountain Winter Recreation Map & Guide* (AMC), *White Mountain National Forest Map & Guide* (AMC), *White Mountains* (Map Adventures), *White Mountain National Forest East* (Trails Illustrated)

Difficulty: Ski mountaineering

Gear: AT, telemark, snowboard

Additional Information: *Avalanche forecast*: Mount Washington Avalanche Center, mountwashingtonavalanchecenter.org; *Weather*: Mount Washington Observatory, mountwashington.org; *Lodging and trail conditions*: AMC Pinkham Notch, 603-466-2727, outdoors.org

HOW TO GET THERE

From the AMC Pinkham Notch Visitor Center on NH 16 (*GPS coordinates*: 44° 15.435′ N, 71° 15.166′ W), it is a 3-mile hike up the Tuckerman Ravine Trail to the floor of Tuckerman Ravine. At 2.4 miles, you will pass the Hermit Lake Shelters and can get information at a staffed AMC caretaker cabin (a.k.a. HoJo's) with a large deck and picnic tables. There is also a staffed U.S. Forest Service snow ranger cabin here.

THE TOUR

Tuckerman Ravine—referred to affectionately as "Tucks" or simply "the Bowl"—is where skiing legends have been made, broken, and made up. It is the home of some of the steepest established backcountry ski and snowboard runs in the country. Tucks usually holds the last snows of the year, when every other place in New England has long since reverted to rock and dirt. Skiers view it as a proving ground or a playground, depending on their abilities.

Tuckerman Ravine is a huge glacial cirque. It is shaped like a teacup or bowl that has been cut in half: the higher you go, the steeper the walls. The area is named for botanist Edward Tuckerman, who explored the White Mountains for two decades in the mid-1800s. Most of the snow that collects in the Bowl is deposited by wind,

TUCKERMAN RAVINE

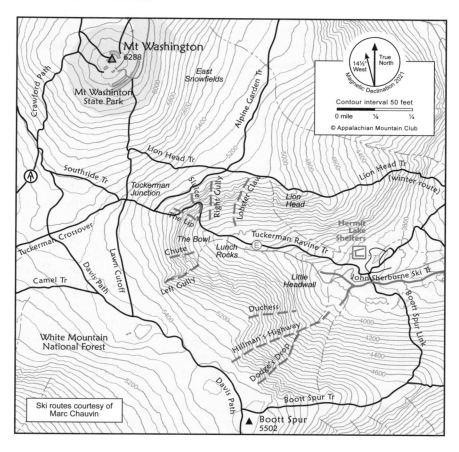

which generally comes out of the west-northwest and carries snow from the Bigelow Lawn and the Mount Washington summit cone. Snow on the floor of the Bowl may reach depths of 75 to 100 feet.

HISTORY OF SKIING IN TUCKERMAN RAVINE

No history of skiing in New England is complete without a look at Tuckerman Ravine over the last century. Indeed, the skiing "firsts" in the ravine serve as milestones in the story of how modern skiing has evolved.

The first recorded skier on Mount Washington was Dr. Wiskott of Germany, who wrote about his 1899 visit on skis to the mountain, though it is not known whether he skied to the summit. Mount Washington was first skied from the summit in 1913 by Fred Harris, the founder of the Dartmouth Outing Club (DOC). He and a group of Dartmouth pals skied what is now the Auto Road. They also skied into Tuckerman

Ravine on the same trip and wrote about it in one of the Boston newspapers. The following year, John Apperson, best known for being the first to ski Mount Marcy in the Adirondacks in 1911, reportedly skied up to Tuckerman Ravine.

The era of ski exploration on the mountain began in earnest in the spring of 1926, when AMC hutmaster Joe Dodge and several of his friends ventured into Tuckerman Ravine on skis, skinning up and skiing the lower slopes of the Head-wall. Among this first crew was Al Sise, a colorful figure who was still ski-racing until his death in 1992 at age 84. Sise once recounted to me the story of his first trip into the Bowl. "We were intimidated by the ravine," he conceded. "It was a mighty impressive place—awe inspiring."

AMC Ski Committee Chair William Fowler proclaimed on a radio show in 1934, "When we consider that this past summer people skied on the Headwall of Tucker-man's as late as July Fourth, we realize that it is one of the seven wonders of New Hampshire, rivaling the Great Stone Face and the Flume."

Sise remembered a time when "there was nobody there—not a soul except us." This quickly changed. The first skiers told their friends, who promptly told other ski-ers about the vast, challenging ski potential of the ravine. Like any religious shrine, Tucks required some sacrifice from its devotees—these first skiers bushwhacked more than 3 miles up Cutler River to reach the Bowl. As skier traffic increased, the U.S. Forest Service (USFS) and AMC were finally persuaded to construct the Fire Trail from Pinkham Notch to Hermit Lake in late 1932. This trail, now known as the Tuckerman Ravine Trail, is still the main thoroughfare for climbing up to the Bowl.

The construction of the Sherburne Ski Trail in 1934 made getting down from the ravine even easier, enabling people to ski from Hermit Lake down to Pinkham Notch in less than 30 minutes. Providing easy access in and out of the Bowl was a turning point in the history of skiing in Tuckerman Ravine.

By the early 1930s, word had spread among the budding ski community about Tuckerman Ravine. In 1930, AMC ran its first ski trip to Tucks. On April 11, 1931, after a run down Right Gully, Dartmouth skiers John Carleton (U.S. Olympic ski team, 1924) and Charlie Proctor (U.S. Olympic ski team, 1928) became the first to ski over the Lip and down the Headwall to the ravine floor. A week later, a group of skiers from Harvard University became the first to ski from the summit over the Headwall. By 1932, the snow trains from Boston to New Hampshire were ferrying more than 10,000 people per season to the North Country, and many of them were coming to ski in Tuckerman Ravine.

American Inferno

The first of three "American Inferno" races was held in the ravine in 1933. The June 1933 edition of the AMC journal *Appalachia* reported:

> The climax of the ski racing season this year was also another step in the conquest of
> Mount Washington under wintertime conditions. Up until this year the Headwall of

Tuckerman Ravine, which is a drop of nearly a thousand feet, had been run by only a handful of people. . . . But this spring the snow was so unusually deep in the Bowl that the angle was perceptibly less and the Ski Club Hochgebirge of Boston [which included some of the best racers of the era] thought the time was ripe to conduct a race they had had in mind for some time—a summit-to-base run, including the Headwall. They christened it the "American Inferno," after a famous course at Murren, Switzerland.

Hollis Phillips of AMC won the race with a time of 14 minutes, 41 seconds. Most of the other 10 skiers finished in about 20 minutes.

Skiing the Inferno was an amazing accomplishment even by today's standards. The racecourse plunged more than 4,200 feet in about 4 miles. The first race started on the summit of Mount Washington, dropped into the Bowl via Right Gully, and continued to Pinkham Notch on the narrow Fire Trail.

As traffic increased into Tuckerman Ravine, skiing standards were pushed to new heights. The Inferno was the best gauge of this progress. In the second American Inferno, held in 1934, legendary Dartmouth racer Dick Durrance astounded the skiing community by winning in 12 minutes, 35 seconds. (Durrance would go on to be a 17-time U.S. ski champion who was an early pioneer of the Alta and Aspen ski resorts.) No one could have predicted how dramatically this speed record would fall. It happened in the most famous race ever held in Tuckerman Ravine—the third American Inferno in 1939.

Toni Matt was an unknown in the American skiing world. A 19-year-old Austrian, he had been brought to the United States to teach at the Cranmore Mountain Ski School in North Conway. He had never heard of Tuckerman Ravine, but when told about the race there, he was game to enter. The race was postponed twice because of bad weather. It was finally run on April 16, 1939. The summit conditions as the racers awaited their start were 0 degrees Fahrenheit with a 60 MPH wind. Matt caught his first glimpse of the Headwall as he climbed it; he had never even seen the Sherburne Trail, which constituted the lower half of the racecourse. By contrast, his competitors, especially Durrance, were veterans of numerous descents of the mountain.

What occurred next was to become one of the greatest moments in ski history. As an observer recounted in the December 1939 issue of *Appalachia*:

> An adequate description of Toni Matt's run cannot fail to take your breath away. From below in the Ravine, he was seen to come tearing down the cone in one long arc, and with one swoop that was hardly a check he dropped over the Lip of the Ravine, came straight down the headwall, across the floor, and on down the brook bed to the Sherburne Trail. On the trail he ran with an ease and abandon that left one gasping. He cut the corners close, never traveling an extra inch. His time of 6:29.2 practically halves any previous time, and he finished looking as fresh as when he left for the ascent four hours before.

Previous page: Skiing steep powder in Tuckerman Ravine. *Photo by Jamie Walter*

Matt finished a full minute ahead of Durrance, who came in second. The young Austrian dynamo simply took the Headwall straight, a feat few have dared to repeat. It is estimated that he hit 80 MPH on his descent. Matt confessed later that he did not plan to schuss the Headwall:

> I figured I'm gonna make three or four turns over the Lip itself and on into Tuckerman Ravine. And before I knew it, I dropped over the Lip and there wasn't any sense in turning; it wouldn't slow me down anyway! I decided it's much safer to go straight than to go by turning on this kind of pitch and I was stupid enough and strong enough to be able to stand up.

A summit-to-base race on Mount Washington has never been held since (bad weather has thwarted several other attempts). Toni Matt died in 1989 at age 69, one month after the golden anniversary of his epic descent. His record time lives on.

Era of first descents

The 1930s were an era of discovery in the Bowl. Skiers from the Dartmouth College ski team would come every spring. The first descents of the classic lines—Right Gully, Left Gully, Chute, Hillman's Highway, and the Lip—occurred during this period, mostly by skiers from Dartmouth and Harvard.

Hillman's Highway was named for Harry Hillman, a Dartmouth skier who enjoyed exploring the less-traveled areas. Sel Hannah, a well-known local skier of the era and a member of the Dartmouth team, told me, "Hillman was a colorful, wild guy and a damn good skier. Everybody would be over on the Headwall, but he used to go up there [to Hillman's Highway] all the time and promote it. So eventually a lot of other guys went over there too." Hannah, for his part, was responsible for the first descent down the Center Headwall in the winter of 1937–1938.

The next major era of exploration in Tuckerman Ravine belonged to one remarkable man. Joseph Brooks Dodge Jr. was born in 1929 and grew up in the shadow of Mount Washington. Brooks, as he was known, was the son of AMC huts manager Joe Dodge and thus had the good fortune to live in Pinkham Notch. This upbringing served Brooks well. He first skied over the Lip at the tender age of 13. He went on to attend Dartmouth College, was a member of that renowned ski team, and earned berths on the U.S. Olympic ski team in 1952 and 1956.

Dodge left his greatest mark on the skiing in his own backyard. Between 1946 and 1952, Dodge had a singular passion: skiing the steepest, boldest, and most elegant lines on Mount Washington and the surrounding mountains. He made first descents of a dozen different routes, most of which were frighteningly steep. Dodge's Drop, which is to the left (as you look up) of Hillman's Highway, is one of his best-known runs. Among his others: Duchess (it had been skied once before him); Cathedral; Lion Head Gullies 1 (a.k.a. Lobster Claw), 2, and 3 (between Right Gully and Lion Head); Sluice; Boott Spur Gullies 1, 2, and 3 (gullies to looker's left of Cathedral); and the Chute Variations (left and right, respectively, of Chute).

His most difficult run was Icefall, an audacious route that only occasionally forms through the cliffs just looker's left of the Lip.

Dodge insisted that he didn't have any agenda in his skiing conquests beyond satisfying his hunger for good skiing. "Each spring, I'd go up and do the ones where the snow was good," he told me. "I didn't have any specific goals to do them all. I just looked for the best skiing. I didn't like to ski where there was another track—I always liked smooth fresh snow."

Dodge had a strong skiing ethic. "I never considered those runs worth a damn unless I could ski top to bottom without a stop," he said. He credited his ski achievements to the special technique that he developed. He insisted that the popular stem christie parallel ski technique required too much space and did not provide the precise, controlled turns needed for skiing steep, narrow gullies. So he devised his "two-pole turn" for the steeps: a quick jump turn, "keeping your tips on the snow at all times and pivoting on the tips of your skis. You can turn very quickly in tight spaces," he explained. Dodge also waited for what he considered to be safe snow conditions: 1 to 1.5 inches of soft snow on a hard surface. He did all his skiing on 7-foot-long, metal-edged hickory skis with cable bindings that were secured by a heel latch.

Dodge went on to be a highly successful civil engineer, helped develop the Wildcat Ski Area, and was an early pioneer of heli-skiing with Hans Gmoser, the founder of Canadian Mountain Holidays heli-skiing company.

Brooks Dodge, who died in 2018 at age 88, raised the bar for skiing in Tuckerman Ravine to new heights. Nearly a century after he began skiing on Mount Washington, only a handful of modern skiers can follow where Dodge led. Dodge's achievements confirm that what matters most in pioneering new mountain descents are creativity, tenacity, and boldness. High-tech equipment is no substitute for skill and passion. When Dodge began skiing in Tuckerman Ravine, there were seven established routes; when he finished, there were nineteen. In the years since he made his mark, no major routes have been established in Tuckerman Ravine of the high standard and enduring quality of those skied by Brooks Dodge.

I asked Dodge if he considered himself to be an extreme skier. "I don't know what people mean by that term," he said with an air of disapproval. "I just thought of it as developing technique that would meet the challenge that I had given myself. I would always do it with a minimum of risk. That was part of the game. I wanted to stick around. If that's what they call extreme skiing—well, I never thought of it that way."

For Dodge, skiing the steeps was a challenge that was equal parts intellectual, aesthetic, and athletic. "I was interested in skiing elegantly, precisely, and well from the top to the bottom," he told me.

Brooks Dodge wasn't looking for glory. He was simply on a quest for the perfect run.

Airing it out: dropping into Tuckerman Ravine. *Photo by Andrew Drummond/Ski the Whites*

THE DHARMA OF TUCKERMAN RAVINE

The pilgrimage to Tuckerman Ravine is the world's grandest, oldest, and biggest celebration of sliding on snow. Nowhere else on Earth do people come together so faithfully and in such numbers to revel in the joys of skiing.

Tucks is anathema to many of the values of modern society. It takes hard work to get there, there are almost no rules, dire consequences can result from mistakes, and you have nothing to show for your courageous efforts save for a fleeting track in the snow. For this, people return again and again. In Tucks, you are free.

Skiing in Tuckerman Ravine today is as exciting and heart-stopping as it ever was. The sensation of climbing the Headwall and standing at the top with your pulse racing and palms sweating as you try to talk yourself into dropping into the fall line repeats with each run that you take. The first time you ski over the Lip into the Bowl is a moment that you remember for a lifetime. As Toni Matt recalled of his maiden voyage: "Going over the Lip is a terrifying experience, especially for the first time. It's like jumping into a 600-foot-deep hole from a speeding car."

Fear. It is an intoxicating part of the Tucks experience. Fear is the mind's rational reaction to being in insane places. At best, fear has a moderating effect on behavior. At worst, it paralyzes you. The best skiers do not claim to conquer fear. They harness its energy, control it, and learn when to heed it.

All the routes in Tuckerman Ravine are for expert skiers and riders. Just because the skier before you skied something effortlessly does not mean that you can follow his or her tracks. The normal rules of gravity apply here: if you leap off a cliff and fall or tomahawk down a rocky couloir, you will likely get hurt.

Warnings heeded, every backcountry skier and rider should make the pilgrimage to Tucks at some point. The skiing, scenery, history, community, and terrain are unmatched. This is a place where ordinary people shed their workaday personae and, for a moment, live large. Some return as heroes in their own minds, proud simply to have survived the hike. Others return humbled or inspired.

Being in Tucks is not a wilderness experience in the traditional sense. On a nice spring weekend, you will be joined by thousands of fellow seekers. You will see people descending the Headwall on everything from skis and snowboards, to inner tubes, rubber boats, plastic sleds, and their rear ends. A circus? Perhaps. But this is the steep culture of Tucks. Enjoy it. This is a celebration, after all, and it wouldn't be complete without the celebrants.

TUCKS FAQ: WHEN TO GO, WHAT TO BRING
The Season
The prime skiing season in Tuckerman Ravine runs from March through May. Winters vary considerably from year to year, so wise skiers will ski according to the conditions, not the calendar. I have skied Tucks on the Fourth of July, although skiing this late is not reliable. By late May, the terrain is usually limited and the ski conditions become progressively more difficult. Warm April days in Boston may offer perfect spring skiing in the ravine. Wait for low avalanche danger before considering going without avalanche safety gear. Even then, keep in mind that "low danger" does not mean *no* danger.

See the "Additional Information" section on page 44 regarding where to find weather and avalanche information for Tuckerman Ravine. The Mount Washington Avalanche Center posts current information and photos of the ravine. Friends of Tuckerman Ravine (friendsoftuckermanravine.org) also offers useful information and advice.

"Are We There Yet?"
It typically takes the fittest hikers about two hours to climb from Pinkham Notch to the floor of the Bowl; slower-moving parties can take three hours or longer, depending on pace. The descent from the Bowl to Pinkham Notch takes about 45 minutes if you can ski all the way from the ravine, down the Little Headwall (which becomes a waterfall in warm weather and after heavy rains), and all the way down the Sherburne Ski Trail. If the Sherburne Trail is closed due to lack of snow and you have to hike, it takes about 90 minutes from the Bowl to Pinkham.

Is It Open?

Tuckerman Ravine is almost always open (the notable exception being spring 2020, when much of the White Mountain National Forest closed due to the COVID-19 pandemic). The U.S. Forest Service (USFS) has jurisdiction over Tucks. In the past, rangers closed the ravine when they deemed snow conditions hazardous. In 1982, following years of criticism from skiers and climbers, the USFS abandoned this policy. In the spirit of mountaineering, each person must now decide for themself what, where, and when they can ski. Even during periods of elevated avalanche danger, you will likely be warned (via a ranger or a posted sign) that conditions are unsafe, but no one will stop you. This is as it should be—long live the freedom of the hills. But with this freedom comes the responsibility to use good mountaineering judgment about when to go and when to go home.

What to Bring

This is a backcountry area. There is no food or shelter in Tuckerman Ravine. Bring plenty of water—consider taking 2 liters on hot days. You can refill your water bottle at a pump near HoJo's, the AMC caretaker cabin (it got its nickname because the steep roofline of the original cabin resembled the iconic Howard Johnson's chain of restaurants and hotels). Pack food and bring storm gear. It is colder and wetter in the Bowl than at the trailhead. Be prepared for winter conditions, particularly if you plan to hike above the Lip. Carry a map and compass, especially if you will be hiking anywhere outside the Bowl (i.e., above treeline)—whiteouts and fog are common around the Mount Washington summit.

If you are climbing and skiing the steeper runs in Tuckerman Ravine, bring avalanche gear (see below), and consider bringing lightweight crampons and an ice ax (Microspikes are not adequate).

Where to Stay

If you plan to spend several days skiing in Tucks, you may as well stay in the neighborhood. For people interested in camping out, Hermit Lake (next to HoJo's) has eight shelters with room for 86 people. Five of the shelters are three-sided, and three are four-sided. There are also three tent platforms in the woods near Hermit Lake. The shelters and tentsites are filled on a first-come, first-served basis. You can buy a same-day permit to stay overnight at Hermit Lake in the AMC Pinkham Notch Visitor Center, so you will know whether there is room for you before you hike up. On spring weekends, all sites are usually filled by Friday night. Camping is forbidden anywhere else in the area. Pets are not allowed overnight.

If cooking over a camp stove and crashing in a sleeping bag is not your style, you can stay in comfort at the AMC Joe Dodge Lodge, located at the trailhead in Pinkham Notch. The epic family-style, all-you-can-eat meals are famous. Call ahead for reservations at 603-466-2727 or visit outdoors.org. Finally, there are numerous inns and hotels within a 15-minute drive of Pinkham Notch. You can obtain information and make reservations by contacting the Mount Washington Valley Chamber of Commerce (877-948-6867, mtwashingtonvalley.org).

How to Ski

The most important thing to bring with you to Tuckerman Ravine is common sense. Use good judgment and be realistic about what you can do here. Rather than being hell-bent on "going over the Lip" at all costs, try another goal: skiing well. Work on making good, controlled turns on lower-angle slopes, gradually moving up to steeper terrain as you improve. Learn to read snow; notice how it changes throughout the day and adapt your technique to the different types of snow that you encounter. Figure out when the snow is best to ski, and learn when and where to back off. You will soon progress from just getting down the Headwall to actually skiing it—one of the greatest thrills in Tuckerman Ravine.

MOUNTAIN HAZARDS

Tuckerman Ravine is not Disneyland. There are real mountain hazards to contend with. More than 160 fatalities have occurred on or around Mount Washington since 1849, including more than 30 people who have been killed skiing in Tucks. Following are some mountain hazards to watch out for.

Avalanche

Avalanches are common in Tuckerman Ravine and throughout the Presidential Range.

Every year, skiers and hikers are caught in avalanches in the Presidential Range; dozens have died or been injured. The most significant avalanche danger in Tuckerman Ravine and in all steep terrain is within 24 hours after a snowstorm. In addition, the ravine is subject to significant wind loading—that is, large amounts of snow can be deposited in the Bowl by wind, even if it is not snowing. That means that even on days when there has not been new snow, there can be significantly elevated avalanche danger. April is the peak month for reported avalanche incidents around Mount Washington.

Check the daily avalanche forecast from the Mount Washington Avalanche Center (mountwashingtonavalanchecenter.org), which is also posted in the Pinkham Notch Visitor Center and at HoJo's. The final assessment of the avalanche hazard rests with each skier. Look for signs of avalanche activity around the Bowl; a recent slide anywhere is a serious warning sign of snow instability. Gullies that are crowned by a new cornice or pillows of smooth snow are probably wind loaded and should be avoided. If you are concerned about the stability of the slope, ski in a different location or confine your skiing to the Sherburne Ski Trail.

Every backcountry skier should take an avalanche course. Find a course near you on the National Avalanche Center website, avalanche.org.

Bulletproof snow

Tucks can be a cruel lover. You may make the long drive and even longer hike only to discover that the sun is not shining and the snow is hard. Skiing the steeps on a hard, icy, "bulletproof" snow surface can be suicidal.

Look where the sun is shining and anticipate whether your route will be in shadow an hour later, by the time you have hiked to the top. If you lose the sun, the snow surface can instantly freeze over. Long sliding falls are a major cause of injury in Tucks.

Icefall

By late spring, icefall becomes a major hazard in Tuckerman Ravine. On warm spring days, refrigerator-sized ice blocks come tumbling down the Headwall. The danger of falling rock and ice is especially high on warm days. Choose your picnic spot carefully—look above you and avoid the most exposed places. Have an escape route (e.g., a large rock you can duck behind). Lunch Rocks is especially exposed to icefall so sit on your pack somewhere else—and heads up.

Crevasses

As spring progresses, crevasses form as snow in the steep gullies and in the Bowl becomes undermined by snowmelt. *Give crevasses and holes a wide berth when skiing or climbing near them.* The hole created by a waterfall that forms on the skier's right side of the Lip is particularly dangerous. Avoid routes that have crevasses. Crevasse falls are extremely serious, and extrication can be difficult or impossible.

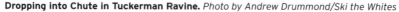

Dropping into Chute in Tuckerman Ravine. *Photo by Andrew Drummond/Ski the Whites*

Sun

The solar assault in the Bowl can be intense. You are simultaneously baked and broiled: sunshine gets you from above, and reflected sun can burn you from below. Wear sunglasses, sunscreen, and lip protection. Serious sunburn is a common problem, even in early spring.

Falling

If you fall when skiing or snowboarding, try to swing your skis or snowboard downhill. Attempt to self-arrest by setting your steel edges into the slope (but avoid the dreaded "tomahawk" caused by a ski edge abruptly biting into the snow) or driving the tip of your ski pole into the snow and putting your weight on it like an ice ax. If you have self-arrest pole grips, drive the pick into the snow and roll onto it to make it bite. Then breathe deep and pray.

SKI AND SNOWBOARD ROUTES IN TUCKERMAN RAVINE

The skiable routes change from day to day and year to year in Tuckerman Ravine. A gully that you skied in perfect corn snow one day may be an icy luge run the next. Let the prevailing conditions—not your fond memories—dictate where you point your skis.

Several critical factors should influence where you ski in Tuckerman Ravine. Snow conditions, the hour of day, the depth of the corn snow, the firmness of the base, and the runout (in case of a fall) should all be considered when deciding where to ski in the ravine. The steepness of each route varies from year to year depending on snow depth. Runouts also change; rocks that menace one year can be buried beneath snow the next.

The steepest routes in Tucks should be skied only in good snow conditions. In midwinter, if the avalanche hazard is low, you may be able to ski powder; more likely, you will find wind-affected "Styrofoam" snow. Corn snow is best and safest, along with dense snow that can be edged. Hard snow, as noted earlier, should be avoided.

Part of the art of skiing in Tucks is anticipating and adapting to the ever-changing personality of the mountain. You can come with a plan, but the mountain always gets the last word regarding what you can do.

Treat the mountain with respect, and you will be rewarded with a great skiing experience.

ROUTES IN THE BOWL

There are a few key orienting points in the ravine. (*Note*: Directional references are as you look up from the bottom of the ravine.) The Tuckerman Ravine Trail delivers you to the floor of the Bowl—this refers to the ravine proper, the bowl-shaped basin of snow into which most of the gullies empty. Lunch Rocks is the large area of boulders on the lower right side of the Bowl. This is the gathering spot (or bleachers) for the vocal crowd of spectators who cheers each skier and applauds the antics of those on the Headwall. Lunch Rocks is also in the line of fire for falling ice and avalanches—stay aware!

The most popular runs on the Headwall vary each year, depending on snow conditions in the ravine. Following are the main routes around the Bowl. The first two routes, the Headwall and the Lip, are the most prominent and popular runs.

Note on ski route data: Information on length of run and vertical drop is drawn from the U.S. Forest Service and from my own measurements. Slope pitch data is from the Mount Washington Avalanche Center.

The Headwall

- *Length of run*: 0.25 miles
- *Vertical drop*: 400 feet
- *Maximum pitch*: 55 degrees
- *Sustained pitch*: 30 degrees
- *Access*: The most popular routes ascend to the left and right ends of the Headwall. Climbing directly below the rock and ice cliffs is inadvisable because of the danger of falling ice, especially in spring.

The most distinctive feature in the ravine is the Headwall (a.k.a. Center Bowl). The Headwall is the broad slope that extends left to right from Chute to the Lip, and from the cliffs above to the floor of the ravine. The Headwall gets progressively steeper as you climb it. It starts at 30 degrees at the bottom, steepens to 40 degrees just below the rock band, and reaches 55 degrees alongside the cliffs in the upper center of the Headwall. You can ski anywhere on the lower section of the Headwall, provided there are no crevasses. See below for routes through the steep upper section of the Headwall. Less experienced skiers can simply climb the lower slopes to the level they feel comfortable and then ski down.

The Lip

- *Length of run*: 0.25 miles
- *Vertical drop*: 600 feet
- *Maximum pitch*: 45 degrees
- *Sustained pitch*: 40 degrees
- *Access*: Climb west above Lunch Rocks toward the right side of the Lip. The slope becomes progressively steeper until you exit the Bowl onto the Alpine Garden, a flat area of grass and sedge above the ravine. As you climb, take note of the location of any crevasses or holes to avoid on the descent.

Skiing over the Lip and into the Bowl is the classic test piece of Tucks. The Lip is on the upper right side of the Bowl, the broad slot that forms above Lunch Rocks and to the right of the rock and ice band. Above the Bowl, you glide gently across the flats of the Alpine Garden and then drop precipitously over the Lip. Earth falls away, sky rushes up to greet you, and your heart lodges in your throat. Late in

STOVEPIPE
CATHEDRAL
DODGE'S DROP
BOOTT SPUR #3
BOOTT SPUR #2
BOOTT SPUR #1
DUCHESS
HILLMAN'S HIGHWAY
EMPRESS
LEFT GULLY
CHUTE VARIATION SOUTH
CHUTE
CHUTE VARIATION NORTH
CENTER GULLY
HEAD
LOWER
SNOWFIELDS
LITTLE HEADWALL

BOOTT SPUR #1
BOOTT SPUR #2
BOOTT SPUR #3
CATHEDRAL
STOVEPIPE
DODGE'S DROP
HILLMAN'S HIGHWAY
DUCHESS
THE
CHRISTMAS
TREE
SHERBURNE

Photo by Alexandra Roberts

Graphics: WiseguyCreative.com. Photography: Aerial Photo NH

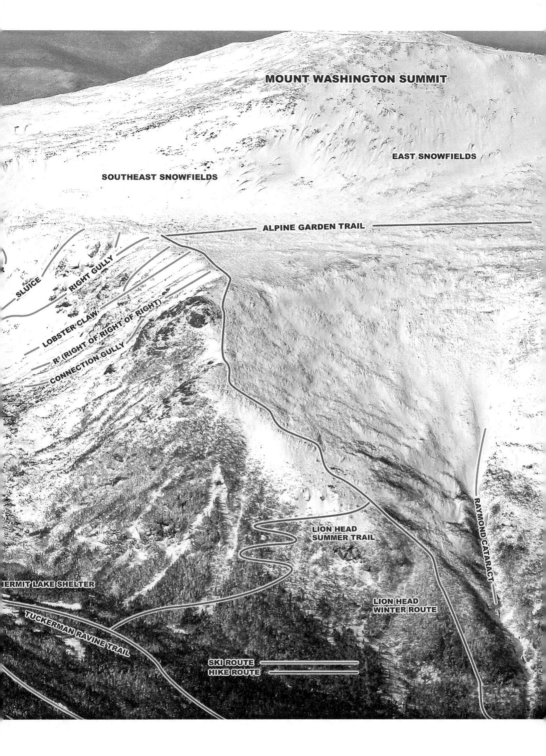

MOUNT WASHINGTON SUMMIT

EAST SNOWFIELDS

SOUTHEAST SNOWFIELDS

ALPINE GARDEN TRAIL

SLUICE

RIGHT GULLY

LOBSTER CLAW

R³ (RIGHT OF RIGHT OF RIGHT)

CONNECTION GULLY

RAYMOND CATARACT

LION HEAD
SUMMER TRAIL

HERMIT LAKE SHELTER

LION HEAD
WINTER ROUTE

TUCKERMAN RAVINE TRAIL

SKI ROUTE
HIKE ROUTE

spring, the Lip melts and separates from the Headwall and is no longer skiable. The U.S. Forest Service closes the Tuckerman Ravine Trail, which ascends through the Lip, when it becomes heavily crevassed in order to prevent unwitting hikers from stumbling into it.

Southeast and East Snowfields

- *Length of runs*: 0.2 miles
- *Vertical drop*: 600–900 feet
- *Maximum pitch*: 30 degrees
- *Sustained pitch*: 25 degrees
- *Access*: Ascend Lion Head Winter Route from Huntington Ravine Fire Road (see sign for Harvard Cabin), or climb Right Gully from Tuckerman Ravine.

Above Tuckerman Ravine, the long, moderate slopes of the Southeast and East Snowfields rise above the Alpine Garden on the Mount Washington summit cone. On clear days, this is the sunniest, most relaxed ski terrain on Mount Washington. It is a good destination for skiers and snowboarders who are getting their backcountry legs under them, provided they have the endurance for the climb.

The following routes are listed in the order they appear, from left to right as viewed from the bottom of the ravine.

Left Gully

- *Length of run*: 0.25 miles
- *Vertical drop*: 700 feet
- *Maximum pitch*: 45 degrees
- *Sustained pitch*: 35 degrees
- *Access*: Climb directly into Left Gully from the floor of the Bowl or traverse across the Headwall below Chute and then climb directly up the gully.

This beautiful, long, classic alpine gully runs from the Bigelow Lawn above Tuckerman Ravine to the floor of the Bowl. Most of Left Gully is hidden behind the large spur ridge left of Chute, just out of view from Lunch Rocks. With its northeastern exposure, this is one of the best and longest-lasting spring runs; I have skied from the top of Left Gully in early July. The headwall at the top of Left Gully occasionally forms a cornice that requires an airborne entrance; without this cornice, the Left Gully headwall is about 45 degrees. If you prefer terra firma, you can put on your skis just below this final steep pitch or on the left side at the top.

After the sheer entrance, the upper part of Left Gully is a wide ballroom. The pitch relaxes and the gully narrows into a 20-foot-wide hourglass between towering rock walls in the center. This bottleneck is the most dramatic feature of the run. The gully then reopens for its final turns all the way to the ravine floor. Like all the gullies, Left Gully is avalanche prone in midwinter, since it gets corniced and wind loaded.

Chute

+ *Length of run*: 0.25 miles
+ *Vertical drop*: 700 feet
+ *Maximum pitch*: 50 degrees
+ *Sustained pitch*: 40 degrees
+ *Access*: Climbing the boot ladder directly up Chute is strenuous and nerve-racking, but this enables you to preview conditions on the run. Many skiers will instead climb Left Gully and descend Chute after carefully scoping their intended line and assessing snow conditions.

Chute is the big, bold, in-your-face line that forms the left edge of the Headwall. The huge top-to-bottom exposure of this gully makes it the most intimidating of all the runs. "Like skiing off the edge of a cue ball" is the apt way Tucks veteran Brooks Dodge III (son of the legendary Tucks pioneer) describes it. Chute starts innocently on the Bigelow Lawn; you cannot see the route from the top. The route steepens gradually as you ski toward the edge of the Headwall, then it suddenly plunges straight down. Once you get started, you cannot turn back. A menacing rock buttress on skier's right bulges into the steep center section of the descent, forming an hourglass. A runnel often develops down the middle of Chute. Unlike the Lip, where skiers frequently take dramatic tumbles but bruise only their egos, a fall in Chute is more likely to have consequences. The lower-angle top section is usually wind scoured, with snow quality improving as you descend into the Bowl. A star-struck audience on Lunch Rocks applauds the skiers with the nerve to ski this run.

Chute has several variations. Brooks Dodge's original Chute Left Variation descended from the snowfield between Left Gully and Chute and went all the way down to the main slope of the ravine. This line rarely has enough snow to ski. Today's more common Chute Left Variation angles from the snowfield on the upper left and enters Chute above the hourglass. Chute Right Variation drifts out toward the center-left side of the Headwall.

Center Headwall and Icefall

+ *Length of run*: 0.2 miles
+ *Vertical drop*: 700 feet
+ *Maximum pitch*: 90 degrees
+ *Sustained pitch*: 60 degrees
+ *Access*: Climb via the Lip and traverse left.

These are the most technical ski routes in Tuckerman Ravine. A snow- and ice-covered cliff band separates the top of the Headwall from the more gradual slopes above the ravine. The Center Headwall runs are actually looker's left of center; dead center on the Headwall is a cliff. The two Center Headwall routes go right and left, respectively, around large rocks. This whole area in the center of the Headwall is disorienting as you ski down into it. The key to skiing here is to locate reference points as you climb. As you ski down, aim for these points so you don't get lost and cliffbound.

The Icefall route forms sporadically through the rock band just looker's left of the Lip. Brooks Dodge Jr., who first skied this line, insisted that this route no longer fills in enough to enable a descent "while remaining in contact with the snow at all times."

These are true extreme ski routes. The descents through Center Headwall and Icefall require intimate local knowledge of the terrain and perfect snow conditions. Skiing or riding through this area requires 5 to 25 feet of mandatory air. These are no-falls routes for experienced Tucks skiers.

Sluice

+ *Length of run*: 0.25 miles
+ *Vertical drop*: 600 feet
+ *Maximum pitch*: 50 degrees
+ *Sustained pitch*: 45 degrees
+ *Access*: Climb straight up Sluice or make an easier climb up neighboring Right Gully. From the top of Right Gully, walk to the Alpine Garden Trail, turn left, walk about five minutes, and Sluice leaves directly from the hiking trail. The top can be difficult to find; step out and confirm that you are on the ski route before heading down.

Sluice lies directly above Lunch Rocks, between the Lip and Right Gully. It is one of the steepest pitches in the Bowl. In its upper section, the slope bulges out and becomes convex before easing back for its direct run at Lunch Rocks. The top of Sluice reaches the Alpine Garden. If you are skiing from the summit, Sluice is the most direct line (but not the easiest) from the Southeast Snowfields into the Bowl. The top section is highly prone to avalanche or sluff.

Right Gully

+ *Length of run*: 0.25 miles
+ *Vertical drop*: 600 feet
+ *Maximum pitch*: 45 degrees
+ *Sustained pitch*: 35 degrees
+ *Access*: Climb the route from the bottom.

An elegant straight chute that begins at Lunch Rocks and rises directly north, Right Gully was one of the first routes to be skied in the ravine. It is wide at the top, narrows midway down and then widens steeply at the bottom where it joins with Sluice. Be extra cautious when skiing in firmer snow conditions. The runout—directly into Lunch Rocks—is unforgiving.

Right Gully is the easiest route to climb out of the ravine if you are headed to the summit. However, this route often gets wind loaded from the gusty summit; avoid skiing here (or any of the gullies) when there is a new cornice on top. Because it faces due south, it tends to have loose, wet snow sluffs and loses its snow early in spring.

Lobster Claw

- *Length of run*: 0.25 miles
- *Vertical drop*: 600 feet
- *Maximum pitch*: 40 degrees
- *Sustained pitch*: 30 degrees
- *Access*: Climb the ski route from the bottom.

This is the next prominent chute to looker's right of Right Gully. It derives its name from the way it breaks into two arching fingers at the top, resembling a lobster claw. The top of Lobster Claw is higher than the Lip, so it affords spectacular views over the ravine. Lobster Claw is about 10 feet wide in its upper section, and the run maintains a comfortable, consistent pitch of 35 degrees. Like Right Gully, this is a sunny south-facing run that builds good corn snow early.

ROUTES AROUND HILLMAN'S HIGHWAY

Rising directly just beyond HoJo's on looker's left is the prominent long alpine gully known as Hillman's Highway. It is the main attraction in an area that features a number of established descents. Following the description of Hillman's Highway below, the remaining route descriptions are listed from Boott Spur to Little Headwall (looker's left to right).

Hillman's Highway

- *Length of run*: 0.6 miles
- *Vertical drop*: 1,400 feet
- *Maximum pitch*: 40+ degrees
- *Sustained pitch*: 30 degrees
- *Access*: From HoJo's, cross the bridge over the Cutler River and turn right (west) on the Sherburne Ski Trail. Follow the trail uphill, bearing left at a fork. You will soon pass a rescue cache. Hillman's Highway is the prominent snow gully that continues all the way up to the ridge.

Hillman's Highway is the longest of the routes around Tuckerman Ravine, with a vertical drop of 1,400 feet. It was first skied by Dartmouth skiers Harold Hillman and Ed Wells in the mid-1930s. Hillman's is less traveled because it is outside of the Bowl and lacks the cheering section found at Lunch Rocks. For many, that is part of its appeal: Hillman's is a place to get away from the crowds.

Hillman's has two entrances at the top. The left fork (when climbing up) is the steepest section of the run, around 43 degrees. The grade on the right fork starts more gradually but then steepens to about 40 degrees and narrows into a rock-lined 30-foot-wide corridor. The run then opens up as much as 50 feet (depending on snow levels) for the lower two-thirds of the descent. There is plenty of room to make turns.

From the top of Hillman's, there are nice views into Tuckerman Ravine of Chute, the Lip, Right Gully, and Lion Head. It is possible to hike out of Hillman's to access Oakes Gulf or to drop down into Tucks (Left Gully is the closest entrance). The reverse is also possible: you can hike out of Left Gully to go to Hillman's. Take care on the Bigelow Lawn to walk on snow and not damage the delicate sedge. When skiing Hillman's, be aware that it can ice over quickly and become a dangerous luge run when it goes into shade. The gully ends at the Sherburne Trail, where you can continue directly to Pinkham Notch.

Cathedral

- *Length of run*: 0.2 miles
- *Vertical drop*: 700 feet
- *Maximum pitch*: 45 degrees
- *Sustained pitch*: 35 degrees
- *Access*: Climb from the bottom, starting on Hillman's Highway.

This narrow couloir plunges down from high on the summit ridge of Boott Spur. It is located on the slope that forms the left (southern) boundary of Hillman's. There are two entrances from the top; the one on skier's right has the easier (lower angle) start. The gully connects with the bottom section of Hillman's Highway. Cathedral has several ice bulges and needs a lot of snow to be skiable. The climb can be ornery, involving post-holing through vegetation at the bottom before reaching the firmer snow. This north-facing line loses sun quickly, so it is best skied at midday when the snow is soft.

Dodge's Drop

- *Length of run*: 0.25 miles
- *Vertical drop*: 700 feet
- *Maximum pitch*: 50 degrees
- *Sustained pitch*: 45 degrees
- *Access*: The easiest access to Dodge's Drop is to climb to the top of Hillman's Highway then hike left to the top of Dodge's.

This ultra-steep gully was Brooks Dodge's signature run. It is the prominent line to looker's left of Hillman's Highway. When Dodge first skied it in the mid-1940s, his friends met him at the bottom and suggested that he give it an alliterative name, in the fashion of Hillman's Highway. "How about Dodge's Drop?" his friend proposed. Dodge liked it. "I'm not unhappy that a run is named after me," Dodge told me, "and I'm pretty happy with that run, too."

As well he should be. Dodge's Drop is a run that seasoned Tucks die-hards aspire to ski. It is an intimidating descent. The top of the chute is almost always corniced.

Brooks Dodge skiing the Headwall. *Courtesy of New England Ski Museum*

There are two entrances that merge into a narrow main gully. The crux is the top turns, which are about 50 degrees and often rocky. After the two upper fingers merge, a narrow chute leads to an ice bulge between some rocks; you must ensure that there is enough snow to ski over the ice flow. From here, the gully opens and the pace relaxes. It goes over some bushes and merges onto Hillman's Highway.

Duchess

- *Length of run*: 0.3 miles
- *Vertical drop*: 800 feet
- *Maximum pitch*: 50 degrees
- *Sustained pitch*: 45 degrees
- *Access*: Climb Hillman's Highway. From the top, hike skier's left onto the prow of the buttress, where Duchess drops down.

The broad rocky buttress that separates Hillman's Highway from the Bowl in Tuckerman Ravine is home to Duchess. Looking up from HoJo's, Duchess lies just right of Hillman's Highway. The most dramatic feature of Duchess is its funnel-like lower section that empties onto the Lower Snowfield. The route was first skied by Brooks Dodge in the mid-1940s. He named it after the Duchess Trail, a faint abandoned path that climbed from the Little Headwall to the top of Boott Spur and passed by the top of what is now the Duchess ski route.

Duchess greets her suitors by terrifying them: as you stand at the top, you look over your ski tips, peering straight down at Hermit Lake, 1,500 feet below. There is no mistaking how high you are and how steep the route is. Making things scarier, you can't see the descent route beyond the first snowfield. The route is wide to start but narrows quickly. The skiable line drifts to the skier's right, then back to the center. The route descends through a series of funnel-like chutes, some just wider than a ski length, before finally emptying onto the Lower Snowfields.

Lower Snowfields

- *Length of run*: 0.3 miles
- *Vertical drop*: 700 feet
- *Maximum pitch*: 40 degrees
- *Sustained pitch*: 30 degrees
- *Access*: From HoJo's, ski up toward either Hillman's Highway or the Little Headwall, and you will run into the Lower Snowfields.

The Lower Snowfields are the broad slope between the Little Headwall and Hillman's Highway. This area can be skied on its own and is a good alternative if conditions on Hillman's are wind loaded or otherwise poor.

Little Headwall

- *Length of run*: 100 yards
- *Vertical drop*: 150 feet
- *Maximum pitch*: 40 degrees
- *Sustained pitch*: 25 degrees

Access: From the bottom of the Bowl, bear right of the Tuckerman Ravine Trail, staying in the Cutler River drainage. The Little Headwall is a short, steep drop that forms halfway down the riverbed to Hermit Lake.

This short pitch forms on the Cutler River between the Bowl and Hermit Lake. When the Little Headwall is in, you can ski from the Bowl directly onto the Sherburne Trail. By springtime, it has usually turned into a waterfall, making it necessary to hike back down to HoJo's on the Tuckerman Ravine Trail. When holes start to appear on the Little Headwall, it is a sign that the snow on the riverbed is undermined and you should hike down.

11 AVALANCHE BROOK SKI TRAIL

This exciting and rugged ski trail lies in the shadow of Mount Washington and features deep woods, frozen cascades, and a fun descent. It connects Pinkham Notch to the ski town of Jackson, New Hampshire.

Distance: 6 miles, AMC Pinkham Notch Visitor Center to Rocky Branch trailhead
Elevation: *Start*: 2,020 feet; *Highest point*: 2,480 feet; *Finish*: 1,200 feet, Rocky Branch trailhead; *Vertical drop*: 1,280 feet
Maps: *White Mountain Winter Recreation Map & Guide* (AMC), *White Mountains* (Map Adventures), *White Mountain National Forest East* (Trails Illustrated)
Difficulty: More difficult
Gear: Telemark

HOW TO GET THERE

The Avalanche Brook Ski Trail departs from Gulf of Slides Ski Trail 0.3 miles from the parking lot at AMC's Pinkham Notch Visitor Center on NH 16 (*GPS coordinates*: 44° 15.435' N, 71° 15.166' W). You must either hitchhike back or drop off a car where you finish at the Rocky Branch trailhead on NH 16 (*GPS coordinates*: 44° 12.288' N, 71° 14.438' W).

THE TOUR

The Avalanche Brook Ski Trail is an exciting run that passes through mixed forest in the heart of the White Mountains. Cut by volunteers of the Appalachian Mountain Club in 1975, the Avalanche Brook Ski Trail was designed to link the growing cross-country ski trail network in the town of Jackson with AMC's ski trail network in and around Pinkham Notch. The original plan was to cut a trail down the east side of NH 16, where the terrain is relatively gentle. When the trail designers could not figure out a way to skirt the precipitous and rocky drop-off around Glen Ellis Falls, they turned their attention to the west side of the valley. The views from the west side were considered superior, but the trail builders had to level out a bothersome sidehill in several places. The result was the Avalanche Brook Trail.

Once the trail was completed, it became possible to traverse the entire length of Pinkham Notch, beginning from what is now Great Glen Trails (next to the Mount Washington Auto Road), and to ski most of the way to Jackson. The trail enjoys steady traffic throughout winter.

This tour showcases alpine forests, numerous frozen cascades, and varied terrain. It offers an enjoyable half day of skiing. The terrain is rolling and is best suited for skiers using Nordic backcountry (telemark) equipment, since there are frequent transitions. When the Avalanche Brook Trail begins its descent, it heads fairly quickly to the valley floor, dropping some 1,300 feet in slightly more than 2 miles. The trail runs parallel to NH 16 and is well marked with blue blazes throughout.

AVALANCHE BROOK SKI TRAIL

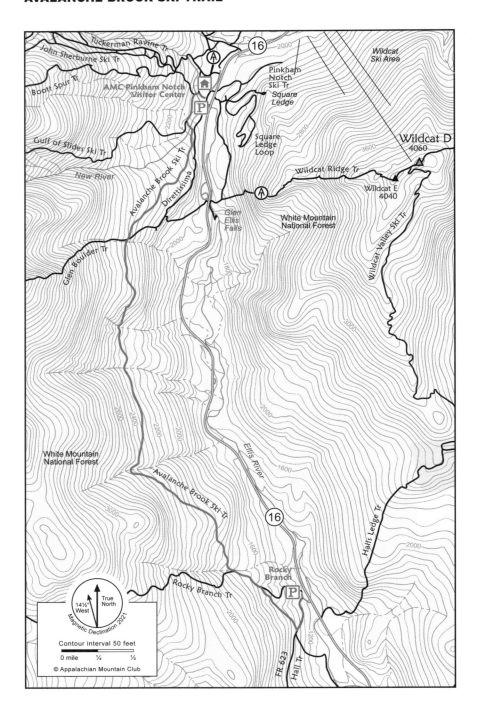

Backcountry skiers cross a snow-laden bridge over a deep ravine on the Avalanche Brook Trail.

The route should be skied from north to south since this maximizes the amount of downhill. You will need to leave a car at the large Rocky Branch trailhead parking area on NH 16, 5 miles south of the AMC Pinkham Notch Visitor Center. Drop your car in the morning, then hitch back to Pinkham Notch with one of the many cars heading to the Wildcat Ski Area.

Starting at Pinkham Notch, take in the beautiful views of Huntington Ravine to the northwest and the craggy summit of Boott Spur, which lies due west. The tour begins on Gulf of Slides Ski Trail, which departs at the south end of the parking lot at the Pinkham Notch Visitor Center. Immediately cross a wooden bridge over the New River and follow Gulf of Slides Ski Trail. After 0.3 miles, Gulf of Slides Ski Trail diverges right and the Avalanche Brook Trail continues to the left, marked by blue blazes. The Avalanche Brook Trail meanders through hardwood forests for 0.7 miles, then climbs steadily toward the Glen Boulder Trail junction at 1.5 miles. The Avalanche Brook Trail then levels out and contours. Glen Boulder itself can be seen above to the west. The trail continues through mixed forest, with beautiful views of the Carter Range across the valley.

Rounding a broad ridge that runs from Slide Peak, the trail descends briefly then contours at 2,300 feet for another mile, crossing a broad frozen brook (where a bridge washed away). After a gradual climb, the trail crosses a wooden bridge over Avalanche Brook, a deep, ravine-like drainage. From this point, the trail plunges downhill for the next 2 miles. AMC crews have done good trail work on this route, adding sturdy bridges that now span most of the deeper drainages.

Once the Avalanche Brook Trail begins its descent, it continues a sustained downhill with plenty of room for turns. The trail is well graded but beware of drainages and open water, especially at the lower elevations. This is a moderately challenging but forgiving route; there is ample room to slow down or bail out on the sides of the trail.

After about 5 miles and a turn-filled descent, pass a junction for the Rocky Branch Trail, a hiking trail that joins the Avalanche Brook Trail for a short distance. Ski downhill another 0.3 miles, and the Rocky Branch Trail diverges to the left. Bear right and continue on the Avalanche Brook Trail for another half-mile until it crosses the Hall Trail (also known as FR 623), a groomed ski trail of the Jackson Ski Touring Foundation (JSTF). If you turn left here, it is 0.3 miles back to the Rocky Branch trailhead parking lot. JSTF generously allows skiers to ski this short piece of the Hall Trail between the Avalanche Brook Trail and the Rocky Branch parking area without the purchase of a trail pass. Downtown Jackson is 9 miles south of the Rocky Branch trailhead on NH 16, where you can finish your tour by a fireplace at one of the local establishments.

⑫ GULF OF SLIDES

Gulf of Slides is a wild, beautiful, and lightly traveled wilderness ravine with great steep skiing. Gulf of Slides Ski Trail is a historic CCC route that links the ravine with Pinkham Notch. The sinewy ski trail is a fine tour on its own.

Distance: 2.5 miles, Gulf of Slides Ski Trail, one way; 0.5 miles, Main Gully, Gulf of Slides

Elevation: *Start/Finish*: 2,020 feet, Pinkham Notch; *Highest point*: 4,000 feet (top of Gulf of Slides Ski Trail/base of Main Gully), 5,000 feet (top of Gulf of Slides); *Vertical drop*: 3,000 feet, top of Gulf of Slides to Pinkham Notch

Maps: *White Mountain Winter Recreation Map & Guide* (AMC), *White Mountains* (Map Adventures), *White Mountain National Forest East* (Trails Illustrated)

Difficulty: Most difficult, Gulf of Slides Ski Trail; Ski mountaineering, Gulf of Slides

Gear: AT, telemark, snowboard

HOW TO GET THERE

Gulf of Slides Ski Trail leaves from the south end of the parking lot at the AMC Pinkham Notch Visitor Center (*GPS coordinates*: 44° 15.435′ N, 71° 15.166′ W).

HISTORY

Skiing in Gulf of Slides has historically been reserved for the smaller number of skiers interested in exploring lesser-known slopes around Mount Washington. Although skiers began venturing into Tuckerman Ravine in the late 1920s, those same skiers did not make their way into Gulf of Slides until the early 1930s. That skiers finally came was inevitable: the snowfields and gullies of Gulf of Slides are visible from numerous vantage points in the Mount Washington Valley and hold obvious promise for skiing.

Al Sise, one of the early Tuckerman skiers, told me that Gulf of Slides was simply "where someone would go to get away from the crowds. It was not as awe-inspiring a place [as Tuckerman Ravine], but it was a nice place to get away from it all and ski."

The first skiers in Gulf of Slides bushwhacked their way up the New River from AMC's Pinkham Notch Camp. It was not a leisurely trip, according to the early accounts. Some skiers accessed the Gulf from the top by climbing up to Davis Path, returning to Pinkham Notch by skiing the snow-filled bed of the New River—no easy feat.

Interest and activity in skiing Gulf of Slides picked up enough in the early 1930s to warrant building a bona fide ski trail. In 1935, master trail designer Charlie Proctor laid out Gulf of Slides Ski Trail from Pinkham Notch, following the north bank of the New River. The trail was cut that same year by the Civilian Conservation Corps, and it has been maintained as a ski trail ever since. The trail was the site of a few races, but because there are no shelters near Gulf of Slides, it was considered a less hospitable place for racing than the more popular trails in the valley. Unlike

GULF OF SLIDES

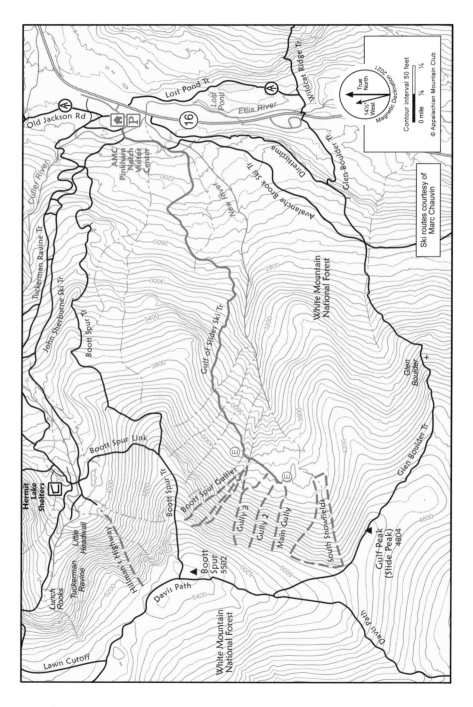

Contour interval 50 feet

© Appalachian Mountain Club

Ski routes courtesy of Marc Chauvin

The long line: skiing Main Gully in Gulf of Slides. *Photo by Cait Fitzgerald*

the Sherburne Ski Trail, which has been widened and rerouted over the years, Gulf of Slides Ski Trail has never been significantly altered.

Lacking crowds, Gulf of Slides has not enjoyed the kind of ski lore of Tuckerman Ravine, where every ski run has a name and reputation. The more popular runs on Gulf of Slides headwall were given rather uninteresting names. The names are less important than the fact that virtually all the gullies and snowfields on the headwall of Gulf of Slides, starting from Boott Spur, have been skied and are skiable.

THE TOUR

The fact that Gulf of Slides remains unknown to many Tucks regulars is precisely its appeal.

Gulf of Slides is a wide ravine between ridges that run off Boott Spur (5,502 feet) and Slide Peak (4,804 feet). The slides for which it is named form along the east-facing headwall and can be seen from NH 16. Gulf of Slides holds some of the latest snow in the White Mountains outside of Tuckerman Ravine. It is a traditional spring skiing destination, with ski activity usually continuing into May.

Gulf of Slides is an extraordinary area. A first reaction on seeing the slides and the snowfield is one of amazement: the wide, open bowl skiing and steep alpine runs more closely resemble the Colorado backcountry than New England. Climbing high up the slides, skiers are treated to panoramic views up and down the valley. There is a wild, untamed quality about the place. It is rewarding just to come here and take in the breathtaking landscape. Skiing the gullies adds to the thrill.

Gulf of Slides Ski Trail starts at the south end of the parking lot at the AMC Pinkham Notch Visitor Center and branches off immediately from the bottom of the Sherburne Ski Trail. The start of the trail is the same as that of the Avalanche Brook Ski Trail; the trails diverge after 0.2 miles, where Gulf of Slides Ski Trail heads right. The trail is about 20 feet wide and climbs steadily; the steepest grade is about 20 degrees. There are nice views to the east of the Carter–Moriah Ridge and Wildcat Ridge as the trail climbs. Near the top, there is a rescue cache with a litter shortly before the trail crosses the New River. There are only fleeting views of the slides themselves until this point.

Gulf of Slides Ski Trail is an enjoyable run in itself. Skied from the top, it is a sustained, 2.5-mile downhill run similar in character to the Sherburne Trail, although narrower and not as steep as the lower sections of the Sherbie. If avalanche danger exists on the slides (see note on page 75), simply skiing the trail is a day well spent. It has the characteristics of the best 1930s-era down-mountain ski trails, full of twists, turns, swoops, and surprises.

On the upper half-mile of Gulf of Slides Ski Trail, you cross the bottom of the skiing routes. After skiing across a bridge and rounding the top of a drainage, the bottom of **Gully #3** meets the trail. Ski a little farther, and come upon **Gully #2**, a prominent sickle-shaped run. Finally, the ski trail feeds directly into the foot of **Main Gully, or Gully #1**. This broad, fan-shaped gully climbs 1,000 feet in a half-mile in a direct line to the ridge. All of these gullies get progressively steeper as they rise; the steepest sections are about 40 degrees.

Carving powder high on Gulf of Slides. *Photo by Corey Fitzgerald/Northeast Mountaineering*

The preferred approach to the gullies is to climb them from Gulf of Slides Ski Trail. This enables you to preview what you will ski and assess conditions. Skiers and snowboarders can climb—booting up if the snow is firm or skinning in wide traverses—as high as they are comfortable and then descend.

For more moderate skiing in this beautiful landscape, continue just beyond (south of) Main Gully through widely spaced spruce trees to the base of **South Snowfields (a.k.a. the Sandbox)** that runs north from Slide Peak. This is a broad lower-angle snowfield with easier skiing than the gullies.

Boott Spur Gullies (a.k.a. the Fingers) are to looker's right of Gulf of Slides, raking the flanks of rocky Boott Spur. These can be reached by climbing from the bottom of Gully #3. It is also possible to enter these gullies from the top by climbing Boott Spur Trail, which leaves the Tuckerman Ravine Trail just above Crystal Cascade, 0.4 miles from the Pinkham Notch Visitor Center. From Pinkham Notch, it is 3.4 miles to the summit of Boott Spur via Boott Spur Trail.

Finally, Gulf of Slides can be accessed by hiking up Hillman's Highway or Left Gully in Tuckerman Ravine and walking south on Davis Path until you can see the gullies and snowfields of Gulf of Slides. This is a much longer approach than Gulf of Slides Ski Trail and requires good weather on the summit.

A trip into Gulf of Slides is a good way to inspire skiers to explore the other possibilities for wilderness skiing in the White Mountains. Gulf of Slides is one of many outlying ravines that are far less traveled by skiers. Oakes Gulf, Ammonoosuc Ravine, King Ravine, and Jefferson Ravine are just some of the many excellent skiing jewels that skiers with a lust for adventure have had to themselves. You need only pick up your map and head out. There is skiing everywhere, and the opportunities for exploring new terrain are limitless.

A word of caution: Gulf of Slides is so named because *it is highly prone to avalanches.* Despite being lower angle than many runs in Tuckerman Ravine, it has long avalanche paths that funnel into dangerous terrain traps. There have been numerous close calls and at least three backcountry skiers have died in avalanches in Gulf of Slides—one was killed in February 2000, and on March 24, 1996, an avalanche claimed the lives of two skiers who were standing at the bottom of Main Gully. Families of the victims of the 1996 avalanche provided funds for one of the Gulf of Slides rescue caches, which is stocked with avalanche probes, shovels, and a litter.

Check the daily avalanche forecast of the Mount Washington Avalanche Center (mountwashingtonavalanchecenter.org). Carry avalanche equipment—a shovel, avalanche beacon, and probes. Observe the terrain for signs of recent slide activity. Gulf of Slides should be avoided just after a snowfall, when its 30- to 40-degree slopes are most likely to slide. This is a remote area and, in the event of an accident, help will take a long time to arrive. Prevention—not skiing slopes that you suspect are unstable—is essential.

⑬ JOHN SHERBURNE SKI TRAIL

The historic Sherburne Ski Trail—the "Sherbie"—is the most popular back-country ski trail in the East. It is easily accessed and packed with turns as it descends from just below Tuckerman Ravine to the AMC Pinkham Notch Visitor Center.

Distance: 2 miles, Hermit Lake Shelters to AMC Pinkham Notch Visitor Center
Elevation: *Start/Finish*: 2,020 feet; *Highest point*: 3,950 feet; *Vertical drop*: 1,930 feet
Maps: *White Mountain Winter Recreation Map & Guide* (AMC), *White Mountains* (Map Adventures)
Difficulty: More difficult+
Gear: AT, telemark, snowboard

HOW TO GET THERE

From the AMC Pinkham Notch Visitor Center on NH 16 (*GPS coordinates*: 44° 15.435′ N, 71° 15.166′ W), take the Tuckerman Ravine Trail 2.4 miles uphill to the Hermit Lake Shelters. The Sherburne Trail starts across the wooden bridge that is next to the Hermit Lake caretaker's building (a.k.a. HoJo's).

THE TOUR

For Tuckerman Ravine skiers, the John Sherburne Ski Trail simply may be the final run after a day of steep skiing in the Bowl. But the Sherbie, as it is affectionately known, is actually a great downhill ski trail and a worthwhile destination in its own right.

Designed and laid out by Charles Proctor and cut in 1934, the Sherburne Trail was named for John H. Sherburne Jr., a well-liked ski racer and member of the Ski Club Hochgebirge of Boston. Sherburne was instrumental in starting the famous American Inferno races in Tuckerman Ravine (see the chapter on Tuckerman Ravine, page 44, for history). He died unexpectedly of tetanus in 1934.

As the popularity of skiing in Tuckerman Ravine increased, it created a critical need for a ski trail that connected the Bowl to Pinkham Notch. Before the Sherburne Trail was built, Tuckerman Ravine was served only by the old Fire Trail, now known as the Tuckerman Ravine Trail (TRT). Skiing was always prohibited on the Fire Trail because it posed a serious threat to unsuspecting hikers ambling up the mountain. Tuckerman Ravine regulars insisted on the development of an alternative to walking downhill with skis for more than 2 miles. The solution was the John Sherburne Ski Trail.

The rules of the road established in the 1930s are still in effect today:

* The Sherburne Ski Trail is reserved for skiing and snowboarding. No snowshoeing or hiking is permitted. Skins are required if ascending.
* The Tuckerman Ravine Trail is the preferred ascent route to Tucks. Skiing downhill is strictly forbidden on the TRT.

JOHN SHERBURNE SKI TRAIL

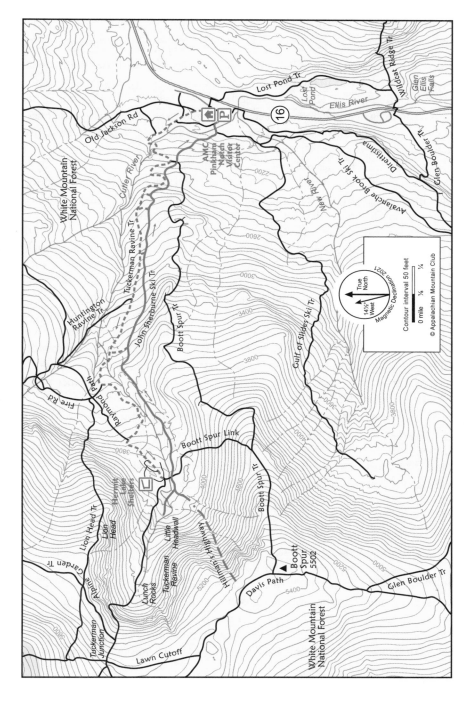

- Skinning uphill is permitted on the Sherburne Trail, but it may not be appreciated by unsuspecting downhillers. Skinners should stay well to the side as downhill skiers may not see you.

The Sherbie is a wide trail that was cut with skiers in mind. There is ample room to choose your own line, and ski and ride it as you like. It catches the frequent storms on Mount Washington and is often replenished with a new layer of snow.

After climbing the TRT, you arrive at the Hermit Lake caretaker's cabin, better known as HoJo's (so nicknamed because its roofline resembled that of the once-popular Howard Johnson's roadside restaurants and hotels). There is also a staffed U.S. Forest Service cabin here, and the snow rangers offer a wealth of knowledge about Tuckerman Ravine and avalanche conditions.

After peering at the steep ski routes of Hillman's Highway and Tuckerman Ravine that beckon in the distance, it's time to down some snacks, don downhill ski clothing, and begin the descent. The actual start of the Sherburne Trail is above HoJo's at the base of the Little Headwall. This enables skiers coming from Tucks to ski a continuous route from the bottom of the Bowl all the way to Pinkham Notch. However, once the Little Headwall melts and becomes a cascade, which tends to be early in spring, the short section of the Sherburne Trail above HoJo's is no longer used. Thus, most skiers access and descend the Sherburne from HoJo's.

Directly opposite HoJo's, see a sign for Hillman's Highway and the Sherburne Ski Trail next to a bridge over the Cutler River. Cross the bridge and you are on the Sherburne. Turn left, and the trail drops gently at the start. The views across the valley to Wildcat Ridge and Carter Dome are worth stopping to admire. There are also impressive views back into both Tuckerman and Huntington ravines to the west and northwest, respectively.

As with many trails of its era, the memorable sections of the Sherbie were all given names by the early skiers. The trail runs parallel to the south fork of the Cutler River but turns sharply southeast away from the drainage 0.6 miles below HoJo's. This turn is known as Windy Corner, and it was once the site of a cabin built by the Harvard Mountaineering Club. Windy Corner got its name because it is blasted by wind from the ravines and was frequently icy and windblown. The U.S. Forest Service relocated the section of the trail at Windy Corner so it would be less exposed to the weather.

As it descends, the Sherburne Trail progressively steepens. At 1.6 miles, the S-turn is reached, so named because the trail swings back and forth. Just below the S-turn is the Schuss, a sharp left turn with a steep, straight drop. This was considered one of the most difficult points of the Sherburne Trail when races were held there. The trail then passes through a sharp, narrow right turn called the Bottleneck, then enters the Glade, an open, moderately steep slope. The final drop is Deadman's Curve, where the trail drops steeply and turns sharply to the

Last run of the day down the Sherburne Ski Trail. *Photo by Cait Fitzgerald*

right. The latter section received its name in the 1930s when a skier was killed here after hitting a tree. The tree was promptly removed.

The steepest sections of the trail (up to 24 degrees) are encountered in the last third of the route. The trail widens to 60 feet at this final section, so there are many options for how to ski it.

The Sherbie can be deceptive. Two miles of turns is a lot of skiing at the end of a long day. This run can be a delight if your legs are fresh and an endurance test if you've blown all your strength in Tuckerman Ravine earlier in the day—hence, its nickname, the "sure burn."

The Sherbie is an excellent introduction to backcountry down-mountain skiing and Eastern trail riding. It is equivalent to an intermediate trail at a downhill ski area, but it is ungroomed, so conditions can make it challenging. The trail is wide enough to make long turns, will certainly introduce you to some unpredictable snow conditions, and calls for some creative thinking in your approach to some of the natural obstacles.

The Sherburne Trail is the gateway to the high church of Eastern backcountry skiing, Tuckerman Ravine. If you are a newcomer to this sport, a side trip into the Bowl to see what you can aspire to ski or ride should provide the incentive to keep training. The thrill of the steeps awaits you just above.

14 GREAT GULF

Airplane Gully and Pipeline Gully are steep, elegant couloirs that descend one of the most dramatic alpine ravines in the White Mountains. Great Gulf Trail descends a broad headwall.

Distance: 2.1 miles, Marshfield Base Station via Cog Railway to Airplane Gully; 5.2 miles, Pinkham Notch via Tuckerman Ravine Trail
Elevation: *Start/Finish*: 2,700 feet, Marshfield Base Station; 2,500 feet, Jewell trailhead; or 2,020 feet, Pinkham Notch Visitor Center; *Highest point*: 5,500 feet (Airplane), 5,533 feet (Pipeline), 5,925 feet (Great Gulf Trail); *Bottom of gullies*: 4,228 feet, Spaulding Lake; *Vertical drop*: Great Gulf gullies, 1,300–1,600 feet; Total tour, 2,800 feet (via Cog), 3,480 feet (via PNVC)
Maps: *White Mountain Winter Recreation Map & Guide* (AMC) is the only map showing the Great Gulf ski routes. The terrain is covered by *White Mountain National Forest Map & Guide* (AMC), *White Mountains* (Map Adventures), and *White Mountain National Forest East* (Trails Illustrated).
Difficulty: Ski mountaineering
Gear: AT, telemark, snowboard

HOW TO GET THERE

Via Cog Railway: The most direct access to Great Gulf is by skiing 2.1 miles up the Cog Railway (fee required, see thecog.com) from the Marshfield Base Station (*GPS coordinates*: 44° 16.205′ N, 71° 21.050′ W) to the Gulfside and Westside trail junction. Alternatively, ski 3.3 miles up the Jewell Trail (no fee, trailhead at hiker parking lot on Base Road, GPS coordinates: 44° 16.033′ N, 71° 21.683′ W) to Gulfside and Westside trail junction.

From Pinkham Notch: Climb to the summit of Mount Washington (4.2 miles via the Tuckerman Ravine Trail or 4.4 miles via the Lion Head Trail Winter Route), from which point it is 0.4 miles north on Gulfside Trail to the junction with Great Gulf Trail. Continue following Gulfside Trail another 0.6 miles north to the Westside Trail junction, which is near the top of Airplane Gully.

Via Auto Road: The Mount Washington Auto Road (mtwashingtonautoroad.com, 603-466-3988, *GPS coordinates*: 44° 17.378′ N, 71° 13.495′ W), which usually opens to cars in mid-May, also offers access to the Great Gulf. Park at the 7.5-mile parking area (*GPS coordinates*: 44° 16.475′ N, 71° 18.162′ W) and hike 0.7 miles around the top of Great Gulf on Gulfside Trail. *Note*: The Mount Washington Auto Road charges a fee to drive up the road.

HISTORY

Great Gulf is the largest glacial cirque in the White Mountains. The walls of this massive ravine extend east 3.5 miles from Mount Washington all the way to Mount Madison. The southern headwall is bounded by the Mount Washington summit cone (6,288 feet) and on the west by Mount Clay (5,531 feet). Great Gulf

GREAT GULF

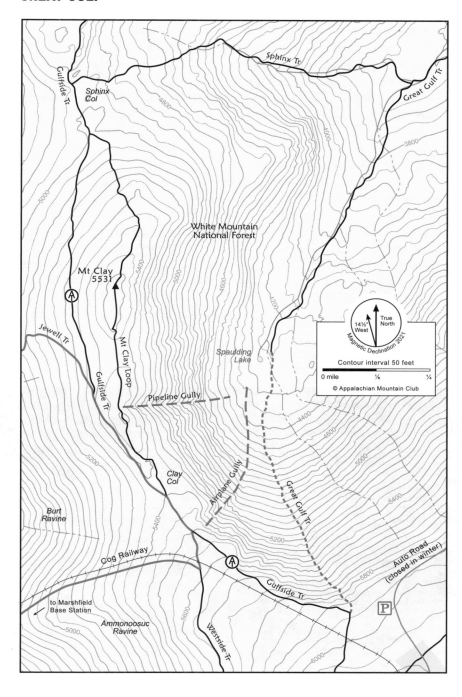

drops more than 1,600 feet from its rim to Spaulding Lake, which lies on the valley floor. This entire area lies within the 5,552-acre Great Gulf Wilderness, established in 1964.

Great Gulf is one of the wildest places in the White Mountains. According to AMC's *White Mountain Guide*, Darby Field, who is credited with the first ascent of Mount Washington in 1642, made the first recorded observation of Great Gulf. The name is credited to Ethan Allen Crawford, who got lost in cloudy weather on Mount Washington in 1823 and reported coming to "the edge of a great gulf." Laura and Guy Waterman wrote in *Forest and Crag* (AMC Books, 1989) that a Boston newspaper observed in 1909: "Until the present summer, the Gulf has remained almost as unknown as it was inaccessible."

For skiers, the remoteness of Great Gulf has been at once its attraction and its deterrent. There is simply no easy way to "get there from here." One indication of its out-of-the-way character is that the ski history of Great Gulf is obscure. Photographer Winston Pote has stunning photos of skiing on the rim of the Great Gulf in 1938 and 1940 (see page xx), but there is no indication that Pote or his friends actually descended into the Gulf. The credit for first descents of all the major routes in Great Gulf may go to Brooks Dodge, the author of numerous firsts in Tuckerman Ravine, who skied six major gullies in Great Gulf in the mid-1940s. Among them were what he called Clay Col Gully (now Airplane) and Clay Summit Gully (now Pipeline).

Skiing one of Great Gulf's steep gullies. *Photo by Brian Mohr/EmberPhoto*

For those skiers who make the effort, Great Gulf holds many rewards. Standing on the rim of Great Gulf, you peer out over the wildest reaches of the White Mountains. The northern peaks of the Presidential Range—Mounts Jefferson, Adams, and Madison—stand like inaccessible beacons from here. To reach them requires traveling along the exposed spine of the White Mountains. They appear so close yet are so far.

The terrain of Great Gulf is remarkably alpine. The skiing options are appropriately intimidating and humbling. A series of couloirs rake the rocky headwall. Many are hidden away, revealing themselves by surprise. You will be hiking or skiing along, when suddenly a spectacular corridor opens beneath you, offering passage through the vertical world of rock and ice. In summer, watery cascades tumble down the sides of Great Gulf. In winter, these become skiable gullies.

In any given winter, some gullies may form and others do not. Such is the fickle character of these high-mountain environs. I have skied couloirs in Great Gulf that have appeared one year, only to vanish until several years later. Each trip into Great Gulf is a surprise.

THE TOURS

Airplane Gully

Airplane Gully is the most prominent and striking line of descent in Great Gulf. The gully gets its name from an incident on October 2, 1990, when an airplane crashed at its top and tumbled down into Great Gulf, killing its three passengers. The wreckage was removed, but it is still possible to see the remnants of metal or glass lying on the ground at the top.

The top of Airplane Gully lies just north of the junction of Gulfside and Westside trails. A truck-size boulder sits slightly northeast of the trail junction; walk or ski toward the boulder (taking care not to step on fragile alpine plants), and, just north of it, a prominent gully plunges down the side of the Great Gulf. From the top of the gully, you see a vast sweep of land. There are views to the west of Mount Mansfield and Camel's Hump in Vermont, to the north of the northern peaks of the Presidential Range, and to the northwest of the rugged Mahoosuc Range in Maine.

Airplane Gully begins with a bang. A cornice often forms on the top, forcing skiers to either ski through it or jump off it. The top of the gully is about 25 feet wide, with a pitch of 44 degrees. The entrance is intimidating, but there is plenty of room for turns—at first. The gully gets narrower as you descend. Large boulders choke off the midsection to about 15 feet in width. Below this waist, the gully doglegs to the left, opens up, and continues plunging all the way to Spaulding Lake. The total vertical drop is about 1,200 feet. Most skiers stop well above Spaulding Lake in order to shorten the hike back up and to avoid the final few hundred yards to the lake, which are brushy.

Pipeline Gully

Mount Clay is the rocky knob that lies north of Airplane Gully. Clay is actually a minor summit of Mount Washington, rising only 150 feet from the surrounding ridge, but it hosts dramatic views and exceptional skiing. The rocky east face of Mount Clay is streaked with skiable gullies, the most prominent being Pipeline Gully. It departs from the Mount Clay summit ridge and plunges straight down to Spaulding Lake.

From Airplane Gully, walk north, cross a flat col, and climb to the top of the next rock pile (this is one of three Mount Clay summits); alternatively, where the Jewell Trail ends in a flat col, turn right (south) and climb the Mount Clay Loop Trail. Pipeline starts in a shallow between two rock summits; it is about 20 feet wide with a gradual entrance, but it steepens and chokes off quickly to the length of a ski. The route remains narrow, drops over an ice bulge that may require a 6- to 8-foot jump (during low snow years this ice bulge may be larger and make Pipeline unskiable), and empties onto a snowfield above Spaulding Lake. Pipeline has a consistent 40-degree pitch.

Other Great Gulf Descents

There are many other skiable gullies along the rim of Great Gulf. Just north of Pipeline is **Hallway**, another skiable steep gully.

A bit south of Airplane is **Spacewalk**, which is a steeper drop-in that joins with Airplane. Continuing south, **Turkey Chute (a.k.a. Batman Gully)** drops into a wide headwall then doglegs left into Airplane below the junction with Spacewalk.

Great Gulf Trail (a.k.a. Mother-in-Law Gully) offers a different experience than skiing the narrow gullies. Great Gulf Trail splits a broad face and plunges down the center of the Great Gulf headwall. Grand views of the whole cirque greet skiers here. With ample snow, this can be a thrilling, steep, and open descent, but in lower snow (which is more typical), the trail and headwall can be rocky, narrow, and treacherous. Great Gulf Trail departs due north from Gulfside Trail, where the latter turns northwest and follows the rim of the gulf. Skiers who descend Great Gulf Trail sometimes opt to climb out via Airplane Gully, which provides a shorter hike to the ridge.

Good mountaineering judgment and extreme caution must be used when skiing anywhere in Great Gulf. Unlike Tuckerman Ravine, you cannot hike up and preview what you are about to ski, you are far from help, and the fastest escape route is up. Whether or not you can ski in Great Gulf on a given day depends entirely on snow conditions. All of the Great Gulf gullies are prone to avalanche and should be avoided for at least 24 hours after storms until the snow stabilizes.

Previous page: Dropping into Great Gulf with the Mount Washington summit behind. *Photo by Brian Mohr/EmberPhoto*

Skiing steep, rocky terrain on bulletproof snow leaves no margin for error. Airplane and Pipeline gullies both have a northeastern exposure. It can take most of the morning before the sun hits them and the snow softens—if it softens at all. A skier was killed and another badly injured after falling in Pipeline Gully in March 2004. Crampons and an ice ax are usually required to climb out of any of the gullies (I've climbed out of Great Gulf both with and without crampons—trust me, you will be very grateful for those sharp points). You should also bring avalanche gear (shovel, transceiver, probes), in addition to your usual backcountry skiing equipment.

Great Gulf is a spring skiing destination. It can be a thrill and a pleasure to ski the steep, soft corn snow on sunny spring days. If you arrive to find dangerous or questionable snow conditions, *back off*—take in the views of Great Gulf but continue your tour to ski safer terrain elsewhere around the mountain.

Your exit options depend on where you started. If you came from Pinkham Notch and through Tuckerman Ravine, you can retrace your steps, dropping one of the classic entrances into Tucks.

If you came from the Cog Railway or the Jewell Trail, you can descend to the Marshfield Base Station via Burt or Ammonoosuc ravines or Monroe Brook (see tour 16, Burt and Ammonoosuc Ravines, page 92). If nothing else is in good shape or you just want a fast exit, you can ski down alongside the railroad tracks. The Jewell Trail is very tight just below treeline and is not recommended for skiing down, but it is a fine hiking route if skiing is not feasible.

A journey into Great Gulf is a venture to the wilder side of the White Mountains. The first taste will spark your imagination about the vast skiing potential of the more remote high terrain of New England.

15 OAKES GULF AND MONROE BROOK

The sunny, south-facing gullies in Oakes Gulf offer wilderness skiing in a stunning remote glacial cirque. Double Barrel is a steep gully located on the west side of the ravine. Monroe Brook is a steep, open skiable drainage.

Distance: *To top of Oakes Gulf:* 2.3 miles from Marshfield Base Station, 2.9 miles from Ammonoosuc Ravine trailhead; 3.7 miles from Pinkham Notch.
Elevation: *Start/Finish:* 2,700 feet, Marshfield Base Station; 2,500 feet, Ammonoosuc Ravine trailhead; 2,020 feet, Pinkham Notch Visitor Center; *Highest point:* 5,100 feet; *Bottom of gullies:* 4,600 feet (Main Gully), 4,300 feet (Double Barrel); *Vertical drop:* 2,700 feet (via ART)–3,080 feet (via PNVC), total tour
Maps: *White Mountain Winter Recreation Map & Guide* (AMC) shows the ski routes. *White Mountain National Forest Map & Guide* (AMC), *White Mountains* (Map Adventures), *White Mountain National Forest East* (Trails Illustrated) all show the terrain but not the ski routes.
Difficulty: Ski mountaineering
Gear: AT, telemark, snowboard

HOW TO GET THERE

Via Ammonoosuc Ravine Trail (ART): From ART (free parking) (*GPS coordinates*: 44° 16.033′ N, 71° 21.683′ W), it is 2.7 miles to AMC's Lakes of the Clouds Hut (or 2.1 miles from Marshfield Base Station, with parking fee), and another 0.2 miles on the Dry River Trail to the top of Oakes Gulf.

Via the Cog Railway: It is 3.6 miles to AMC's Lakes of the Clouds Hut if you ski up the Cog Railway and turn right (south) on the Westside Trail and Crawford Path to the hut. *Note:* The Cog Railway (thecog.com) charges skiers a fee to access its property.

From Pinkham Notch (*GPS coordinates*: 44° 15.435′ N, 71° 15.166′ W): It is 4.6 miles to AMC's Lakes of the Clouds Hut via the Tuckerman Ravine and Tuckerman Crossover trails, and about 4 miles via Hillman's Highway and Davis Path.

THE TOUR

Oakes Gulf is a large glacial cirque that bounds the south side of the Mount Washington summit cone. It resembles a giant horseshoe ringed by 5,000-foot peaks. Oakes Gulf has a special appeal among the remote ravines. This south-facing basin is a sunny getaway from the more traveled ski destinations such as Tuckerman Ravine. The ski gullies in Oakes Gulf are shorter and not quite as steep as found elsewhere, but the beauty and isolation of this place, combined with the soft spring snow, make for a memorable day of backcountry skiing.

Oakes Gulf is defined by Boott Spur (5,502 feet) on the east and Mount Monroe (5,371 feet) on its western boundary. It cradles the Presidential Range–Dry River Wilderness, a 27,380-acre tract of land established as a wilderness area by Congress in 1975. Oakes Gulf is named for William Oakes, a botanist who began studying the White Mountains in 1825. Brooks Dodge skied four or five gullies in Oakes Gulf

OAKES GULF AND MONROE BROOK

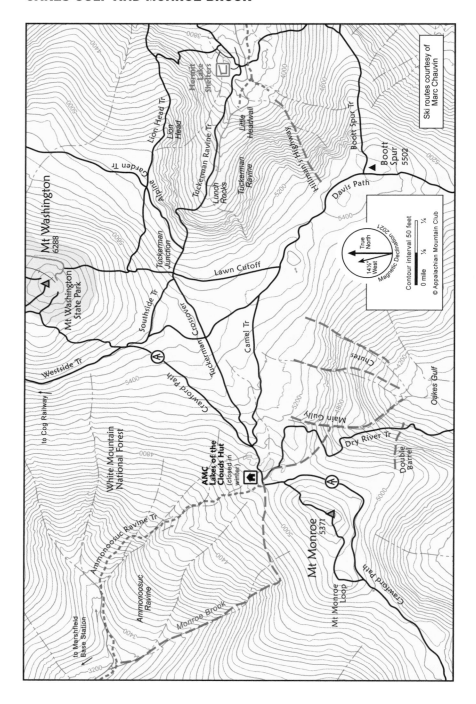

Ski routes courtesy of Marc Chauvin

Mt Washington 6288

Mt Washington State Park

Hermit Lake Shelters

Lion Head Tr

Lion Head

Alpine Garden Tr

Tuckerman Ravine Tr

Tuckerman Ravine

Lunch Rocks

Little Headwall

Hillman's Highway

Boott Spur Tr

Boott Spur 5502

Davis Path

Tuckerman Junction

Lawn Cutoff

Contour interval 50 feet

True North

14½° West

Magnetic Declination 2021

0 mile ¼ ½

© Appalachian Mountain Club

Southside Tr

Tuckerman Crossover

Camel Tr

Chutes

Oakes Gulf

Westside Tr

Main Gully

Dry River Tr

Crawford Path

to Cog Railway

White Mountain National Forest

AMC Lakes of the Clouds Hut (closed in winter)

Double Barrel

Mt Monroe 5371

Ammonoosuc Ravine Tr

Ammonoosuc Ravine

Monroe Brook

Mt Monroe Loop

Crawford Path

to Marshfield Base Station

Obeying the laws of gravity in Oakes Gulf. *Photo by Jerimy Arnold*

in the mid-1940s, which may have been the first ski descents here—the ski history, like the place itself, is obscure.

The extra effort required to reach Oakes Gulf keeps traffic to a minimum. The most direct route to Oakes Gulf is from the west side of Mount Washington via Ammonoosuc Ravine Trail. The trail becomes a steep, narrow tunnel through tight trees at the top; it is easiest to remove skis and walk up the steep pitches (see tour 16, Burt and Ammonoosuc Ravines, page 92, for other ways to access and exit the west side of Mount Washington, including skiing up the Cog Railway or climbing Monroe Brook). At Lakes of the Clouds Hut (closed in winter), continue on the Dry River Trail following signs and rock cairns 0.2 miles to a height-of-land. As you begin to descend from here, you are sliding into Oakes Gulf.

Main Gully

The most popular ski route in Oakes Gulf is Main Gully. The Dry River Trail drifts right, and an obvious snow gully heads directly down to the valley floor. The gully begins gently and steepens briefly to about 38 degrees. This passageway is very wide, so skiers can feel comfortable swinging longer turns or traversing. Main Gully drops 500 vertical feet before reaching light vegetation. Most skiers stop at this line of scrub and hike back up this or another nearby gully. For more vertical, take a higher entrance into Main Gully, angling uphill from the Dry River Trail. There is about 1,000 vertical feet of skiing from the top of the gully to the very bottom of Oakes Gulf.

What the sun giveth in Oakes Gulf, it also taketh: Oakes Gulf is a fun spring ski, but it can turn to glop after an extended spell of warm, sunny weather.

Double Barrel

For skiers who lust for the thrills found in Tuckerman Ravine but don't want the crowds, Oakes Gulf offers Double Barrel. This is a steep gully with two distinct channels that plunge down into the gulf from a long ridge off Mount Monroe. To reach Double Barrel, you can hike up from the bottom of Oakes Gulf or take a high traverse from the Main Gully around the west side of the bowl. You may have to scramble across some bushes, but you will eventually arrive at a snowy chute that drops all the way to the ravine floor. This is the left "barrel" of Double Barrel. It is 45 degrees at the top, moderating as you descend. This left side of the gully is about half the length of the right side, and a narrow rock ridge separates them.

The right side of Double Barrel begins at the rim of Oakes Gulf, at about 5,000 feet. The right chute pinches off into a 5-foot wide sliver between large rocks midway down and you cannot see what lies beyond. This right "barrel" starts at about 38 degrees, quickly steepening to 45 degrees. It then opens up and empties out onto the valley floor about 800 vertical feet below. As with any steep mountaineering gully, it is advisable to hike up from the bottom to assess snow conditions.

The hike up the west flank of Oakes Gulf is worthwhile just for the views. Nearby ski areas such as Wildcat and Attitash appear insignificant here. Mount Washington appears as a large white dome to the north. The summits of Boott Spur meld into the sprawling Bigelow Lawn which tumbles down into Oakes Gulf over a rocky buttress with long skiable chutes. **Central Buttress** is the most popular steep descent. These chutes are most easily reached by climbing Hillman's Highway.

Oakes Gulf suddenly looks much bigger than it did from the valley floor. This is a place you could return many times to explore on skis or a snowboard without coming close to exhausting its potential.

The walk along the Mount Washington summit ridge over to Oakes Gulf on a calm, clear day is spectacular. But the remoteness of Oakes Gulf often deters skiers and with good reason. The Mount Washington summit area is not the place to be during a storm or a whiteout. If bad weather is moving in, make an early exit and head back down a trail that gets you below treeline quickly. Note that Lakes of the Clouds Hut is closed in winter. Be sure to carry a map and compass or GPS and know how to use them, because whiteouts on this ridge are common.

From the bottom of Oakes Gulf, you can climb Main Gully next to the Dry River Trail and return to Lakes of the Clouds Hut. From the top of Double Barrel, you can walk a short distance due east to intersect Crawford Path, which is marked by rock cairns. Turn right, and you will arrive back at the hut.

Monroe Brook

From Lakes of the Clouds Hut, a popular return route to the Marshfield Base Station is to ski Monroe Brook, a steep, wide-open corridor of snow down the northeast face of Mount Monroe that offers 1,800 vertical feet of excellent skiing. To reach it, contour over from Lakes of the Clouds Hut for a quarter-mile, then drop into the prominent drainage. The bottom of Monroe Brook ends in a 0.3-mile bushwhack to Ammonoosuc Ravine Trail, 1 mile east of the Marshfield Base Station.

Both of the routes described here—Oakes Gulf and Monroe Brook—are active avalanche zones. Avoid them if avalanche risk is elevated, be alert, and have avalanche safety equipment.

16 BURT AND AMMONOOSUC RAVINES

This alpine tour on the west side of Mount Washington offers wide open skiing on snowfields and steep drainages with breathtaking views of the Presidential Range summits.

Distance: 2.1 miles, top of Burt Ravine; 2.3 miles, top of Ammonoosuc Ravine, via Cog.
Elevation: *Start/Finish*: 2,700 feet, Marshfield Base Station or 2,500 feet, Jewell and Ammonoosuc Ravine trailhead; *Highest point*: 5,500 feet (top of Burt Ravine), 6,288 feet (summit of Mount Washington/top of Ammonoosuc Ravine); *Vertical drop*: 2,800–3,588 feet, total tour
Maps: *White Mountain Winter Recreation Map & Guide* (AMC) is the only map that shows the ski routes. The terrain is covered by *White Mountain National Forest Map & Guide* (AMC), *White Mountains* (Map Adventures), and *White Mountain National Forest East* (Trails Illustrated).
Difficulty: Ski mountaineering
Gear: AT, telemark, snowboard

HOW TO GET THERE

The fastest access to the west side of Mount Washington is to ski up the Cog Railway from the Marshfield Base Station (*GPS coordinates*: 44° 16.205′ N, 71° 21.050′ W). The Cog is reached via Base Road, which departs from US 302, 5 miles west of Twin Mountain. *Note*: The Cog Railway (thecog.com) charges skiers a fee to access its property. The Ammonoosuc Ravine Trail and Jewell Trail offer free access from hiker parking lot on Base Road (*GPS coordinates*: 44° 16.033′ N, 71° 21.68′ W).

THE TOUR

This is a tale of two sides of the same mountain. On the east side of Mount Washington lies Tuckerman Ravine, the world-renowned extreme sports playground, a magnet for thrill seekers. Then there is Mount Washington's West Side Story: just over the ridge from Tucks lie skiable snowfields and ravines that comparatively few skiers explore. The West Siders plunder their snow stashes on Mount Washington in amazed delight, thankful that their snowy sanctuary remains out of the limelight. But word has gotten out about the remarkable ski terrain on the quiet side of Mount Washington, and on sunny spring days the West Siders turn out in force when the corn snow goes off.

The west side of Mount Washington is dominated by two glacial cirques. Burt Ravine is a compact and well-defined horseshoe-shaped bowl on the northwest corner of the Mount Washington summit cone that drains into Clay Brook. Ammonoosuc Ravine is an enormous 1.5-mile-wide slope that lies due east of the Mount Washington summit, bounded by Mount Monroe on its south end. Ammonoosuc Ravine drains into the Ammonoosuc River. In good conditions, both ravines offer great skiing with some of the most spectacular scenery in the East.

BURT AND AMMONOOSUC RAVINES

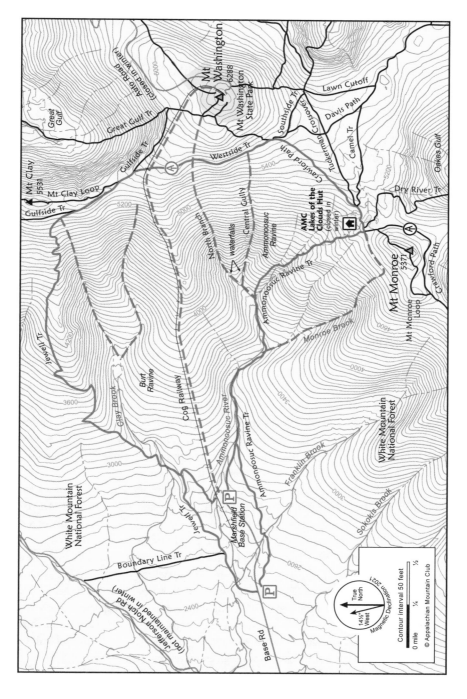

Conditions in Burt and Ammonoosuc ravines are largely determined by how the wind blows. Most years, prevailing westerly winds scour the west side and deposit the snow in Tuckerman Ravine and Great Gulf, leaving the west side a vast rock field plastered in wind-hammered snow and ice. But some years, nor'easters blow out of the east and load the west side, transforming rocky slopes into huge snowfields.

A big attraction of the west side is that it offers the fastest access to the summit of Mount Washington. Most skiers ascend via the Cog Railway, a fast and straight uphill ski that charges 2 miles from the Marshfield Base Station to the Skyline Switch at the junction with the Westside Trail, which, as its name suggests, traverses the west side of the Mount Washington summit cone. From the Westside Trail, a turn to the north (left, when you are skiing uphill) delivers you to the top of Burt Ravine within minutes; a turn south (right) puts you atop the longest descent line in Ammonoosuc Ravine.

Burt Ravine can also be accessed by the Jewell Trail, which ascends the northern shoulder of Burt Ravine; it is 3.3 miles to the top of Burt from the free hiker parking lot on Base Road. The Jewell Trail climbs at a moderate grade through the woods, offering periodic views of the surrounding peaks and ravines. Most of the trail is pleasant, but the last half-mile before treeline is tight and brushy, requiring lots of bending and turning to avoid getting skewered by spiky limbs. Skinning up alongside the Cog is less woodsy but more direct. The climb from the Marshfield Base Station to the Westside Trail takes about two and a half hours via the Jewell Trail and about two hours via the Cog Railway.

Ammonoosuc Ravine can also be reached via the Ammonoosuc Ravine Trail (ART) from the free hiker parking on Base Road. It is 2.7 miles to AMC's Lakes of the Clouds Hut and another 1.0 miles on Crawford Path to the top of Central Gully. The top part of ART is steep and can be slow going, especially if a lot of blowdown or new snow obscures the trail. Most people boot up this last section. Another option is to ascend Monroe Brook, a major drainage that crosses Ammonoosuc Ravine Trail a mile from the Marshfield Base Station. Note that Monroe Brook becomes very steep at the top and may require crampons to ascend.

Finally, walking on the tracks of the Cog is not recommended and is not for the faint of heart or the short-legged. The railroad ties are spaced unevenly, and you can injure yourself easily if you fall between or off the tracks. After the snow melts, the ground alongside the Cog is typically muddy and unpleasant to walk on.

The Cog Railway was the dream of Sylvester Marsh, a resident of Campton, New Hampshire, who made his fortune in Chicago's meatpacking industry. After getting lost near the summit of Mount Washington in 1852, Marsh decided there should be an easier way to reach the top of New England. He dreamed up the world's first mountain-climbing railroad. When he presented his idea to the New Hampshire legislature, lawmakers dismissed him as a crank, saying, "He might as well build a railway to the moon." Undeterred, Marsh pressed on with his plan.

While Marsh soldiered on, the dream of providing motorized access to the summit of Mount Washington was realized—by automobile. In 1861, the Auto Road to the summit opened on the east side of Mount Washington. The train followed close behind: on July 3, 1869, "Old Peppersass" (so named because it resembled a pepper sauce bottle) became the first mountain-climbing cog railway in the world, ascending the west side of the mountain. The train quickly became the preferred mode of transport up the 6,288-foot peak and has carried 5 million passengers to the summit since it began operating. The Cog has had only one major accident. In 1967, the train derailed about a mile below the summit and passenger cars plummeted downhill into a rock, killing eight people and injuring 72.

Owners of the Cog have made several unsuccessful attempts to attract skiers. From 2003 to 2006, the Cog operated in winter, bringing skiers a mile up the mountain so that they could ski down alongside the tracks. In the late 1980s, there was a proposal for the Cog to transport skiers up Mount Washington so that they could ski into Tuckerman Ravine. The proposal was met with a storm of protest from the U.S. Forest Service, which insisted that Tucks be preserved as a backcountry ski experience. Today, skiers and snowshoers travel the snow-covered Cog in quiet solitude.

Burt Ravine was named for Henry M. Burt, the founder and publisher of *Among the Clouds*, a daily newspaper that was established in 1877 on the summit of Mount Washington. From where the Cog crosses the Westside Trail—or where the Jewell Trail meets Gulfside Trail—ski along the top of Burt Ravine and choose whichever open line appeals to you.

The view from the top of Burt Ravine is inviting: a beautiful long, wide, moderate open slope beckons you forward. The slope is a consistent 30 degrees, a perfect angle for intermediate skiers to link continuous turns. The run descends 2,200 feet in about a mile. There are two distinct skiable drainages that merge into Clay Brook. It is an exhilarating descent with breathtaking views of the full sweep of the Presidential Range. The best exit from Burt Ravine is to skin back up it, cut over to the Cog once you can see the tracks, and then ski down Ammonoosuc Ravine, Monroe Brook, or alongside the Cog back to the Marshfield Base Station.

Ammonoosuc Ravine—or "Ammo"—is awe inspiring by its sheer size. The ravine is the headwaters of the mighty Ammonoosuc River, which flows into the Connecticut River at Woodsville, New Hampshire. When climbing the Cog, stop at Jacob's Ladder, the trestle high up on the mountain, to peer into Ammonoosuc Ravine; this is also the best vantage point to check conditions lower in the ravine.

Jacob's Ladder, which is at treeline, marks an important decision point in your tour. Snow and weather conditions may change markedly here, and you may need crampons to continue ascending. Assess the conditions of the mountain and of your group and decide whether you want to proceed uphill or head down via one of the routes described here.

When it is fully snow covered, Ammo offers one of the longest skiable descents in the White Mountains—nearly 3,000 vertical feet of continuous skiing. Under the right conditions, the top of the ravine can be a mile-long snowfield that funnels into the Ammonoosuc River. The most popular ski routes are two prominent drainages: **North Branch** is the closest to the Cog, and **Central Gully** descends the middle of the ravine. Starting from Crawford Path on the summit of Mount Washington, ski due west, crossing the Westside Trail (which may be indistinct under the snow) and continuing downhill. See a large clearing on the valley floor—this is what you are skiing toward. The clearing is where the two drainages converge; there are no trees there because they have been knocked down by avalanches that blast down the ravine. You can't see the lower section of Ammonoosuc Ravine until you are about halfway down the face. When it comes into view, stop and assess which drainage is skiable before continuing. By early April, the lower parts of the drainage steadily revert into spectacular waterfalls and open brooks. Ski whichever line has continuous snow in it.

The Ammo slopes have a sustained 30-degree pitch, getting steeper at the bottom. In hard snow, Ammonoosuc Ravine should be avoided because of the potential for taking a long, dangerous slide on its massive open slopes. In low snow, or if the west side has been wind scoured, large ice bulges appear lower down in the Ammo drainages (remember, they are waterfalls), making them dangerous and unskiable.

The bottom line is this: you can only hope to ski Ammo—you cannot count on it. Your final decision will be made when you get there and assess the conditions.

Once you have descended Ammo and are on the valley floor, turn around and ogle the vast playground you have just skied. It is an awe-inspiring vantage point. This is also an obvious terrain trap for avalanches—take note of the enormous destructive forces that have ripped through here.

Continue descending on what is now the frozen Ammonoosuc River for as long as you can. When the snow ends, sidestep through tight trees on your left (south). You will quickly reach Ammonoosuc Ravine Trail, which runs alongside the river and brings you back to Marshfield Base Station (1.4 miles) or ART trailhead (1.9 miles). Skiing the trail here is like descending through a fun, zany, twisting obstacle course that keeps you dodging and weaving. Give a friendly audible warning to snowshoers and other hikers so that they are not startled by you zipping down the trail.

If you choose not to ski Ammonoosuc Ravine, you can continue around the top of the ravine past the AMC Lakes of the Clouds Hut (closed in winter) to reach Monroe Brook. Contour around from the hut to the first major drainage; this is Monroe Brook. The brook begins very steeply, but it quickly widens and the angle moderates into a long, fun, 1,800-vertical-foot descent with many turns. It ends in a short bushwhack that delivers you to Ammonoosuc Ravine Trail, close to where Ammo skiers also join the trail.

If it is too late in spring or the snow is unstable so that none of these descent routes are skiable, you can always safely hike down Ammonoosuc Ravine Trail

Charging down Ammonoosuc Ravine in perfect corn snow.

from Lakes of the Clouds Hut or ski down alongside the Cog, which is an enjoyable intermediate ski. Depending on where you are on the summit ridge or in Ammo, Ammonoosuc Ravine Trail may be the fastest, most protected exit to get below treeline. As noted earlier, the top of the ART can be difficult to follow in new snow, and the upper trail is too steep and narrow for skiing. This is an emergency exit, not a great ski route.

Avalanches are a serious concern in Burt Ravine, Ammonoosuc Ravine, and Monroe Brook. As already noted, there is ample evidence of destructive avalanches that pour down Ammo. To play it safe, wait for spring corn snow to ski these routes. The earlier in winter you go, the more unstable the snow will be. Be sure to check the daily Mount Washington Avalanche Center forecasts (mountwashingtonavalanchecenter.org), which cover the entire Presidential Range. West side skiers should carry avalanche safety gear, including a shovel, probes, and avalanche beacon.

A day in Burt and Ammonoosuc ravines is beautiful and thrilling. You can link hundreds of turns here without the crowds or the fear factor that goes with skiing the steeps of Tucks or Great Gulf. Spending a sunny spring day experiencing Mount Washington's version of West Side Story will expand your horizons about the many faces of skiing on New Hampshire's highest peak.

⑰ KING RAVINE

This is a high alpine ski tour into the wild, dramatic King Ravine on the north face of Mount Adams to ski Great Gully.

Distance: 4.3 miles to top of Great Gully Trail
Elevation: *Start/Finish*: 1,306 feet, Appalachia parking lot; *Highest point*: 5,490 feet, top of Great Gully Trail; *Vertical drop*: 4,184 feet
Maps: *White Mountain National Forest Map & Guide* (AMC), *White Mountains* (Map Adventures), *White Mountain National Forest East* (Trails Illustrated)
Difficulty: Ski mountaineering
Gear: AT, telemark, snowboard

HOW TO GET THERE

Appalachia (*GPS coordinates*: 44° 22.288′ N, 71° 17.363′ W) is a major trailhead and parking lot located on US 2, 1 mile west of Randolph and just east of Lowe's Store. Air Line Trail departs from Appalachia and connects with Short Line, King Ravine Trail, and Great Gully Trail.

THE TOUR

King Ravine is among the wildest and most beautiful glacial cirques of the Presidential Range. It lies on the north face of Mount Adams (5,797 feet), the second-highest peak in the Northeast after Mount Washington. The ravine can be seen from US 2, the snow in its north-facing gullies often lingering into June. As snow on the surrounding peaks melts, a prominent gully in King Ravine takes the form of the number 7. This is Great Gully, which some skiers simply call The Seven.

King Ravine was named for Thomas Starr King, a minister in Boston and San Francisco who in 1859 wrote *The White Hills*, an influential book about the White Mountains. Mount Starr King, just outside the town of Jefferson, is also named after him. King led the first party of white men to explore this huge cirque in 1857. King named it Adams Ravine, but it was later changed to bear his name. King Ravine Trail was built in 1876.

King Ravine is a 3-mile ski from the trailhead—about the same distance as a trip into Tuckerman Ravine—but it sees few visitors in winter due to its remoteness. Its rocky headwall is raked by gullies and snowfields. This is its allure to skiers.

The trip into King Ravine begins at the busy Appalachia trailhead on US 2, the gateway to the Northern Presidentials. Hikers depart from here for the summits of Mount Madison and Mount Adams. You have several trail options. The shortest route to King Ravine is to start out on Air Line Trail, then connect with Short Line. From Appalachia, pass the trailhead kiosk, cross under a power line and look to your right for a small sign for Air Line.

Alternatively, Valley Way, which proceeds straight ahead from the power line, may add a few minutes to your trip but is an exceptionally pretty trail, following the

KING RAVINE

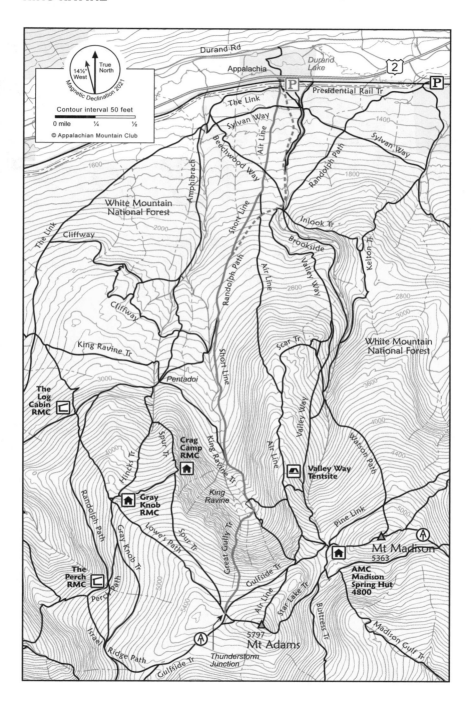

Royal skiing in King Ravine with Mount Madison as a backdrop.

cascading Snyder Brook and passing three different falls. After 0.9 miles on Valley Way, turn right onto Randolph Path and join Short Line in 0.4 miles. Randolph Path and Short Line coincide for another 0.4 miles, then Short Line bears left and proceeds gradually uphill for a mile until it joins with King Ravine Trail. Until this point, the trail is open and wide and climbs at a gradual, pleasant grade.

Shortly after starting up King Ravine Trail, you come to the beautiful Mossy Falls, where Cold Brook shoots out from between boulders that choke the drainage. From here, the character of the skiing changes. The trail steepens and narrows, necessitating sidestepping up short sections. The trail can be rocky and tight. Glimpses of King Ravine appear and vanish, making the climbing more urgent. After 0.4 miles on King Ravine Trail, the forest releases its grip and you emerge into the open among giant boulders strewn on the floor of the ravine. In front of you are the gully-raked walls of King Ravine. It is a stunning expanse of snow, rock, and ice. This is the climactic end of the Northern Presidential Range, where it crashes down into King Ravine.

The floor of the ravine looks like a place where maniacal giants have been playing catch with boulders. Weave your way up through the massive rocks until you arrive at the foot of the prominent gully on the right side of the ravine that climbs all the way to the ridge. From here, Great Gully Trail ascends this couloir for 1 mile. Great Gully is shaped like an hourglass: a wide fan at the base of the ravine rises to where it pinches off to about 10 feet wide between rocks. Above the pinch, the gully gets progressively wider. You can either boot straight up Great Gully or skin up, zigzagging up a snowfield to the right of the gully until merging into the main gully just above the rock pinch. You may need crampons to climb safely if the snow is firm.

Great Gully Trail tops out at a giant rock cairn marking the intersection of five different trails. This is Thunderstorm Junction, which lies between the summits of Mounts Adams and Sam Adams, one of four lesser summits of Mount Adams. On a clear day, the views up here seem endless. You are in a snowy desert dotted by rocky summit cones. Continue due south for a few hundred yards to where you can peer over the entire Great Gulf, the name given to the massive 3.5-mile-long ring of glacial cirques that extends from Mount Washington all the way to where you stand.

The descent into King Ravine begins gradually. Keep your head up to admire the hundred-mile views as you glide across this broad ridge. Great Gully begins as a 100-foot-wide slope with a steep headwall on skier's left that you can ski down or skirt around on easier ground to the right, as you like. The upper section of Great Gully is a consistent 35 degrees. It steepens to 40 degrees at its crux, the rocky choke. If the choke does not have enough snow, you can skirt around to the left to ski a broad snowfield to the bottom. This is an exciting alpine descent through rock, snow, and ice.

A word of caution: It is common to find fresh avalanche debris at the base of Great Gully, a sign of how active this environment is. Climbers and hikers have been caught in avalanches in King Ravine on multiple occasions. Carry avalanche equipment with you (shovel, transceiver, and probes), assess snow conditions, and if the snowpack is too unstable, abandon your plan to ski in the gullies. The same caution applies to attempting to ski here in bulletproof snow conditions. A winter hiker died in 2013 after falling down King Ravine, and in 2010 an AMC caretaker hiking above King Ravine slipped and slid 1,500 feet down the ravine headwall on hard snow. Miraculously, he had only minor injuries.

This north-facing gully takes a long time to soften. If you get to King Ravine and the snow is unstable or hard, *back off*. It is still a beautiful and worthwhile tour just to ski around and see the ravine.

Descending King Ravine Trail is just survival skiing until Mossy Falls. Take it easy, sidestep as needed, and pick your way down carefully for the first 0.4 miles. Below the falls, the trail widens and the grade relaxes. Short Line is a fun ski, with room enough to make turns all the way back to your car.

A ski tour into King Ravine is a trip to the wild side. Enjoy going where few others go and experiencing this majestic place.

⑱ ZEALAND FALLS HUT TOURS

AMC's Zeland Falls Hut serves as a base for skiing in and around the Pemigewasset Wilderness. The ski tours from the hut access a beautiful and dramatic landscape of ice cliffs, waterfalls, and high-alpine ponds.

Distance: 6.9 miles, Zealand Falls Hut via Spruce Goose Ski Trail to Zealand Trail, one way; 6 miles, Zealand Falls Hut via Zealand Road to Zealand Trail, one way
Elevation: *Start*: 1,500 feet; *Highest point*: 2,600 feet, Zealand Falls Hut; *Vertical drop*: 1,100 feet
Maps: *White Mountain National Forest Map & Guide* (AMC), *White Mountains* (Map Adventures), *White Mountain National Forest West* (Trails Illustrated)
Difficulty: Moderate
Gear: Nordic backcountry/telemark, AT
Additional Information: AMC Hut Reservations, 603-466-2727, outdoors.org

HOW TO GET THERE

From the junction of NH 3 and NH 302 in the town of Twin Mountain, drive east 2.3 miles on NH 302 to a sign for the Zealand Campground on the right. Parking is in a plowed lot on the north side of NH 302, a quarter-mile east of the trailhead (*GPS coordinates*: 44° 15.913′ N, 71° 29.660′ W). The route begins on the unplowed and gated Zealand Road (FR 16).

THE TOUR

A ski trip to the AMC Zealand Falls Hut provides access to the best ski terrain of the three self-service AMC winter mountain huts (the other year-round huts are at Carter Notch and Lonesome Lake). From Zealand Falls Hut, skiers can take a variety of excellent day trips that travel into the 45,000-acre Pemigewasset Wilderness, or embark on an ambitious Pemi Traverse.

The route to the hut begins on gated and unplowed Zealand Road (FR 16) and continues on Zealand Trail. There are two ways to reach Zealand Trail: ski on Zealand Road for 3.2 miles to the junction with Zealand Trail, or take Spruce Goose Trail 4.1 miles to reach the same trail junction. Zealand Road often has logging trucks on it and may be plowed part of the way; this changes year to year (check the AMC website for Zealand Road updates). When there is logging, take Spruce Goose Trail. Otherwise, you may prefer the shorter ski on the road. Climbing skins are not needed to reach the hut; waxable or waxless Nordic backcountry (light telemark) skis will be faster and more enjoyable; AT skis and skins will work too.

To ski Spruce Goose Trail, start out on Zealand Road, cross the Ammonoosuc River on a bridge, pass a trailhead sign for Flat Iron Ski Trail, and 50 feet later come to the well-signed Spruce Goose Ski Trail. The Young Adult Conservation Corps constructed this trail in 1977 so that skiers could be separated from snowmobilers on Zealand Road (snowmobiles have since been rerouted onto their own trail,

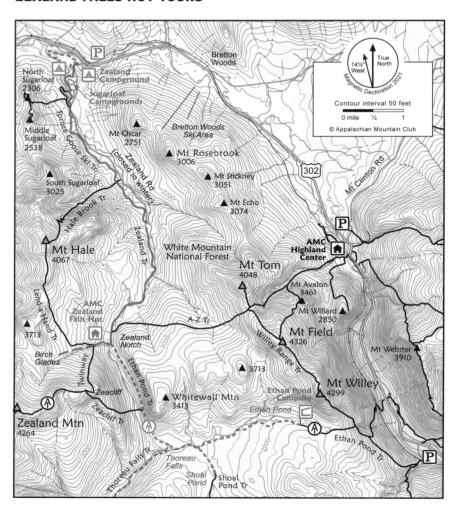

which lies east of the road). Spruce Goose Trail, which is marked with blue blazes, winds its way through the woods parallel to the road, between 100 to 600 feet away.

At 0.8 miles from the start, Spruce Goose Trail passes through the Sugarloaf II campground. Bear to the right side of the campground and turn right at a sign for Trestle Trail, which puts you out onto Zealand Road for several hundred feet, where you cross Zealand River on a bridge. Other trails crisscross this area; keep your eyes open for the blue blazes of Spruce Goose Trail. Reenter the woods on the right just beyond the bridge, where Spruce Goose Trail continues on easy, rolling terrain through the woods before ending at the Zealand Campground and rejoining Zealand Road at another bridge.

A notch above: skiing through Zealand Notch on the edge of the Pemigewasset Wilderness.

From the last bridge, you leave the road and continue to the hut on Zealand Trail. It is 2.7 miles from the bridge to the hut, following an old railroad grade for about a mile. The trail passes alternately through tunnels of birch and tall, sparsely wooded second-growth forest. Zealand Notch comes into view as the trail winds around beaver ponds and open meadows, evidence of the wildlife that has repopulated the area.

The AMC Zealand Falls Hut lies at the top of a knoll just west of the trail. You will need to remove skis and boot up the steep final pitch to the hut. The hut was built in 1932 and was renovated in 1989. In 1972, it became the first AMC hut to stay open through the winter. It was built to link the western AMC huts with those in the Presidential Range, part of AMC hutmaster Joe Dodge's plan to space each hut a day's hike apart. It gets its name from the cascades on Whitewall Brook, which are just below the hut. There are beautiful views from the hut out to the surrounding mountains. A woodstove warms the dining room, but the sleeping quarters are unheated, making this a unique way to go winter camping—indoors. There are several nice glades to ski near the hut. The Caretaker Glades—a favorite of Zealand Hut staff—are just west of the hut as you ski toward Lend-a-Hand Trail. About 0.8 miles up Zeacliff Trail is the top of a long birch glade that can be skied back down toward the hut.

Zealand Notch Ski Tours

Zealand Notch is one of the more dramatic land formations in the White Mountains. It was once a typical V-shaped, stream-eroded valley, but the ice sheets that covered New England gouged their way down to the ocean and left Zealand Notch with the characteristic U-shape of glacial valleys. The notch becomes more impressive as you ski through it. The steep rock walls of Whitewall Mountain tower overhead to the north, the tree-covered slopes of Zealand Mountain rise to the south, and in between the blocky refuse of the glacier lies strewn about the valley floor. A ski tour through the notch usually involves stopping every few minutes just to marvel at the views.

The trip through Zealand Notch to Thoreau Falls and Shoal Pond is a classic White Mountain ski tour.

From the Zealand Falls Hut, Ethan Pond Trail follows the old bed of J.E. Henry's Zealand Valley Railroad. Henry was the most famous and colorful logging boss in New Hampshire history. In 1884, Henry opened the Zealand Valley Railroad, which plied the route now traveled by Zealand Road (FR 16), from NH 302 all the way through Zealand Notch to Shoal Pond—a distance of more than 10 miles. Henry employed as many as 250 people, housing them in small villages established deep in the woods of the Zealand Valley. Little trace now remains of these logging camps. Even the town of Zealand, once a bustling business center that had its own post office (it was located just west of the current Zealand Campground), has vanished into the brush.

Henry left a legacy of ecological devastation in the Zealand Valley. Beginning in 1886, large quantities of slash caused the first of several catastrophic fires that swept through the valley all the way up the slopes of Whitewall and Zealand mountains. The clear-cutting and fires prompted one writer to dub the area "Death Valley." An 1892 editorial from the *Boston Transcript* observed:

> The beautiful Zealand Valley is one vast scene of waste and desolation; immense heaps of sawdust roll down the slopes to choke the stream and, by the destructive acids distilled from their decaying substance, to poison the fish; smoke rises night and day from fires which are maintained to destroy the still accumulating piles of slabs and other mill debris. (C. Francis Belcher, *Logging Railroads of the White Mountains*)

The ecological recovery of the Zealand Valley is nothing short of remarkable. As you ski the trail to the AMC Zealand Falls Hut today, the forest has regenerated with birches and other second-growth trees, and the area is now home to the largest lynx population in the state. Only hints remain of the past destruction.

Ethan Pond Trail, which is part of the Appalachian Trail, offers passage through Zealand Notch, contouring at 2,500 feet along the sparsely vegetated sides of Whitewall Mountain. The mountain's name is presumably derived from the chalky color of the cliffs on its flank. Old scars from the huge fires that swept through here at the beginning of the twentieth century are still visible on the rocks. The trail offers clear views of Mount Hale and the Mount Hancock–Carrigain ridge and glimpses of the expanse of wilderness that lies just beyond the southern end of the notch.

Skiing across the slopes of Whitewall Mountain can be disconcerting if the snow is icy. The trail narrows and drops off somewhat steeply, keeping you on your edges on exposed sections.

From the southern end of Zealand Notch, you have several choices. If you are going to Thoreau Falls, turn right on Thoreau Falls Trail and reach the falls in 0.2 miles. Thoreau Falls is an icy, snow-covered cascade that drops off precipitously, providing a sweeping view of Mount Bond, Mount Guyot, and the Zealand Ridge. During good snow years, it's possible to ski the falls, but you may have to bushwhack back up because the trail is difficult to find.

There are two mountain ponds worth visiting.

Ethan Pond is about 5 miles from Zealand Falls Hut. The ski tour follows the Appalachian Trail over old railroad beds to a beautiful high-mountain pond at 2,800 feet.

Shoal Pond is 3.5 miles from the hut. At 2,600 feet, Shoal Pond is isolated and pretty. After skiing through the deep woods, the sensation of coming out onto a long, white, empty clearing with expansive views of Mounts Carrigain and Hancock is breathtaking.

Pemi Traverse

A north-south traverse of the Pemigewasset Wilderness is one of New England's classic long-distance backcountry ski tours. You can do this 21-mile ski tour from NH 302 to the Kancamagus Highway/NH 112 in a single day, skiing fast and light, or you can spend a night at Zealand Falls Hut. You must first drop a car at the Lincoln Woods parking lot on the Kancamagus Highway (White Mountain National Forest parking permit required, available from WMNF Visitor Center in North Woodstock, New Hampshire).

The Pemi Traverse is a demanding but rewarding wilderness adventure. The route travels through a remote area of rivers, waterfalls, and old logging railroads. The tour involves moderate skiing but challenging navigation, as trails in the Pemigewasset Wilderness are minimally maintained and lightly blazed. From the Zealand Falls Hut, the preferred route of the Pemi Traverse follows the Thoreau Falls Trail to East Side Trail. You typically alternate skiing on the frozen North Branch and on Thoreau Falls Trail—when you can find it. At the southern end of Thoreau Falls Trail you will need to ski across the frozen East Branch of the Pemigewasset River; the footbridge was removed in 2018. This is a true wilderness experience far off the beaten track. Enjoy the solitude.

19 GREELEY PONDS

This is a relaxed ski tour into the beautiful Greeley Ponds, which are nestled beneath ice cliffs and towering rock walls.

Distance: 4.4 miles, Kancamagus Highway/NH 112 to Lower Greeley Pond, round trip; 6.8 miles, Livermore Road trailhead, Waterville Valley to Lower Greeley Pond, round trip
Elevation: *Start*: 1,800 feet, Kancamagus Highway; *Highest point*: 2,245 feet, Upper Greeley Pond; *Vertical drop*: 445 feet, Greeley Pond tour
Maps: *White Mountain Winter Recreation Map & Guide* (AMC), *White Mountains* (Map Adventures), *White Mountain National Forest West* (Trails Illustrated)
Difficulty: Moderate
Gear: Nordic backcountry

HOW TO GET THERE

Parking for the Greeley Ponds cross-country ski trail is 4.7 miles east of the Lincoln Woods Visitor Center on the Kancamagus Highway (NH 112). Parking for about ten cars is available on the south side of the road (*GPS coordinates*: 44° 01.780′ N, 71° 31.243′ W). Additional parking is available at the major trailhead for the Greeley Ponds hiking trail, 0.3 miles farther east. See "Other Options" on page 110 for Livermore Road trailhead directions.

THE TOUR

The Greeley Ponds are a picturesque mountain oasis. The ski tour into the ponds follows a dedicated cross-country ski trail that crosses the Greeley Ponds hiking trail several times. The ski trail is blazed with blue plastic diamonds; the hiking trail sports yellow painted blazes. The popular Greeley Ponds hiking trail is used heavily by hikers and snowshoers, so the cross-country ski trail, which extends past the upper pond and rejoins the hiking trail just before the lower pond, is a welcome option.

From the ski trail parking lot, the cross-country ski trail climbs gently through open hardwoods to where it intersects the Greeley Ponds hiking trail in Mad River Notch at 1.3 miles, where the Mount Osceola Trail diverges to the right (west). This is also the boundary of the 810-acre Greeley Ponds Scenic Area, established in 1964 by the U.S. Forest Service to protect this beautiful wild area.

Remain on the ski trail, and in 0.3 miles you reach Upper Greeley Pond. The mountain pond is a stunning white canvas that erupts from the soft green confines of the forest. The landscape is dominated by breathtaking views of the cliffs and ice floes that tumble down from East Osceola (4,161 feet). Ski across the frozen pond or follow the hiking trail around the west side if the ponds are not completely frozen. From the south end of the pond, follow the blue-blazed ski trail through a pleasant downhill section for 0.3 miles until it reconnects with the hiking trail (yellow blazes) just before reaching Lower Greeley Pond.

GREELEY PONDS

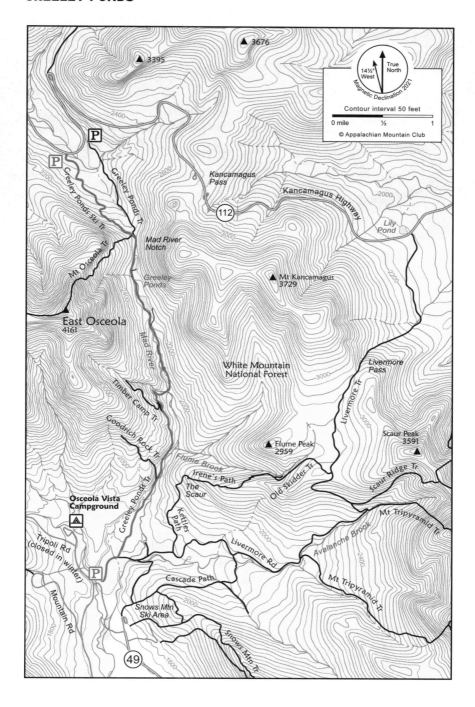

A skier on Lower Greeley Pond admires the cliffs on the east face of Mount Osceola.

Trees jut up through the ice from the bogs at either end of Lower Greeley Pond. Dramatic gullies appear as gashes torn into the forest cover on the face of East Osceola as it plunges into the pond. Nature puts on a dramatic performance here. Enjoy the show.

Skiing south from Lower Greeley Pond, you descend a fun wide logging road alongside the swirling Mad River. A mile south of the pond, the Greeley Ponds Trail was rerouted away from the river following a 2011 flood. It now climbs and descends a hillside, crossing Timber Camp Trail and ending at Livermore Trail 1.7 miles later. The Livermore Road trailhead in Waterville Valley is 0.3 miles farther.

OTHER OPTIONS

Many skiers access the Greeley Ponds from Waterville Valley. The Livermore Road/ Greeley Ponds cross-country ski parking area is 1.9 miles north of the Tripoli Road/ NH 49 junction. Follow Tripoli Road 1.3 miles to the ski area access road, bear right, and go 0.5 miles. Turn right and cross the bridge, then bear left. Parking is available for about 50 cars (*GPS coordinates*: 43° 57.962′ N, 71° 30.823′ W). It is a 3.4-mile ski from the Livermore Road parking area to Lower Greeley Pond via the Greeley Ponds Trail. A White Mountain National Forest (WMNF) parking permit is required at the Livermore Road trailhead, which can be purchased at the WMNF Visitor Center off I-93 Exit 32 in North Woodstock.

20 SAWYER POND

This is a moderate ski tour into beautiful Sawyer Pond, located just outside the Pemigewasset Wilderness.

Distance: 12 miles, Kancamagus Highway/NH 112 to Sawyer Pond to Sawyer Pond Trail to Meadow Brook Connector, round trip
Elevation: *Start*: 1,800 feet, Kancamagus Highway; *Highest point*: 2,000 feet, Sawyer Pond Trail; *Vertical drop*: 200 feet
Maps: *White Mountain Winter Recreation Map & Guide* (AMC), *White Mountain National Forest Map & Guide* (AMC), *White Mountains* (Map Adventures), *White Mountain National Forest West* (Trails Illustrated)
Difficulty: Moderate
Gear: Nordic backcountry

HOW TO GET THERE

Sawyer River Trail begins at a small parking pullout on the Kancamagus Highway/ NH 112, 0.6 miles east of Lily Pond and just west of the Sugar Hill scenic overlook (*GPS coordinates*: 44° 01.305′ N, 71° 26.335′ W).

THE TOUR

The ski tour into Sawyer Pond is an opportunity to kick and glide on easy ground en route to a beautiful and remote mountain waterway. Much of the route rides the beds of the old logging railroads that crisscross this region, and part of the trip follows snowmobile trails. This means you can use lightweight backcountry skis and move fast.

From the Sawyer River Trail parking lot, pass a trailhead sign and ski ahead on Sawyer River Trail for 0.3 miles and across the frozen Swift River, being careful to test the ice first. Upper Nanamocomuck Ski Trail joins from the left and follows Sawyer River Trail for 0.3 miles before diverging to the right. Ski straight ahead on Sawyer River Trail, and you soon join a well-established snowmobile trail. As you fly down the trail, you feel the sensation of what it must have been like to look out from the logging trains that plied this route more than a century ago. Views into the 45,000-acre Pemigewasset Wilderness appear and disappear throughout this stretch.

At 2.0 miles, you reach a junction with Hancock Notch Trail. Sawyer River Trail continues straight ahead beyond the trail sign, but it is poorly blazed and hard to follow. The better option is to follow the snowmobile trail as it takes a hard right here. Ski on the snowmobile trail around a wide bend on a fast and scenic cruise, taking in views of Mounts Tremont and Carrigain. After skiing down a hill and across a road bridge, you come to a junction with Sawyer River Road, a major snowmobile thoroughfare that comes in from NH 302 (skiing Sawyer River Road to this point is another way to access Sawyer Pond). Cross a small wooden footbridge

SAWYER POND

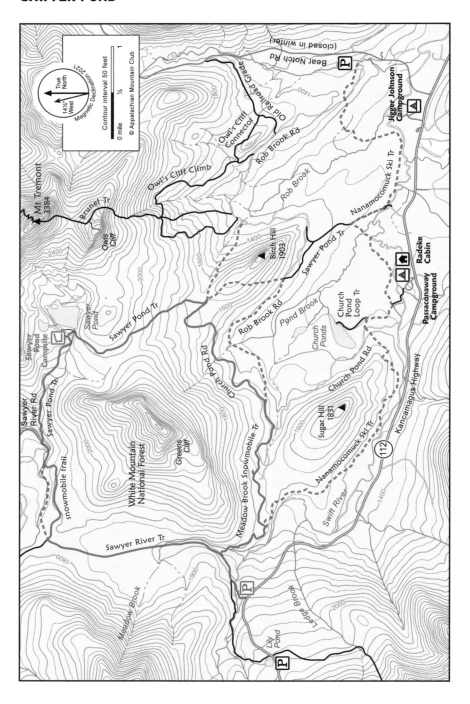

over Sawyer River on the right, and you are on Sawyer Pond Trail, a foot trail that follows logging roads on rolling terrain through the woods. The trail is obvious but poorly blazed. There are also a number of small drainage crossings.

In 1.5 miles, you emerge onto Sawyer Pond. This area, comprising two ponds and 1,130 acres, was one of the original six designated scenic areas in the White Mountain National Forest in 1961.

Mountain ponds are special places. The deep woods give way to the bright open expanse of snow and ice. Owl's Cliff and Mount Tremont rise up from the large mountain pond. The Sawyer Pond Campsite is tucked in the woods on the west shore of the pond.

This gentle tour is an opportunity to take in the details of the woods in winter. Note the way the snow sparkles in afternoon light and how fungi form on the sides of dead trees and become a platform for snow to settle. Animal tracks crisscross your path. One time when I skied this tour, I followed a fox track down the trail for a surprisingly long distance.

Sawyer Pond Trail departs from the southwest corner of the pond and angles generally southeast. Once again, the trail is not well blazed but the trail corridor is reasonably well defined. You pass large glacial erratics in the forest that appear to have cleaved from nearby cliffs on the high peaks of the Pemi.

In 1.9 miles, the hiking trail intersects diagonally with Church Pond Road (FR 318), a snowmobile trail. Turn right here and follow this snowmobile trail to a large snowmobile crossroads called Swan's Crossing. Bear right onto Meadow Brook Trail, which leads back to Sawyer Pond Trail, where you skied earlier in the day. Turn left on Sawyer Pond Trail, recross the Swift River, and return to your car.

This 12-mile tour takes a full day. Plan to be on the trail by 9 A.M. in order to finish in daylight.

Gliding across Sawyer Pond toward the cliffs of Mount Tremont.

㉑ RECOMMENDED SKI TOURS IN NEW HAMPSHIRE

New Hampshire is home to numerous other excellent ski touring opportunities. Below are some additional moderate tours for those who want to get out and enjoy the ungroomed wilds.

21a. PINKHAM NOTCH TOURS, Pinkham Notch, New Hampshire

Pinkham Notch is renowned as the gateway to the steep skiing wonderland of Tuckerman Ravine. But it is also home to several easy and beautiful ski tours.

The following tours begin at the AMC Pinkham Notch Visitor Center, which offers meals and a wealth of information, both published and anecdotal. The AMC Joe Dodge Lodge, located next door, accommodates more than 100 guests. The original Pinkham Notch Camp was first constructed in 1920 and used as a three-season base of operations for the Appalachian Mountain Club. It opened in winter for the first time in 1929–1930. When the Pinkham Notch Highway (now NH 16) was plowed from Jackson that winter, it marked "the beginning of a new era in winter travel," according to Winston Pote, who skied and photographed the White Mountains during those years.

The plowing was a source of contention at the Jackson town meeting that year. "Who would want to go up there in the winter anyway?" demanded some of the residents, as reported by Pote in his excellent chronicle, *Mount Washington in Winter*.

The advent of a plowed road to Pinkham Notch eliminated an arduous 12-mile snowshoe from Jackson, but driving a car didn't necessarily make the going easier. Pote describes what it took to drive in the mountains in those days:

> Winter road conditions, despite the improved snowplowing, remained troublesome. High winds formed deep drifts in the mountain passes. Snow alternately thawed and refroze, and by March there were deep ruts of ice, sometimes filled with water. One always carried shovels, and an ax came in handy if one met another car in the same rut and had to chop out a path around it.

Fortunately, it is easier to reach Pinkham Notch these days. Once there, skiers can access the ski tours to Square Ledge and Connie's Way and enjoy relaxed backcountry skiing in a grand environment. Square Ledge Ski Trail is on the east side of NH 16 and offers spectacular views of Mount Washington and the Northern Presidential Range. Connie's Way Ski Trail is a cross-country ski tour on rolling terrain in the shadow of New Hampshire's highest peak.

The Square Ledge Ski Trail departs across NH 16 from the AMC Pinkham Notch Visitor Center. Cross the road and ski diagonally left (northeast) across a snowy field to reach the start of the Square Ledge Ski Trail (signed). The trail enters the forest and climbs moderately but steadily; climbing skins are helpful. As the trail bends around to the south, you take in jaw-dropping views across the valley of

PINKHAM NOTCH

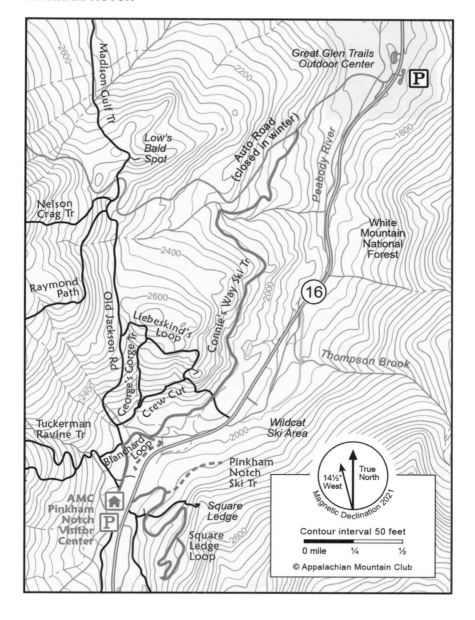

Mount Washington, Gulf of Slides, and Huntington Ravine. The majesty of the Presidential Range provides the backdrop for this entire tour. The trail also swings by Square Ledge, an impressive cliff that is popular with rock climbers. The tour has an elevation gain/loss of 300 feet, making for a fun descent on the return leg.

Connie's Way is a gentle out-and-back tour through a beautiful landscape. Light backcountry or cross-country skis are best and skins are not needed.

Connie's Way was created in memory of Connie Waste. A member of the AMC Pinkham Notch crew, Connie died of a heart attack in 1975 while playing touch football with her crewmates. She was 19. The following year, her friends created 2.4-mile-long Connie's Way as a living memorial. Her brother, Bill Waste, who worked for AMC for many years, reflects about Connie's Way, "The serenity, the beauty, and the peace you can get in the woods there is definitely in the spirit of who she was."

From the Pinkham Notch Visitor Center (where free maps of these ski tours are available at the front desk), ski briefly on the Tuckerman Ravine Trail, then ski Old Jackson Road for 0.3 miles. Turn right on Link Trail and then left on Blanchard Loop to Connie's Way (all junctions are signed). Kick-and-glide through a conifer forest, climbing gently for a mile. The trail passes by giant boulders and tall crags split by long crack systems. This is troll country—the dramatic features are an interesting diversion to stop, admire, and explore. Across the valley is the Wildcat Ski Area. The crowds there make you appreciate your solitude here. The trail ends at the Mount Washington Auto Road, where you turn around and retrace your tracks.

This tour is especially nice early in the day. Morning light filters through the trees, illuminating the birches and accentuating the white snowcaps on the peaks to the west.

Distance: 2.5 miles, Square Ledge Ski Trail, round trip; 5.8 miles, Connie's Way Ski Trail, round trip

Vertical drop: 200 feet

Difficulty: Moderate

Location: The AMC Pinkham Notch Visitor Center is located on NH 16, 11 miles south of Gorham, New Hampshire, and 9 miles north of Jackson (*GPS coordinates*: 44° 15.435′ N, 71° 15.166′ W).

Additional Information: AMC Pinkham Notch Visitor Center, 603-466-2727, outdoors.org

21b. PEMIGEWASSET RIVER TOURS, Lincoln, New Hampshire

These popular and gentle ski tours are ideal for beginning backcountry skiers. The East Branch of the Pemigewasset River has skiable trails that run alongside both of its banks: The Lincoln Woods Trail runs along the west bank, and the Pemi East Side Trail travels the opposite bank. Both trails start and finish at the Lincoln Woods Visitor Information Center located on the Kancamagus Highway, where you can obtain information.

PEMIGEWASSET RIVER

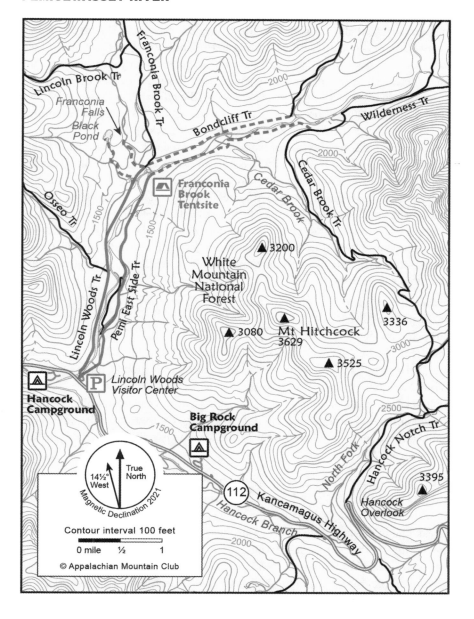

Lincoln Woods Trail: From the information center, ski across a suspension bridge and turn right onto Lincoln Woods Trail. The wide, flat trail follows the bed of a logging railroad that last ran in 1948. The trail is groomed on weekends by the U.S. Forest Service (USFS) up to the wilderness area boundary (2.9 miles in), so it should make for fast cross-country skiing. The Pemigewasset River meanders alongside the trail, offering glimpses of the peaks beyond. After crossing a bridge over Franconia Brook, a sign informs you that you are entering the official Pemigewasset Wilderness Area, a 45,000-acre preserve created by Congress in 1984. The trail grooming ends here and most skiers turn around retrace their tracks.

Pemi East Side Trail: This former truck road was used in the 1940s to haul timber out of the Pemigewasset Wilderness. It is now an easy, scenic ski tour alongside the Pemigewasset River. From the Lincoln Woods information center, descend a short path to the trail. From here to the wilderness area boundary in 2.8 miles, the trail follows a narrow road that is groomed for skiing by the USFS. There are intermittent views of the river and into the roadless Pemigewasset Wilderness as you ski. Just before the gate at the wilderness boundary, pass by the Franconia Brook Campsite (24 sites). Past the gate, the trail narrows into a footpath. Most skiers turn around and retrace their tracks at the gate.

Distance: 6 miles, round trip (both tours)
Vertical drop: 200 feet
Difficulty: Moderate
Location: The Lincoln Woods Visitor Information Center (*GPS coordinates*: 44° 03.821′ N, 71° 35.323′ W) is located beside a large parking lot 5.6 miles east of the White Mountain National Forest Visitor Center in North Woodstock.
Additional Information: White Mountain Visitor Center, fs.usda.gov/whitemountain. White Mountain National Forest parking permit is required at the Lincoln Woods trailhead and can be purchased at the White Mountain Visitor Center off I-93 Exit 32 in North Woodstock.

21c. CHAMPNEY FALLS, MOUNT CHOCORUA, Conway, New Hampshire

Mount Chocorua is a 3,500-foot peak renowned for its craggy summit. It is said to be the most photographed of all the White Mountains, more closely resembling a peak one might find in the Swiss Alps than among the typical glacial domes of the Northeast. The best section of the mountain for skiing is between the parking lot and the beautiful Champney and Pitcher falls. This is also a popular day hike.

From the parking lot, the route ascends Champney Falls Trail, a moderate logging road that is marked with yellow blazes. After about a half-mile, the trail climbs onto the shoulder of Champney Brook via a sharp turn—to be noted for the descent. The route soon rejoins the logging road and continues to a trail junction with Champney Falls Loop at 1.4 miles; bear left onto the loop trail that drops slightly to Champney Falls and Pitcher Falls. This trail to the waterfalls is a half-mile jug handle off the main hiking trail.

CHAMPNEY FALLS

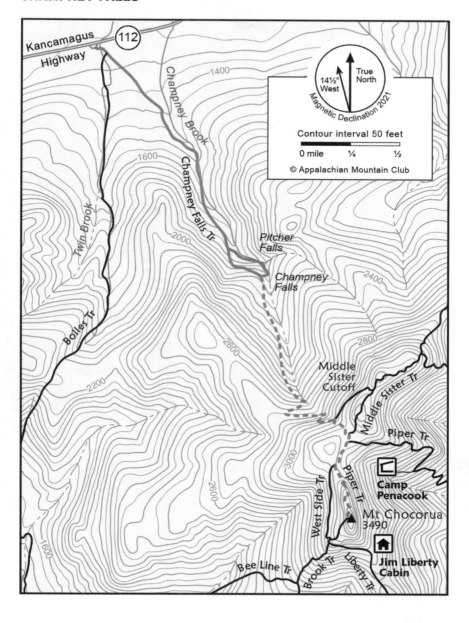

Visiting the spectacular Champney and Pitcher falls is a White Mountain high-light. Champney Falls, a 70-foot cascade, is named for White Mountain landscape artist Benjamin Champney (1817–1907). Pitcher Falls is the more striking winter attraction: a 35-foot curtain of ice that forms inside a small box canyon. It looks as if the bedrock simply broke apart, with the water frozen in time as it spilled over the lip of the vertical wall. This is also a popular ice climbing area. Watch out for slush and water beneath the falls as you ski around taking in the gorgeous winter landscape. The return trip from Champney Falls to the parking lot is an enjoyable mix of trail and glade skiing.

Distance: 3.4 miles, round trip
Vertical drop: 600 feet
Difficulty: Moderate
Location: The large trailhead parking lot is marked by a brown USFS sign, "Champney Falls/Bolles Trail," on the Kancamagus Highway (NH 112), 11.5 miles west of NH 16 (*GPS coordinates*: 43° 59.403′ N, 71° 17.948′ W). A White Mountain National Forest parking permit is required at this trailhead and can be purchased at the WMNF Visitor Center off I-93 Exit 32 in North Woodstock.

21d. MONADNOCK STATE PARK, Jaffrey, New Hampshire

Mount Monadnock holds a special place in the hearts of New Englanders. Standing alone like a beacon over southern New England, it is the gateway to the mountain ranges farther to the north. The mountain has been sketched and painted by numerous artists and written about by dozens of writers and poets. Among its best-known fans were Ralph Waldo Emerson and Henry David Thoreau, who visited the mountain often from their homes in Concord, Massachusetts.

Monadnock State Park currently operates about 8 miles of backcountry ski trails. These trails offer a relaxed introduction to backcountry skiing. Skiers will enjoy the gentle, ungroomed ski trails that crisscross the base of the mountain. The park's cross-country ski trails do not appear on hiking trail maps, and ski trail junctions are denoted by a number, so the free cross-country ski map (available online and at the park store and visitor center) is essential for navigating. The tour to Gilson Pond is a highlight, providing a classic tour through a New England forest, with the Monadnock summit coming in and out of view.

The 4-mile round-trip tour from the park headquarters to Gilson Pond traverses open forest and large stands of white birch trees, along with lovely alpine scenery. Old stone walls dart off in different directions, the remnants of previous generations that have inhabited and farmed this historic mountain. This is pleasant kick-and-glide touring best enjoyed on lightweight cross-country skis.

Previous page: Admiring the rainbow hues of Pitcher Falls on Mount Chocorua.

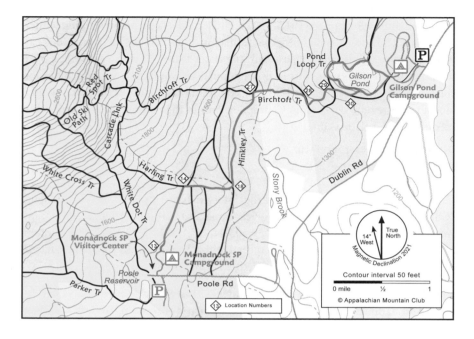

Gilson Pond is an intimate open space within the forest. You can follow Pond Loop Trail around the pond (it is 0.8 miles to circumnavigate the pond) to take in different perspectives on the Pumpelly Ridge of Mount Monadnock.

Only 90 minutes from Boston, Mount Monadnock offers a quick escape for urbanites hungry for a wilder landscape.

Distance: 4 miles, round trip

Vertical drop: 200 feet

Difficulty: Moderate

Location: From Jaffrey, take NH 124 west 2 miles to Dublin Road and turn right at the sign for Monadnock State Park. Turn left on Poole Memorial Road just beyond the campus of Monadnock Christian Ministries. Trails begin from the parking lot at the end of the road (*GPS coordinates*: 42° 50.729′ N, 72° 05.300′ W).

Fee: Monadnock State Park charges a day-use fee on weekends and holidays, but not on weekdays.

Additional Information: Monadnock State Park, nhstateparks.org

2 MAINE

22 ACADIA NATIONAL PARK

One of Acadia's many scenic ski tours follows the famous carriage roads and a hiking trail to the summit of Sargent Mountain, where there is skiing on large snowfields overlooking the Atlantic Ocean. Other Acadia mountains also feature good backcountry skiing.

Distance: 5.6 miles, Parkman Mountain parking area to Sargent Mountain summit, via most direct route, round trip
Elevation: *Start*: 400 feet; *Highest point*: 1,367 feet, Sargent Mountain; *Vertical drop*: 967 feet
Maps: *Acadia National Park Map* (AMC), *Acadia National Park* (Map Adventures, Trails Illustrated). Maps are for sale at park headquarters.
Difficulty: Moderate
Gear: Telemark, cross-country, AT, snowboard
Additional Information: Acadia National Park, 207-288-3338, nps.gov/acad; Acadia Winter Trails Association/Friends of Acadia, friendsofacadia.org

HOW TO GET THERE

From the north, follow ME 198 to the Parkman Mountain parking area (*GPS coordinates*: 44° 19.748′ N, 68° 17.601′ W), a half-mile north of Upper Hadlock Pond. Park headquarters is just west of Eagle Lake on ME 233.

ACADIA NATIONAL PARK

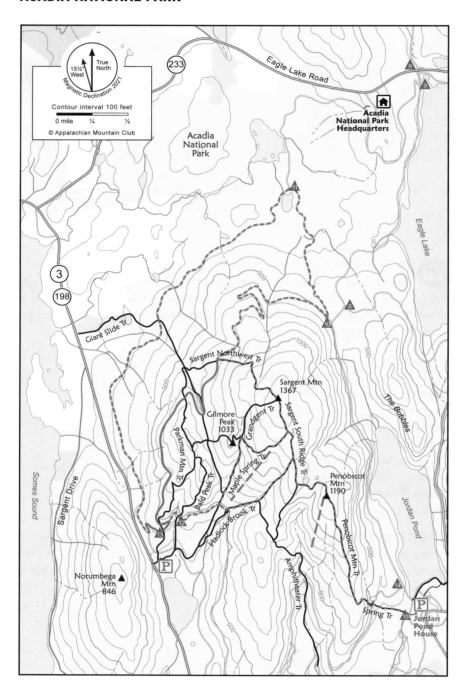

Contour interval 100 feet

0 mile   ¼   ½

© Appalachian Mountain Club

True North

15½° West Magnetic Declination 2021

Eagle Lake Road

233

Acadia National Park

Acadia National Park Headquarters

Eagle Lake

3

198

Giant Slide Tr

Sargent Northwest Tr

Sargent Mtn 1367

Gilmore Peak 1033

Grandgent Tr

Sargent South Ridge Tr

The Bubbles

Parkman Mtn Tr

Bald Peak Tr

Maple Spring Tr

Penobscot Mtn 1190

Somes Sound

Sargent Drive

Hadlock Brook Tr

Penobscot Mtn Tr

Jordan Pond

P

Norumbega Mtn 846

Amphitheater Tr

Spring Tr

P

Jordan Pond House

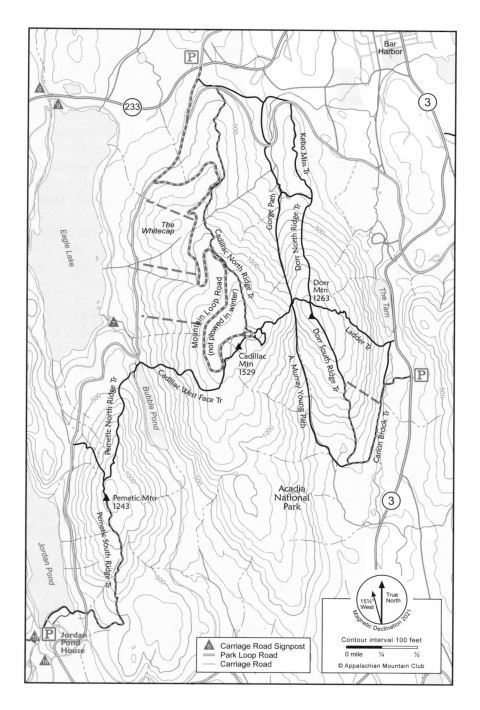

The Whitecap

Eagle Lake

(233)

P

Bar Harbor

(3)

Kebo Mtn Tr

Gorge Path

Dorr North Ridge Tr

Cadillac North Ridge Tr

Mountain Loop Road (not plowed in winter)

Cadillac Mtn 1529

Cadillac West Face Tr

Bubble Pond

Pemetic North Ridge Tr

Dorr Mtn 1263

Ladder Tr

The Tarn

P

Dorr South Ridge Tr

A. Murray Young Path

Canon Brook Tr

Acadia National Park

(3)

Pemetic Mtn 1243

Pemetic South Ridge Tr

Jordan Pond

P Jordan Pond House

True North
15½° West
Magnetic Declination 2021

Contour interval 100 feet

0 mile   ¼   ½

© Appalachian Mountain Club

△6 Carriage Road Signpost
Park Loop Road
Carriage Road

HISTORY

Acadia National Park offers one of the most unique settings in the country for backcountry skiing. Mount Desert Island sits in the Atlantic Ocean just off the coast of Maine. From the island's bare, dome-shaped summits, skiers have a 360-degree view of miles of rugged Maine coastline and outlying islands. This is a rare opportunity to ski snowfields over the ocean. Or you can savor an afternoon of easy cross-country skiing.

Acadia is also special for its cultural history. It was once a summer haven for blue-blood families such as the Fords, Carnegies, Vanderbilts, Astors, and Morgans. Maine Highway 3 leading into neighboring Bar Harbor was once known as "Millionaires' Row." The most popular ski routes in the park travel over paths originally laid to accommodate the horse-and-buggy ramblings of the Rockefellers and their friends. In 1917, John D. Rockefeller Jr. hired the noted landscape architect Frederick Law Olmsted, designer of New York's Central Park and Boston's Emerald Necklace, to design and oversee construction of 45 miles of carriage roads. This elaborate network of roads took a quarter-century to build. Rockefeller later donated most of these carriage roads to the federal government when Acadia National Park was created. These paths are now a unique hallmark of Acadia. No motorized transport, including snowmobiles, is allowed on the carriage roads.

Skiers in Acadia will appreciate the craftsmanship of these paths. They are lined with shark's tooth–shaped slabs of pink granite. Known as "Rockefeller's Teeth," these stones were quarried locally and cut by hand. Turns and curves on the 16-foot-wide paths were designed to direct the attention of horse-and-buggy passengers to scenic vistas. When bridges were needed, Rockefeller saw to it that they received no ordinary treatment. The 17 bridges on the carriage roads, an attraction in themselves, were built with stones painstakingly cut by local masons. The carriage roads were extensively rehabilitated from 1992 to 1995.

THE TOURS

A classic ski tour in Acadia would include a taste of all its unique features, along with good skiing. Sargent Mountain fits the bill. Sargent is a 1,367-foot peak lying directly across from Cadillac Mountain (1,529 feet), the highest point on the East Coast. The carriage road that forms a horseshoe around the north slopes of Sargent Mountain ascends higher (780 feet) than any other carriage road in the park. Most cross-country skiers in the park glide along the carriage roads, which are groomed when there is enough snow. Backcountry skiers are rewarded for stepping off the beaten track to climb and ski the summit of Sargent Mountain.

From the north side of the Parkman Mountain parking lot, turn right. Within 100 feet, you come to a junction with a carriage road (junctions are signed and numbered). You may turn right here if you want a more direct route to Sargent Mountain via Around Mountain Carriage Road (turn left at Junctions 13 and 12;

Skiing Acadia powder over the Atlantic Ocean. *Photo by Lincoln Benedict*

it is 2.8 miles to the summit). If you want a longer tour, turn left and ski Around Mountain Lower Loop, which, when combined with a trip to the Sargent summit, forms a 9.8-mile loop. Should you choose the latter route, you will ski for 3.2 miles on flat terrain before coming to carriage road junction 11, where you turn right. Climb for 200 feet, cross six small bridges that span a wandering stream, and then make a sharp right at junction 10 onto Around Mountain Lower Loop, which climbs gently along the north face of Sargent Mountain. After 1.7 miles, Sargent Northwest Trail leaves on the left, leading to the summit in 0.7 miles.

While skiing the carriage roads, note the intricate stonework that forms the borders and bridges along each path. It is also worth looking over your shoulder where the path turns to see where the original landscape architects were directing your attention. The path affords nice views to the west of Somes Sound, the only natural fjord on the eastern seaboard.

Sargent Northwest Trail can be negotiated easily without climbing skins. Be aware that snow conditions on the summit slopes can be icy and somewhat treacherous and it will be easiest to carry your skis the short distance from treeline to the summit when this is the case. From the summit, the Atlantic Ocean glistens to the south, the horizon broken only by occasional coastal islands. The windswept summit ridge tells the story of the glacier that shaped the landscape. The icecap, estimated to be 2 miles thick, slid over Acadia from the north, leaving deep north-south scratches in the rocks and grinding the island mountains into the characteristic domes that form the park's skyline. The lakes below were merely puddles that formed where the earth was scooped out by the glacier as it ground its way into the ocean.

From the summit, walk south along the ridge and ski Maple Spring Trail until the Maple Spring, then ski a snowfield on skier's left. After crossing Grandgent Trail, stay left of Maple Spring Trail on the ridge above a stream. You can ski through the trees down to the Hemlock Bridge and come to the Upper Hadlock Carriage Road Loop. Turn right and return to intersection 12, where you turn left again, then right at 13, and the Parkman Mountain parking lot will appear on your left shortly.

Another option from the Sargent Mountain summit is to hike or ski along the ridge and take Hadlock Brook Trail, which can be skied all the way to the bridge by Hadlock Falls. Turn right when you hit the carriage road.

If you want to stay up high and sample more skiing, walk the summit ridge from Sargent over to Penobscot Mountain and ski the snowfields to the southwest or ski Penobscot Mountain Trail for a long downhill with views of the Amphitheater Carriage Road Loop.

Snow conditions in Acadia are difficult to predict. The coastal climate may cause it to snow in Acadia when there has been little precipitation elsewhere in Maine, or it may rain here when snow has dumped in the interior of the state. You can check groomed ski trail conditions at the website of Friends of Acadia Winter Trails Association (friendsofacadia.org). Another source of ski information is Cadillac Mountain Sports in Bar Harbor (207-288-4532), where you can also buy maps and rent skis.

The best skiing in Acadia is generally from February through early March, although there is often snow by Christmas. Good skiing can be found on north-facing trails and slopes well into March, long after south-facing slopes have melted.

The rule of thumb in Acadia is *don't wait*—ski the snow when it falls. Lacking a recent storm, it is still worth defying the pessimists and heading out. At best, you may be surprised to find great skiing; at worst, you may have to settle for hiking and savoring Acadia's world-class views.

CROSS-COUNTRY SKIING IN ACADIA

Acadia is home to some of the most scenic cross-country skiing on its groomed carriage roads. The packed snow stays longer, which helps extend the ski season. Volunteers with the Acadia Winter Trails Association groom and set ski tracks on about 35 miles of the carriage road network when snowfall exceeds 4 to 6 inches. You may also cross-country ski and snowshoe on unplowed auto roads in the park. Be careful, as snowmobiles are also permitted to use most of the auto roads. Check the park website for updates on trail conditions and grooming.

OTHER OPTIONS

Pemetic Mountain (1,243 feet) offers a reliable snow cache as well as a mile-long descent, one of the longest skiable downhills in Acadia. The tour follows Pemetic South Ridge Trail and takes in a beautiful summit vista. Park at the Jordan Pond House, ski up the road a short distance, and turn on the Bubbles and Jordan Pond Path. In 0.4 miles, turn left on Pemetic South Ridge Trail. Ski 1.2 miles up to the summit and return via the same route.

Cadillac Mountain can offer good skiing from the auto road, which climbs 3.5 miles to the summit from a parking turnout on ME 233. The auto road is shared with snowmobilers, so trail conditions may be icy or choppy. Ski up the auto road or North Ridge Trail. When skiing down the auto road, look to the west for skiable snowfields. There is a particularly nice run off the snowfields on the Whitecap, a prominent knoll to the west.

Dorr Mountain (1,263 feet), named for "father of Acadia" George Dorr, is the second-highest peak on Mount Desert Island. The southeastern face of Dorr Mountain has open slopes that make for excellent steeper skiing after big storms. To ski this tour, drive approximately 2.5 miles on ME 3 from downtown Bar Harbor. Just uphill from the Tarn and on the left is a plowed parking pullout. The Cannon Brook trailhead is across the street. To access Dorr Mountain, ski down from the trailhead into the Gorge. Follow the Cannon Brook Trail approximately 0.3 miles along the base of Dorr Mountain then switchback up the southeast face. Alternatively, ski up Dorr South Ridge Trail and after about 0.75 miles look for open pitch-pine glades to ski. Enjoy skiing over the Atlantic Ocean.

23 RUMFORD WHITECAP AND BLACK MOUNTAIN

Rumford Whitecap features a mile-long treeless summit plateau with panoramic views of the surrounding Mahoosuc Range. There is a mix of low-angle summit glades and steeper pitches off the summit and in the woods. Black Mountain is home to the Black Mountain of Maine Ski Area. Black and White Glade, a project of Granite Backcountry Alliance and Mahoosuc Land Trust, is an exciting multi-glade tour linking both mountains.

Distance: 2.75 miles, East Andover Road to Rumford Whitecap summit; 6 miles, Black Mountain summit to East Andover Road
Elevation: *Start*: 675 feet (East Andover Road trailhead), 970 feet (Black Mountain of Maine base); *Highest points*: 2,201 feet (Rumford Whitecap), 2,354 feet (Black Mountain); *Vertical drop*: 1,300–1,500 feet
Maps: Download maps from granitebackcountryalliance.org
Difficulty: Most difficult
Gear: AT, telemark, snowboard
Fee: If you start this tour at Black Mountain of Maine Ski Area, you must purchase a lift ticket or an uphill skiing pass. See skiblackmountain.org about ticket prices and designated uphill ski routes.
Additional Information: Granite Backcountry Alliance, granitebackcountryalliance.org

HOW TO GET THERE

East Andover Road trailhead, 52 East Andover Road, Rumford, ME (*GPS coordinates*: 44° 33.000′ N, 70° 41.023′ W): From Bethel, drive 12 miles on US 2 East, then 3 miles on ME 5 North. Turn right on Andover Road, then left on East Andover Road. The trailhead parking lot is on your left in 0.2 miles.

   Black Mountain of Maine, 39 Glover Road, Rumford, ME 04276 (*GPS coordinates*: 44° 34.905′ N, 70° 36.800′ W): From Rumford, head west on Spruce Street, turn right on Isthmus Road, and turn left on Glover Road.

THE TOUR

Rumford Whitecap features a unique mile-long open summit with 360-degree views and excellent skiing. The mountain is visible for miles and has long tempted skiers, though for many years it was not obvious where to ski. That changed in 2019 when Granite Backcountry Alliance (GBA) partnered with Mahoosuc Land Trust, whose 1,200-acre Rumford Whitecap Mountain Preserve extends across Whitecap to near the top of Black Mountain. Volunteers with GBA, Mahoosuc Land Trust, and the Angry Beavers (the local glade cutters of Black Mountain of Maine) teamed up to create multiple glade zones on both Black Mountain and Rumford Whitecap. The result is a spectacular two-mountain tour that can be accessed via a historic community-run ski area. The tour is also the product of an innovative partnership that showcases recreation opportunities on conserved land.

RUMFORD WHITECAP AND BLACK MOUNTAIN

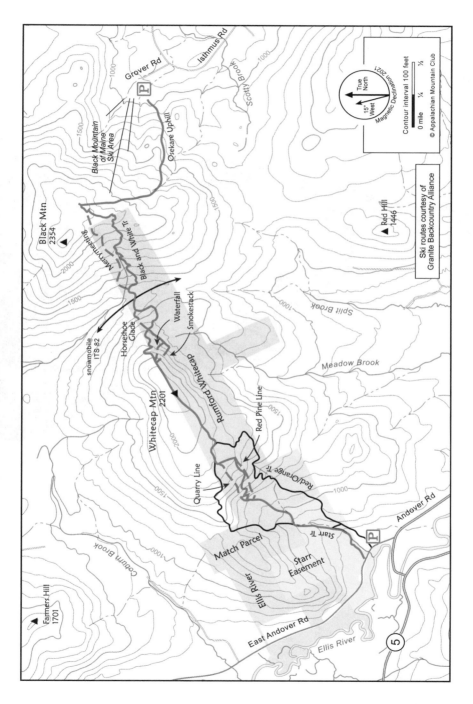

The ski tours on Rumford Whitecap and Black Mountain can be done in several ways. Skiers can simply ski Rumford Whitecap, enjoy the summit views and glades, and return to East Andover Road. Or skiers can start and finish at Black Mountain of Maine (BMOM), riding the lift or skinning up the mountain on designated uphill routes (inquire with BMOM about ticket prices and designated uphill ski routes). Or you can do the full Black and White tour, a grand traverse linking both mountains, which requires a car shuttle. I describe the full tour here.

Starting at BMOM offers a taste of this historic Maine ski area that is best known for its Nordic skiing. The mountain has hosted numerous national cross-country ski championships, and the modern base lodge includes a cross-country ski museum. The cross-country trails weave around the base of the mountain. The ski area is largely volunteer run and has the relaxed feel of a community gathering place. Whether skinning or riding the lift, the backcountry tour begins above the top lift shack. Skin uphill from the lift and look out for blue GBA blazes. The trail to Black & White Glade departs to the left as you climb.

The Merrymeeting Glade off the backside of Black Mountain is about a mile long and drops 900 vertical feet. It threads through a classic New England forest at a moderate angle and is packed with turns. It ends at a snowmobile trail, which you cross and then begin climbing Rumford Whitecap. As you climb, you ascend through the inviting Horseshoe Glade. Accept the invitation, take a fast lap, and continue climbing. You finally emerge onto the open summit plateau of Rumford Whitecap. Soak up the panorama, which is reason enough to do this tour in good weather.

The north end of the summit has fun low-angle glades to ski. The east face features several steep pitches, Waterfall and Smokestack, which begin on the open slopes of the summit but quickly plunge 500 vertical feet into a birch forest. GBA cautions that these steep runs "contain significant risk of avalanche so please be prepared with, at minimum, beacon, probe, and shovel." Heed these words if skiing these steep lines.

As you traverse the summit plateau, you feel as if you are floating over Maine. You are actually skiing across an extensive wild blueberry patch that is much beloved by locals in the summer. The entire Whitecap summit contains fragile and rare plant communities of statewide significance. Users should ski on marked trails and within the designated skin track and glade areas, and avoid vegetation. Look out for the blue GBA blazes that lead you downhill, ultimately ending on a snowmobile trail. You finally emerge on East Andover Road where there is a parking lot.

The highlight of this tour is skiing on top of Rumford Whitecap and taking in some of the best scenery and skiing in western Maine.

Previous page: Maine-lining: skiing the summit snowfields of Rumford Whitecap.

24 LODGE-TO-LODGE SKIING IN THE 100-MILE WILDERNESS

Maine's 100-Mile Wilderness is home to outstanding lodge-to-lodge ski touring. These tours traverse a gently rolling landscape of lakes and high mountains. The trip features easy skiing along groomed trails and staying at full-service AMC backcountry lodges. These lodges also offer gear shuttles so you can ski fast and light.

Distance: 31.5 miles total, four-lodge tour: 8.2 miles, Medawisla Lodge to West Branch Pond Camps; 8.5 miles, West Branch Pond Camps to Little Lyford Lodge; 6.5 miles, Little Lyford Lodge to Gorman Chairback Lodge; 8.3 miles, Gorman Chairback Lodge to winter parking lot

Elevation: *Start*: 1,275 feet, AMC Medawisla Lodge; *Highest point*: 1,775 feet, Shaw Mountain Trail; *Vertical change*: 500 feet, Medawisla to Little Lyford Lodge

Maps: AMC Lodge-to-Lodge Ski Map (download at outdoors.org/mainelodges), *100-Mile Wilderness Map & Guide* (AMC), *Baxter State Park & Katahdin Iron Works* (Trails Illustrated)

Difficulty: Moderate

Gear: Cross-country or light backcountry for lodge-to-lodge tour. If driving to one lodge for backcountry skiing, AT, telemark, or snowboard gear can be used.

Additional Information: AMC Reservations, 603-466-2727, outdoors.org/mainelodges

HOW TO GET THERE

Greenville is the logistics center for the Appalachian Mountain Club (AMC) lodges. From Greenville, the winter parking lot (*GPS coordinates*: 45° 28.043′ N, 69° 24.840′ W) for the AMC Little Lyford and Gorman Chairback lodges is approximately 10 miles east, and Medawisla Wilderness Lodge and Cabins is about 25 miles northeast of town. If you need to shuttle people, cars, and gear to and from the lodges, contact Northwoods Outfitters in Greenville (*GPS coordinates*: 45° 27.557′ N, 69° 35.471′ W), where you can also buy or rent skis and other equipment (866-223-1380, maineoutfitter.com). Shuttles are arranged by AMC when you make lodging reservations. AMC's website has updated information about visiting the Maine lodges.

THE TOUR

The 100-Mile Wilderness is the final stretch of the 2,184-mile-long Appalachian Trail (AT). Until recently, backcountry skiers had little reason to venture into this area, since the so-called wilderness, which runs from Monson, Maine, to Katahdin, historically has been owned by timber companies and subjected to industrial logging. The only protected land outside of Baxter State Park was the narrow Appalachian Trail corridor, a ribbon of green amid a threatened landscape.

LODGE-TO-LODGE SKIING IN THE 100-MILE WILDERNESS

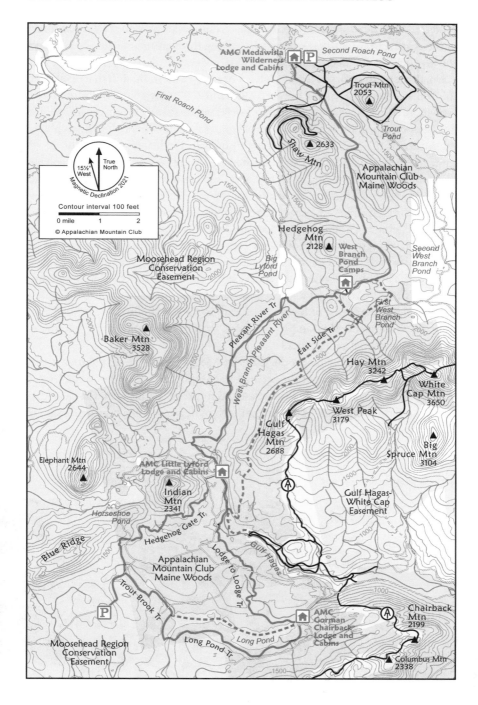

But that was last century. In a stunning turn of events, everything has changed. A large swath of northern Maine between Greenville and Baxter State Park has been protected from development. The 100-Mile Wilderness is now one of the best places in the Northeast for anyone who relishes skiing through remote wild lands while staying in rustic full-service wilderness lodges.

No, this isn't an environmentalist's fever dream. The seismic shift that resulted in this transformation occurred between 1997 and 2007, when 6 million acres of forest—more than a quarter of Maine's land—was put up for sale by timber companies. This sudden sale of the largest forest ecosystem east of the Mississippi River placed the future of the 100-Mile Wilderness in danger. Environmental organizations came to the rescue. In 2003, AMC launched the Maine Woods Initiative, which has resulted in the conservation of 70,000 acres of land north and east of Greenville. AMC also built 120 miles of recreation trails and opened three wilderness lodges: Little Lyford, Gorman Chairback, and Medawisla. The Maine Woods Initiative stitches together an uninterrupted 63-mile-long corridor of conservation land that covers 600,000 acres from just outside Greenville all the way to the northern part of Baxter State Park. This is the single largest conservation and recreation investment in the club's history and one of the most significant conservation efforts in Maine.

Maine's North Woods got a further boost in 2016, when President Obama designated 87,500 acres east of Baxter State Park as the Katahdin Woods and Waters National Monument. This land was donated by Roxanne Quimby, the founder of Burt's Bees personal care products.

One of the immediate by-products of the AMC Maine Woods Initiative is that Maine is now home to one of the premier lodge-to-lodge ski routes in the United States. The route showcases both the past and future of Maine, from the clear-cuts visible on distant hillsides, to the bright green of new growth, a reassuring sign of nature's resilience.

Gorman Chairback Lodge and Long Pond.

Skiers crossing West Branch Pond en route to spending the night at West Branch Pond Camps. The Appalachian Trail runs along the ridge in the background.

Skiers can experience Maine's wilderness lodges in a variety of ways. One option is to visit just one lodge and explore the surrounding area from this base camp. Two of the four lodges—Medawisla and the private, family-owned West Branch Pond Camps—are accessible by car. Each has miles of groomed and ungroomed ski trails that you can explore while returning to the same place. This means you can bring a quiver of skis and ski a variety of terrain.

Another option that avoids having to shuttle a car is to ski lodge-to-lodge between Little Lyford and Gorman Chairback. Both lodges, which are accessible only on skis, share the same winter parking lot. Each of these lodges also has its own trail network for those wishing to explore during the day but stay put at night.

The ultimate option is a lodge-to-lodge ski traverse between all four wilderness lodges. This requires at least four nights. You ski on groomed trails from lodge to lodge, and you must arrange a shuttle so that your vehicle is waiting at your final destination.

Why ski lodge-to-lodge? In our hyperconnected age, going off-grid and skiing through wilderness to a remote lodge may seem like a throwback to another era. That is precisely the appeal. This is a journey. As you move through the mountains and lakes of northern Maine, your attention is focused entirely on the stunning landscape around you. Your skis kick and glide in a comfortable rhythm while your muscles flex and stretch. The palette of each day ranges from white to deep green.

The snow is dappled with animal tracks. You feel as if you are all alone gliding in the crisp winter air. And then you catch the scent of woodsmoke. As if by magic, a log cabin emerges from the forest. You have arrived at your next destination. At night, look up to see stars flickering brilliantly in the ink-black sky.

The full lodge-to-lodge ski traverse can be skied in either direction. I describe the lodges from north to south, as I skied them.

Medawisla Wilderness Lodge is the largest and newest of the AMC Maine lodges. The original hunting lodge, which included seven cabins, was built in 1953 and closed in 2012, then torn down. AMC then invested $6 million to build a state-of-the-art ecolodge, including nine cabins and a bunkhouse, which opened in 2017. The interior showcases Maine craftsmanship, featuring gorgeous tables and chairs handmade from curly maple. From the dining room windows there are expansive views of Second Roach Pond. For those staying longer at Medawisla, take time to ski on the lodge's 35-mile network of groomed cross-country ski trails. And be sure to ski across snow-covered Second Roach Pond and take in the sweeping views of the frozen white wilderness. Medawisla is the Abenaki word for loon, and the 1981 film *On Golden Pond* featured the sound of singing loons, which was recorded on Second Roach Pond.

The ski trail that you follow between lodges is groomed, and you can opt to have your gear shuttled by snowmobile (highly recommended). This enables you to use lightweight waxable or waxless skis, the same equipment you would use at a cross-country ski center. You need carry only a day pack with the usual backcountry essentials, such as repair gear, food, extra clothing, and first aid supplies. If you are skiing to more than one lodge, I recommend that you leave the heavy skis and climbing skins behind—this is cross-country skiing, albeit in a wild landscape.

From Medawisla Lodge, start the 8.2-mile trip to West Branch Pond Camps by skiing 1.3 miles on Emmit Brook Trail, then turning onto Lodge-to-Lodge Trail (a.k.a. the groomed Long Ridge Road). The trail reaches a height-of-land on the shoulder of Shaw Mountain, from where you should turn around and take in the views. The imposing snow-covered tabletop summit of Big Spencer Mountain (3,215 feet) crowns this landscape. This vista orients you to the wild country in which you are traveling. From this high point, continue on rolling terrain and then begin a fun descent on the wide trail. As you round each bend, the vista changes. New valleys open then close. You finally come out to a trail junction; look for signs or blazes pointing left to West Branch Pond Camps (or WBPC). A 6-foot-wide spur trail snakes through the woods before emerging at the weathered cabins of West Branch Pond Camps.

Previous page: Skiing to Gorman Chairback Lodge through a snow-laden forest.

West Branch Pond Camps is privately owned by Eric Stirling, the fifth generation of his family to run the hunting and fishing lodge. This is the only privately owned camp on the lodge trip, and it offers a welcome touch of local culture and lore. We stayed in rustic century-old log cabins beside the frozen First West Branch Pond. I joined Stirling as he cooked our dinner on a woodstove in the dining cabin. Stuffed trophy heads adorned the walls. Stirling pointed outside to Whitecap Mountain (3,650 feet), which overlooks the camp, and he noted that the Appalachian Trail crosses its summit. Stirling, a bearded, congenial man, gave voice to what I felt as I relaxed from the day's ski. "My hope," he told me, "is that skiers take away from here a sense of something that's been unchanged through the generations."

The next day, you strike out on the 8.5-mile trip to AMC Little Lyford Lodge. The route follows the Pleasant River Trail, which weaves alongside its frozen namesake. Midway down the trail is an expansive meadow with beautiful views of Baker Mountain (3,528 feet), which was acquired by AMC as part of the Maine Woods Initiative. The trail becomes more serpentine as you move south until you finally glide past the two Little Lyford Ponds. You finally arrive at Little Lyford Lodge and Cabins, which was originally built in 1874. We relaxed and sipped tea on the wood deck and enjoyed dinner served in front of giant picture windows.

From Little Lyford Lodge, I took a side trip by skiing over to Gulf Hagas, the "Grand Canyon of Maine." It is 2.2 miles from Little Lyford Lodge to the Head of the Gulf; the first mile is on the groomed Lodge-to-Lodge Trail, and the remainder follows Head of the Gulf Trail, a hiking trail on which you may need to snowshoe or walk (the lodge offers free snowshoes). From Head of the Gulf, proceed 0.3 miles on the trail to an overlook at Billings Falls and peer down into the deep gorge. This is troll land, with wild trees clinging to the sides of the frothing chasm. Below lies a primeval sight of frozen waterfalls, open pools of rushing water, and beautifully sculpted snow that swirls along the floor of the gorge in the most fantastical ways. Returning to Little Lyford Camp from the churning Gulf Hagas, you will savor this comfort in the wilds.

From Little Lyford to Gorman Chairback Lodge, it is a 6.5-mile ski south on the well-signed Lodge-to-Lodge Trail. The trail weaves through tall conifers that appear like Christmas trees under a heavy mantle of snow. On this shortest leg of the ski traverse, you emerge at Gorman Chairback, a refurbished 1867 hunting lodge with a breathtaking perch alongside Long Pond. I stayed in a century-old octagonal log cabin that included a library and a view onto the lake.

From Gorman Chairback Lodge, there are two options for your return to the winter parking lot where you left your car: ski 8.3 miles via Long Pond Trail, or, if conditions permit, ski across the frozen expanse of Long Pond, which is about 2 miles shorter.

If you exit from Little Lyford Lodge, you follow Hedgehog Gate Trail, which leads to the winter parking lot. Enjoy this classic, twisty skiing finale to your tour through the heart of the 100-Mile Wilderness.

25 MAINE HUTS & TRAILS

Maine Huts & Trails offers some of the best hut skiing in the East. Ski on groomed trails that wind through the mountains of western Maine and stay at modern backcountry huts. Skiers on light gear can tour for days through a wild landscape.

Distance: 2.2 miles, Long Falls Dam/Flagstaff trailhead to Flagstaff Lake Hut; 12 miles, Flagstaff Lake Hut to Poplar Stream Falls Hut; 3.3 miles, Airport Trailhead in Carrabassett Valley to Poplar Stream Falls Hut; 11.7 miles, Flagstaff Lake Hut to Grand Falls Hut; 14.4 miles, West Forks trailhead to Grand Falls Hut; 3.1–3.6 miles, to Stratton Brook Hut depending on trailhead
Elevation: *Trailheads:* 1,058 feet, Big Eddy/Grand Falls trailhead; 883 feet, Airport trailhead, Carrabassett Valley; 1,294 feet, Route 27/Stratton Brook trailhead; *Huts:* Stratton Brook Hut, 1,880 feet; Poplar Falls Hut, 1,314 feet; Flagstaff Lake Hut, 1,202 feet; Grand Falls Hut, 1,049 feet
Maps: *Maine Huts & Trails* (download trail maps at mainehuts.org)
Difficulty: Moderate
Gear: Cross-country
Additional Information: Maine Huts & Trails, 207-265-2400, mainehuts.org

HOW TO GET THERE

The Long Falls Dam trailhead for the Flagstaff Lake Hut is in North New Portland, Maine, 23 miles up Long Falls Dam Road (*GPS coordinates*: 45° 11.220′ N, 70° 09.540′ W). The Airport trailhead for the Poplar Falls Hut is in Carrabassett Valley (*GPS coordinates*: 45° 05.340′ N, 70° 13.200′ W). The Route 27/Stratton Brook trailhead for the Stratton Brook Hut is also in Carrabassett Valley (*GPS coordinates*: 45° 04.860′ N, 70° 19.020′ W). The trailhead for the Grand Falls Hut is on ME 201, near West Forks. Current directions for parking and skiing can be found at mainehuts.org.

THE TOUR

Maine Huts & Trails is a nonprofit organization that was founded with a bold vision: to build mountain huts spanning 180 miles in western Maine. The original plan was to build a hut route extending from the Mahoosuc Mountains near Bethel, through the Rangeley Lakes and Flagstaff Lake, all the way to Moosehead Lake in Greenville. Poplar Falls Hut outside the town of Carrabassett Valley was the first to open in 2008, followed by Flagstaff Lake Hut, Grand Falls Hut, and Stratton Brook Hut.

The grand vision of Maine Huts & Trails (MHT) bumped up against hard realities in 2019 when the nonprofit organization nearly ran out of money, leaving the future of MHT uncertain. I chose to keep it in this book on faith that the organization finds a way forward and keeps its beautiful huts open. Check mainehuts.org for the current status of the huts.

MAINE HUTS & TRAILS

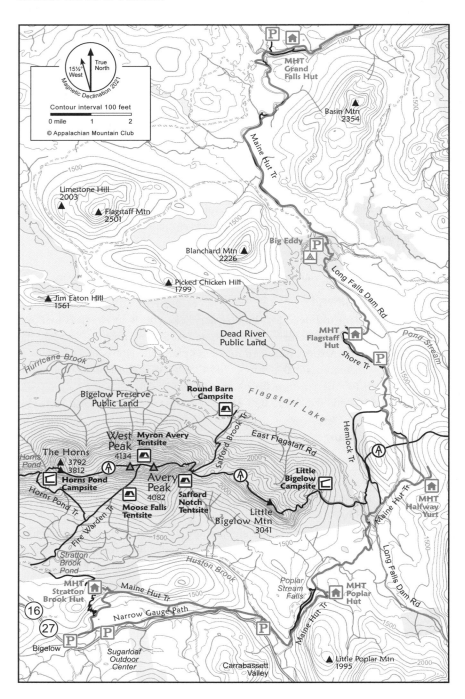

Grand view: gazing at Grand Falls, a majestic 40-foot high waterfall on the Dead River.

I have a soft spot for hut skiing. It combines two seemingly incompatible experiences: being far out in the wilds while enjoying the comfort and warmth of home. Western skiers and Europeans have been reveling in the joys of winter huts for generations. But easterners, for odd reasons, have been slow to catch on. One explanation is that Eastern mountains are relatively accessible, diminishing the need for huts. Another reason may be that backcountry suffering has been too honored a tradition in New England, an anachronistic by-product of the Puritan work ethic.

In an impassioned essay entitled "A Plea for Huts" that appeared in the 1942 *American Ski Annual*, James Laughlin wrote:

> We must have huts in America for high-mountain touring. Not just occasional isolated huts here and there, but groups of two and three (and later more) related huts in our principal mountain areas. Until we have them, the run of American skiers will never know what it means to tour, and, as anyone knows who has toured abroad, touring is the real cream of skiing. . . . The ultimate in ski pleasure is to get off into the "big stuff," a high range far away from the world below, a world to itself of sun and snow, where, likely enough, the only tracks you will see will be those you make yourself. . . . So here's to our chain of American huts! Soon may they come!

It was not soon enough. It took until the mid-1980s, when the Tenth Mountain Trail in Colorado was established, for American skiers to truly understand the pleasures of which Laughlin wrote. The beautiful log cabins sprinkled around the high mountains of Colorado and linked by ski trails have been a huge success. Those who ski them return as converts to the cause of going light and lodging in style in the wilderness.

Maine Huts & Trails was the brainchild of Larry Warren, the former CEO of Sugarloaf Ski Area. In 1974, he dreamed up the idea of a wilderness hut-to-hut ski

Preparing to set off from Flagstaff Lake Hut on Maine Huts & Trails.

and hiking trail for western Maine. It was an era when many people were going back to the land, and Warren thought backcountry skiing was on the brink of going big. He also wanted to bring environmentally sustainable development and jobs to a rural part of Maine that faces continual economic challenges. Right idea, wrong time—it took 35 years before the first Maine hut opened.

MHT introduced a new style of skiing and backcountry travel to the East. The trail between huts is a groomed carpet of corduroy snow. Some fast gliding down the track is all it takes to reach what is euphemistically called a "hut." You will be pleasantly startled by the structure that greets you far out in the Maine Woods.

MHT lodges are a showcase for green design. Odorless composting toilets handle waste, wood-fired boilers heat water for radiant floor heat and showers, and electricity is partly generated by a small windmill at Flagstaff Lake Hut and a hydro turbine in a brook at Poplar Falls Hut. The dining rooms feature beautiful tables and rustic chairs crafted by Maine furniture makers. The huts have similar amenities throughout: interiors crafted from Maine pine with stuffed leather chairs facing a woodstove; solar- and hydro-powered lights and plumbing; semiprivate and bunkroom lodging.

MHT has offered gear shuttling between huts (for a fee), which enables skiers to travel fast and light, but the future of this service was in question at the time of this writing.

A few highlights of skiing this unique hut-to-hut trail system:

At Flagstaff Lake Hut, the bright white canvas of the vast lake shines through the windows. You glide out onto the lake to admire the frosted ridgeline of Bigelow Mountain, which stands watch over a large undeveloped area.

On the ski between Flagstaff Lake Hut and Poplar Falls Hut, the snowy summits of the Bigelow Preserve cap the vista. A little farther on, you ski across the Appalachian Trail.

A scenic highlight of the network is Grand Falls, located near the Grand Falls Hut. The river is 100 feet wide and drops 40 feet in a thunderous cascade. Ice plasters the surrounding rock walls and trees. The natural spectacle is breathtaking and mesmerizing.

MHT offers easy access to a wild and remote landscape. During other seasons, the trail and huts are open to bikers, paddlers, and hikers. But the trail is about more than just skiing and riding. Former MHT executive director Dave Herring told me, "The huts preserve public access to a remote corridor and create a model of ecotourism that hopefully will create a sustainable source of economic development for western Maine."

To really enjoy the groomed trails, use lightweight cross-country skis without metal edges, much as you would at a cross-country ski center. This is especially feasible if there is a hut-to-hut snowmobile gear shuttle. The trails are rolling but never pushy, so they are suitable for fit, intermediate skiers who are comfortable skiing for four to five hours. The huts and trails are also great for families. And don't feel that you have to change huts each night. It is enjoyable to take a relaxed pace, staying more than one night at a hut and exploring surrounding mountains and lakes on day trips.

In Europe, comfortable lodging is as much a part of the mountain culture as skiing and climbing. Who would have dreamed: *la dolce vita*—the good life, as Italians say—right in western Maine.

26 KATAHDIN AND BAXTER STATE PARK

Baxter State Park is home to some of the most awe-inspiring mountain scenery and terrain in the United States. Ski mountaineering routes in the Chimney Pond area and ski touring around Russell Pond are some of the classic ski routes in the park. A north-south traverse of the park makes for a spectacular multiday trip.

Distance: 13 miles, Abol Bridge (parking area on Golden Road) to Roaring Brook bunkhouse; 3.3 miles, Roaring Brook to Chimney Pond; 7 miles, Roaring Brook to Russell Pond; 43 miles, north-south park traverse, Matagamon Gate to Abol Bridge

Elevation: *Start/Finish*: 590 feet, Abol Bridge; *Highest point*: 5,267 feet (Katahdin summit—Baxter Peak), 2,914 feet (Chimney Pond campground); *Vertical drop*: 2,353 feet, Katahdin to Chimney Pond

Maps: *100-Mile Wilderness Map and Guide* (AMC), *Katahdin* (Map Adventures), *Baxter State Park* (Trails Illustrated)

Difficulty: Ski mountaineering, Katahdin; Moderate, Roaring Brook, Russell Pond, and other lowland routes

Fees and Regulations: Baxter State Park charges fees for camping within the park. Contact the Baxter State Park Authority for information on visiting the park in winter. Applications for overnight stays in the park and payment must be received one week before your arrival.

Additional Information: Baxter State Park Authority, 64 Balsam Dr., Millinocket, ME 04462, 207-723-5140, baxterstatepark.org

HOW TO GET THERE

Follow I-95 north to the Medway exit (Exit 56), then go west 10 miles on ME 157 to Millinocket. Follow signs to the park. It is 20 miles from Millinocket to a large plowed parking area (*GPS coordinates*: 45° 50.111′ N, 68° 57.700′ W) just before Abol Bridge on the Golden Road (the plowed logging road just outside the park boundary).

"THE MOUNTAIN OF THE PEOPLE OF MAINE"

Man is born to Die, His Works are Short-lived
Buildings Crumble, Monuments Decay, Wealth Vanishes
But Katahdin in All Its Glory
Forever Shall Remain the Mountain of the
People of Maine.

—Governor Percival P. Baxter

"It was vast, Titanic, and such as man never inhabits," wrote Henry David Thoreau of his 1846 ascent of Katahdin. Like Katahdin, Baxter State Park has a way of reorienting one's sense of space and time. Covering 209,501 acres, the park is home to 46 mountain peaks and ridges, 18 of which are more than 3,000 feet tall. Although Baxter State Park is not the largest tract of wild lands in New England (that distinc-

KATAHDIN AND BAXTER STATE PARK

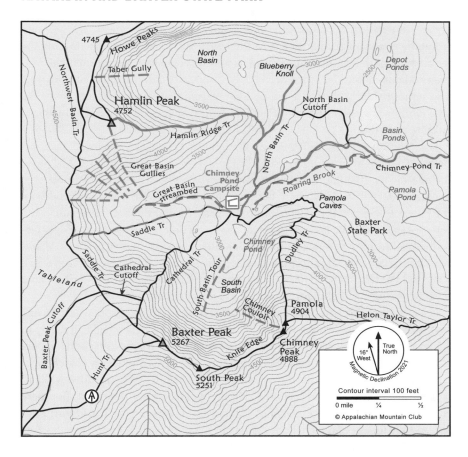

tion lies with the 785,000-acre White Mountain National Forest in New Hampshire and Maine), it feels bigger and wilder than any other place. That is partly because of its remoteness—the park is a full day's drive from urban centers such as Boston or Portland, and it is surrounded by thousands of miles of forest and rivers. The vastness of the place often stuns New Englanders, who are more accustomed to the tighter confines of the northern woods.

Baxter State Park is arguably home to the best wilderness skiing in the East. With its numerous mountains, valleys, and lakes, it is unmatched in the region as a destination for extended ski expeditions.

The crown of Baxter State Park, Katahdin, roars up out of the rolling terrain of northern Maine in a cacophony of ice, rock, and snow. At 5,267 feet, it is the highest point in Maine. It also serves as the northern terminus for the Appalachian Trail. Katahdin is stunning in its severity, a striking contrast to the undulating lake-pocked countryside around it. "What a place to live, what a place to die and be buried in! There certainly men would live forever, and laugh at death and the grave," Thoreau wrote of Katahdin in *The Maine Woods*.

Katahdin is incongruous for a New England peak. Its serrated ridgeline and the long, sweeping gullies that plunge from its summit are more reminiscent of the Alps than a Maine mountain. Its massive size is at once awe-inspiring and intimidating. The summit ridge is part of a 4-mile-long plateau that rises 4,500 feet above the surrounding lowlands. This so-called Tableland is bounded by a number of glacial cirques, or basins.

Katahdin, an Abenaki or Penobscot word meaning "greatest mountain," is comprised of a series of summits that ring the horseshoe-shaped Great Basin. The peaks include Baxter (the highest), South, Chimney, Hamlin, Howe, and Pamola. The Penobscot feared the mountain, believing that Pamola was a wrathful god with the power to destroy those who climb the peak. Today, the most dramatic—and feared—feature of the mountain for hikers and climbers is the Knife Edge. Described as "the most spectacular mountain trail in the East" in AMC's *Maine Mountain Guide*, the Knife Edge is a mile-long section of the summit ridge between South Peak and Pamola. Lying at nearly 5,000 feet, the Knife Edge narrows to 24 inches in some sections and plunges thousands of feet on either side.

Just as remarkable as the park itself is the fact that so large a place exists in Maine that isn't being relentlessly logged. The defenders of the park fought tirelessly to achieve this distinction, and it took a former governor of Maine to make it happen.

Baxter State Park was conceived in an unprecedented act of love and stubbornness. Percival P. Baxter, governor of Maine from 1921 to 1925, crusaded while in office to preserve the lands around Katahdin by making it a state park. But mere governors were no match for Maine's real power brokers: the timber barons, who successfully fought him off. Unbowed, Baxter made an audacious end run: he simply bought the lands and gave them to the state to preserve as a park. Between 1930, when he purchased Katahdin itself, and 1962, Baxter bought and donated more than 200,000 acres of land to the state of Maine. The land is protected by the former governor's covenant, which declared that the park would "forever be left in its natural wild state, forever be kept as a sanctuary for wild beasts and birds, and forever be used for public forest, public park, and public recreational purposes." Today, Baxter Park is the fourth-largest state park in the nation.

SKI HISTORY OF KATAHDIN

The first recorded ascent of Katahdin was in 1804 by Massachusetts surveyors Zackery Adley and Charles Turner, who later became a U.S. congressman. Henry David Thoreau climbed it in 1846 and wrote about it in his classic book, *The Maine Woods*.

The ski history of Katahdin is more obscure. The first recorded winter ascent of Katahdin was made in 1892. In March 1926, Arthur Comey, a noted blazer of the Appalachian Trail, Appalachian Mountain Club (AMC) member, and influential

Soaring over Maine: dropping into the Great Basin Gullies of Katahdin. *Photo by Jamie Walter*

city planner, made the historic first descent of Katahdin on skis via the Saddle Trail. He was accompanied by noted mountaineer and mathematician Robert Underhill, though Underhill removed his skis for the last few hundred feet. Comey also reported skiing in North Basin and descending some of the Great Basin Gullies. Comey and other AMC skiers also skied Katahdin in 1928.

Comey wrote of dropping onto the steep Saddle Trail, "The greatest thrill of all comes when one dips the ski-points over its rim." He was both humble and humorous in his description of his technique: "If the runner is a bit tired and not particularly expert, he will probably use the 'Sitz-Telemark' turn, said to have been invented by Professor Sitz for just such occasions."

Comey was an early pioneer of creative approaches to Eastern skiing. Outdoor historians Laura and Guy Waterman recount in *Forest and Crag* that Comey "skied through krummholz, over rocky ridges, and even up fire tower ladders." Comey was a phenomenally prolific skier. By his own account, he logged 1,115 miles on skis during three winters. But he was also a contentious figure among mountaineers. The Watermans recounted that he had a "skyrocketing temper" that resulted in his being banned from the Bemis Crew, a gung-ho group of top New England climbers in the 1920s. One of his partners observed, "The trouble with Arthur Comey is that I can never tell which way he will jump, except that it is generally the way I don't want him to."

After Comey's early ski exploits, virtually no recorded ski history of Katahdin exists for another half-century. In 1980, a group from the University of Maine at Orono, which included Dave Getchell and Tad Feffer, skied Taber Gully in North Basin, along with the next gully north. These elegant 30- to 40-degree couloirs may have been skied earlier, but no record of the descent exists. In 1984, some ski patrollers from nearby Squaw Mountain are reported to have skied Black Gully, a steep ice-climbing route that ascends Baxter Peak. This 50-plus-degree couloir would rate as an extreme ski descent. In 1986, telemark skiers Dick Hall, Winslow Ayer, Gary Faucher, Roger Zimmerman, and Dean Mendell skied the Chimney Couloir, Katahdin's classic climbing gully that ascends South Peak.

VISITING BAXTER STATE PARK IN WINTER

First-time winter visitors to Katahdin may be surprised to find themselves confronting one of its challenges before leaving home: navigating the rules and regulations of Baxter State Park. In the past, a trip to Baxter State Park was like going on a date with your mother along—park authorities wanted information about everything from your gear, your partners, and your medical history to your mountaineering experience. Trips had to be planned months in advance.

Mountaineers have long groused about Baxter's rules and regulations. Guy and Laura Waterman, writing in the climbing journal *Off Belay* in 1977, charged that the rules "stifle the 'freedom of the hills' so successfully that many climbers simply avoid Katahdin rather than submit."

Park authorities explain in their literature that the purpose of the regulations is "to promote safety of all persons using the Park and to protect the Baxter State Park Authority and its staff from unnecessary search and rescue efforts." Baxter State Park is separate from the Maine state parks system and is governed by its own rules and rangers.

Former park director Buzz Caverly insisted that the rules exist to protect the fragile natural resources. He explained that the park is closed during April and May (unfortunately, the best and safest time for spring skiing) to "give the resources a rest." When I asked him why mountaineers couldn't rely on their own judgment to travel freely in the park, he replied bluntly, "We don't agree with the philosophy that you have the right to die in the mountains." Despite these precautions, two dozen people have died on Katahdin since 1962.

Times change, and so does Baxter State Park. Baxter has relaxed some of its more onerous requirements, but there are still plenty of hurdles to leap. Following are the basics.

Baxter State Park has special rules and regulations that govern entry into the park in winter (defined as December 1 to April 1). These include submitting an application and payment at least one week prior to arrival; registering for climbing or skiing above treeline; designating a "trip leader"; and providing a day-by-day itinerary of where visitors intend to stay. The maximum group size is 12 people,

Katahdin at first light from Hamlin Peak. *Photo by Jamie Walter*

and the park now allows solo travel by special advance registration. Park rangers have stopped requiring certain equipment (such as helmets and ropes for skiers), and they no longer open and close climbing and skiing routes based on weather and safety issues.

"We are trying to give that responsibility back to the user," said Marcia Williamson, former interpretive specialist at Baxter State Park. "We make recommendations. It's up to you to make the decisions."

This is a welcome change. Nevertheless, the rules and regulations for Baxter change periodically. Suffice it to say that *a trip to Baxter State Park should be planned at least one month in advance.* Applications for winter use are accepted starting November 1. If you are even considering a trip to Baxter, contact the Baxter State Park Authority to inquire and make arrangements. If you plan to ski in any of the basins (that is, off-trail above treeline), this is considered "technical climbing" and you must register as a technical climber or skier with the ranger at Chimney Pond. As of this writing, helmets are strongly recommended for skiing above treeline.

The park concedes that its paperwork requirement can be onerous. But, as a park naturalist told me, "It's an exercise in expedition planning and accountability. We take it seriously." The rules of the park are rooted in Governor Baxter's deeds of trust. "He said that protection and preservation of the resource—the flora and fauna—comes first. Recreation is of secondary importance," explained Williamson.

The silver lining for those who successfully negotiate the gauntlet of requirements is that you typically have the park to yourself. The crowds that have overrun places like Tuckerman Ravine are absent here. Enjoy the solitude.

SKI ROUTES IN BAXTER STATE PARK

Winter visitors to the park need not set an ambitious itinerary. It is enough to ski around and take in the grandeur of the mountains. Weather and snow conditions will determine what you are able to accomplish above treeline. The bunkhouses, with their views of the summits, are a good base from which to take day trips.

Two areas of major interest to skiers are the areas around Chimney Pond and Russell Pond. The Chimney Pond region is the most popular destination for winter climbing in the park. It lies at the foot of Katahdin in the heart of the Great Basin. Skiers can make reservations to stay at the bunkhouse, to camp in a lean-to, or to pitch a tent, all next to Chimney Pond. The Chimney Pond bunkhouse can feel a bit dank and crowded when it is full, but with the woodstove roaring, it is a warm refuge. Still, some people prefer tents or lean-tos to the close quarters of the bunkhouse.

The Approach

The long ski in from the Golden Road is the first test of your commitment and your packing prowess. It is a 13-mile ski from where you park at Abol Bridge to Roaring Brook (the route is generally packed out by snowmobiles used by the rangers) and another 3.3 miles to Chimney Pond, the base of Katahdin. Most people take two days to reach Chimney Pond, but if you are up for a very long day, you can knock out the 16.3-mile approach in one push. In either case, you need an early start.

From the Abol Bridge parking area, take Abol Stream Trail a short distance to a picnic area then turn left on an unplowed road that is a snowmobile trail. In a few minutes, you will reach the main tote road, which is also a snowmobile trail, where you turn right to ski to the Togue Pond Gate. Turn left at Togue Pond and continue skiing on a relatively flat, snow-packed road. Heavily laden parties often drag their gear in plastic kiddie sleds, which works reasonably well if you are going only as far as Chimney Pond (the flimsy sleds are unsuitable in deep snow elsewhere in the park). Ski pulks work even better. Bring wax for this part of the tour; plodding across the flats using climbing skins makes it painfully slow going. Pro tip: Bring a blister kit (2nd Skin or equivalent) and if your backcountry boots are uncomfortable, consider using waxless cross-country skis for the long approach and carrying your backcountry skis and boots in your gear sled.

Enjoy the scenery, strike up conversation, zone out. Use this long approach to put physical and spiritual distance between your everyday world and Katahdin. Be here now.

The ski from Roaring Brook to Chimney Pond is strenuous. The Chimney Pond Trail climbs 1,400 feet in 3.3 miles (by contrast, the approach to Roaring Brook rises only 1,000 feet in 13 miles). Most people carry in food and gear for a week, which increases the grunt factor. The day or two to ski in and the day to ski out explains why winter trips to the park usually require a week (not to mention the drive to and from Millinocket).

The reward for the trip to Chimney Pond is the humbling view of South Basin, a north-facing glacial cirque that wraps like a horseshoe around Chimney Pond. Large snowfields drop from the upper cliffs of the Cathedral Buttress on the west side of the ravine, and on clear days, you can see the summit of Baxter Peak.

Chimney Pond & South Basin

An enjoyable moderate tour from Chimney Pond is to ski the mile-long streambed down to Basin Pond. Follow the Saddle Trail as it cuts east through the campground and you will quickly come upon a 15-foot-wide streambed. Turn right and start skiing. The trail makes a meandering descent toward Basin Pond, picking up speed just before emptying out onto the pond.

For more dramatic scenery, ski south across Chimney Pond and up onto the steep slopes of South Basin. You can ski up to the base of the gullies that ascend Baxter Peak and Pamola, going as high as you feel comfortable then skiing down. One of the better routes ascends the drainage that flows from Chimney Pond toward the base of the Chimney, a prominent gully in the left corner of the ravine. Note that the South Basin slopes are steep and avalanche prone, so you must exercise care in deciding where to travel (see "Avalanches" on page 157).

The **Chimney Couloir** is a true ski-mountaineering descent of the steep gully that separates Pamola (4,904 feet) from Chimney Peak (4,888 feet). "It combines technical mountaineering and skiing for one of the best ski descents in the U.S.," says Andrew Drummond, founder of Ski the Whites and a prolific ski mountaineer. The lower two-thirds of the couloir is typically skiable in good winters; the top is scoured and not skiable. Skiers can traverse over from Chimney Pond and boot up the gully (crampons and avalanche gear required) to an obvious ice bulge at about 4,350 feet. This is a good spot from which to ski. Like the steep descents on Mount Washington, skiing the Chimney requires solid mountaineering and skiing skills and the right conditions. The reward is a classic North American ski-mountaineering descent.

North Basin

Another moderate ski tour from Chimney Pond is the trip over to North Basin. This is a beautiful traverse that links Katahdin's two most dramatic ravines, South and North Basin. North Basin is lightly traveled, especially in winter. It is a wild, remote place, with spectacular walls and gullies that rise 1,500 feet to the summit of Howe Peaks. The northern rock face, known to climbers as Taber Wall, is a massive cliff.

The route into North Basin follows the North Basin Trail. From the Chimney Pond campground, ski down the Chimney Pond Trail toward Basin Pond, and at 0.3 miles, you will see the junction with the North Basin Trail on the left. The trail climbs through a spruce forest and soon rounds the lower buttress of Hamlin Ridge, passing a junction with the Hamlin Ridge Trail. The trail is moderately graded but can be rocky in light snow cover. The trail then contours into North Basin and climbs Blueberry Knoll. This is a spectacular vantage point providing views into both North Basin and South Basin. The North Basin Trail ends here, but you can bushwhack another 0.2 miles to the floor of North Basin, where there are two small ponds. You can ski around the floor of the ravine right up to the cliff wall.

Several prominent gullies tumble down the headwall that forms the western edge of North Basin. **Taber Gully** is the dramatic swath in the center of the horseshoe. It is a classic 1,000-foot couloir, a straight shot from the Tableland to the valley floor. To ski Taber Gully, the best approach is to climb 1.5 miles up the Hamlin Ridge Trail to the summit of Hamlin Peak (4,752 feet). This is a breathtaking hike with expansive views into both North and South Basin. Taber Gully begins steeply, at about 40 degrees, then eases back to a consistent 30- to 35-degree pitch all the way down. The gully is spacious at the top and bottom but narrows to about 15 feet in the center. This is a thrilling descent in a wild landscape.

Great Basin

Some of the best skiing on Katahdin is found in the gullies on the north wall of the Great Basin, the yawning glacial cirque bounded by Hamlin Peak on the north and Pamola on the south; South Basin is located on the southern side of the Great Basin. Between Hamlin Peak and the Saddle Trail, a series of snow gullies stripe the flanks of the Great Basin.

Starting with the **Saddle Trail** (itself a fine ski, and the route taken by Arthur Comey in his 1926 ski descent of Katahdin), there are seven more gullies en route to Hamlin Peak. These Great Basin Gullies all have a similar character: each drops 800 to 1,000 vertical feet and averages about 30 to 35 degrees, steepening to near 40 degrees at the top. The gullies are all 20 to 30 feet wide. They face south and southeast, the perfect exposure for forming corn snow. Standing at the top of the Great Basin Gullies, you peer directly across at the dramatic ice cliffs that pour 2,000 feet down the flanks of Pamola. During the course of the day, observe how the ice changes color as the sun moves. Dropping into the Great Basin, you have the sensation of flying over all of Katahdin.

The easiest access to the Great Basin Gullies is to climb the Hamlin Ridge Trail; the first gully drops down directly from the summit of Hamlin Peak. These gullies are clearly visible from Chimney Pond. All the gullies empty into a prominent streambed on the floor of the basin that you can ski right back to the Chimney Pond campground.

Skiers can also access the Great Basin gullies from the bottom. The lower slopes are at a moderate angle, so skiers can climb and ski based on their comfort level. From the campground, head out either on the Saddle Trail or the streambed and ski up into the Great Basin. Break off to the right (north), ski across the floor of the

Great Basin, and you are at the foot of the gullies. The skiing here is world class, but there are potential dangers, notably avalanches (see "Avalanches," page 157).

Russell Pond

The Russell Pond area is a ski adventure of a different character than the high-alpine skiing on Katahdin. Russell Pond is a peaceful crossroads in a vast, upheaved landscape. The pond lies in a valley pockmarked with numerous lakes, all linked by small brooks. A trip to this area is a worthwhile wilderness ski tour on gentle terrain that brings you deep into the interior of Baxter State Park.

From Roaring Brook Campground, skiers take Russell Pond Trail, which crosses the Wassataquoik Stream and its drainages a number of times in the first 4 miles. Three miles from Roaring Brook, Wassataquoik Stream Trail (listed on some older maps as Tracy Horse Trail) diverges to the right. Skiers can take either trail to reach Russell Pond Campground. Wassataquoik Stream Trail travels over flatter terrain than Russell Pond Trail in this section, following an old tote road and passing two lean-tos 5.4 miles after Roaring Brook. Camping is permitted at the shelters. The trip to the Russell Pond Campground is 6.8 miles via Russell Pond Trail and 7.2 miles via Wassataquoik Stream Trail.

Russell Pond is the gateway to Baxter State Park's northern peaks. From the pond, there are views south to Katahdin and north to Traveler Mountain and Pogy Mountain. It is an exceptionally pretty area. Wildlife is abundant here; sightings of moose, pine marten, and other animals are common. Russell Pond Campground has a bunkhouse and lean-tos. Reservations are required for both. From the Russell Pond area, day trips can be made into the remote Northwest Basin and to the many lakes that lie to the west and east to view the remains of century-old logging activity.

Despite the moderate skiing on a trip to Russell Pond, skiers must still consider a winter ski trip anywhere in the park to be a serious undertaking. Severe weather can set in for days, making travel impossible. Extra food should be brought in anticipation of such unpredictable events.

Baxter Park Traverse

Traversing Baxter State Park is among the grandest and most ambitious backcountry ski expeditions in the East. This trip combines the isolation and rugged beauty of far northern Maine with the jaw-dropping drama of Katahdin. Traversing the park from north to south makes Katahdin the goal of your journey. Allow at least five to six days for the trip. It is possible to stay in bunkhouses (cabins with woodstoves) each night—if you stay on schedule. Anticipate moving slower than expected; when I traversed the park, the northern trails were fiendishly difficult to follow, often appearing and vanishing before our eyes. We planned to stay in the bunkhouses, but we ended up camping in lean-tos when we didn't cover the miles that we expected. Be prepared to camp and travel in severe weather. You should be competent with off-trail navigation because you may spend much of

Dawn patrol: first tracks in the Great Basin Gullies. *Photo by Jamie Walter*

your time bushwhacking until you reach Roaring Brook. The forest here is fairly open, making off-trail travel quite reasonable.

The best time for undertaking this north-south tour is February and March. Rivers will have frozen by then (Wassataquoik Stream is a major crossing), and parts of the trail may even have been recently skied or snowshoed. Start your tour south of Matagamon Gate, due west of Patten, Maine. The perimeter road is plowed to just beyond the Matagamon Wilderness Campground, which is just east of the bridge that crosses the East Branch of the Penobscot River. From there, the route goes 4.1 miles along the unplowed perimeter road to the bunkhouse at Trout Brook Farm. The route then continues 7 miles to the South Branch Pond bunkhouse (5 miles of this is on the snowmobiled perimeter road) and another 9.7 miles to the Russell Pond bunkhouse.

Some of the highlights of this area include the views of the wild and craggy Traveler Mountains. It is 7 miles from Russell Pond to the bunkhouse at Roaring Brook, and a 3.3-mile ski to Chimney Pond. Your final day is a 16.3-mile trip out to the Golden Road and Millinocket.

It is possible to eliminate a first day of skiing on snowmobile trails by arranging a 9-mile snowmobile ride from where you park at the Matagamon Wilderness Campground to Trout Brook Crossing; from there, it is a 2-mile ski to the South Branch Pond bunkhouse. You will need to have your car shuttled to where you will exit the park on the Golden Road. Inquire with Baxter State Park for the names of local people who provide these car and snowmobile shuttle services.

AVALANCHES

The steep ski routes around Chimney Pond and the Great Basin require a high degree of skiing and mountaineering skill. *The slopes and gullies of Katahdin are highly avalanche prone.* I met one climbing party that had just triggered an avalanche on a climbing route on Katahdin, sending the climbers tumbling 300 feet. Snow instability is typically highest just after snow- or rainstorms.

Some rangers at Chimney Pond dig snow pits and offer informal advice about avalanche hazard. But these rangers are not trained avalanche forecasters and are not a reliable source of information about snow stability. At least one member of your party should be experienced in avalanche hazard evaluation, and all skiers planning to venture onto steep terrain should carry avalanche rescue equipment, including shovel, probes, and avalanche transceiver. Choose your routes conservatively, and back off if you are uncertain about the conditions. *Avalanches on Katahdin are common!*

SKIING SAFE

The most important skill for skiing steep terrain is to use your head. Skiing gullies that are icy or have bulletproof hard snow is suicidal. An innocuous slip on a steep, icy gully can result in a terrifying slide-for-life with no chance for self-arrest. With a little sun or soft snow, the same gully can be an enjoyable, forgiving, and reasonably safe descent. Baxter Park is not like a ski area; there is no easy way out if you get injured. Mounting a rescue operation out here requires scores of people, and it takes a very long time.

Use conservative mountaineering judgment. Bring crampons (smaller traction devices like Microspikes are not adequate) and an ice ax if you plan to climb and ski steep terrain above treeline. Assess your skills and the conditions before committing to a route. Even if you back off a coveted descent, you will have countless consolation prizes—incredible views, thrilling hikes, and camaraderie with friends—just for being in this magical place.

3 VERMONT

27 STRATTON POND
This gentle ski tour on the Catamount Trail brings you to the beautiful and tranquil Stratton Pond, located in the Green Mountain National Forest.

Distance: 7.8 miles, Kelley Stand Road to Stratton Pond, round trip
Elevation: *Start/Finish*: 2,218 feet; *Highest point*: 2,743 feet; *Vertical drop*: 525 feet
Maps: *Green Mountain National Forest South* (Trails Illustrated), *Catamount Trail, Section 5* (download map at catamounttrail.org)
Difficulty: Moderate
Gear: Nordic backcountry
Additional Information: Catamount Trail Association, 802-864-5794, catamounttrail.org

HOW TO GET THERE
From West Wardsboro, drive west on Stratton Arlington Road, continuing on Arlington Road to Kelley Stand Road. Pass the Grout Pond parking area and continue straight ahead about 0.75 miles to where the plowing ends. There is a large snowmobile and hiker parking area here (*GPS coordinates*: 43° 03.663′ N, 72° 58.069′ W). To reach the Catamount Trail, continue uphill on the snow-covered road for 0.25 miles, and turn right at a blue plastic Catamount Trail blaze.

HISTORY
Stratton Pond is an unspoiled pocket of wild country at the southern end of the 400,000-acre Green Mountain National Forest. It is the largest body of water along

Previous page: A skier carves a turn below the summit of Mount Mansfield in Vermont.
Photo by Brian Mohr/EmberPhoto

STRATTON POND

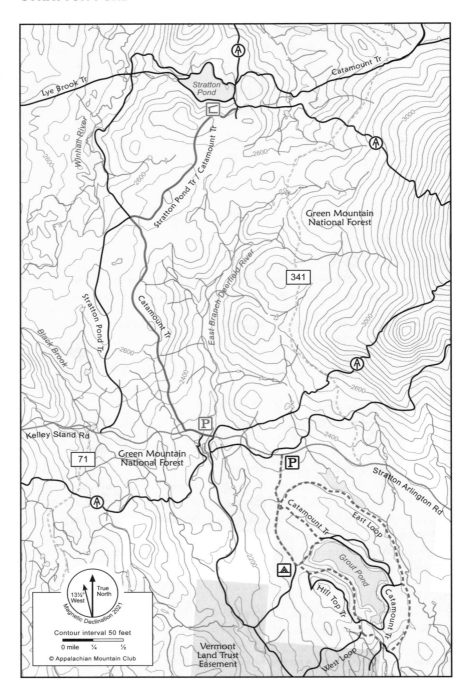

the 270-mile Long Trail (LT). The pond lies on the undeveloped west side of the bustling Stratton Mountain Ski Area. From Stratton Pond, you would never know there was anything besides trees and wildlife inhabiting the long, flat-topped mountain that dominates the skyline.

Stratton Pond receives the most annual overnight use of any place on the LT. To meet the demand, the Green Mountain Club (GMC) built a beautiful two-story post-and-beam shelter in 1999 that sleeps twenty people (this replaced an earlier shelter that was removed in 1997). No fee is charged for staying in the shelter in winter (but wood fires are prohibited), and there are no reservations—it is first come, first served.

Stratton Mountain occupies a special place in the history of the Eastern mountains. In 1909, James P. Taylor, a principal at Vermont Academy in Saxtons River, stood atop Stratton, peered out over the surrounding Vermont forests and mountains, and conceived of a long hiking trail that would run the length of the state. He helped found the Green Mountain Club in 1910, and by 1930, Taylor's dream—and the Long Trail—were a reality. It was also on the summit of Stratton Mountain that Benton MacKaye is said to have conceived of the Appalachian Trail (AT).

Stratton Mountain holds yet another spot in history: in 1840, Senator Daniel Webster of Massachusetts, a renowned orator, addressed 10,000 to 15,000 people on Kelley Stand Road at the foot of the mountain as he campaigned for "Tippecanoe and Tyler Too"—the Whig ticket of William Henry Harrison, who became the ninth U.S. president, and John Tyler, who became the tenth U.S. president when Harrison died of pneumonia after just 32 days in office. There is a roadside historical marker about this event.

THE TOUR

Several routes lead to Stratton Pond from the south. Hikers favor the LT, which coincides with the AT here. This 7-mile-long route to the pond climbs over Stratton Mountain. Hikers can also take a much less strenuous route by heading in on the rolling Stratton Pond Trail, which departs from Kelley Stand Road, 0.75 miles west of the Catamount Trail; it is 4.7 miles from your car to the pond via this route. Skiers take a variation on this route—the Catamount Trail (CT) offers a quiet, scenic glide that is 3.9 miles from the Kelley Stand Road parking area to the pond. To fully enjoy a day tour to the pond, go light—waxable or waxless cross-country skis without metal edges are fine for skiing this moderate terrain.

From Kelley Stand Road (which is also the LT/AT trailhead for Stratton Mountain), head uphill on the unplowed road for 0.25 miles. This is a busy snowmobile trail, so be sure to stay to one side of the road to avoid becoming a hood ornament. Where the road flattens out, the CT departs north (right) onto a logging road. After 0.9 miles, the trail forks: The logging road bears right, and the CT heads to the left. Look for the blue Catamount Trail blazes to guide you here. The trail follows a logging road again, and after another mile, intersects the Stratton Pond Trail, which

Skiers glide across snow-covered Stratton Pond to take in the views and sunshine.

is marked by painted blue blazes but no trail sign. Take a sharp right turn here and head into the woods; the CT follows the Stratton Pond Trail from this junction to Stratton Pond. (Do not continue straight ahead on the logging road; this is a previous CT route, which has since been relocated. The unmaintained old CT vanishes a short distance ahead.)

The combined Stratton Pond/Catamount Trail takes a delightful, serpentine meander through a mixed forest. Birches and spruce line the trail, and you duck and weave through the woods like other forest creatures. In 1.5 miles, you reach a junction of the LT/AT and see a sign pointing uphill to the GMC Stratton Pond shelter. The shore of Stratton Pond lies just 0.1 miles downhill.

Stratton Pond is a stunning white canvas amid a sea of green. Skiing out onto the pond, you can look back at Stratton Mountain, which appears as a long, frosted tabletop rising from the far end of the pond. From your quiet vantage on Stratton Pond, it is hard to imagine that just beyond the top of the mountain lies a bustling city in the woods—the "Upper North Side," as New Yorkers have been known to call it—complete with multilevel parking garages and crowded lift lines. That realization only reinforces the sense that Stratton Pond is a gem in the wilderness. You can ski around on the pond if it is frozen or ski the North Shore Trail, which hugs the north edge of the pond.

Stratton Pond is a showcase for the 300-mile-long Catamount Trail. It is an elegant ski path in the wilderness that serves up a scenic feast.

OTHER OPTIONS

Grout Pond Recreation Area is one of the more popular areas for backcountry skiing in southern Vermont. Located on 1,600 acres of wild land, the area has more than 10 miles of trails that are exclusively for cross-country skiing and snowshoeing. To access the ski trails you will need to ski on a snowmobile trail for about a mile. The ski tour around Grout Pond is about 5 miles long and follows East Trail, and then Pond Trail, which becomes part of the Catamount Trail on the west side of the pond. The terrain is generally flat, and views over the pond are excellent. You can also follow the CT south past Grout Pond to access the beautiful and vast Somerset Reservoir.

28 MOUNT ASCUTNEY

This community-run ski area offers excellent downhill skiing and panoramic views while you earn your turns.

Distance: 2.5 miles, base to ski area summit, round trip
Elevation: *Start*: 800 feet; *Highest point*: 2,200 feet; *Vertical drop*: 1,400 feet
Maps: Available online from Ascutney Outdoors, ascutneyoutdoors.org
Difficulty: More difficult
Gear: AT, telemark, snowboard
Additional information: Ascutney Outdoors, ascutneyoutdoors.org

HOW TO GET THERE

Ascutney Outdoors Center (449 Ski Tow Road, Brownsville, VT 05037) is about 15 minutes from Interstate 91. From the north, take Exit 9 onto VT 5 south through Windsor, then turn right onto VT 44 west to continue into Brownsville. From the south, take Exit 8 to VT 5 north then veer left to Back Mountain Road to Route 44 west into Brownsville (*GPS coordinates*: 43° 27.825′ N, 72° 27.977′ W).

HISTORY

Ascutney is a skiers' mountain that refuses to die. Which is good—Mount Ascutney has great ski terrain. Snow, on the other hand, is fickle here. The mountain, rising up alongside Interstate 91, is a monadnock, a mountain that stands alone. This solitary sentinel beckons skiers heading north from the cities to the mountains.

The first skiers who flocked to Mount Ascutney traveled under their own steam. In 1933, the Civilian Conservation Corps established a camp on the mountain and, among its projects, constructed a ski jump. In 1946, the Mount Ascutney ski area opened. The ski area was bedeviled by years of low snow and chronic mismanagement and went in and out of bankruptcy over the ensuing decades. In 2010, the ski area closed for good and sold off its lifts. That's when the community took over.

In 2015, the town of West Windsor purchased the mountain, and a community nonprofit, Ascutney Outdoors, stepped forward with a new vision for the storied mountain. Skiing would continue, but it would be low tech and low cost. The entire mountain, which is run by volunteers, is now open to skiers and riders who skin up and ski down. In 2018, a simple but elegant base lodge, the Ascutney Outdoors Center, was built for skiers and mountain bikers to gather. In 2020, a T-bar opened on the lower 435 vertical feet, which is groomed and used for races, school groups, and recreational skiing. The upper 1,000 feet of the mountain is ungroomed and reserved for skiers and riders traveling under their own steam.

MOUNT ASCUTNEY

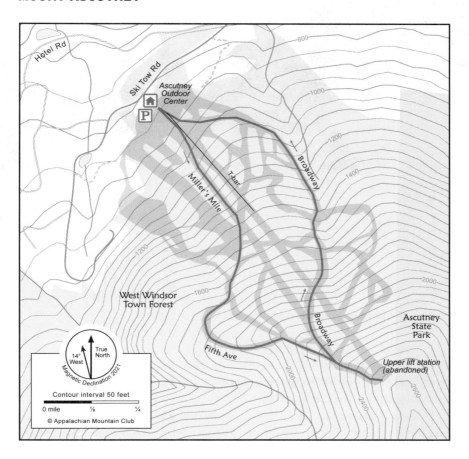

THE TOUR

Ascutney today looks a lot like its earliest days, when skiing was a self-powered and joyful community affair. Many of the former ski area's trails are well maintained and are a pleasure to ski both uphill and downhill. As you skin up Ascutney, you can't help but stop and admire the 100-mile views of southern Vermont and New Hampshire.

At the top of the ski area trails sit the rusting remains of a ski patrol shack and lift station. It has a ghostly, postapocalyptic feel. But your attention is quickly diverted to the 360-degree views. The ski areas of Okemo and Killington are visible off in the distance, and the White Mountains of New Hampshire feel close enough to touch.

Earning your turns on an Ascutney powder day.

Ascutney's maintained ski trails are in fine shape and are skiable even with relatively low snow. Broadway is the main descent route. It is wide enough to share with other skiers yet still get fresh tracks.

As climate change and financial pressures increase on smaller ski areas, the community-powered skiing model being pioneered at Ascutney may well be the solution.

RASTA BACKCOUNTRY ZONES

The Rochester/Randolph Area Sports Trails Alliance (RASTA) formed in 2013 when a group of residents around Rochester, Vermont, came together to share ideas about how they could promote backcountry recreation in their rural community, which lies adjacent to the 400,000-acre Green Mountain National Forest (GMNF). Angus McCusker, RASTA's executive director, says the early discussions focused on addressing a simple question: "What can we do to invite others to come and recreate that would also help the town economically?"

In 2014, RASTA sponsored a backcountry forum to open the conversation, and hundreds of people attended from around the state. It was clear that they had tapped into a strong desire to create backcountry recreational opportunities in areas where none existed. RASTA volunteers cut the first glade zones in nearby Braintree Mountain Forest in fall 2014 (see tour 29, Braintree Mountain Forest, page 169). That partnership between RASTA, private landowners Paul Kendall and Sharon Rives, and the New England Forestry Foundation became the model for RASTA's future projects.

Fruits of their labors: skiing the RASTA glade zones of Brandon Gap. *Photo by Brian Mohr/ EmberPhoto*

RASTA found receptive partners in the U.S. Forest Service (USFS) staff at the GMNF, led by Holly Knox, now a recreation program manager with the Green Mountain and Finger Lakes National Forests. One incentive for collaboration was to rein in illegal glade cutting, a New England tradition that forest officials frowned upon.

RASTA's partnership with the USFS was a first: never before had backcountry skiers banded together to work with public land managers anywhere in the country. Hikers and mountain bikers had worked collaboratively with the USFS and others, but skiers have long had a culture of secrecy and independence that kept them from partnering and sharing their stashes. RASTA's partnership with the USFS was hailed and emulated. "That was a breakthrough," says Tyler Ray, who was inspired by RASTA to found Granite Backcountry Alliance in New Hampshire and Maine.

"I'm proud of the collaborative effort that made this a success," says Knox of the GMNF partnership.

RASTA continues to inspire other groups of backcountry skiers to come together and create public glade zones. RASTA is a chapter of the Vermont Mountain Bike Association (vmba.org) and the Catamount Trail Association (catamounttrail.org), which continues to add new chapters of RASTA-inspired community skiing groups around Vermont. RASTA has created first-rate backcountry skiing zones. But it has created something much bigger, something that endures long past the last snowstorm.

When I ask Angus McCusker what he is proudest of about RASTA, he replies simply, "Friendships. Community."

RASTA's backcountry ski zones are works in progress. The descriptions in this book highlight some of the skiing in each zone as of this writing. For the latest information and maps of RASTA's backcountry zones, consult rastavt.org.

29 BRAINTREE MOUNTAIN FOREST

Braintree Mountain Forest is an excellent Vermont glade zone created by volunteers of the Rochester/Randolph Area Sports Trails Alliance (RASTA) in partnership with the New England Forestry Foundation (NEFF). Skidoo Mountain offers lower-angle skiing with nice views of Braintree Mountain and features a warming hut open to skiers. Twin Peaks offers steeper trail skiing.

Distance: 2.1 miles, parking lot to Skidoo summit, one way; 2.3 miles, parking lot to Twin Peaks, one way
Elevation: *Start/Finish*: 1,250 feet, parking lot; *Highest point*: 2,873 feet (Twin Peaks), 2,880 feet (Skidoo Mountain); *Vertical drop*: 1,650 feet
Map: Download trail map from RASTA (rastavt.org)
Difficulty: More difficult, Skidoo Mountain; Most difficult, Twin Peaks
Gear: AT, telemark, snowboard
Additional Information: Rochester/Randolph Area Sports Trails Alliance, rastavt.org

HOW TO GET THERE

Braintree Mountain Forest is located off Exit 4 on I-89. Drive 2.5 miles on VT 66 and continue straight on VT 12A at the intersection. Drive another 2.5 miles then bear left onto Riford Brook Road and continue 2.6 miles. Trailhead parking can be found at 2576 Riford Brook Road, Braintree, VT 05060 (*GPS coordinates*: 43° 56.628′ N, 72° 45.022′ W).

HISTORY

The roots of the modern backcountry skiing revolution in New England started in a humble farmhouse at the foot of Braintree Mountain in Vermont. That is the home of Paul Kendall and Sharon Rives, whose family has owned land there since 1951. In 2013, the couple donated 1,547 acres of the Braintree Range to the New England Forestry Foundation (NEFF), a conservation organization. The land includes four peaks that each reach about 3,000 feet in elevation. Kendall—who has twice skied the 300-mile Catamount Trail and, together with his wife, built 15 miles of trails on their land—had a vision of conserving the land and turning it into a community resource. He explains, "Our strategy had been, 'Build it and they will come.' We knew that if we created the resource, not only the land but the trail system, that it would be an inviting attraction to people."

Enter Zac Freeman, who made Kendall's vision a reality. Freeman grew up in Braintree and had been exploring Braintree Mountain (3,026 feet) on skis since he was young. When he asked Kendall if he could create some glades to ski on their land, Kendall was all for it. This was exactly the kind of use that he hoped to support.

BRAINTREE MOUNTAIN FOREST

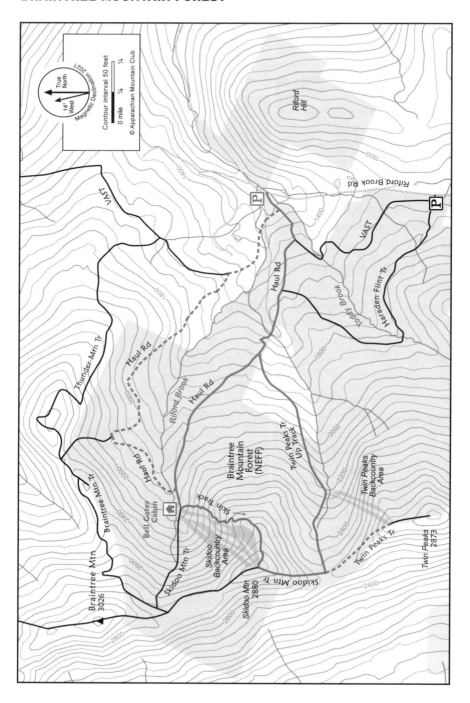

Freeman says of the collaboration that led to opening Braintree Mountain Forest to skiing: "It's a really unique opportunity for a rural working-class town without tourism around it to offer something that would otherwise not be available."

Freeman was a moving force in the Rochester/Randolph Area Sports Trails Alliance (RASTA), which formed in 2013 and made glading Braintree Mountain Forest (BMF) its first project. The BMF glade zone was cut by RASTA volunteers in fall 2014 and spring 2015 under the supervision of foresters from NEFF, who viewed glading as good forest management. BMF quickly became the model for community skiing ventures throughout the Northeast.

Frank Lowenstein, chief conservation officer for NEFF, says that community skiing fits the larger environmental mission of NEFF. "In the long term, we need to find ways to recreate that are not carbon intensive and that don't require lots of mechanized equipment. Backcountry skiing is a wonderful example of this. We can enjoy the forest and mountains without anything except what is strapped to our feet."

The result of this innovative community partnership is the beautiful glades on Skidoo Mountain (2,880 feet) and Twin Peaks (2,873 feet) in Braintree Mountain Forest.

THE TOUR

From the Riford Brook Road parking lot, bear left onto Haul Road for 1.6 miles until you reach Bell Gates cabin. This simple cabin was originally a camp owned by the Bell Gates Lumber Company of Jeffersonville, Vermont, which logged in the area before going out of business about two decades ago. RASTA volunteers renovated the unheated cabin to use as a shelter for skiers. The skin track to the Skidoo summit departs directly from the Bell Gates cabin.

The skin track climbs at a comfortable grade, ascending through softwoods and emerging into a beautiful birch glade on the summit of **Skidoo Mountain**. From the summit, the soft contours of the Braintree Range unfold below and around you. As you head downhill, the slope starts gradually, enabling you to get into a leisurely rhythm as you weave through the well-spaced trees. The pace quickens as the slope steepens, but the pitch never gets too pushy, making the skiing accessible to a variety of skill levels. The forest is spacious enough that you can charge down a fast fall line or swing leisurely turns. A 700-vertical-foot descent delivers you back to the Bell Gates cabin.

Another glade zone descends from just below the summit of **Twin Peaks**. The skin track departs from Haul Road about halfway between the parking lot and the Bell Gates cabin. The descent from Twin Peaks stays in the fall line and is a bit steeper and shorter. It is more of a trail than an open glade, with several nice north-facing lines.

Braintree Mountain Forest showcases the best of community-supported skiing. The success of the glading effort became the model for RASTA's subsequent partnership with the Green Mountain National Forest to create the wildly popular glade zones in Brandon Gap. And that, in turn, inspired New Hampshire skiers to form

Carving powder in Braintree Mountain Forest. *Photo by Kyle Crichton*

Granite Backcountry Alliance, which has pioneered community-supported skiing in New Hampshire and Maine.

Paul Kendall quotes St. Francis of Assisi as his inspiration: "Start by doing what is necessary, then do what is possible, and suddenly you are doing the impossible."

"That summarizes it. We started with the necessity to protect our own self-interest, the land around us. Then we went to what was possible, acquiring other land and opening it up to recreation for everybody. Then RASTA came around the corner. No one ever dreamed of that."

Kendall marvels at the synergy of people and place that has launched a conservation and recreation movement. "These were impossible dreams. You just do what you can do, do what's possible, and all of sudden, stuff you never thought you could do, you've done."

30 BRANDON GAP

Brandon Gap consists of four glade zones at two trailheads spread out over three miles of the Long Trail. This popular area is one of the best examples of community-supported skiing in the Northeast.

Distance: 1.6 miles, Bear Brook Bowl (BBB) parking area to BBB Ridge summit, one way; 1.1 miles, BBB parking to No Name summit, one way; 1.6 miles, Long Trail (LT) parking area to Goshen Mountain summit, one way
Elevation: *Start/Finish*: 1,800 feet (BBB parking), 2,200 feet (LT parking/Goshen Mountain); *Highest point*: 3,125 feet (Bear Brook Ridge), 3,290 feet (Goshen Mountain); *Vertical drop*: 500–1,300 feet, depending on zone
Map: Download trail map from RASTA (rastavt.org)
Difficulty: More difficult, Sunrise Bowl; Most difficult, other terrain
Gear: AT, telemark, snowboard
Additional Information: Rochester/Randolph Area Sports Trails Alliance, rastavt.org. For information about staying at the nearby Chittenden Brook Hut, contact Vermont Huts Association, vermonthuts.org

HOW TO GET THERE

The Brandon Gap backcountry ski zones originate from two parking areas. On VT 100, drive 1 mile south of Rochester, Vermont, and turn onto VT 73 west, Brandon Mountain Road. Drive 8 miles and see a parking area on the south side of VT 73 with a sign for Brandon Gap/Bear Brook. The Bear Brook Bowl and No Name Backcountry Area start here, 8107 Brandon Mountain Road, Rochester, VT 05767 (*GPS coordinates*: 43° 50.451′ N, 72° 56.770′ W). Goshen Mountain and Sunrise Bowl start 1 mile west on VT 73 at a parking lot on the south side of the road for the Long Trail, 3255 Gap Road, Goshen, VT 05733 (*GPS coordinates*: 43° 50.365′ N, 72° 58.103′ W).

THE TOURS

Brandon Gap has become one of Vermont's most popular backcountry ski destinations, which is remarkable when you consider what and where it is. The soft rounded mountains that bound VT 73 in the middle of the Green Mountain National Forest are devoid of iconic summits such as Mount Mansfield or Camel's Hump, and this area is not close to any major tourist destinations. This is a story of "if you build it, they will come."

In 2016, hundreds of volunteers flocked to Vermont from around the Northeast to create the backcountry ski glades of Brandon Gap, investing 1,700 hours of volunteer labor into the effort. After waiting out a snowless first winter, skiing at Brandon Gap took off in winter 2017–2018.

BRANDON GAP

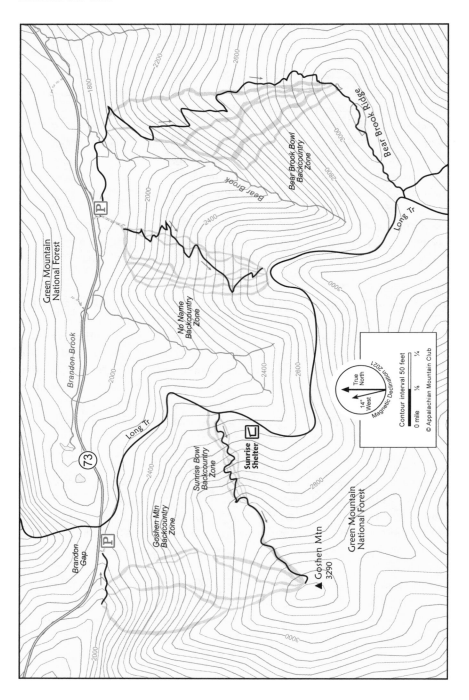

Reap what you sow: A powder day in RASTA's Brandon Gap backcountry zones. *Photo by Brian Mohr/EmberPhoto*

Skiers can choose among four different glade zones in Brandon Gap:

No Name Backcountry Zone (Vertical drop: 1,100 feet): This is a set of braided glade lines that depart from the Brandon Gap/Bear Brook trailhead. Climb on a dedicated uphill trail with yellow plastic RASTA blazes. The trail switchbacks as it steepens and crosses a number of the ski lines near the top. The uphill track ends at a kiosk near the Long Trail at about 2,800 feet.

The descent starts gradually, then steepens over a series of short drops. These are excellent steep fall-line runs with interesting rolls that pack lots of turns. The glade lines all lead back to the skin track at the bottom. Just above the parking lot, you can turn right and traverse alongside VT 73 to make your way to Bear Brook Bowl. You may need to remove skis to cross a broad stream at the bottom of the BBB skin track.

Bear Brook Bowl (Vertical drop: 1,300 feet): Bear Brook Bowl is a longer and larger backcountry area located in a north-facing bowl. The skin track has an intimate feel as it winds through old-growth birch glades. Look for signs of wildlife such as moose and deer scat. At the top, there is enough room and terrain for many skiers to find fresh lines. This is steeper, expert terrain with lots of interesting features, from rollovers to boulders.

Sunrise Bowl (Vertical drop: 500 feet): Sunrise Bowl and Goshen Mountain start at the Long Trail parking lot, a mile west of Bear Brook Bowl on VT 73. Skin up the LT, turning right after 0.75 miles and following a skin track up through Sunrise Bowl. Fifty yards in from the LT, there is a kiosk with maps and yellow RASTA trail blazes mark the way. Sunrise Bowl features several braided glade lines. This is the most moderate ski terrain in Brandon Gap.

Goshen Mountain (Vertical drop: 1,300 feet): Continue climbing above Sunrise Bowl to reach the top of Goshen Mountain (3,290 feet), from where you can see the back of Braintree Mountain Forest, a distant RASTA glade zone. Breadloaf Wilderness and the spine of the Green Mountains extend to the north. Goshen Mountain is naturally open. You choose your own line through a spacious hardwood forest. The trail rolls downward and steepens toward the bottom.

OTHER OPTIONS

Skiers at Brandon Gap can stay at the Chittenden Brook Hut, which is a 2-mile ski from the glade zones. The hut is operated by Vermont Huts Association (vermonthuts.org), and reservations fill early in winter. As of this writing, RASTA plans to create an extensive glade zone above the hut.

CAMEL'S HUMP

Camel's Hump (sometimes spelled Camels Hump) is the most iconic and beloved mountain in Vermont. The distinctive profile of this peak—depicted on the Vermont state quarter, among other places—has come to symbolize the unique character of the state. It is the only undeveloped 4,000-foot peak in Vermont—which means it is the only big mountain that you can ski all the way around without running into a chairlift.

Throughout history, many an entrepreneur has fantasized about the commercial prospects for Camel's Hump. There was a proposal in the 1930s to build a highway over the summit. There have been other proposals to build ski resorts and communications towers on the mountain. But the state of Vermont, determined to avoid creating another alpine Disneyland on one of its highest peaks, declared the summit a State Natural Area in 1965 and extended protection to the rest of the mountain in 1969 by making it part of Camel's Hump Forest Reserve. The summit was designated a National Natural Landmark in 1968.

The effort to preserve Camel's Hump began in 1911, when Colonel Joseph Battell of Middlebury, Vermont, made a gift of 1,000 acres, including the summit, to the state in an effort to protect the undeveloped view from his home. Camel's Hump State Park currently covers about 21,000 acres and is the largest state park in Vermont.

Camel's Hump is visible from downtown Burlington and from many miles farther away, from highways to mountaintops. A debate has raged for years about what the summit most closely resembles. The Green Mountain Club *Long Trail Guide* recounts the story:

> The Waubanaukee Indians called Camel's Hump "the saddle mountain," and Samuel de Champlain's explorers named it *le lion couchant*, translated "the couching [not crouching] lion" or, in more contemporary language, "the sleeping lion." Either name is more descriptive of the mountain's profile seen from the east or west than is Camel's Hump, a name amended by Zadock Thompson in 1830 from the less genteel "Camel's Rump" listed on Ira Allen's 1798 map.

The first recorded ski on Camel's Hump was in February 1912, when J. R. Norton and a friend named Aldrich skied to within 100 feet of the summit. Camel's Hump has enjoyed a loyal following among local skiers ever since. One reason will be obvious to any visitor: the mountain is blessed with an abundance of snow (an average of about 18 feet of snow falls here annually). The mountain is also fortunate to have relatively open forests, making it possible to weave off the trails and through the glades. Finally, Camel's Hump is simply a strikingly beautiful landscape. Peering out from its rocky summit on a crisp winter day is an experience that remains with you.

Following are three tours that capture distinctly different personalities of this mountain.

31 MONROE TRAIL

The Monroe Trail is a popular hiking route up Camel's Hump, which has one of the most spectacular summits in Vermont. There is good skiing both on the trail and in the glades that flank it.

Distance: 7.4 miles, round trip
Elevation: *Start/Finish*: 1,300 feet; *Highest point*: 4,078 feet; *Vertical drop*: 2,778 feet
Maps: *Camel's Hump* (Green Mountain Club), *Northern Vermont Hiking & Biking Trails* (Map Adventures), *Mount Mansfield/Stowe* (Trails Illustrated)
Difficulty: Most difficult
Gear: AT, telemark, snowboard

HOW TO GET THERE

From Exit 10 on I-89, drive into Waterbury and turn right on Winooski Street. Cross the bridge over the Winooski River, and turn right on River Road. Drive 4 miles, turn left on Camel's Hump Road, and drive 3 miles to the end (avoid turning onto one of the many side roads). Where the plowing ends at the last house, see signs pointing left to the Camel's Hump winter parking lot (*GPS coordinates*: 44° 18.943′ N, 72° 50.470′ W).

THE TOUR

An ascent of Camel's Hump in winter is one of Vermont's most exhilarating mountaineering adventures. Whether you are traveling on skis, snowshoes, or a snowboard, the thrill lies in being able to experience this remarkable landscape. The climax of this tour is standing atop the wild, windswept, icy summit of Vermont's third-highest peak.

The Monroe Trail begins at the site of the old Couching Lion Farm. Professor Will S. Monroe, a botanist who planted a variety of trees on the mountain, left this farm to the state of Vermont. Among the trees that he introduced here were white spruce, red and Scotch pine, Douglas fir, and Norway spruce, which were the source of the wood for the caretaker cabin that was built in 1973. Professor Monroe, his sister Katherine, and his dogs are buried in a small cemetery just north of the unplowed summer parking lot.

From the winter parking lot, walk back down to the road, turn left, and ski 0.3 miles on the gated unplowed road that leads to the summer parking lot. The Monroe Trail starts at a trail register and enters the woods on fairly flat terrain, which steepens moderately and maintains an even grade as it heads southwest alongside a brook. After 1.3 miles, you come to a junction with the Dean Trail, which departs to the left for Wind Gap and the Green Mountain Club (GMC) Montclair Glen Lodge. Stay right on the Monroe Trail, which continues uphill until it reaches the base of a cliff band, then traverses left, finally crossing the Alpine Trail at 2.5 miles.

MONROE TRAIL

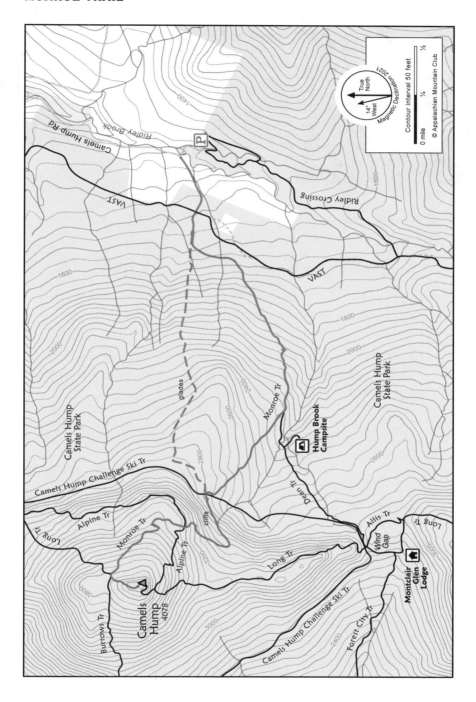

Skiing Camel's Hump powder. *Photo by Kyle Crichton*

The Monroe Trail narrows and continues straight ahead, reaching the Long Trail (LT) at the former Camel's Hump hut clearing in 3.1 miles. This was the site of a hotel that went broke and then burned down in 1875.

Remove your skis at this clearing and leave them behind before you turn left onto the LT. The final 0.3 miles up the LT to the summit is narrow, windy, and steep, and the summit cone of Camel's Hump is too icy and rocky to ski. When you approach treeline, it is time to don storm gear.

The views from the top of Camel's Hump are breathtaking. On a clear day, you can see nearly all of Lake Champlain, Mount Washington in New Hampshire, and Giant Mountain in the Adirondacks. Mount Mansfield and the Worcester Mountains beckon to the north, and Killington Peak lies to the south. Most impressive is the vast sweep of wild land that surrounds Camel's Hump itself. The south end of the summit cone ends in a huge cliff. The summit is one of three peaks in the Green Mountains that are home to arctic alpine vegetation, which is typically found only near the Arctic Circle. When walking around the summit, take care to step only on rocks and not on fragile vegetation.

After hiking back down to the clearing, put on your skis and get ready to descend. The initial pitch back to the Alpine Trail junction is narrow and hectic. The trail opens up slowly below this point, but it is typically packed out by snowshoers. Hang on.

The best skiing on Camel's Hump is found by simply skiing the open woods that line the trail. Some of the best glades are found at the end of the cliff band. At 2,800 feet, where the Monroe Trail takes a sharp right and heads downhill, continue straight ahead for several hundred yards until the forest opens, then bear right (east) and choose your own line down through the glades. Enjoy a 1,500-vertical-foot, 1.5-mile-long glade run that delivers you back to the Monroe trailhead (*GPS coordinates*: 44° 18.982′ N, 72° 50.972′ W).

The quest for the perfect glade run will keep you coming back to Camel's Hump time and again.

32 HONEY HOLLOW TRAIL

The Honey Hollow Trail, part of the Catamount Trail, mixes fun backcountry downhill sections with skiing on gentle logging roads. It is a good introduction to Camel's Hump skiing.

Distance: 6.6 miles, Camel's Hump Nordic Center to Duxbury Road
Elevation: *Start*: 1,400 feet; *Highest point*: 1,900 feet; *Finish*: 360 feet; *Vertical drop*: 1,540 feet
Maps: The Catamount Trail Association map shows the entire Honey Hollow Trail (Section 20 of the Catamount Trail) but not the trails of Camel's Hump Nordic (CHN). The CHN trail map, available at the CHN parking lot or at camelshumpskiers.org, is essential for navigating through the groomed trail network to reach the start of the Honey Hollow Trail. Also, *Mount Mansfield/ Stowe* (Trails Illustrated).
Difficulty: More difficult
Gear: Nordic backcountry/telemark
Fee: Skiers must buy a trail pass from the CHN to gain access to the Honey Hollow Trail via the CHN network. Trail fees are paid on the honor system at the parking lot.
Additional Information: Camel's Hump Nordic, camelshumpskiers.org; Catamount Trail Association, 802-864-5794, catamounttrail.org

HOW TO GET THERE

This tour requires a car drop at the finish. The trail starts at Camel's Hump Nordic (CHN), located at 1125 Bert White Road, Huntington, VT 05462. From Exit 11 on I-89, drive into Richmond, turn south on Huntington Road, and continue for 8 miles. Once in Huntington, turn left onto East Street, bear right at all forks, and continue uphill as East Street becomes Bert White Road. The large CHN parking lot is on the left, 2.7 miles from Huntington (*GPS coordinates*: 44° 22.305′ N, 72° 54.025′ W).

To drop off a car at the finish: From Richmond, drive east on US 2 to Jonesville, turn right onto Cochran Road, drive across the bridge, and turn immediately left onto Duxbury Road (a.k.a. River Road). A plowed parking area for the Honey Hollow Trail is 2.2 miles ahead on the right, just past (east of) Honey Hollow Road (*GPS coordinates*: 44° 22.300′ N, 72° 54.023′ W). Don't forget to carry the keys to this car with you on the trail (unlike my ski partners, who have left their keys in the car at the CHN parking lot—twice)!

THE TOUR

The Honey Hollow Trail is a great sampler of the ski adventures that Camel's Hump has to offer. This tour is part of the 300-mile Catamount Trail that runs the length of Vermont. Originally cut in 1980 by former Camel's Hump Nordic Ski Center owner

HONEY HOLLOW TRAIL

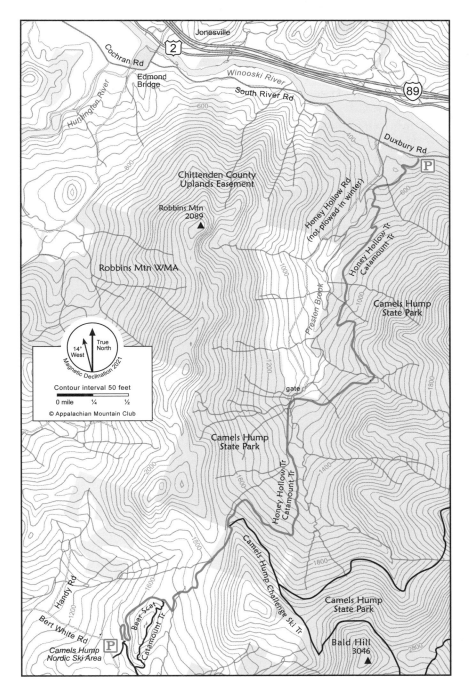

Dave Brautigam and state forest rangers, the Honey Hollow Trail drops a thrilling 1,500 feet from the flanks of Camel's Hump to the Winooski River. This tour has three distinct sections: a gentle ski through the trails of Camel's Hump Nordic, a fast descent through the backcountry, and a rolling ski tour on logging roads and woods trails. Due to the rolling nature of the trail and frequent transitions, this tour is best skied on telemark equipment.

The fierce loyalty of Camel's Hump skiers is conveyed by the history of the Camel's Hump Skiers' Association. The association came into existence in 1996 when the Camel's Hump Nordic Ski Center closed. Local skiers were determined to preserve the cross-country ski trails that weave through the lower forests of Camel's Hump, so they decided to maintain and operate the ski trail system themselves. After obtaining permission from 22 local landowners to keep the trails open, the nonprofit skiers' cooperative opened for business in winter 1996–1997. Volunteers continue to maintain more than 35 miles of trails on 1,500 acres. CHN pays for its equipment through yearly memberships and trail fees, which you pay on the honor system in the parking lot. This cooperative has been a unique Vermont solution that has maintained access to a cherished mountain.

From the CHN parking lot, buy a trail pass at the hut and pick up a trail map. The CHN maps are essential for navigating the ever-changing labyrinth of trails that lead to the start of the Honey Hollow Trail (and since you've already bought a trail pass, you may want to take extra time to enjoy skiing around the groomed trails). From the parking lot, head out on Bear Scat Draw. At a trail junction, see the blue Catamount Trail blazes with the trademark cat's paw that indicates Catamount Trail (CT) North. Turn sharply left, following signs to Big Baldy. Follow these blue blazes as they climb gently uphill, before the Catamount Trail finally turns left off the groomed Big Baldy trails to enter the ungroomed backcountry part of the trail. Continue climbing past a cabin (skins are not essential—waxless or waxable skis should be adequate) until you reach a sign marking the town forest boundary. Continue straight ahead, following the CT blazes.

The Honey Hollow Trail begins with some long, straight downhill drops punctuated by hairpin turns. Stay on your toes and look for warning signs posted on the trees that alert you to sudden direction changes. The trail has a nice drop-and-roll rhythm, where downhills alternate with flat stretches. You are making your way down into the Preston Brook drainage (a.k.a. Honey Hollow), which flows from the summit of Camel's Hump.

After about a mile and many turns, the Honey Hollow Trail emerges onto an unplowed road, where you turn left and follow it downhill. At the bottom of a long, fast schuss, pass through a gate, then immediately turn right and pass through another gate. You then begin climbing a wide, well-graded logging road for 0.6 miles. The trail is well marked with blue CT blazes.

Skiing beneath Camel's Hump on the Honey Hollow Trail.

From here to the end of the tour, the trail likely will be well packed, as this is a popular area for snowshoers, dog walkers, and cross-country skiers. At the top of the hill, the road ends and the Honey Hollow Trail continues into the woods to the left. Follow the trail as it twists downhill through the forest until it emerges onto another logging road, where you turn right. This wide road heads downhill and gets steadily faster until finishing at the Honey Hollow parking area. It is a wind-in-your-hair finale to a great mountain tour.

33 BALD HILL

Bald Hill offers easily accessible and excellent glade skiing on Vermont's iconic peak.

Distance: 2.6 miles, Burrows Trail trailhead to Bald Hill summit, round trip
Elevation: *Start*: 1,800 feet, Burrows Trail trailhead; *Highest point*: 3,000 feet, Bald Hill Ridge; *Vertical drop*: 1,200 feet
Maps: *Northern Vermont Hiking & Biking Trails* (Map Adventures), *Camel's Hump* (Green Mountain Club), *Mount Mansfield/Stowe* (Trails Illustrated)
Difficulty: Most difficult
Gear: AT, snowboard, telemark

HOW TO GET THERE

From Huntington Center: Turn east on Camel's Hump Road and travel 3.5 miles to where the road dead ends in the Burrows trailhead parking lot (*GPS coordinates*: 44° 18.298′ N, 72° 54.458′ W).

THE TOUR

Bald Hill is a prominent peak on a ridge extending due west from the summit of Camel's Hump. It has long been a favorite powder preserve of this mountain's loyal band of skiers. It offers the best of Camel's Hump: expansive views of Vermont's iconic peak, easy access, and first-rate glade skiing.

The Camel's Hump faithful have a long history of unofficial glading on Bald Hill. Rather than crack down on the tree trimming, the state of Vermont has officially recognized the creation of backcountry ski glades on Bald Hill in its management plan for Camel's Hump State Park. This rising popularity means that on powder days and weekends, the Burrows Trail parking lot fills early.

The easiest access to Bald Hill is via the Burrows Trail, a popular hiking route up Camel's Hump. Ski up the blue-blazed Burrows Trail for 1 mile, and where the trail turns sharply right and crosses a drainage, bear left onto an obvious but unmarked herd path. It likely will have snowshoe and ski tracks. Look up and you can see the ridgeline of Bald Hill. Ascend this trail for 0.6 miles until attaining the ridge. This ridgeline is dotted by three distinct peaks. The actual summit of Bald Hill (3,046 feet) is to the right (north), but to reach the most popular skiing, turn left (south) on the ridge. Detour left around the second peak to a spectacular viewpoint over Wind Gap and the Camel's Hump summit. This vista alone makes the trip worthwhile.

The prime skiing on Bald Hill is located just beyond the third peak (about 2,900 feet). Bear right (northwest) around the peak and the forest opens below you. Descend here and enter the area known as the Ballroom. Drop in where you please and leave your signature between the large spacious trees. The open glades extend down to 2,200 feet. There are numerous descent lines here to lap. The skiing is fun and fast.

BALD HILL

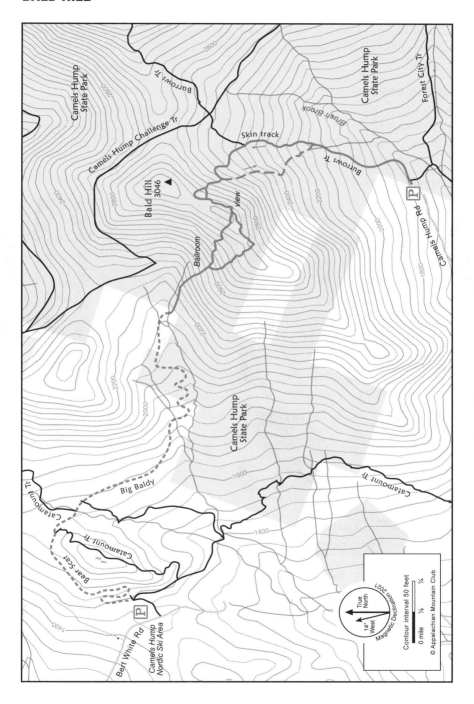

When returning to the Burrows trailhead, stay high in the forest to maximize glade skiing and minimize skiing the busy Burrows Trail.

Bald Hill and its glades are a community treasure. This is some of the best downhill skiing on Camel's Hump, offering a rollicking ride through a wild and beautiful landscape.

OTHER OPTIONS

It is also possible to reach Bald Hill on groomed trails through the trail network of the Camel's Hump Nordic Center in Huntington (camelshumpskiers.org). This approach is about 2 miles and delivers you to the base of the Ballroom glades.

Ballroom dancing on Bald Hill, Camel's Hump.

BOLTON BACKCOUNTRY

Bolton Valley sits high atop the Green Mountains, reaping some of Vermont's deepest and most reliable snow. Skiers first began coming to Bolton Valley in the 1920s, when a forester and conservationist from Boston named Edward Bryant started purchasing land around Bolton Mountain (3,670 feet) and cutting ski trails. He built cabins—one of them, Bryant Camp, still stands—and skiers began making the pilgrimage to his backcountry paradise. When the Deslauriers family opened the Bolton Valley ski resort in 1966, Bryant Camp became the hub of a thriving backcountry ski network. Soon the Catamount Trail passed by, and the Long Trail is not far away.

BOLTON BACKCOUNTRY

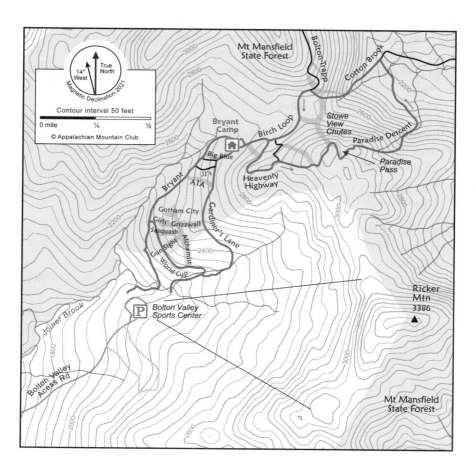

The Bolton Backcountry has continued to grow, and it is now protected. In 2011, when much of the prized Bolton Backcountry was on the verge of being sold to a private buyer, skiers and land conservationists swung into action and formed Friends of Bolton Valley Nordic and Backcountry. They worked with the Vermont Land Trust to raise $1.8 million to purchase the land and transfer it to the state of Vermont in 2013. This beloved powder trove is now part of the Mount Mansfield State Forest.

Today, the Bolton Backcountry is a bustling center of activity. Skiers come in search of powder, glades, and community.

Skiers looking for full-day adventures head out on the Woodward Mountain Trail or the Bolton–Trapp Trail, detailed in the following sections. Others come to ski Bolton's legendary glades. Bolton reveals more of itself with each return trip.

Below are a few of the classic shorter tours in the Bolton Backcountry. All of these tours begin at the Bolton Valley Sports Center, where trail passes and maps can be purchased.

Paradise Pass

Ski past Bryant Camp to Paradise Pass. From here, ski straight ahead past the Paradise Pass trail sign into the north-facing Cotton Brook Basin. There are numerous open lines through widely spaced hardwoods, with runs of 800 vertical feet. At the bottom of the runs, see the red-blazed Cotton Brook Trail. Skin up and climb out Cotton Brook Basin to the Bolton–Trapp Trail to return to Bolton Valley.

Stowe View Chutes

Ski past Bryant Camp to a height-of-land known as Stowe View (3,000 feet). The actual viewpoint is a cliff; backtrack on the trail 100 feet and enter skier's left of the viewpoint into an open forest and several long powdery chutes. Enjoy the north-facing powder, then skin up on Cotton Brook Trail to return to Bolton Valley.

Gardiner's Lane

This is a forest thruway that links a series of low-angle glades, including JJs, A1A, and Gotham City (named for Ann Gotham, leader of the Friends of Bolton Valley Nordic and Backcountry). This trail is named for Gardiner Lane, the longtime director of the Bolton Nordic center who cut many of the trails.

Following page: Diving into the Bolton Backcountry.

34 WOODWARD MOUNTAIN TRAIL

This is a high-elevation ski tour from the top of the Bolton Valley Ski Area down to Little River State Park in Waterbury. Skiers can also ski partway out the trail to access excellent glades, then backtrack to Bolton Valley. The trail features prime glade skiing and spectacular mountain views.

Distance: 5.6 miles, top of Bolton Valley Ski Area to Little River Road parking area, one way

Elevation: *Start/Highest point*: 3,099 feet; *Finish*: 450 feet; *Vertical drop*: 2,650 feet

Maps: *Mansfield Region Backcountry Trail Map* (MapleRidge Solutions), *Northern Vermont Hiking & Biking Trails* (Map Adventures). Maps are for sale at the Bolton Valley Nordic Center.

Difficulty: More difficult+

Gear: AT, telemark, snowboard

Fee: This trail begins at the top of the Bolton Valley Ski Area. A single-ride lift ticket is available at ticket windows and at the Bolton Valley Sports Center, located in the Sports Center building, for those who intend to ski only the Woodward Mountain Trail. Check the Bolton Valley website for its uphill skiing routes.

Additional Information: Bolton Valley Sports Center, 802-434-6876, boltonvalley.com

HOW TO GET THERE

If you are skiing to Little River State Park, you will need to leave a car at the end. Take Exit 10 on I-89, turn briefly onto VT 100 south, then right onto US 2 west. In 1.3 miles, watch for a sign for Little River State Park and turn right onto Little River Road. In 0.9 miles, just after another sign for Little River State Park, see a snowmobile trail and parking area on the left (*GPS coordinates*: 44° 21.919′ N, 72° 46.670′ W). Leave one car here, taking care to avoid blocking the trail. If there is no room to park here, continue another 0.7 miles on Little River Road to a major snowmobile parking area on the left and leave a car here instead (*GPS coordinates*: 44° 22.107′ N, 72° 46.173′ W).

To reach Bolton Valley Ski Area, backtrack to US 2, turn right (west), drive 6.6 miles, see a sign for the Bolton Valley Ski Area, and turn onto the Bolton Valley Access Road. Drive 4.2 miles, passing the Timberline base area, and park at the main ski resort (*GPS coordinates*: 44° 25.218′ N, 72° 51.097′ W). Purchase a single-ride lift ticket to ski the Woodward Mountain Trail at a ticket window or at the Sports Center.

HISTORY

The Woodward Mountain Trail is one of the finest high-elevation backcountry ski tours in Vermont. It descends nearly 3,000 vertical feet in 6 miles. This tour has it all: great views, powder bowls, fun skiing, glades, and long downhill cruising.

WOODWARD MOUNTAIN TRAIL

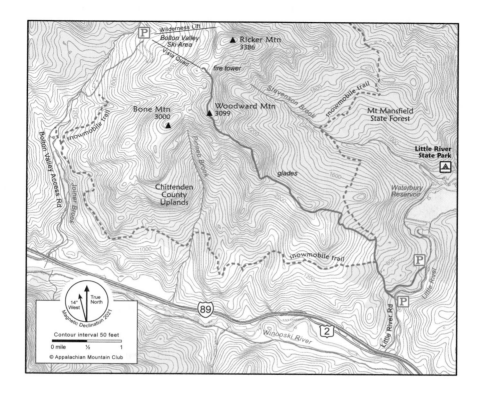

The Woodward Mountain Trail was originally conceived in the early 1970s at the same time as the Bolton–Trapp Trail. The late Gardiner Lane, founder of the Bolton Valley Nordic Center, recalled that there was a grand plan for a network of backcountry ski trails that could be linked together and even used for hut-to-hut skiing. The Bolton–Trapp Trail was cut in 1972, and that same year Lane and some friends blazed the Woodward Mountain Trail. The trail descended from Ricker Mountain to the Waterbury Reservoir and overlooks the historic Ricker Basin. From the 1790s to the early twentieth century, this basin was a thriving farm community with schools, homes, and cemeteries. In 1927, the nearby Winooski River catastrophically flooded. The state responded by building a large earthen dam in Waterbury, which permanently submerged much of the old farm community beneath Waterbury Reservoir. Remains of the abandoned towns are now part of Little River State Park, where the Woodward Mountain Trail ends.

Vermont State Forester Ed O'Leary blazed the trail in 1972, but Lane could not muster a large enough crew to cut the trail. So the blue blazes went unused. Though the Woodward Mountain Trail appeared on some old maps, it mostly existed as a gleam in Lane's eye. In 1992, when Lane was 78 years old, he and his friend Clem Holden—they dubbed themselves the "Old Goats"—decided to hunt for buried treasure. They went hiking and rediscovered many of the old blazes, but they were unable to connect the trail all the way to Waterbury and got lost twice trying. The Old Goats abandoned the idea once and for all. Or so they thought.

In 1994, Lane received a letter from some local backcountry skiers. The letter included a picture of an old trail sign that the younger skiers had discovered in the woods while bushwhacking up from Little River State Park. It was a sign that Lane had placed twenty years before! An excited Lane recounted, "Like the explorers Freemont and Lewis and Clark, the Old Goats and the Young Catamounts were stimulated and reactivated the work on the Woodward Mountain Trail."

The "Young Catamounts" included Catamount Trail Association members Jerry Lasky, Cilla Kimberly, John Riley, and Rich and Sheri Larsen. They promptly sought and obtained permission from the state to recut the trail, and a small army of saw-wielding skiers forged their way down Woodward Mountain in several passes between 1996 and 1997. Following a snowstorm in March 1997, the Old Goats and Young Catamounts together made the first descent of the Woodward Mountain Trail. Lane was 83 and Holden was 73 on the inaugural run. "The trail was steep, the snow was deep, the hearts were beating fast," wrote Lane of the adventure.

THE TOUR

This backcountry tour begins incongruously on a chairlift; the lift ride is the coldest part of the tour. From the top of the appropriately named Vista Quad, ski straight ahead toward the prominent fire tower. Climbing the fire tower to take in the views is a required part of this tour! The panorama at the top is breathtaking. The full sweep of Lake Champlain, the largest inland body of water outside the Great Lakes, unfolds below you. There are views of the ski trails on Whiteface, Sugarbush, Mad River Glen, Pico Peak, Killington, Stowe, and Bolton Valley. Giant Mountain, with its prominent Eagle Slide, and Mount Marcy, New York's highest peak, crown the Adirondack skyline across the lake. To the north, the Mount Mansfield summit appears as a huge rocky dome that has been blasted white. Bolton Mountain is the round, wooded summit just south of Mansfield. The nearby radio tower is located on Ricker Mountain. Finally, look to the southeast to take in the landscape of this ski tour: the long, rolling wooded ridgeline of Woodward Mountain continuing all the way down to the Waterbury Reservoir.

From the fire tower, the Woodward Mountain Trail starts discreetly as a narrow opening in the woods, but the path is well defined and clearly marked with blue plastic blazes. The trail initially drops like a crazed rabbit in an abrupt swoop to the southeast (toward the reservoir), twisting and turning down a narrow trail. The trail then turns right (southwest), passing just above beautiful, isolated Goose Pond. After a series of quick turns, the trail widens then climbs gently but steadily

Riding the powder bowls on the Woodward Mountain Trail. *Photo by Kyle Crichton*

up a ridge. This wooded ridge running from northwest to southeast is Woodward Mountain. The mountain has four peaks, all of which you ski over or around.

The Woodward Mountain Trail snaps back and forth twice before arriving at a small clearing, where it then proceeds to the east-southeast. The trail meanders through a high fir and spruce forest. Broken and twisted treetops are evidence of the powerful weather that pounds this high-elevation forest. This is a stunning ramble through numerous dark hollows that appear and vanish along the broad ridge. You are alone up here in a wild place. Bobcat and moose tracks crisscross the route.

A short downhill through a stand of white birch trees brings you to a large clearing at about 2,800 feet. Camel's Hump appears across the valley to the south. After taking in the views, the trail begins to rock and roll. You begin a series of moderate descents through the trees where you can swing turns or simply ski straight if you prefer. Camel's Hump appears more regularly now, alternating with views into the wild and trailless Ricker Basin on the north side of Woodward Mountain. At about 2,700 feet, ski around a prominent knoll that is one of the peaks of Woodward Mountain (the actual summit, which is unmarked, is 3,099 feet). As you descend, you can pause and turn for impressive views back up the trail.

Powder and smiles on the Woodward Mountain Trail.

The trail descends past a number of north-facing bowls. You likely will see ski tracks dropping off to the left (north) of the trail into what have become a favorite haunt of local powder skiers. You can stop and yo-yo one of these bowls and then climb out to rejoin the Woodward Mountain Trail (you need climbing skins for this). Resist the temptation to ski all the way down into Ricker Basin; there is no easy exit out the bottom. Many skiers come to ski these bowls and then backtrack on the Woodward Mountain Trail to Bolton Valley. The skiing here is that good.

If you are continuing to Little River after skiing the bowls, keep your skins on as the trail climbs over yet another summit knob. Look for double blazes, which signal abrupt direction changes in the trail. At about 2,400 feet, the trail runs into a rocky outcropping on your left. The trail doubles back to the left up a short ramp to get over this small knoll. From here, there are views to the west of the Worcester Mountains and Elmore Mountain. Just beyond, you come upon Gardiner Lane's old brown trail sign indicating the direction and distance to Little River Campground and Bryant Camp, which is located within the Bolton Valley Ski Area. The Woodward Mountain Trail makes a sharp right here and drops downhill.

The lower sections of the trail are south facing, and the snow quality may be completely different than what you found up higher. A long gradual descent brings you to a clearing where you bear right onto an old logging road. You are not done yet—more than a mile of continuous turns are yet to come. Watch out for water bars and open water on this section of trail.

You finally emerge into a large clearing and a snowmobile trail, where you turn right, then come quickly to a junction with another major snowmobile thoroughfare where you bear left (downhill), soon passing a cabin on the right. Continue straight, following the snowmobile trail as it steepens. If you parked at the unmarked snowmobile trailhead on Little River Road, continue straight down to your car. If you parked at the major snowmobile parking lot farther north on the road, turn left on the snowmobile trail that diverges about 300 yards above Little River Road and continue on flat ground to the parking lot.

A word of caution: There is no easy access on or off the middle of the Woodward Mountain Trail, and you are miles from help. Your party should be equipped to deal with any mishaps. Don't be fooled by the fact that the trail is only 6 miles long. It crosses rugged terrain and you may be breaking trail. This trip is a full-day commitment, and you should start early to ensure that you can finish in daylight.

One of the unique and noteworthy aspects of the Woodward Mountain Trail is that it was cut and is still maintained by an informal but dedicated network of local backcountry skiers. This is skiing created by and for friends. That is Gardiner Lane's fitting legacy.

Upon finishing the Woodward Mountain Trail, you will undoubtedly agree with Lane, who reflected after completing the first descent: "Rejuvenation offsets exhaustion when you know you have skied an historic trail through many miles of beautiful wilderness without any mishaps."

35 BOLTON-TRAPP TRAIL

This beautiful and exciting ski tour starts at the Bolton Valley Ski Area, crosses the shoulder of Bolton Mountain, and descends into the Nebraska Valley in Moscow, with the option of finishing at the famous Trapp Family Lodge. This tour is one of the most popular and challenging sections of the 300-mile-long Catamount Trail.

Distance: 6.5 miles, Bolton Valley Ski Area to Nebraska Valley Road; 9.4 miles, Bolton Valley to Trapp Family Lodge
Elevation: *Start*: 2,050 feet, Bolton Valley Sports Center; *Highest point*: 3,300 feet; *Finish*: 1,000 feet (Nebraska Valley Road), 1,350 feet (Trapp Family Lodge); *Vertical drop*: 1,950–2,300 feet, depending on destination
Maps: *Mansfield Region Backcountry Trail Map* (MapleRidge Solutions), *Northern Vermont Hiking & Biking Trails* (Map Adventures), *Bolton Valley Backcountry & Nordic Map* (free at Bolton Valley Sports Center or download at boltonvalley.com), Catamount Trail, Section 22 map (download at catamounttrail.org)
Difficulty: More difficult
Gear: AT, telemark, snowboard
Fee: You must purchase a cross-country ski trail ticket at the Bolton Valley Sports Center to use its trail system to access this route.
Additional Information: Bolton Valley Sports Center, 802-434-3444, boltonvalley.com; Trapp Family Lodge, 802-253-8511, trappfamily.com; Catamount Trail Association, 802-864-5794, catamounttrail.org

HOW TO GET THERE

Bolton Valley (4302 Bolton Valley Access Road, Bolton Valley, VT 05477): From the south, take Exit 10 on I-89; from the north, take Exit 11. Follow the signs on US 2 to the Bolton Valley Ski Area. Turn onto Bolton Access Road and drive 4.2 miles to the Bolton Valley Ski Area. The Bolton Valley Sports Center is located on the west side of the parking lot in the Sports Center building (*GPS coordinates*: 44° 25.308′ N, 72° 51.120′ W).

Trapp Family Lodge (700 Trapp Hill Road, Stowe, VT 05672): From Exit 10 on I-89, take Route 100 north toward Stowe. After 7.5 miles, turn left onto Moscow Road. If you are leaving a car at Trapp Family Lodge, turn right onto Barrows Road, pass Stowe Junior/Senior High School, then turn left at the stop sign, following signs to the lodge (*GPS coordinates*: 44° 27.845′ N, 72° 44.752′ W).

Nebraska Valley Road: If you are ending your tour on Nebraska Valley Road in Moscow (part of Stowe), pass Barrows Road, bear sharply right after Trapp Hill Road, cross a bridge, and continue on Nebraska Valley Road for another 4.2 miles. Pass a small plowed parking pullout on the left with a sign for Mount Mansfield State Forest, and park in a second plowed pullout 0.1 miles beyond (*GPS coordinates*: 44° 28.073′ N, 72° 47.822′ W). This is where the Bolton–Trapp Trail comes

BOLTON-TRAPP TRAIL

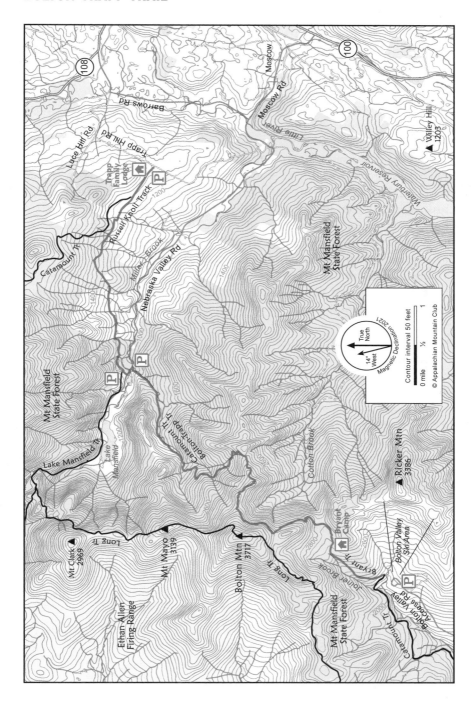

out. If this parking pullout is full, continue another 0.1 miles to a larger plowed parking area at the corner of Old County Road.

THE TOUR

The ski tour between the Bolton Valley Ski Area and the Trapp Family Lodge is one of the most popular backcountry adventures in Vermont. One reason for its renown is that it lies in the heart of Vermont ski country. This region is home to numerous ski areas due to the abundance of snow here and the quality of the terrain. These attributes are showcased on this tour.

The Bolton–Trapp Trail traverses a remarkable breadth of terrain. Beginning at the groomed cross-country trails of the Bolton Valley Ski Area, the Bolton–Trapp Trail travels through a wild, high-mountain landscape, descends a powdery basin, then offers the option of ending at the Trapp Family Lodge, one of the most famous cross-country ski centers and ski lodges in the U.S. Bolton Valley is the highest cross-country ski center in the state and is a reliable preserve of powder even when the valleys are dry. An added bonus is that this is part of the Catamount Trail, the 300-mile backcountry ski trail that runs the entire length of Vermont.

A logistical challenge of this tour is the 30-mile car shuttle between Bolton and Stowe. The Catamount Trail Association (catamounttrail.org) periodically runs a weekend shuttle for this tour, or you can post a shuttle request on its Facebook page.

The idea of linking the Bolton and Trapp Family cross-country centers belonged to Johannes von Trapp, the founder of the Trapp Family Lodge. Von Trapp proposed to Gardiner Lane, founder of what was then the Bolton Valley Cross-Country Ski Center, to undertake a joint effort to link their respective cross-country trail networks with an ambitious, over-the-mountain backcountry ski route. In spring 1972, the two men, each accompanied by a trail crew, flagged and cut their way up opposite sides of Bolton Mountain. They used old logging roads and abandoned trails wherever possible.

Von Trapp, who still owns the Trapp Family Lodge along with his children, Sam and Kristina, describes himself as someone who "skis to get out into the woods more than for the sake of skiing." In the early 1970s, he imagined that the future of cross-country skiing would be ski touring in the backcountry and that the Bolton–Trapp Trail would become a centerpiece of the Trapp family ski trail network. He envisioned an ambitious European-style hut-to-hut trail system that would extend from Waterbury to Bolton to Stowe. It was a nice dream, but he was way off the mark. Skiers flocked to the groomed trails of cross-country centers, and until recent years, the backcountry trails were only lightly used.

Facing page: Finding powder on the Bolton–Trapp Trail.

The Bolton–Trapp Trail begins at the Bolton Valley Sports Center, which is on the opposite side of the parking lot from the chairlifts. (Skiing the route from the Stowe side would make most of the tour an uphill climb.) You must purchase a cross-country trail ticket before heading out, since you ski through the groomed Bolton cross-country ski trail network to reach the Bolton–Trapp Trail. The folks at Bolton Valley are a helpful source of information on route conditions. Plan to start this tour by 10 A.M. and allow four to five hours to ski to Nebraska Valley Road, longer if you are headed all the way to Trapp Family Lodge. Snow conditions and group fitness level will affect these times.

From the Sports Center, ski out on Broadway, quickly turn right (uphill) on World Cup, then turn right on the ungroomed Bryant Trail and continue climbing, following signs for Bryant Camp. Bryant Trail gradually rises while the ski resort and the lift lines recede behind you.

Just over a mile from the Sports Center you arrive at the historic Bryant Camp, a rustic cabin that sleeps eight (you can book an overnight stay through the Vermont Huts Association, vermonthuts.org). The camp was built around 1927 by Ed Bryant, a conservationist and ski enthusiast from Boston who purchased 4,000 acres of land in this area. Ski enthusiasts would hike in several miles and stay at the cabin for several days while skiing and exploring the mountains. Bryant Camp was restored in 2016. This is the last outpost of civilization before the trail heads up into the hills.

From Bryant Camp, continue uphill and turn left on Birch Loop. The trail rises gently, then forks: Birch Loop continues left and the Bolton–Trapp Trail heads off to the right. The blue plastic Catamount Trail blazes will reassure you that you are headed the right way. After about 100 yards, Cotton Brook Trail leaves to the right, dropping more than 6 miles to end at Cotton Brook Road. The Bolton–Trapp Trail continues north and is clearly blazed in blue.

The Bolton–Trapp Trail switchbacks up into a grove of well-spaced birch trees with panoramas of the eastern Green Mountains. Don't miss skiing this glade—God didn't put the spaces between those trees for nothing. From here, the trail climbs moderately then contours below the summit of Bolton Mountain (3,717 feet). At 2.1 miles, the trail passes Raven's Wind on the left, which returns to Bolton Valley. Just past this junction you ski over the highest point on the Catamount Trail (3,310 feet).

After a series of short, steep climbs and drops, the trail swings around sharply to the east (right), where it follows the top of a ridge that separates Cotton Brook Basin from Nebraska Valley. Be sure to make this turn—don't be confused by other ski tracks that head out into local powder stashes (of which there are many in this area). The Bolton–Trapp Trail snakes through tightly spaced trees here and is often exposed to the full force of the elements. Take in the views of Camel's Hump and the Worcester Mountains from a clearing at the end of the ridge. This is a nice lunch or snack spot. If you are getting buffeted by weather up here, you can forge ahead as the trail soon drops off sharply to the north into a protected valley.

From the end of the ridge, the Bolton–Trapp Trail begins a series of long descending switchbacks into Nebraska Valley. Skiing down is a delight in good conditions. The forest is quite open, and Nebraska Valley is often a powder basin. If one skier goes ahead, marking where the trail is, others can ski the fall line through the glades, dovetailing with the trail when it suits them. If you like what you find up high, you will enjoy the rest of the tour—there are 3 more miles of downhill skiing in which to play.

The trail has a number of stream crossings, which may be open if there is light snow cover or if it is late in the season. After taking some final wide switchbacks through the forest and crossing a large stream, the trail parallels Miller Brook for the remainder of the route to Nebraska Valley Road. The trail drops quickly and passes a small camp on the right before entering a large clearing. This was the site of a farm in the 1930s and 1940s. From here, the trail bears left, following an abandoned town road that once served the farm. It is a steady downhill from here to the trailhead.

Miller Brook is worth stopping to admire as you ski alongside it on the old town road. It constricts into a dramatic narrow gorge and has a waterfall near the old farm site then continues as a boulder-choked stream down into Nebraska Valley.

Once at Nebraska Valley Road, you have two choices. I highly recommend that you leave a car here and end your tour, as most skiers do. The best skiing is behind

Skiers heading out on the Bolton–Trapp Trail.

you. Another option is to continue to the Trapp Family Lodge. If you continue, don't underestimate what's ahead—you have another 3 miles of moderate skiing before you can rest.

If you continue to the Trapp Family Lodge, take off your skis, turn left, and walk up the road for 100 yards. Turn right on Old County Road, and immediately see blue plastic blazes on your right, where you put skis back on and reenter the woods. Ski another half-mile and reemerge onto Old County Road, where you must walk a short distance past a house on the left and an open field on the right before continuing straight ahead past some homes. Put your skis back on where the plowing ends. Ski uphill on the improved woods road, and 1.4 miles after Nebraska Valley Road, you connect with the groomed Russell Knoll Track of the Trapp cross-country trail network. Turn right and follow signs to the lodge, which is another 1.5 miles away. You finish on the gorgeous open pasture of the Trapp Family Lodge, with huge views of the Worcester Mountains in front of you and the classic gabled roof of the lodge ahead. Trapp Family Lodge does not charge a fee for skiers who use its trails to exit from this route.

This is a demanding ski tour. The area between Bolton and Stowe is relatively remote, which is one of the primary attractions of this route. The trail is not groomed and is not patrolled by either Trapp Family Lodge or Bolton Valley. Skiers on this route should be prepared to bail themselves out if problems arise. When it is icy in the north-facing Nebraska Valley, the trail is arduous and dangerous and not worth skiing. It is best to get information on trail conditions at the Bolton Valley Sports Center before heading out.

The prize for skiers on this tour is the chance to traverse a wild landscape in the heart of the Green Mountains. This untamed backyard of Vermont ski country is a gem.

MOUNT MANSFIELD REGION

Mount Mansfield (elevation 4,393 feet) is the highest mountain in Vermont. Viewed from the east and west, the ridgeline of the mountain resembles the profile of a face, hence the names given to the various features along the ridge, from south to north: Forehead, Nose, Upper Lip, Lower Lip, Chin, and Adam's Apple. According to the Green Mountain Club's *Long Trail Guide*, the Abenaki originally named the mountain Mose-o-de-be-Wadso (mountain with the head of a moose). The current name was adopted from the nearby town of Mansfield, which is now defunct.

Mount Mansfield has captured the imagination of skiers since the early 1900s. It was first climbed on skis on February 1, 1914, when Dartmouth librarian Nat Goodrich ascended via the Toll Road. Goodrich was accompanied by Appalachian Mountain Club trailsman C.W. Blood, who wore snowshoes. Blood descended the mountain nearly as fast as his skiing partner. Goodrich offered in explanation, "I had a lot of fun, but my stops, voluntary and otherwise, were very frequent."

Numerous ski trails were cut on both sides of Mount Mansfield beginning in the early 1930s. Many of these trails were incorporated into the network of what is now Stowe Mountain Resort, located on the northeast slopes of the mountain. What the ski area left behind, backcountry skiers claim today.

Mount Mansfield is now home to one of the most extensive networks of backcountry ski trails in the Northeast. Many of these trails are maintained by dedicated local volunteers. Much of the history of skiing on Mount Mansfield, and indeed in the United States, can be found in the storied ski trails that are described in this section.

The ski tours in the Mount Mansfield region offer a variety of exciting trail skiing and glade skiing. The old-growth forests are an ideal setting for skiers who enjoy weaving through the hardwoods and finding their own lines of descent. The history, quality, and variety of terrain make this entire region an essential destination for skiers in search of the classic New England ski experience.

36 TEARDROP TRAIL

The Teardrop is a classic down-mountain trail that was cut in the 1930s by the Civilian Conservation Corps. It leaves just south of the Nose of Mount Mansfield and descends the steep, powdery west face of the mountain.

Distance: 2.4 miles, Underhill Center winter parking lot to top of Teardrop, one way
Elevation: *Highest point*: 3,900 feet; *Bottom*: 1,600 feet; *Vertical drop*: 2,300 feet
Maps: *Mansfield Region Backcountry Trail Map* (MapleRidge Solutions), *Northern Vermont Hiking & Biking Trails* (Map Adventures)
Difficulty: Most difficult
Gear: AT, telemark, snowboard

HOW TO GET THERE

From Stowe: From the Stowe Mountain Resort downhill ski area (*GPS coordinates*: 44° 31.815′ N, 72° 47.118′ W), purchase a lift ticket and take the Fourunner Quad chairlift to the Octagon Café. Or, from the Mansfield Base Lodge, ski uphill (check stowe.com for current uphill skiing policy and routes). From the Octagon, ski or walk up the Toll Road to the top, passing giant radio antennae until a junction on the right with Long Trail south. Ski on the Long Trail (LT) for 100 yards, staying right at a sign for Forehead Bypass. Continue straight on the LT, and where the hiking trail bends left, bear right into the woods for about another 100 yards, eventually intersecting the top of the Teardrop Trail.

From Underhill Center: From Pleasant Valley Road, turn right onto Mountain Road, drive to where the plowing ends, and park (*GPS coordinates*: 44° 31.310′ N, 72° 51.223′ W). Ski up the unplowed road toward Underhill State Park for about a half-mile. An unmarked trail departs on the right (east) that connects directly with the bottom of the Teardrop Trail. This is the most popular access point for the Teardrop so there likely will be ski tracks to follow.

HISTORY

In 1937, encouraged by the popularity of its ski trails in Stowe, the Civilian Conservation Corps (CCC) turned its energies to the "other side" of Mount Mansfield. Burlington-area skiers clamored for ski routes on Mansfield that didn't require driving all the way around to Stowe. So the U.S. Forest Service issued orders to the CCC to cut a trail that dropped from the summit of Mount Mansfield to the sleepy town of Underhill on the west side of Vermont's highest peak. Stowe's master trail engineer, Charlie Lord, was then serving on the technical staff of the CCC. He laid out the Teardrop Trail, and the CCC trail builders went to work. Vermont State Forester Perry Merrill gave the trail its name because, as Lord told me before he died in 1997, the trail was so fast "it made tears run from your eyes."

Underhill residents once had visions of a ski development on par with the alpine ski resort in Stowe. In the late 1930s, slopes were cut on the west side of Mount

TEARDROP TRAIL

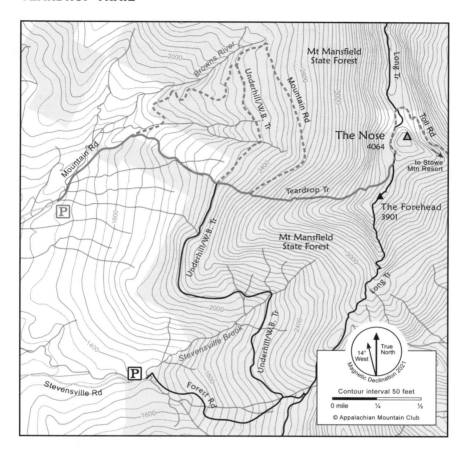

Mansfield. A 1,000-foot rope tow was installed, and lights were put on the slopes for night skiing. Snow trains from New York City arrived in Burlington, where buses took skiers either to Underhill Center or Stowe. "A variety of practice runs, trails which vary in rating from beginner to advanced expert, and the well-known Underhill Ski School combine to make this a mecca for New York's snowbirds," declared the 1939 guidebook, *Skiing in the East: The Best Trails and How to Get There*. But the Underhill ski scene was eclipsed when the single chairlift began operation in Stowe in 1940. Stowe's chairlift rose 2,000 vertical feet up Mount Mansfield to the Octagon, a newly built warming hut. The Underhill slopes were the site of several intercollegiate ski meets in the early 1940s, but the operation was abandoned soon after World War II.

The Teardrop was described in one account as "the pièce de résistance" of the trails in the Underhill area. *Skiing in the East* proclaimed it "one of the most thrilling trails in the East." It originally linked to a trail to the Halfway House for a total descent of 3 miles. An 800-foot rope tow was at one time in operation at the base of it, along with a warming hut and snack bar.

Despite the quality of this run, the Teardrop never achieved the popularity of the legendary Nose Dive, Chin Clip, and Bruce trails on the "front" side of the mountain. Early Stowe skiers such as Lord, Craig Burt Jr., and the rest of their crowd simply felt it was too much hassle to climb the mountain, ski down the Teardrop, and then climb up again to return home. It was left to skiers from Underhill and Burlington to ski and maintain the trail. Ironically, the Teardrop has probably achieved more renown today among backcountry skiers than it did in its early years.

What's so special about an abandoned downhill trail that goes down the wrong side of the mountain? Its loyal following would agree on one thing: powder. While weekend warriors may be scraping their way down icy slopes on the front side of the mountain, backcountry skiers and riders can float through knee-deep fluff on the back side. The Teardrop is often a reliable powder stash even when the lowlands are dry.

Like many CCC ski trails, the Teardrop has a distinctive personality. Turns were placed strategically to keep the route interesting and challenging, and the trail moves with the contours of the mountain. It banks, dips, turns, and rolls along with the mountain, keeping it unpredictable throughout its entire length. Just as importantly, the trail was located where the snow dumped most heavily and lasted longest. There were no snowmakers or groomers 70 years ago to replenish the trail after a day's ski, so skiers had to place the trail where Mother Nature could help.

THE TOUR

The Teardrop has evolved from a cult classic to one of the more popular backcountry ski tours in northern Vermont. The trail is heavily skied, but it is still wide and powdery enough that many skiers and riders can find their own untracked lines.

The Teardrop's popularity has not diminished its appeal, but it has increased the options for how to descend. There are now numerous glade variations from the Teardrop. It's also worth noting that the Teardrop is a steep ascent that requires full-length, full-width skins. *Please never walk in the skin track!*

The most popular approach to ski the Teardrop is from Underhill Center, but you can also access the trail from Stowe Mountain Resort (see "How to Get There," page 206). When skiing from Stowe Mountain Resort, the top of the Teardrop is intentionally discreet and difficult to find. Local skiers have left the top of the trail obscure partly to keep skier traffic down as well as to prevent Long Trail hikers from unwittingly detouring down the ski trail. The narrow top of the trail, which is skied only if you are coming from Stowe, is the most challenging part. A tight chute threads among stunted trees, and this section is often windblown and icy. But the trail opens steadily into a 20-foot-wide swath heading west. The trail slabs across the north side of a buttress that runs from the Forehead. There is a double fall line

Finding buried treasure on the Teardrop Trail.

to contend with for the first half of the run. Looking back up the trail, there is an impressive view of the cliffy western face of the Forehead.

The Teardrop begins its descent with a gradual traverse, then begins snapping back and forth across the fall line. Right-angle turns force you to keep swooping around blind corners while the trail twists downhill. Steep drops alternate with gradual runouts, with barely enough time to catch your breath in between. Skiing the Teardrop is like paddling a good whitewater run: you drift slowly through a calm section, get lured unwittingly into the next chute, pick up speed, then work the subtle currents in the river as you fly down the big drops. The Zen of negotiating all these forms of "whitewater" is the same: stay centered, relaxed, balanced, and move with the terrain. Go with the flow.

The Teardrop drops quickly, and after 1 mile it intersects with the CCC Road, a popular cross-country ski trail in Underhill State Park. Turn left on the CCC Road and go about 20 yards, where the CCC Road ends and the Teardrop bangs a hard right and continues downhill for another 0.8 miles. This lower section begins with the steepest drop yet, descending a sometimes-bony headwall. The trail then moderates and proceeds downhill at a more relaxed pace all the way to Mountain Road in Underhill Center.

The Teardrop covers a full range of downhill skiing terrain, from narrow chutes to open powder skiing to tighter tree shots. You can pull out all the stops on the Teardrop and try everything in your bag of tricks. This action-packed variety is what makes the route so interesting and fun to ski. The Teardrop has transformed from a historical relic to a trail where skiers vie with each another to claim first tracks after a storm. The passions that this route inspires are understandable—when conditions are right, it is one of the best powder runs in New England.

As with all trails, the challenge of the Teardrop is dictated by the snow conditions, which in turn are largely affected by the amount of skier traffic. On a good weekend, dozens of skiers may be tearing it up. To really capture the spirit of this old trail, catch it just after a storm, preferably midweek.

③⑦ BRUCE TRAIL

The Bruce Trail descends 2,000 feet down the south side of Mount Mansfield, ending on the trails of the Stowe Mountain Resort Cross-Country Ski Center. This legendary down-mountain ski run was cut in the 1930s by the Civilian Conservation Corps.

Distance: 4 miles, Octagon Café to Stowe Mountain Resort Cross-Country Ski Center

Elevation: *Start*: 3,640 feet; *Finish*: 1,100 feet; *Vertical drop*: 2,540 feet, Octagon to cross-country center

Maps: *Mansfield Region Backcountry Trail Map* (MapleRidge Solutions), *Northern Vermont Hiking & Biking Trails* (Map Adventures)

Difficulty: Most difficult

Gear: AT, snowboard, telemark

Fee: The Bruce Trail is reached via the alpine or cross-country trails of Stowe Mountain Resort, and you may need to purchase a trail pass depending on where you start. You can either skin up from the alpine ski area (check stowe.com for the latest uphill skiing policy and fees) or ride the Fourrunner Quad chairlift to the start of the Bruce Trail, which requires a lift ticket. If you ski up from the Stowe Mountain Resort Cross-Country Ski Center, you must purchase a cross-country trail pass.

Note: Even though you start and finish this trail at ski areas, the Bruce Trail is not patrolled or maintained by Stowe Mountain Resort. This is a backcountry trail, and in the event of a mishap, you may be billed for rescue.

Additional Information: Stowe Mountain Resort Cross-Country Ski Center, 802-253-3000, stowe.com

HOW TO GET THERE

Option 1: From Stowe Mountain Resort downhill ski area (*GPS coordinates*: 44° 31.815′ N, 72° 47.118′ W), take the Fourrunner Quad chairlift to the top, where the Octagon Café is located (you must first purchase a lift ticket). The Bruce Trail leaves from the Toll Road just behind (west of) the Stone Hut. Alternatively, ski up the trails of Stowe Mountain Resort to the top of the Bruce Trail (check stowe.com for current uphill skiing policy). It is about a 2-mile ski up from the Mansfield Base Lodge to the Bruce Trail.

Option 2: Purchase a trail pass from the Stowe Mountain Resort Cross-Country Ski Center (*GPS coordinates*: 44° 30.348′ N, 72° 45.710′ W) and ski the Burt Trail to the Bruce Trail, which you can climb and descend.

HISTORY

On June 9, 1933, a contingent of the Civilian Conservation Corps (CCC), the Depression-era federal jobs recovery program, arrived in Waterbury, Vermont, just down the road from Mount Mansfield. Vermont State Forester Perry Merrill,

BRUCE TRAIL

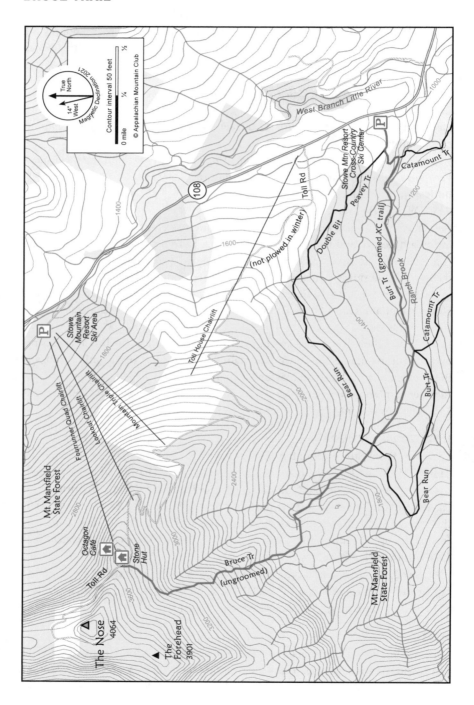

himself an avid skier, had just the project for these eager young men: he would have them cut a ski trail from near the summit of Mount Mansfield almost to the Mountain Road in Stowe. This was the Bruce Trail, named for a well-known local lumberman. It was the first ski trail on Mount Mansfield.

The Bruce Trail was an immediate hit with skiers. On February 11, 1934, it was the site of Mount Mansfield's first ski race. The race was won in 10 minutes, 48 seconds by Burlington golf champion Jack Allen. Charlie Lord, who directed the CCC in cutting the trail and later become the master designer of Mount Mansfield's downhill ski trail system, came in second place. Lord recounted in his notes: "Snow very fast, took numerous spills (planned sitzmarks I guess). . . . Enjoyed the race even though nearly done us in." Mount Mansfield's first officially sanctioned race was held two weeks later. Two thousand people lined the Bruce Trail to watch Dartmouth skier Dick Durrance win the race in 5 minutes, 7 seconds, a full minute faster than the runner-up (Durrance also won the ski jumping and slalom races that day). The Bruce Trail and Nose Dive, on the opposite side of Mount Mansfield, were two of the main skiing attractions on the mountain.

The real center of skiing on Mount Mansfield in the early days was not a trail but a cabin. In 1932, Stowe lumberman and skier Craig Burt Sr. fixed up an old logging camp and turned it into the ski accommodations known as the Ranch Camp. When Lord and his CCC contingent were deciding where to cut the Bruce Trail, they put it where they did partly because it would end at the front door of the Ranch Camp, which is also where the CCC crew was quartered while they built the trail. The Ranch Camp also served as the first headquarters of the Mount Mansfield Ski Club.

Early skiing on Mount Mansfield was intimately connected with life at the Ranch Camp. Ski maps of Mount Mansfield from the 1930s graphically depict how ski trails radiated out from the Ranch Camp like spokes from a hub. The camp was located at the junction of the Steeple, Houston, and Bruce trails—all of which were recut and restored in the 1990s, largely thanks to the efforts of John Higgins, the late director of the Stowe Mountain Resort Cross-Country Ski Center.

Ranch Camp life was the precursor of modern ski bumming. According to Hal Burton, formerly on the board of directors of the Mount Mansfield Ski Club, the cook at the Ranch Camp "always had a huge iron vat of good New England baked beans on the stove. There were always a lot of very happy skiers inside. We felt privileged to have snow because there weren't any snowmakers in those days." It cost $1 for three meals, and $1 for lodging. In its heyday, Ranch Camp consisted of three buildings with bunks for 44 skiers.

"Ranch Camp was a distinctive institution and its clientele really loved to 'get back into the woods,'" wrote Lord. "It had an atmosphere all its own and I suspect that even today it would have appeal, although it probably wouldn't make much money."

The Ranch Camp operated as a ski hut until 1950. Its demise occurred under unfortunate circumstances. In the late 1960s, the Ranch Camp buildings were oc-cupied by squatters, mostly young hippies fleeing urban blight. The Burt Lumber

Company, owner of the property, disapproved of the situation but was unsure how to handle it. The company finally opted for a definitive solution: in September 1970, the company burned down the buildings. There are now only traces of the onetime forest enclave of Mount Mansfield skiers. The legendary home to Stowe's first skiers is now memorialized by a sign alongside the Burt Trail in the Stowe Mountain Resort Cross-Country Ski Center.

With the Ranch Camp as a base of operations in the 1930s, a 3-mile climb up the Bruce Trail and a run down was considered a pretty good day. But in 1937, the first commercial rope tow opened on the eastern slopes of the mountain, and in 1940, a 6,300-foot single chairlift opened, capable of carrying 200 skiers per hour up the mountain (since replaced by the Fourrunner Quad). The Bruce Trail, on the undeveloped south side of the mountain, was quickly abandoned in favor of the lift-served trails.

The Bruce Trail continued to be skied occasionally in the 1950s and 1960s, and locals periodically cut back the underbrush. In the 1980s and early 1990s, the Bruce became a favorite powder run for telemark skiers, but it was still lightly skied. Getting first tracks was easy.

Today's explosion of interest in backcountry skiing has resulted in a new life for the Bruce Trail, which is now used daily as a lift-served backcountry run. This marks a revival of the spirit of the venerable trail. Skiers and riders have come full circle, dusting off this buried treasure to once again appreciate how it shines.

Maintained by local volunteers, the Bruce Trail and the Teardrop Trail endure as crown jewels in the network of down-mountain trails cut by the CCC. A ski down the Bruce will make it clear why skiers of another era traveled so far for this prize.

THE TOUR

From the top of the Fourrunner Quad chairlift, ski straight ahead to the Stone Hut. The Stone Hut was built by the CCC in 1936 to serve as a warming hut for skiers. You can stay overnight in the hut, which sleeps twelve (Stone Hut reservations are very popular and are now done by lottery. Make plans well in advance and follow instructions at vtstateparks.com/stonehut.html). Follow the path to the right past the front door of the Stone Hut, then turn left where you emerge on the Toll Road. The Bruce Trail departs from the Toll Road in about 100 feet. Where the Toll Road jogs slightly left, the Bruce goes straight. The top of the Bruce Trail is unmarked, and there may or may not be a ski area boundary sign, though there probably will be tracks. Pass the sign (if it's there), drift downhill a few feet, and the trail will be obvious.

The Bruce Trail starts with a bang: a seven-foot wide pipeline plunges straight downhill for about 80 feet then makes an abrupt 90-degree turn to the right. If you survive this initiation, you'll do fine on the rest of the run. The trail then widens to about 15 feet. It alternately traverses and drops and is full of quick corners and

Following page: Skiing the Bruce Trail, Mount Mansfield's first ski trail.

surprises. Stay on your toes and expect the unexpected. Most of all, enjoy the quirky sense of humor of this trail.

There are views of Mount Elmore and the Worcester Mountains to the east as you descend. About a mile down the trail, you turn right and suddenly come upon a sharp horizon line. The short, steep pitch below is the Elevator Shaft, the heart-stopping crux of the run. There is a gentle runout at the bottom of this pitch just in case you build up too much steam above.

The Bruce Trail descends a valley with southeastern exposure. Because of this, it tends to have less consistent snow conditions than the Teardrop Trail, which has northern and western exposure. It is common to encounter a wide range of snow types when skiing the Bruce, which adds to its interesting personality. Its sunny aspect makes it a friendly place to stop and enjoy the views.

Beyond the Elevator Shaft, there are still several miles of turns on more moderate terrain. The Bruce Trail travels through some long, open birch glades before finally coming to a well-marked intersection with the Overland Trail after 1.1 miles. The Bruce continues straight ahead with plenty of turns for the next half-mile, until you reach a junction with Bear Run, a groomed trail that is part of the Stowe Mountain Resort Cross-Country Ski Center. Continue straight ahead on the Bruce, which is a groomed trail from this point, and take care to give room to cross-country skiers on the trail. A half-mile later, the Bruce officially ends at the Burt Trail. Continue another 1.5 miles on the groomed Burt Trail.

There are several options for how to finish. You can return to the alpine ski area by following "To Lift" signs that direct you back to the Toll House double chairlift. Or you may exit at the cross-country ski center, where you can take a Mountain Road shuttle bus back to Stowe Mountain Resort ski area.

THE RANCH VALLEY GRAND TOUR

You can extend your backcountry skiing by taking a grand tour of the Ranch Valley. This is a beautiful and worthwhile adventure that will add both scenery and turns to your day. As you descend the Bruce Trail, turn right onto the Overland Trail. The red-blazed Overland Trail climbs steadily (climbing skins are helpful) into an area of giant boulders known as the Devil's Cauldron. Continue climbing until you reach a junction with the Underhill Trail. If you turn right on the Overland here, in 0.25 miles you reach the Devil's Dishpan, a wild place where a cliff is cleaved open. You can peer into the cleft and even ski down into it. From here, the Overland Trail descends to Underhill Center (see the description of this route in tour 40, Nebraska Notch and Dewey Mountain, page 228).

To return to the Stowe Mountain Resort Cross-Country Ski Center from the Underhill Trail junction, remove skins, turn left, and follow the red-blazed Underhill Trail as it contours gently through the forest. You pass through beautiful alcoves with icefalls and giant rocks. Be sure to look back at the sweeping views of Mount Mansfield and the whole Ranch Valley. Continue skiing through old-growth birches, passing junctions with the Burt and Dewey trails, both of which return to the Stowe Mountain Resort Cross-Country Ski Center, the Burt Trail making the nicer descent route. However, it's worth continuing on the Underhill Trail to reach the best downhill skiing: the Steeple Trail, 0.6 miles ahead. Pass the Upper Steeple Cutoff (this links with the Dewey Trail) and continue until you reach the four-way junction of the Underhill Trail, Lower Steeple Cutoff, and the Steeple Trail. You are intersecting the Steeple in the middle; the upper third of the trail is above you and starts from the Skytop Trail (see tour 39, Steeple Trail, on page 223, for a description of the whole trail). Swing many turns down the Steeple Trail until it ends on the Dewey Trail. Turn right, and you will quickly arrive on the groomed Burt Trail at the Stowe Mountain Resort Cross-Country Ski Center. Turn right again on the Burt Trail, and ski back to the cross-country center in 1.5 miles.

The Ranch Valley Grand Tour is a multicourse feast that encompasses every type of skiing, from a powder descent, to backcountry touring in a wild and beautiful landscape, to double-poling or skating your way home on groomed trails. Bon appétit.

③⑧ SKYTOP TRAIL

This high-elevation ridge trail with spectacular views of Mount Mansfield and the surrounding peaks connects numerous backcountry ski trails of the Trapp Family Lodge and Stowe Mountain Resort Cross-Country Ski Center.

Distance: 2.8 miles, Skytop Trail from Rob George Saddle to Dewey Saddle, one way; 9.8 miles, Skytop Trail tour from Trapp Family Lodge, round trip; 8.3 miles, Skytop Trail tour from Stowe Mountain Resort Cross-Country Ski Center, round trip
Elevation: *Start*: 1,100 feet (Stowe Mountain Resort Cross-Country Ski Center), 1,350 feet (Trapp Family Lodge); *Highest point*: 2,960 feet; *Vertical drop*: 1,610 feet (Trapp Family Lodge), 1,860 feet (Stowe)
Maps: *Mansfield Region Backcountry Trail Map* (MapleRidge Solutions), *Northern Vermont Hiking & Biking Trails* (Map Adventures)
Difficulty: Moderate/more difficult
Gear: Telemark, AT, snowboard
Fee: The Skytop Trail can be reached from either the Trapp Family Lodge or Stowe Mountain Resort cross-country ski centers. You must purchase a trail pass from whichever ski center you begin your tour.
Additional Information: Trapp Family Lodge, 802-253-8511, trappfamily.com; Stowe Mountain Resort Cross-Country Ski Center, 802-253-3000, stowe.com

HOW TO GET THERE

The Stowe Mountain Resort Cross-Country Ski Center (*GPS coordinates*: 44° 30.348′ N, 72° 45.710′ W) is located 5.5 miles up the Mountain Road (VT 108) from the village of Stowe. To reach the Trapp Family Lodge Cross-Country Ski Center (*GPS coordinates*: 44° 27.873′ N, 72° 44.727′ W), drive 2 miles up the Mountain Road in Stowe, turn left on Luce Hill Road, and continue for about 2 miles to the top of a long hill.

HISTORY

Cut by the Burt Lumber Company in the late 1930s, the Skytop Trail was originally used by skiers who wanted to make a loop trip from the Ranch Camp, the fabled skiers' lodge that was located in what is now the Stowe Mountain Resort Cross-Country Ski Center, to Conway Trail (now the Burt Trail). Craig Burt Sr., owner of the Burt Lumber Company, was an important force in the expansion of skiing in the Mount Mansfield area. Known as the "father of Stowe skiing," Burt was an avid skier himself, although according to the account of his son, Craig Burt Jr., he was no expert. His son told me how his father used to go ski touring with 8-foot-long double-grooved wood skis and one pole, which he used for braking. "His idea of

SKYTOP TRAIL

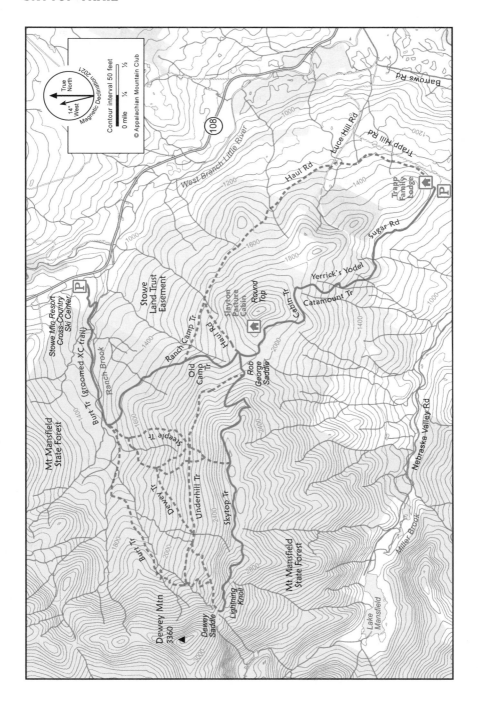

fun was to take his skis, one ski pole, and a shotgun and go out for a rabbit hunt," recalled Burt. "He would bushwhack around, but he seldom came home with a rabbit."

The elder Burt had his loggers open up trails in areas where they had already built logging roads. He wanted to link existing roads and trails to create a large network on which skiers could spend a full day touring. He was partly motivated by the fact that his sons were enthusiastic skiers. Burt was responsible for a number of other ski trails and related developments on Mount Mansfield (see tour 37, Bruce Trail, for this history).

When Johannes von Trapp began looking into opening a lodge and cross-country ski center in the Mount Mansfield valley in the 1960s, it occurred to him that the abandoned 1930s-era ski trails would be perfect for developing again. In spring 1969, he climbed up to the Skytop ridge and went in search of the old blazes. He found most of them and even came across an old first-aid cache in Dewey Saddle. Von Trapp says that he tried to have the new Skytop Trail follow the old route as much as possible. He credits the high quality of the wilderness trails in today's Trapp Family network to the fact that Craig Burt Sr. was so meticulous in the way he cut logging roads. These woods roads were well leveled and cut with a moderate grade since they had to be negotiated by oxen or horses.

THE TOUR

The Skytop Trail is one of the prettiest ski tours in Vermont. The trail follows a 1.6-mile-long ridge that lies in the heart of the rugged Mount Mansfield region. Traveling along the lee side of the ridge, it is common to find fresh powder on Skytop even when snow is sparse in the valleys below. With its knolls, hollows, and high clearings, Skytop is a small, romantic world, a place to retreat to from the madding crowds.

The Skytop Trail offers pristine forest skiing at a high elevation with superb views. Add to this its relatively easy access—it can be reached from two cross-country ski centers in Stowe. Skytop is also a gateway to other excellent backcountry trails such as the Steeple, the Dewey, and the Burt trails. All of this combines to make the Skytop Trail an excellent introduction to backcountry skiing.

Your first decision on this ski tour is to decide which direction to ski Skytop. The fastest approach is to climb on groomed trails from either Stowe Mountain Resort or Trapps. This brings you to the Rob George Saddle, from where you would ski the trail from east to west. The saddle, named for the farmer who once lived there, is a large clearing with views of all the surrounding peaks. If you climb to Skytop from the Rob George Saddle, you would ski to Dewey Saddle and descend the Burt Trail to the Underhill Trail, which is a fun, moderately steep and twisty run; this is the most challenging section of the tour. Alternatively, you can climb the Burt Trail and ski Skytop east to Rob George Saddle. Approaching this way usually takes about an hour longer to reach the ridge, but you can enjoy the solitude of climbing on backcountry trails. Finally, you can simply ski out Skytop as far as you like, then turn around and backtrack the way you came. Either way, skiing the full Skytop Trail takes most of a pleasant day.

If you start at the Stowe Mountain Resort Cross-Country Ski Center, the fastest approach is to ski up to the Rob George Saddle via Old Camp Trail. If you are skiing west to east, climb on either the Burt or the Dewey trail to Dewey Saddle (3.3 miles), from where you climb to Lightning Knoll (2,960 feet), the highest point on the Skytop ridge, and take in views of the whole Ranch Valley on the south side of Mount Mansfield.

To reach the Skytop Trail from the Trapp Family Lodge, ski to the Slayton Pasture Cabin, where you can stop for a snack and hot chocolate. Then follow Cabin Trail a short distance to the Rob George Saddle, which is 2.6 miles from Trapp Family Lodge. As you look at Mount Mansfield from the saddle, the Skytop Trail goes off to the left. The trail quickly enters the forest and begins to climb steadily on old woods roads. Climbing skins are not essential but helpful, especially in deep snow. After a half-mile of climbing, the trail turns sharply south and begins to contour until it reaches the long ridge that gives the tour its character and its name. A sign indicates a scenic vista at the beginning of the ridge where there are views to Camel's Hump.

The Skytop Trail travels on rolling terrain between 2,800 and 2,900 feet along the top of the ridge. The trail meanders around small knolls and snakes its way through white and yellow birches. The forested ridge refracts the southern light, throwing zebra-like stripes across the snow and the forest floor. The feeling up here is quiet and magical. Moose, deer, and other animals prance around freely on the ridge, unaccustomed to seeing people.

Heading out on the Skytop Trail. *Photo by Brian Mohr/EmberPhoto*

About 1.5 miles from the Rob George Saddle, you reach the junction of the Skytop and Steeple trails. If you are ready to begin your trip back, the Steeple is a fast, fun, but steep descent that you can take to the Underhill Trail and loop back to Trapp's, or you can continue skiing all the way down to Stowe Mountain Resort Cross-Country Ski Center (see tour 39, Steeple Trail, page 223 for more details). If you are continuing west along the Skytop Trail, you eventually come to Lightning Knoll, 1.4 miles past the Steeple. Stop here and ski to the overlook, where you can take in a beautiful vista of Mount Mansfield. Just beyond Lightning Knoll, notice a caution sign on a tree. This is your only warning that you are about to drop steeply on a narrow trail into Dewey Saddle, the col that separates Dewey Mountain, a trail-less peak, from the Skytop ridge. Many skiers opt to sidestep down this steep section. Dewey Saddle marks the end of the Skytop Trail and the start of the Burt Trail.

The Burt Trail is a fun descent through an open hardwood forest. This was formerly the Conway Trail, one of the popular down-mountain ski trails cut by Craig Burt Sr. that fed into the Ranch Valley. Conway was the name of a logging camp in the valley. The Burt Trail soon comes to a junction with the Dewey Trail then the Underhill Trail. The Dewey Trail offers the option of a slightly longer ungroomed downhill run back to the Stowe Mountain Resort Cross-Country Ski Center. Beware of stream crossings lower down on both the Dewey and the Burt trails.

The best option for returning to the Trapp Family Lodge after skiing down the top of the Burt Trail is to return on the red-blazed Underhill Trail. This is a mostly flat, ungroomed ski 2.7 miles back to the Rob George Saddle. All junctions are clearly marked with trail signs.

39 STEEPLE TRAIL

The Steeple Trail is a thrilling, steep descent of a classic 1930s-era down-mountain ski trail in the shadow of Mount Mansfield.

Distance: 1.2 miles, from Skytop Trail (top) to Burt Trail (bottom), one way; 9 miles, from Trapp Family Lodge, round trip; 6.7 miles, from Stowe Mountain Resort Cross-Country Ski Center, round trip
Elevation: *Start/Highest point*: 2,800 feet; *Finish*: 1,100 feet (Stowe Mountain Resort Cross-Country Ski Center), 1,350 feet (Trapp Family Lodge); *Vertical drop*: 1,450–1,700 feet depending on starting point
Maps: *Mansfield Region Backcountry Trail Map* (MapleRidge Solutions), *Northern Vermont Hiking & Biking Trails* (Map Adventures)
Difficulty: Most difficult, Upper Steeple; More difficult, Lower Steeple
Gear: AT, telemark, snowboard
Fee: You must purchase a trail pass wherever you begin this tour
Additional Information: Stowe Mountain Resort Cross-Country Ski Center, 802-253-3000, stowe.com; Trapp Family Lodge, 802-253-8511, trappfamily.com

HOW TO GET THERE
The Steeple Trail can be reached via the groomed ski trails of either the Stowe Mountain Resort Cross-Country Ski Center (*GPS coordinates*: 44° 30.348′ N, 72° 45.710′ W) or Trapp Family Lodge (*GPS coordinates*: 44° 27.873′ N, 72° 44.727′ W).

HISTORY
If you mention "Stowe" and "steeple," most people naturally assume you are referring to the stately white tower of the Stowe Community Church that has stood watch over the town since 1863. But for skiers in search of a religious experience, the Steeple they have long sought in Stowe is a fabulous, steep, powder-choked trail that resides high in the Ranch Valley. This is the Steeple Trail, one of Vermont's earliest, and still among its best, backcountry ski trails.

The Steeple Trail was cut by volunteers in 1937 at the same time as the Perry Merrill Trail, which is still in use today as an alpine ski trail within Stowe Mountain Resort. The Steeple was intended to expand the variety of ski tours around Mount Mansfield. All the new ski trails were connected, providing interesting and varied ski touring. An article about skiing in Stowe in a 1938 issue of *The Ski Bulletin* explained:

> Since the Trails Committee [of the Mount Mansfield Ski Club] has made an effort to take advantage of as many connections as possible and to develop circular routes, most of the trails are interconnected. . . . The Trails Committee developed its work with the purpose of meeting three needs: first, an outstanding down-mountain racing trail, such as the Nose Dive, and a jump; second, a system of trails that intermediate skiers would find interesting, yet within their ability; and third, trails for skiers who add to their skiing the love of photography or of the all-day trip.

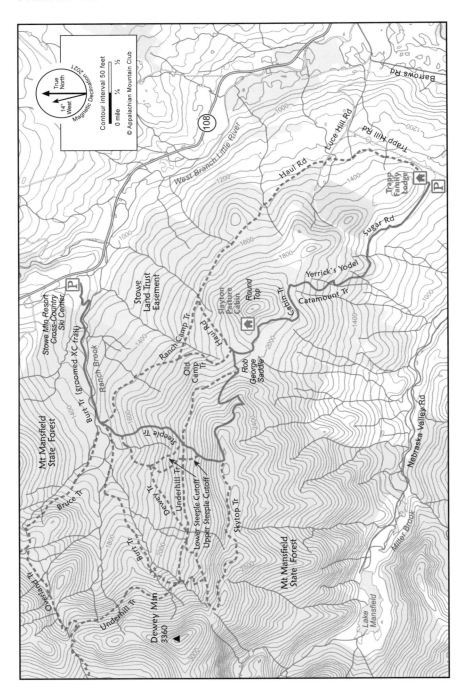

Many of the ski tours around Mount Mansfield were intentionally designed as ambitious outings. People had traveled far to Stowe, and to them, a good ski tour should take a full day. There were plans to link the trails of the Ranch Valley south to Bolton Mountain (later achieved with the Bolton–Trapp Trail) and to extend north all the way to Morristown.

The Steeple, along with the Bruce Trail, started directly from the Ranch Camp, a rustic cabin used as a base for adventuring by Mount Mansfield's earliest ski bums (see tour 37, Bruce Trail, page 211, for a history of the Ranch Camp). The Steeple rises 1,400 feet to where it meets the Skytop Trail. *The Ski Bulletin* asserted in 1938, "The Steeple Trail is not designed as a racing trail, but is a fast run requiring controlled skiing." A 1939 ski guidebook described the Steeple as "a fast run with excellent scenic effect. The upper half-mile is very steep and trees have been left in several places, making controlled skiing a necessity." It was rated as an "expert and intermediate" run.

There are several explanations about how the Steeple got its name. By one account, skiers thought it was "steeper than hell" or "like the side of a steeple." Another version of the story is that the peak it descends was once called Steeple Mountain.

By the 1950s, the Steeple Trail had vanished into the forest. Unlike the Bruce Trail, which could be accessed by a chairlift, the Steeple required a tithe of sweat equity from its devotees. Like so many trails that required skiers to earn their turns, the Steeple simply disappeared.

Then came the resurrection. In the mid-1990s, John Higgins and Jeff Baldwin, then the director and head groomer of the Stowe Mountain Resort Cross-Country Ski Center, found and recut the Steeple with the help of local volunteers. Higgins, a ski history buff who died in 2001, told me that his motivation was simple. "We wanted to ski it," he declared. "We had always skied off the Skytop Ridge. We had heard about the Steeple, but we didn't know where it went." His friends dismissed the notion that there was an old down-mountain trail there and bet him a case of beer that it didn't exist. Sufficiently intrigued and motivated, Higgins found old maps, and then he and Baldwin rediscovered some of the old tin-can trail blazes on the trees. He won his bet and restored a great ski run to boot. Higgins and Baldwin were also responsible for restoring the Houston Trail—which runs from the Mount Mansfield Toll Road to the old Ranch Camp site—and for recutting the Dewey Trail (formerly the Edson Dewey), which parallels the Burt Trail almost to the Dewey Saddle. This labor of love by these latter-day trailblazers restored the luster to the Ranch Valley. Today, it is again a thriving hub of backcountry skiing in the East.

THE TOUR

The top of the Steeple leaves from the Skytop Trail. If you want to ski the Steeple from the top, the approach is the same as for Skytop. From the Stowe Mountain Resort Cross-Country Ski Center, head out on the groomed Burt Trail, skiing alongside the scenic Ranch Brook. At 1.5 miles, you come to a major junction of five

Finding religion: the Steeple Trail brings out the faithful. *Photo by Brian Mohr/EmberPhoto*

trails. To reach the Skytop Trail from here, ski up the wide, groomed Ranch Camp Trail, then turn right on Old Camp. This delivers you to the large, scenic clearing known as the Rob George Saddle, where you can pick up the ungroomed Skytop Trail, which you can ski to the top of the Steeple (see tour 38, Skytop Trail, page 218, for details). If you are starting from Trapps, ski past the Slayton Pasture Cabin on Cabin Trail to the Rob George Saddle, and the entrance to the Skytop Trail is on your left. The distance to the top of the Steeple Trail via either the Stowe Mountain Resort or Trapp Family Lodge cross-country ski centers is about 4 miles and typically takes about two hours to reach the start.

For a shorter tour that still packs plenty of downhill turns, you can ski just the lower two-thirds of Steeple. From the Rob George Saddle, ski out on the ungroomed, red-blazed Underhill Trail for 1.3 miles until the junction with the Steeple. This bypasses the steepest 650 vertical feet of the Steeple, which is half the vertical on this tour. Another way to reach this midway junction on the Steeple is to ski up the Dewey Trail from the Stowe Mountain Resort Cross-Country Ski Center. From the five-way junction on the Burt Trail, ski 0.8 miles up the Dewey Trail to a three-way junction with the Lower Steeple Cutoff and the Upper Steeple Cutoff. You can continue up the Dewey, which climbs moderately but takes a more circuitous route via the Underhill Trail to the Steeple. Or you can take the Lower Steeple Cutoff, which climbs steeply to join the Steeple at the Underhill Trail. Finally, you can take the Upper Steeple Cutoff, which crosses the Underhill Trail and connects with the Steeple at 2,300 feet, just below the steep headwall near the top of the trail. The Upper Steeple Cutoff is a steep climb; it is normally skied as a downhill variation when starting from the top of the Steeple.

Finally, you can ski the Steeple Trail as part of a Ranch Valley Grand Tour. See the description of this full-day outing in tour 37, Bruce Trail, page 216.

Starting from the Skytop Trail, the Steeple draws you in slowly. It drifts down through tall birch trees, steadily picking up speed. Suddenly, the trail narrows and drops precipitously over a steep headwall. This section is stumpy and rocky and needs a good deal of snow to be skiable. Climbing straight up the Steeple is not recommended because you likely will scrape off the snow that you plan to ski in this section. Below the headwall, the Upper Steeple Cutoff enters just below a giant rock, where the Steeple jogs to the right. The Steeple stays in the fall line but eases off here, and you can take more leisurely turns through the trees. Giant old birches grace the trail for you to carve turns around.

After 0.4 miles, the Steeple crosses the Underhill Trail where the Lower Steeple Cutoff also joins. Below here, the Steeple moderates, but there are plenty of turns yet to come. A solid snowplow with a few good turns to check your speed should suffice on this section. Higgins recut the trail leaving plenty of trees, making this lower section an enjoyable low-angle glade. You finally return to the junction with the groomed Burt and Bruce trails. Cross-country skiers may ogle you curiously here, wondering why you are covered in snow and smiling from ear to ear.

The Steeple is a thrilling classic run that alternately hurtles and rolls down the mountain. Throughout the tour, you are treated to nice views over the Ranch Valley and to the Green Mountains beyond. The prize of the Steeple is reserved for those who invest the effort required to reach it. Once you ski it, you are sure to become one of the faithful.

40 NEBRASKA NOTCH AND DEWEY MOUNTAIN

Two tours that share a trailhead showcase the excellent skiing on the west side of Mount Mansfield. The first is a ski tour into the dramatic and scenic Nebraska Notch. The second tour is on the Overland Ski Trail and accesses excellent glade skiing on Dewey Mountain.

Distance: 4.8 miles, Stevensville Road trailhead to Nebraska Notch, round trip; 2.5 miles, Stevensville Road trailhead to top of Dewey Mountain glades, round trip
Elevation: *Start*: 1,400 feet, Stevensville Road; *Highest point*: 1,800 feet (Nebraska Notch), 2,800 feet (Dewey Mountain glades); *Vertical drop*: 400 feet (Nebraska Notch), 1,400 feet (Dewey Mountain)
Maps: *Mansfield Region Backcountry Trail Map* (MapleRidge Solutions), *Northern Vermont Hiking & Biking Trails* (Map Adventures)
Difficulty: More difficult, Nebraska Notch; More difficult+, Dewey Mountain
Gear: AT, telemark, snowboard

HOW TO GET THERE

From Underhill Center: Take Pleasant Valley Road north for 0.2 miles, then turn right (east) onto Stevensville Road and follow for 1.1 miles. Where the main road turns sharply left onto Maple Leaf Road, drive straight ahead for 1.7 miles until you reach the parking lot for Nebraska Notch and the Overland trails (*GPS coordinates*: 44° 30.365′ N, 72° 50.660′ W). This parking lot is often filled by 10 A.M. on weekends, so get an early start. There is a small overflow winter parking lot on the corner of Maple Leaf Road.

Warning: The final mile of Stevensville Road to the trailhead parking lot is narrow, uphill, and often icy. Road signs recommend snow tires and 4-wheel-drive vehicles. Do not attempt this road in bad conditions unless you are confident that your vehicle can make it. Have a shovel and tow cable in your car, just in case.

THE TOUR

Nebraska Notch is the east-west passage between Mount Clark (2,969 feet) and Dewey Mountain (3,360 feet). It is an exceptionally pretty area, one of those gems you stumble across in your mountain travels that keeps drawing you back. At one time a road passed through the notch, allowing passage from Stevensville (now part of Underhill Center) to Moscow (part of Stowe). It was a rough winter road that was eventually abandoned, the only trace of it being the ski and hiking trail described here.

According to one local inn owner, "In most places, people cut roads up the valleys. But in Vermont, there was always some guy who had a girlfriend over the next ridge, so he cut a road over the top of the mountain." If that is the case, the labor of a lovelorn Vermonter is now a plum for skiers. This ski tour is a memorable half-day trip combining dramatic vistas with nice skiing.

NEBRASKA NOTCH AND DEWEY MOUNTAIN

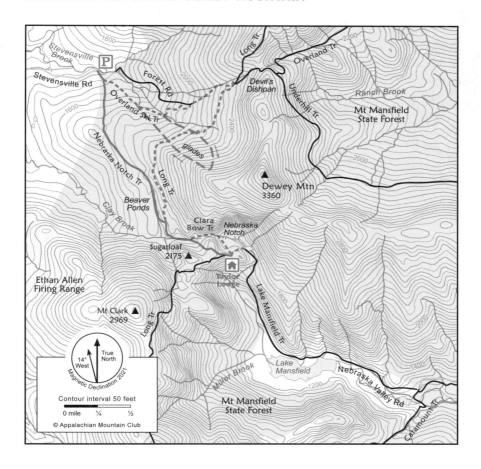

The Nebraska Notch Trail starts at the Stevensville Road trailhead in Underhill Center, which is a busy backcountry skiing hub for several excellent ski tours on the west side of Mount Mansfield. From this trailhead, a sign directs you to the right for Nebraska Notch Trail (signs may also refer to Taylor Lodge, which you pass on this tour). The trail forks after 0.2 miles; the Overland Ski Trail heads left, and the Nebraska Notch Trail heads right. I'll say more about the Overland Ski Trail later.

Continue on the Nebraska Notch Trail, which is marked with blue blazes, rising gently through open hardwoods. The grade is gradual enough that it typically does not require climbing skins. At 1.4 miles, the trail turns left and crosses a bridge; a sign beneath the treadway indicates that it was built by the Underhill Boy Scouts. Cross the bridge, and in about 25 feet an unmarked trail departs to the right, which goes

Backcountry skiing beneath the cliffs of Nebraska Notch.

directly out onto the first large beaver pond formed on Clay Brook. This is a useful shortcut because it eliminates a short climb and descent on the Long Trail (LT).

The ski across the pond is scenic and is a worthy destination unto itself. Nebraska Notch towers overhead. The bright white, open landscape of the pond, fringed by tall spruce and fir trees, provides a dramatic contrast with the tour in the woods. The pointy summit of Sugarloaf (2,175 feet) looms. Follow the shoreline around the left of the pond, finally reentering the woods at the left (north) point of the pond. Just 25 feet from the pond, pick up the LT and proceed straight ahead on rolling terrain.

The second pond offers more views of Nebraska Notch. At the east end of the second pond is a trail junction. You could turn around here and retrace your tracks, which would make for an enjoyable 4-mile round-trip tour with moderate skiing.

If you proceed, you ascend a steeper trail that requires climbing skins. Clara Bow Trail continues straight ahead, and the LT proceeds right for 0.4 miles to Taylor Lodge. Clara Bow Trail, described as "rough" on the sign, is a drainage strewn with house-sized boulders. The trail is among the wildest in the state—you scramble among the boulders, and at one point you must climb a short ice-encrusted ladder out of a cave. Clara Bow Trail is also sparsely blazed and difficult to follow and is not recommended for skiing.

The better choice is to follow the well-marked LT to the right. The LT makes a short, steep climb to a saddle then drops suddenly to Taylor Lodge, a three-sided wooden shelter maintained by the Green Mountain Club. The descent to Taylor Lodge is a narrow trail that is difficult to ski. I recommend that you walk down this short, steep section.

Taylor Lodge was constructed in 1978 and named for James P. Taylor, the founder of the Green Mountain Club. It is a spacious shelter that includes a porch, picnic tables, a loft, and sleeping room for fifteen. From Taylor Lodge, there is a view of Lake Mansfield below and the Skytop ridge up to the northeast. Lake Mansfield itself is humanmade, the dam having originally been built to enhance local fishing. The lake lies in the Nebraska Valley, the only glacial cirque in Vermont, which has long attracted the attention of geologists.

The main event is the east side of Nebraska Notch, which lies just beyond Taylor Lodge. From the lodge, follow signs to Lake Mansfield. The trail drops quickly to the beaver ponds, at which point you can turn left and ski on or alongside the ponds.

This side of Nebraska Notch is a primeval place. Stunted tree trunks stick up out of the white expanse of the beaver ponds. Black rock walls striped with fangs of ice soar overhead. Dull blue ice floes pour down from the summit of Dewey Mountain. It appears that the earth has been cleaved open here to reveal its bowels. The valley floor is dotted with glacial erratics that lie willy-nilly, as if hurled from the side of the mountain by some angry giant. On a sunny day, small ice avalanches cascade down the cliff. Birds shriek maniacally, streaking low across the valley bottom and then soaring upward on thermals. This is an otherworldly place made more dramatic in its winter guise.

To return, backtrack your route past Taylor Lodge, and hike up over a short hill and drop steeply (again, you might need to walk) to the ponds that you crossed on the other side. Once back on the Nebraska Notch Trail, you can ski a gentle downhill on the trail or through the open trees. This is a delightful, moderate downhill run on which you can link turns at your own pace. Steady ski and snowshoe traffic can make the trail feel as if it has been groomed. Enjoy the fast ride out from this magical hidden backcountry world.

DEWEY MOUNTAIN

The Nebraska Notch Trail wins for scenery, but Dewey Mountain offers more exciting skiing. The Dewey Mountain glades are reached via the Overland Ski Trail, which is blazed red and climbs through a striking birch forest. Skin up the Overland Ski Trail until a stream crossing at 1,800 feet, then bear right and follow a herd path and open woods to about 2,800 feet on the side of Dewey Mountain. From here, you can descend through a wide open birch forest for 1,000 vertical feet, rejoining the Overland Trail for the final ski back to the parking lot.

It is possible to ski a loop linking the Nebraska Notch and Dewey Mountain tours. Ski the Nebraska Notch Trail 1.5 miles to the LT and turn left (north) on the LT. Ski along the LT, which has a number of small stream crossings. In .75 miles, you reach the birch glades on Dewey Mountain. Choose a line and enjoy the descent.

41 STERLING VALLEY

Sterling Valley features exciting glade and trail skiing in scenic and historic mountain terrain.

Distance: 5.3 miles, Sterling Ridge Loop, round trip
Elevation: *Start/Finish*: 1,600 feet; *Highest point*: 3,200 feet; *Vertical drop*: 1,600 feet
Maps: *Mansfield Region Backcountry Trail Map* (MapleRidge Solutions), *Northern Vermont Hiking & Biking Trails* (Map Adventures)
Difficulty: More difficult
Gear: AT, snowboard, telemark

HOW TO GET THERE

From VT 100, turn onto Sterling Valley Road and drive 4.6 miles to Sterling Gorge Road. Plowed parking areas can be found on Sterling Gorge Road (*GPS coordinates*: 44° 32.367′ N, 72° 43.180′ W) or by continuing straight 0.1 miles on Sterling Valley Road at the Sterling Forest trailhead (*GPS coordinates*: 44° 32.523′ N, 72° 43.192′ W).

HISTORY

Just over a ridge from the jet-set ski resort of Stowe lies a pristine valley laced with open glades and backcountry ski trails. This is Sterling Valley, a prized local backcountry ski destination and a fine example of community-supported skiing. The town of Stowe, which owns Sterling Forest, invested in the area as a backcountry skiing destination by building trails and plowing parking areas. Local skiers have embraced it as a place to ski for an hour or a day.

Sterling Forest consists of 1,530 acres of public conservation land in Stowe that was purchased from former IBM Chairman Thomas Watson in 1995. The Vermont Department of Forest, Parks, and Recreation owns the land above 2,500 feet, which is part of the Mount Mansfield State Forest and includes the Long Trail.

Skiers today are plying the forgotten byways of the former town of Sterling, which was chartered by the Republic of Vermont in 1782. The first landowners were Revolutionary War veterans, and the town once had five school districts and several sawmills, but no post office, church, or store. The mountain ridges that protect Sterling Valley ultimately proved too inhospitable to support community life. The last farmers left the valley in the 1930s, and the town of Sterling was absorbed by Stowe and other neighboring towns.

The mountainous terrain that was so challenging for early settlers is now attracting a new generation. The highlight of the skiing in Sterling Forest is the open hardwood glades that grace the mountainsides. For skiers, there are few things as alluring as giant birch trees with a blank white canvas between them. That characterizes much of the terrain here.

STERLING VALLEY

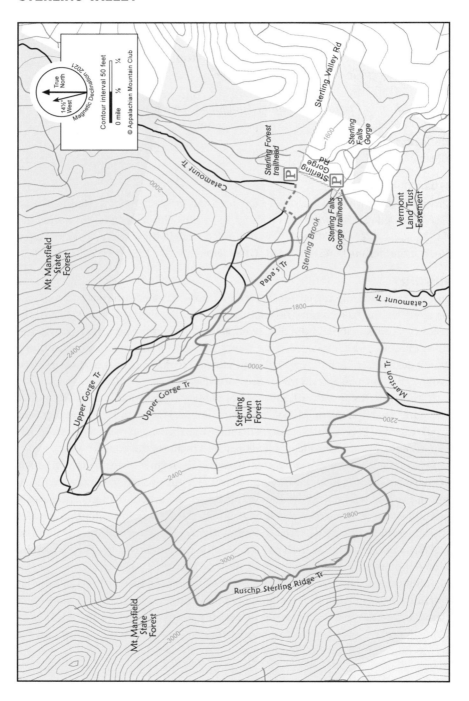

THE TOUR

There are many ways to ski Sterling Forest. A popular easy tour is to ski Upper Gorge Loop to Papa's Trail, a 3.7-mile round trip that starts and finishes at the Sterling Forest trailhead parking lot on Sterling Valley Road. This loop is easy rolling terrain that is best skied on lightweight metal-edged backcountry or telemark skis.

Downhill skiers and riders looking for steep and deep come to ski the powder off Ruschp Sterling Ridge Trail. There are three options here: skiing the glades on either the south or north end of Sterling Ridge or skiing the full Sterling Ridge traverse, which I describe here.

From the Sterling Gorge trailhead, take the footbridge or the road across the beautiful rocky chasm that is Sterling Gorge (*Note*: there is more parking at the Sterling Forest trailhead on Sterling Valley Road, where you can also begin this tour). Ski across a field following the blue plastic Catamount Trail (CT) blazes. The distinct profile of Sterling Ridge looms above. On the far side of the field, enter the woods as the trail becomes an old logging road, still following signs and blazes for the Catamount Trail South and Marston Trail. A short distance later, the CT diverges left; continue skiing straight ahead on Marston Trail. A mile from the parking lot, the yellow-blazed Ruschp Sterling Ridge Trail diverges right. The trail, which was cut in 2013 by local trail builder Hardy Avery, is named for Sepp Ruschp, the legendary Austrian ski instructor who founded the ski school at Stowe.

Ruschp Sterling Ridge Trail ascends for 0.8 miles through large open hardwoods. The upper section of the trail steepens until finally attaining Sterling Ridge. From here, you can turn right or left on the ridge and descend back through the forest that you climbed through, weaving through the trees and plunging through the powder.

For a longer tour, turn right (north) and continue along Sterling Ridge. In the first 0.4 miles you pass two viewpoints. The second one has spectacular views over Mount Mansfield and Spruce Peak, home of Stowe Mountain Resort, as well as Madonna Peak, home to Smuggler's Notch ski area. From your solitary perch on the ridge, peer down at the busy mountain metropolis that you left behind, with its hotels and skating rinks. Continue along the ridge, following Ruschp Sterling Ridge Trail.

After skiing on the ridge for a mile and enjoying intermittent views of the surrounding valleys, you reach a saddle. Look for yellow blazes and signs that point downhill, to the right. Follow Ruschp Sterling Ridge Trail as it broadens and snakes downward like the best down-mountain trails, such as the Bruce Trail on Mount Mansfield. This is classic Eastern trail skiing with plenty of room to make turns. As you reach the bottom, you cruise through gorgeous low-angle birch glades. You soon arrive at Upper Gorge Loop, the main thoroughfare in Sterling Forest. Bear right and ski across several bridges before turning sharply right on Papa's Trail (if you ski straight ahead, you reach the Sterling Forest trailhead on Sterling Valley Road), finally returning to the Sterling Gorge parking lot.

Carving sharp turns in soft snow in Sterling Valley.

42 WILLOUGHBY STATE FOREST

Willoughby State Forest offers a stunning ski tour with glade zones on Mount Hor and Bartlett Mountain. The Tour de Hor features fine glade skiing and world-class views of Lake Willoughby and the towering ice cliffs on Mount Pisgah.

Distance: 5.5 miles, Mount Hor and Bartlett Mountain tour, round trip
Elevation: *Start/Finish*: 1,300 feet; *Highest point*: 2,650 feet (Mount Hor), 2,045 feet (Bartlett Mountain); *Vertical drop*: 745–1,350 feet
Maps: *Northeast Kingdom* (Green Mountain Club), *Northern Vermont Hiking & Biking Trails* (Map Adventures). Download map of ski trails from Northeast Kingdom Backcountry Coalition, nekbc.org.
Difficulty: More difficult, Bartlett Mountain; Most difficult, Mount Hor
Gear: AT, telemark, snowboard

HOW TO GET THERE

From the south end of Lake Willoughby on VT 5A, drive south 0.6 miles to a large plowed parking area on the west side of the road (*GPS coordinates*: 44° 42.639′ N, 72° 01.447′ W). The CCC Road leaves from here.

HISTORY

Lake Willoughby, known as the "Lucerne of America," is the centerpiece of one of the most beautiful landscapes in Vermont. The comparison to Switzerland's famous Lake Lucerne, which is ringed by the Alps, is apt. The fjord-like appearance of Lake Willoughby is created by the steep granite slabs of Mount Pisgah to the east and Mount Hor to the west. The mountains rise precipitously from the water and appear like an open jaw—known as Willoughby Notch—swallowing up the southern end of the lake. The area has been designated a National Natural Landmark, a Vermont Natural Area, and is included in the Vermont Fragile Area Registry.

Willoughby Notch was formed about 2 million years ago when 10,000 feet of ice covered northern New England. As the ice sheet ground its way south to the ocean, it rode up the north side of mountains and calved off the south side. This phenomenon is evident on Mount Hor and on Wheeler and Haystack mountains. Willoughby Notch formed when a finger of the huge glacier reamed out an area of softer rock between Mounts Hor and Pisgah. Some of the glacial till formed the height-of-land at the south side of the lake. The final advance of the glacier pushed the rocks that were New England's mountains all the way to Long Island in New York.

Lake Willoughby and its surrounding peaks are steeped in colorful history. According to *Willoughby Lake: Legends and Legacies*, by Harriet F. Fisher, the lake is most likely named for the Willoughby brothers, lumbermen who held first title to lakefront property. The surrounding mountains draw their name from the bible. As Fisher notes, "Mount Pisgah is the place where the Lord sent Moses to view the Promised Land. . . . Aaron died at Mount Hor after the Lord commanded him to go there."

WILLOUGHBY STATE FOREST

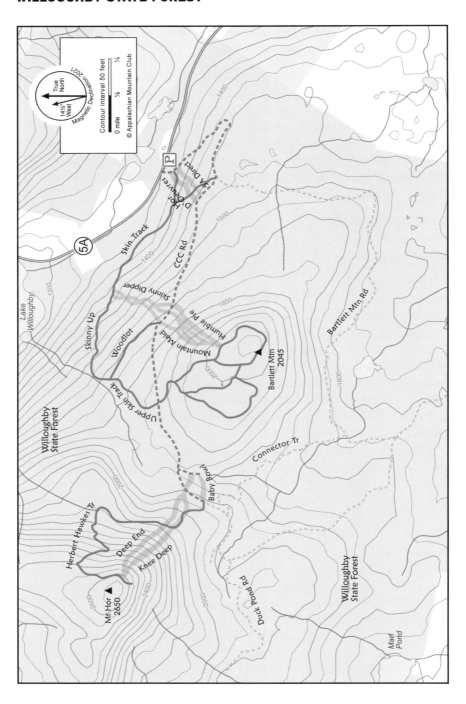

Contour interval 50 feet

True North

14½° West

Magnetic Declination 2021

© Appalachian Mountain Club

0 mile   ⅛   ¼   ⅜   ½

5A

Lake Willoughby

Willoughby State Forest

Skin Track

For Denyers

5A Direct

CCC Rd

Skinny Dipper

Skinny Up

Woodlot

Humble Pie

Mountain Maid

Upper Skin Track

Bartlett Mtn 2045

Bartlett Mtn Rd

Connector Tr

Baby Bowl

Herbert Hawkes Tr

Deep End

Knee Deep

Mt Hor 2650

Duck Pond Rd

Willoughby State Forest

Mud Pond

The lakefront road (now VT 5A) was built by a local tavern owner around 1850. He went broke putting in the road, but it may have helped bring people to his pub. In the 1870s, a 40-passenger steamship began operation on the lake. The boat continued operation until the early 1900s.

THE TOUR

Backcountry skiing in this area got a major boost in 2016, when the Northeast Kingdom Backcountry Coalition (NEKBC), a community-based group of local skiers, secured permission from the Vermont Department of Forests, Parks, and Recreation (FPR) to create glade zones in Willoughby State Forest. NEKBC volunteers and FPR staff cut a variety of glades, ranging from very steep lines on Mount Hor to intermediate runs on Bartlett Mountain. I describe the "Tour de Hor": skiing both mountains in one tour.

Skiing in Willoughby State Forest is like skiing in nature's art museum. Each vista is more impressive than the last. Mount Hor features 1,000-foot cliffs that plunge directly into Lake Willoughby. This precipitous drop-off to the east makes the mountain a particularly dramatic perch from which to view the surrounding scenery.

Starting from the parking lot on VT 5A, ski up the wide CCC Road, which is groomed for cross-country skiing. Climb south for about 200 feet and bear right at a junction, heading back toward the lake. Ski due west, quickly coming to a sweeping view of Mount Pisgah and Lake Willoughby. Stop to take in the magnificent vista—it is one of the best on the tour.

Across the lake is the 1,000-foot-high ice wall that forms on the west face of Mount Pisgah. Look closely and you may see ice climbers crabbing their way skyward. Willoughby, as this climbing area is known, boasts some of the most demanding ice climbs in the United States. This enormous curtain of blue and white ice extends about 1 mile. Beyond it are the rolling hills of the Northeast Kingdom.

As you continue west on the CCC Road, the forest opens up on either side the road, and you likely will see ski tracks. This is the midpoint of the Bartlett Mountain glade zone (more on these following a description of skiing Mount Hor.)

At 1.8 miles, pass a large sign for Willoughby State Forest. Turn right at this sign, and immediately come to another sign for the Herbert Hawkes Trail. This trail is named for the director of the Westmore Association Trails Committee who originally proposed a path up Mount Hor. The trail that now bears his name was cut around 1970, shortly after the state of Vermont purchased some 5,000 acres of land including Mount Hor, which became part of Willoughby State Forest. This state forest, established in 1928, covers 7,300 acres and encompasses Mount Hor, Mount Pisgah, Bartlett Mountain, and other peaks.

Skin up the Herbert Hawkes Trail, which follows a woods road for much of its way. Follow blue blazes along a wide forest path, and meander gradually up through the forest. Bear right at one point where an old woods road continues directly ahead up the hill and the Herbert Hawkes Trail veers off to the north. At 0.4 miles, the trail takes a sharp left turn up a small drainage. The trail steepens, until finally arriving at a trail junction at 0.7 miles. This is the summit ridge of Mount Hor.

For a scenic detour, turn right (north) on the summit ridge. In 0.3 miles, you pass a junction with Moose Mountain Trail; in 0.6 miles, reach East Lookout, which is about 100 feet farther downhill. You would be wise to remove skis here and walk down to the viewpoint—it is the top of a cliff!

East Lookout offers views directly across at the stunning Willoughby ice cliffs. Look straight down, and you are peering into the jaws of Willoughby Gap, which you now stand atop.

Back at the Herbert Hawkes Trail junction, turn left and ski 0.3 miles to the south summit of Mount Hor, a wild place with gnarled trees, evidence of the intense weather that buffets this peak. From the top, there are view of a series of ponds, including Vail and Duck ponds. Off in the distance are Burke Mountain, Hazen's Notch, and several of the northern Green Mountains.

You have several descent options from the summit of Mount Hor. The moderate option is to descend the way you came up, following the Herbert Hawkes Trail. The trail follows a sidehill at the start until turning left and dropping down through open hardwoods. You can ski virtually anywhere and be assured of crossing your tracks from the climb. This is a fun couple miles of cruising.

The other option from the top of Mount Hor is to ski the steep glade lines cut by the NEKBC. Knee Deep and Deep End are expert runs that plunge down the rocky flanks of Mount Hor through a well-gladed forest. The steep summit section gives way to lower-angle glades at bottom. Once back at the CCC Road, continue

Admiring the mile-wide ice cliffs of Mount Pisgah in Willoughby State Forest.

across the road and finish with the short moderate glades of Baby Bowl. It is an 800-vertical-foot descent from the summit to the bottom of Baby Bowl.

Skin back up to the CCC Road, turn right (east), and ski a quarter-mile to a trail junction with the Bartlett Mountain Loops. Turn right and ski up this groomed ski trail 0.3 miles, stopping to take in the views, which get better as you ascend. From the top of Bartlett Mountain there is another breathtaking panorama of the ice cliffs.

Trail signs mark the different glade zones below with names like Humble Pie and Mountain Maid. These are braided lines that you can weave between. Excellent intermediate skiing leads you back to the CCC Road. Continue across the road into Skinny Dipper, a delightful intermediate glade named for a famous nude beach on the south end of Lake Willoughby.

At the bottom of Skinny Dipper, turn right and ski the skin track toward the parking lot. Just above the cars, drop down to your car via two final glades, Hors D'Oeuvres and 5A Direct. This is a fun finale to your Tour de Hor.

43 BIG JAY

The descent of the steep, trailless east face of Big Jay is a stunning and exciting backcountry powder run.

Distance: 3.5 miles, Jay Peak to Big Jay Summit to VT 242, one way
Elevation: *Start/Finish*: 1,577 feet (VT 242), 1,800 feet (Jay Peak Ski Area); *Highest point*: 3,858 (Jay Peak), 3,779 feet (Big Jay); *Vertical drop*: 2,000–2,281 feet
Maps: *Northern Vermont Hiking & Biking Trails* (Map Adventures), *Vermont's Long Trail* (Wilderness Map/Green Mountain Club). These maps show the terrain, but not the ski tour.
Difficulty: Most difficult
Gear: AT, telemark, snowboard
Fee: You can access Big Jay from Jay Peak Resort, either by purchasing a lift ticket and taking the tramway to the summit or by skiing uphill through the Jay Peak trail network (check jaypeakresort.com for current uphill skiing policy). Big Jay is outside the ski area boundary and Jay Peak Resort does not provide information about this ski tour.

HOW TO GET THERE

Option 1: Take VT 242 to Jay Peak Resort, where you can park (*GPS coordinates*: 44° 56.320′ N, 72° 30.299′ W). Purchase a lift ticket and ride the aerial tramway to the summit or skin up. See ski directions below.

Option 2: Ski up from VT 242 into the Big Jay basin, where there are extensive natural glades to ski. From the top of Jay Pass on VT 242, drive south about 1.8 miles until you see a parking pullout on the right (north) side of the road (*GPS coordinates*: 44° 53.743′ N, 72° 31.372′ W), which is across the street from a gated logging road. From the parking pullout, ski north up a logging road to the boundary of the Jay State Forest (sign), continuing uphill into the horseshoe-shaped Big Jay basin.

HISTORY

Hikers and skiers have long peered out from the summit of Jay Peak into the wild and seemingly inaccessible reaches of the surrounding mountains. There are views from the rocky summit out over the Cold Hollow Mountains, a trailless mountain range to the south, as well as glimpses of Mount Mansfield and the Adirondacks.

One nearby mountain is particularly alluring. As you step off the Jay Peak aerial tramway, you peer directly at the steep flanks of Big Jay, the trailless peak to the southwest. The sister peaks are joined by a long ridge that curves around to form a horseshoe. A large trackless basin lies between the two mountains. Skiers have long been probing this basin in search of powder shots. The most captivating prospect is a prominent white chute that splits the east face of Big Jay.

For many years, the few intrepid skiers who ventured out to Big Jay would describe to disbelieving friends the powdery riches they had to themselves. But as

BIG JAY

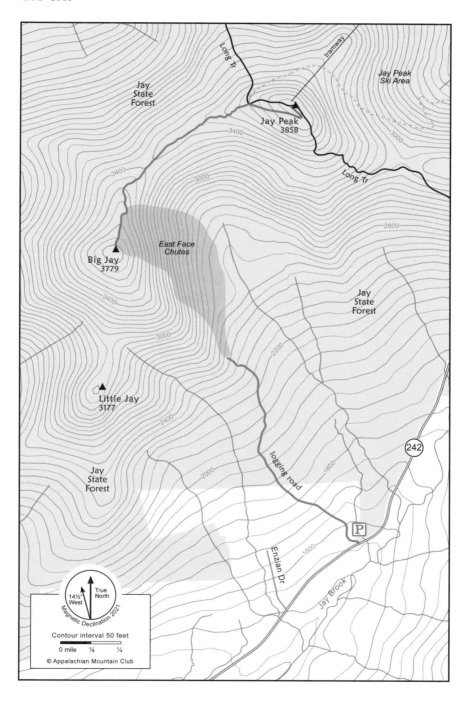

Jay State Forest

Long Tr

tramway

Jay Peak Ski Area

3000

Jay Peak
3858

Long Tr

3400

3400

3000

2600

East Face
Chutes

Big Jay
3779

Jay State Forest

3400

3000

2200

Little Jay
3177

242

2400

logging road

1800

Jay State Forest

2000

2000

P

Enzian Dr

1600

Jay Brook

True North

14½°
West

Magnetic Declination 2021

Contour interval 50 feet

0 mile   ⅛   ¼

© Appalachian Mountain Club

skiers and snowboarders pushed their quest for adventure farther into untamed lands, word about the powder fields hidden on Big Jay spread like fire in dry grass.

If you are on a quest for steep and deep, Big Jay is your promised land.

Jay Peak Resort has long boasted of having the greatest natural snowfall in the East. That is debatable, but Jay Peak is typically better endowed with snow than are mountains to its south. It is also less traveled than the big resorts in central and southern Vermont, which translates into reliable fresh tracks for powderhounds who make the trip to this outpost on the Canadian border.

Big Jay is the second-highest peak without a maintained trail in the Green Mountains. The mountain is home to a variety of plant and wildlife habitats, including the peregrine falcon, Canada lynx, and Bicknell's thrush, which lives on the summit. The mountain was included as part of 5,337 acres that was purchased in 1993 and 2001 by the Green Mountain Club (GMC), with the help of the Vermont Housing & Conservation Board, for the Long Trail Protection Campaign. This parcel, which is now part of the Jay State Forest, also includes 1.3 miles of the Long Trail. The GMC holds a conservation easement on Big Jay, ensuring that the mountain will remain undeveloped.

Protecting Big Jay from those who would love it to death has proven challenging. This wild mountain has suffered repeated indignities at the hands of skiers, all in the name of "improving" an experience that has never needed any help. In 1998, a Jay Peak Resort crew cut an illegal trail all the way to the summit of this wild mountain to make it easier to ski. This explains why there is now a trail to the summit of this officially trailless peak. The resort paid a fine and had to remediate the damage. In 2007, two Northeast Kingdom men cut a 2,000-foot gash down the face of Big Jay through a beautiful glade. They received a suspended sentence and were ordered to perform community service. Their line is now known as Jailhouse Chute.

Skiers bear a special responsibility to do no further harm to Big Jay. To be clear: *There should be no further trail cutting on Big Jay.* The natural corridors provide plenty of room for skiers and riders, and the special character of this mountain derives from its remoteness and its natural state. If you can't hack it, don't hack it.

Big Jay remains a memorable ski descent in a beautiful, if altered, environment.

THE TOUR

From the Jay Peak aerial tramway, follow signs to descend on Northway Ski Trail. Follow the ski trail around a hairpin turn, continue for another 100 yards, and arrive at a wood fence, behind which is a clearly marked ski area boundary. Signs warn that you are leaving the ski area and entering Jay State Forest. The sign also notes that the backcountry access gate is "not open, closed, or patrolled" and strongly recommends that you depart for Big Jay no later than 1 P.M. If you ski beyond this point, you may be billed for rescue if one is needed. Suffice it to say that you have been warned. Just because you are starting at a ski area, do not treat this as a casual

Big air on Big Jay. *Photo by Arnaud Côté Boisvert*

resort run. This is a bona fide backcountry tour and you should carry the appropriate clothing, food, equipment, and repair gear in case of mishaps.

The trail to Big Jay begins beyond the ski area boundary signs. It is 1 mile from the ski area boundary to the Big Jay summit, almost entirely on an unmarked, unblazed trail. Begin by descending a well-defined trail for about 50 feet. This is the Long Trail (LT), Vermont's 272-mile hiking trail. After about 50 feet, turn sharply left off the LT and proceed on an unmarked trail that heads southwest toward Big Jay. *Do not continue on the white-blazed Long Trail* (it is 7.6 miles of slogging to the nearest road if you do). The trail to Big Jay stays atop a well-defined ridge, descends for about 220 feet to a saddle, then climbs steeply for 400 feet to gain the summit. You need climbing skins or snowshoes to negotiate this trail. The trail generally follows the south side of the ridge, affording good views into the bowl between Jay Peak and Big Jay. Avoid the temptation to veer to the north side of the ridge; it does not lead to the summit and might lure you into the inaccessible Black Falls basin. On the final steep section of the climb, spectacular views extend from Mount Washington in New Hampshire to Mount Marcy in New York. You are overlooking some of the wildest stretches of the Vermont mountains here. That is one of the appeals of this tour.

Follow the herd path and stop just north of (i.e., before you reach) the Big Jay summit. This is the easiest access point to the East Face, where the best skiing is. Bear gently right as you start descending (if you ski from the summit, you will want to bear left as you descend). You suddenly arrive in the large chute that is visible from Jay Peak. A prominent shot plunges straight downhill. Enjoy your first of many face shots here. This steep shot soon opens into Jailhouse Chute. There are multiple lines of descent through the trees. Passageways open and close below you. This is the magic of Big Jay, where each skier and rider finds his or her own personal adventure, mining this peak for the deepest powder you are likely to find anywhere.

As you continue your descent, you are aimed directly at Jay Peak. Take your time and enjoy the ride. Do not descend all the way to the valley floor, where there is a stream, as this can be a slog in deep, unbroken snow. Instead, take a traverse line to the right about 150 feet above the valley floor. Keep traversing to the right (south), breaking over the shoulder of Big Jay. The hardwood forest opens as you traverse out. Continue bearing right until you finally pick up logging roads that head down to VT 242, emerging approximately 1.8 miles south of Jay Pass. From here, you can hitchhike back to the ski area to retrieve your car.

There is much more skiing in the Big Jay basin than just the east face of Big Jay. As you ski out, take note of the extensive natural hardwood glades on your right on the flanks of Little Jay. For those who access the Big Jay basin by skiing up from VT 242, these extensive glades will reward you with many fine runs.

On your return, show off your photos to your disbelieving friends of just how deep it can get in the Eastern outback.

This section includes a number of excellent ski tours in Vermont worth exploring. Community-supported ski zones are proliferating throughout the state. Check the website of the Catamount Trail Association (catamounttrail.org) to see if there is a glade zone near you. The 300-mile Catamount Trail itself offers excellent easy skiing throughout the Green Mountain State.

44a. DUTCH HILL, Readsboro, Vermont

Dutch Hill Ski Area was among Vermont's earlier ski resorts, operating from 1944 to 1985. The small ski area had a T-bar, J-bar, and a rope tow, but it could not compete with the larger resorts and was eventually abandoned. The land became part of the Green Mountain National Forest (GMNF), which explored ways to expand recreation opportunities. In 2017, backcountry skiers formed the Dutch Hill Alliance of Skiers and Hikers (DHASH), a chapter of the Catamount Trail Association. DHASH volunteers cleared old ski trails and cut new glades under GMNF direction. Dutch Hill (2,469 feet) is a ski area again—for backcountry skiers and riders. The skin track to the top is 0.9 miles. The gentle Dutch Meadows is a beginner trail; those looking for steeper terrain will find it on Yankee Doodle and its adjoining glades. The steepest run is Lift Line. New terrain continues to expand as volunteers restore old trails.

Distance: 2 miles, parking lot to summit, round trip

Vertical drop: 564 feet

Difficulty: Moderate/More difficult

Location: 910 VT Route 100, Readsboro, VT 05350 (*GPS coordinates*: 42° 49.165′ N, 73° 00.360′ W)

Additional Information: Dutch Hill Alliance of Skiers and Hikers, dhash4vt.org

DUTCH HILL

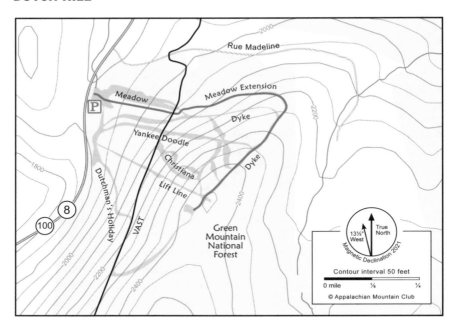

44b. DOVER TOWN FOREST, Dover, Vermont

The Southern Vermont Trails Association (SoVTA) has created a variety of back-country skiing zones for skiers of all abilities in the Dover Hills, the area between Mount Snow and Haystack. The volunteer group, a chapter of the Catamount Trail Association, partners with the town of Dover, Dover Town Forest Conservation Commission, U.S. Forest Service, and Mount Snow to create backcountry terrain that is open to the public. Baby Town Frolic is a family-friendly low-angle back-country zone near the parking lot that is skiable with just a few inches of snow. Chutes and Ladders—so named for how it progresses from tighter pine trees to open maple stands—is a series of north-facing, 800-vertical-foot braided lines that descend the Rock River Ravine. Other zones to visit are Grandma's (500 vertical feet) and Chicken Little (700 vertical feet). SoVTA is expanding so check sovta.org for the latest maps and directions.

Distance: 0.5 miles to Chutes and Ladders

Vertical drop: 300–800 feet

Difficulty: Moderate/More difficult

Location: Clinton Bond Trail, East Dover, VT 05341 (*GPS coordinates*: 42° 58.142′ N, 72° 49.253′ W)

Additional Information: Southern Vermont Trails Association, sovta.org

DOVER TOWN FOREST

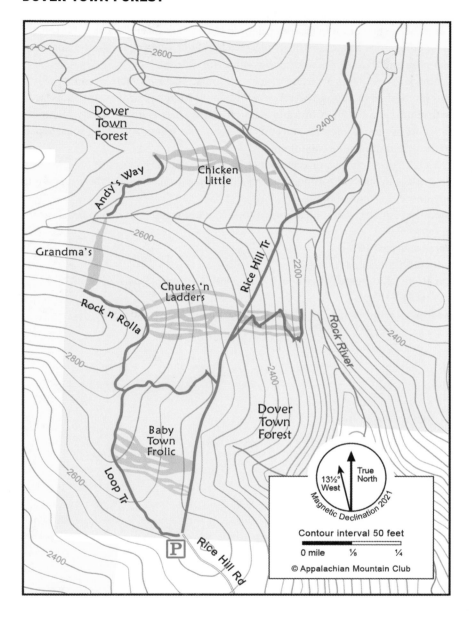

Dover Town Forest

Andy's Way

Chicken Little

Grandma's

Rock n Rolla

Chutes 'n Ladders

Rice Hill Tr

Rock River

Baby Town Frolic

Dover Town Forest

Loop Tr

2600

2400

2200

2800

2600

2400

P

Rice Hill Rd

True North

13½° West

Magnetic Declination 2021

Contour interval 50 feet

0 mile   ⅛   ¼

© Appalachian Mountain Club

44c. MERCK FOREST, Rupert, Vermont

There are a variety of gentle ski tours through the historic and beautiful Merck Forest, with the option to stay overnight in one of eight backcountry cabins. A ski ascent of Antone Mountain (2,607 feet) is a highlight, offering views over southern Vermont and the Adirondacks along with a fun descent.

Merck Forest offers a variety of easy ski tours. The 3,100-acre preserve, which was established by George Merck, the founder of Merck Pharmaceuticals, is laced with more than 30 miles of trails for hiking and cross-country skiing. The tours range from gentle slides down woods roads, to a ski trip to a working sugarhouse, to the ascent of Antone Mountain.

Merck Forest offers a nice introduction to backcountry skiing. It can also be a great place to take kids skiing or hiking. The opportunity to make this a hut skiing adventure is an added bonus.

Distance: 5 miles, visitor center to Antone Mountain summit; also many shorter options

Vertical drop: 810 feet

Difficulty: Moderate

Location: 3270 Route 315, Rupert, VT 05768 (*GPS coordinates*: 43° 16.453′ N, 73° 10.347′ W).

Additional Information: Merck Forest & Farmland Center, 802-394-7836, merckforest.org

MERCK FOREST

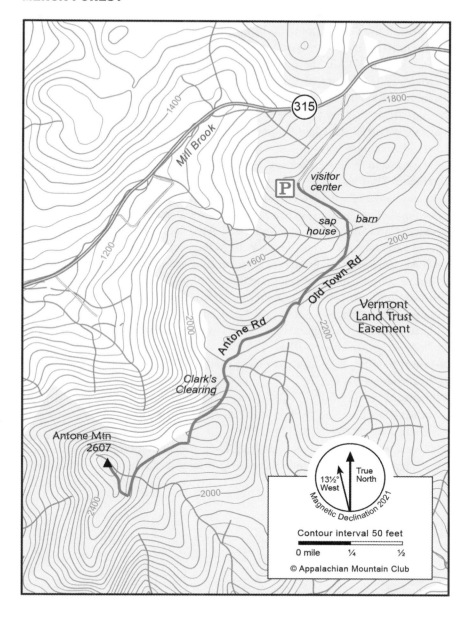

44d. MOOSALAMOO NATIONAL RECREATION AREA, Ripton, VT

The Moosalamoo National Recreation Area, designated in 2006, comprises 16,000 acres within the Green Mountain National Forest. Both the Long Trail and the Catamount Trail traverse this area, which is bounded on the north by VT 125 and on the south by VT 73. The easy tour from the Rikert Ski Touring Center to the Blueberry Hill Outdoor Center is especially pretty and is part of the 300-mile-long Catamount Trail. It features skiing on ungroomed trails with a scenic midpoint at the Sugar Hill Reservoir.

Start the tour at the Chatfield parking area, which is on FR 67 (a.k.a. Brooks Road), just south of VT 125 and opposite the Rikert Ski Touring Center. Follow the ungroomed Widow's Clearing Trail, which is well marked with blue plastic Catamount Trail blazes. Ski 1.9 miles to Widow's Clearing, the former site of a farmhouse where there is an old foundation and numerous stone walls. Continue following the Catamount Trail blazes through several trail junctions until you reach Dave and Carol Smith Trail, a groomed trail of the Blueberry Hill Outdoor Center. Take this to Horseshoe Trail, which leads to the beautiful open white expanse of the Sugar Hill Reservoir. From here, you can either return to your car, making this a 10-mile round trip, or you can continue into the Blueberry Hill trail network (blueberryhilltrails.com, donation appreciated). The Widow's Clearing parking area on Goshen Road is another possible starting point for a ski tour. This is also the base for skiing the ungroomed USFS Wilkinson Trails, Water Tower Trails, and the Robert Frost Interpretive Trail.

Distance: 10 miles, to Sugar Hill Reservoir; other variations possible

Vertical change: 500 feet

Difficulty: Moderate

Location: USFS Chatfield Parking Area, Brooks Road, Ripton, VT 05766 (*GPS coordinates*: 43° 56.797′ N, 72° 59.177′ W).

Additional Information: Catamount Trail Association, catamounttrail.org; Moosalamoo Association, moosalamoo.org. Both websites have downloadable maps.

MOOSALAMOO NATIONAL RECREATION AREA

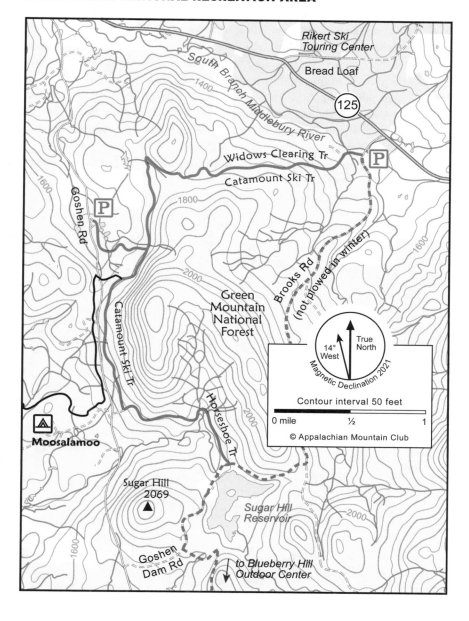

Rikert Ski
Touring Center

Bread Loaf

125

South Branch Middlebury River

Widows Clearing Tr

Catamount Ski Tr

P

Goshen Rd

P

1400

1600

1800

2000

Catamount Ski Tr

Brooks Rd
(not plowed in winter)

1600

Green
Mountain
National
Forest

True
North
14°
West
Magnetic Declination 2021

Contour interval 50 feet

0 mile   ½   1

© Appalachian Mountain Club

Horseshoe Tr

2000

Moosalamoo

Sugar Hill
2069

Sugar Hill
Reservoir

2000

1600

Goshen
Dam Rd

to Blueberry Hill
Outdoor Center

44e. CHITTENDEN BROOK HUT, Rochester, Vermont

The Chittenden Brook Hut, opened by the Vermont Huts Association in 2018, is poised to become a hub for hut-based skiing in Vermont. The USFS has approved plans by the Rochester/Randolph Area Sports Trails Alliance (RASTA) to create an extensive backcountry ski zone around the hut. Chittenden Brook Hut is also a 2.5-mile ski to RASTA's outstanding Brandon Gap backcountry zone (see tour 30, Brandon Gap, page 173). To reach the hut, ski 2.2 miles from the trailhead parking area on VT 73 on the unplowed and gated Chittenden Brook Road. The hut has propane heat and cooking facilities. Chittenden Brook Hut requires advance reservations and fills early in winter, so plan ahead.

Location: 6501 Brandon Mountain Road, Rochester, VT 05767 (*GPS coordinates*: 43° 51.137' N, 72° 53.957' W).

Additional Information: Vermont Huts Association, vermonthuts.org

CHITTENDEN BROOK HUT

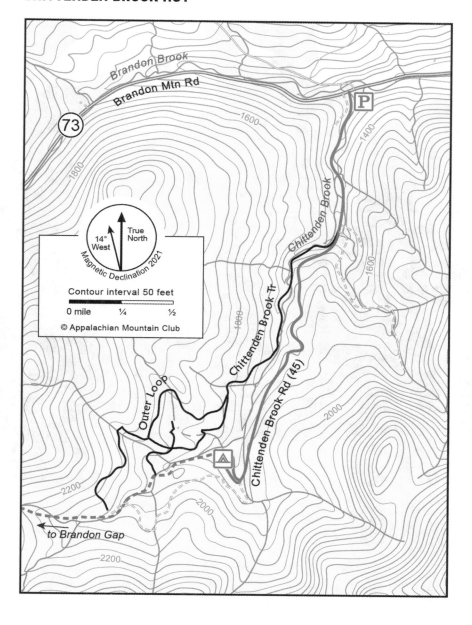

Contour interval 50 feet

0 mile   ¼   ½

© Appalachian Mountain Club

Skiers at the top of Dutch Hill peering over southern Vermont. *Photo by W. Neil Fisher*

4 NEW YORK

THE ADIRONDACKS: A SKI HISTORY

The Adirondack Mountains are one of the great ranges of the East. The mountains lie within the 6-million-acre Adirondack State Park, the largest park in the continental United States. Those who journey to the top of New York immediately will sense that this region is distinctly different than the Green Mountains of Vermont or the White Mountains of New Hampshire. The Adirondacks comprise a majestic, almost incongruous landscape. In contrast to the softly rounded glacial domes that characterize most summits in New England, the jagged Adirondack skyline appears strikingly alpine. There are the Wolfjaw Mountains gaping skyward like a hungry animal; Giant Mountain with a huge eagle-shaped slide torn into its east face; Gothics, its towering flanks raked by landslides; and Mount Marcy, the crown jewel of New York, capping the state like an enormous ice cream cone.

The Adirondacks are unique: they are the only mountains in the eastern United States that are not geologically part of the Appalachian chain, which extends from Georgia to Maine. The Adirondacks form part of the Canadian Shield, an area of igneous and metamorphic rock that underlies about half of Canada. The mountains are young by geological standards. Indeed, mountain formation is still actively under way here. Earthquakes occur with some regularity, and landslides periodically tear holes in the endless green carpet. Avalanches occasionally race down the steepest slopes. This is a living landscape.

The Adirondacks have an unusual political status. In 1885, the New York State legislature created the Adirondack Forest Preserve with the stipulation that it "shall be forever kept as wild forest lands." In 1892, the legislature created Adirondack State Park, which included the Forest Preserve plus all privately owned land within a somewhat arbitrarily drawn "blue line" (for the blue pencil used to indicate the area on the state map). In 1894, responding to environmental abuses, New Yorkers voted to include the "forever wild" clause in the state constitution. The Adirondacks thus became the only wild lands in the country that enjoy such constitutional protection. With such strict control come some headaches, as skiers have discovered when they have tried to cut or maintain trails wide enough for skiing (the law prohibits the cutting of mountain trails wider than about 10 feet).

SKIING IN THE ADIRONDACKS

Skiing came to the Adirondacks for an unlikely reason. Lumber baron John Booth of Ottawa arrived in Saranac Lake in 1892 to visit his daughter, who was being treated for tuberculosis. Booth brought with him a pair of skis. Local residents were excited, and a carpenter, Napoleon Bailey, who was familiar with skiing from his native Wisconsin, began making skis and selling them. A major impetus for skiing came in 1904 when the Lake Placid Club opened in winter. The club, according to its brochure, was "an informal university in the wilderness, a meeting and working area that combined civilization with leisure and beauty, access to the vitalizing forces of nature, and contact with many of those contributing to the nation's growth." The Lake Placid Club brought over European ski instructors to lead trips into the mountains. This established skiing as a pastime in the Adirondacks, at least for the club's blue-blooded clientele.

Two of the early pioneers of Adirondack skiing were Irving Langmuir and John S. Apperson, both of whom worked for General Electric in Schenectady, New York. Langmuir, who is best known as the winner of the 1932 Nobel Prize for chemistry, began skiing the northeastern peaks in 1906, which makes him the first major ski mountaineer in North America. In 1907, he skied Wittenberg Mountain in the Catskills, and the following year he skied up Mount Greylock in Massachusetts. Langmuir met Apperson in 1910, and the two men became fast friends. Langmuir shared his enthusiasm for skiing with Apperson, and Apperson introduced Langmuir to the Adirondacks.

Apperson made the first recorded ski ascent of Mount Marcy in 1911 with two partners. Apperson and Langmuir continued to pioneer routes throughout the Adirondacks. They skied Gothics in 1927, and Apperson is credited with the first ski ascent of Basin and Saddleback mountains that year.

A milestone in Adirondack skiing came in 1912, when the famous Arctic explorer Fridtjof Nansen came to Lake Placid with his daughter. Being Scandinavian, they opted to tour around on skis, rather than using the snowshoes favored by most people in the area. Nansen and his daughter celebrated Christmas in Lake Placid and then skied up Whiteface Mountain, a feat that amazed many locals.

The man who made the biggest impact on Adirondack skiing, however, was Herman "Jackrabbit" Smith-Johannsen. Born in Norway in 1875, he first began visiting the Adirondacks in 1915 from New York City, where he worked.

Jackrabbit was known for his skiing prowess and his marathon ski tours. In 1919, he moved his business (he was a mechanical engineer importing heavy equipment) to Montreal and installed his family at the Lake Placid Club, visiting them on weekends. That winter, he skied Marcy, Algonquin, and Whiteface. The following year, he teamed up with Langmuir and Apperson for an assault on the as-yet-unskied Mount Haystack. Climbing from Upper Ausable Lake, Langmuir eventually turned back. Apperson and Jackrabbit continued, arriving at the summit just as the sun set. Jackrabbit waxed poetic about that moment, as Alice Johannsen quotes him in her biography of her father, *The Legendary Jackrabbit Johannsen*:

> We stood there together on the top of Haystack and looked over there towards the setting sun. The sky was a wonderful rose. To the northwest trailed the peaks of the Great Range, with Giant in the far distance. All the intervening peaks were basking in the sunset glow. High overhead rode the full moon, which we knew would give us plenty of light as we picked our way down again through the thick forest back to our camp on the Upper Ausable.
>
> It was a sight neither of us would ever forget, for in that moment we saw the world below us as though it were frozen in time. There was no past, no future, just the present. And it was unspeakably beautiful!

Jackrabbit's most enduring contribution to Adirondack skiing is the spirit and attitude with which he approached the mountains. Where others saw obstacles, Jackrabbit saw opportunities. An English skier wrote of a 1922 outing with him: "Mr. Johannsen is a believer in his skis. . . . When there is snow, he skis in that, but he has no unreasonable prejudices against rocks, stumps or roots, provided they are white in parts at least."

Jackrabbit's other daughter, Peggy Johannsen Austin, described his technique for me: "His pièce de résistance was what he called 'bushwhacking.' He could hop around like a rabbit, and that's why he got his name 'Jackrabbit.' He always said, 'Never stay on two skis at once. Always jump—keep moving your weight back and forth all the time so you're never stuck in a rut.' That was his technique. He really did float and hop around trees."

Jackrabbit believed that long tours were the essence of the ski experience. That sensibility continues among Adirondack skiers who think nothing of a 14-mile tour up Marcy and back or of even longer excursions. Jackrabbit Johannsen died in 1987 at age 111. He skied until age 108 and is said to have attributed his longevity to his motto, "Ski, ski, ski!"

In 1932, the Winter Olympics were held in Lake Placid for the first time. The Winter Games featured cross-country skiing but no downhill events. It further catalyzed the growth and development of Nordic skiing in the region.

Herman "Jackrabbit" Johannsen, circa 1932. *Courtesy of Peggy Johannsen Austin collection.*

The 1930s was the era of down-mountain skiing in the Adirondacks. It was during this period that the Wright Peak Ski Trail was cut and the Van Hoevenberg Trail up Mount Marcy was widened for skiing (for more on this history, see tour 47, Wright Peak Ski Trail, on page 273 and tour 49, Mount Marcy, on page 284). In 1938, Lake Placid residents financed the cutting of Whiteface Ski Trail on Little Whiteface Mountain. With a 2,700-foot vertical drop, this 2-mile-long down-mountain run became the first Class A race trail in the Adirondacks. Whiteface Trail was an anomaly: it was built on land owned by a timber company, so it could be cut wide and fast. The cutting of ski trails elsewhere in Adirondack State Park was sharply limited by conservation restrictions, so skiing remained limited to a die-hard core of outdoorspeople.

Jim Goodwin, who began guiding trips in the Adirondacks in the 1920s and served in the famous ski troops of the U.S. Army Tenth Mountain Division in World War II, told me, "The tragedy was that because of the 'forever wild' laws, the Adirondacks had to lose out on having decent ski trails cut like the CCC [Civilian Conservation Corps] was cutting in Vermont. So skiing in the Adirondacks really fell way behind."

The down-mountain ski era began to fade as small lift-serviced ski areas began popping up around the Adirondacks and in New England. Marble Mountain Ski Area opened near Lake Placid in 1948. It was replaced a decade later by Whiteface Ski Area, the largest Adirondack ski resort to date. The venerable down-mountain Whiteface Ski Trail was incorporated into the Whiteface Ski Area (the current Wilderness Trail roughly follows its course). People all around the Northeast quickly embraced chairlifts and abandoned the old ski trails, leaving them to grow in.

SKI TO DIE

Development restrictions in the Adirondacks had an unintended effect: they spawned a "forever wild" style of skiing. Narrow-trail skiing was elevated to a high art. Adirondack skiers began to strike out for the highest, wildest terrain on their cross-country skis. They redefined the sense of what is possible on free-heel skis.

In the early 1970s, a small group of local rock climbers led by the late Geoff Smith of Plattsburgh started venturing into the High Peaks on skis. Dubbing themselves the American Eider Schussboomers, this wild-eyed group of mountaineers adapted their bold, exploratory mindset to backcountry skiing. They thought nothing of barreling down a narrow mountain trail on their skinny wooden cross-country racing skis. Inadvertently, they became phenomenally good skiers.

As friendly competition grew among this clan of skiers, they adopted a new name. The moniker "Ski to Die Club" captured the group's boldness, commitment, and sense of humor. "A lot of the competitiveness of climbing—the camaraderie, the goading—carries over into skiing," Smith told me. Take, for example, the Ski to Die notion of "turnbacks."

"A turnback is when you ski something so horrific or frightening or so rotten that the guy you're with just looks at it, packs his backpack, turns around, and leaves. There are many reasons not to ski something, but the idea of getting a turnback— *that* makes it even better," he said. Long before the term *extreme skiing* was coined, Ski to Die Club members were aiming their skinny skis down landslides, streambeds, narrow trails, and virtually anywhere they could think to slide.

The Ski to Die Club, whose elusive members still roam the highest peaks in search of the most elegant lines and best ski tours, captures the low-glitz, high-adventure soul of Adirondack skiing. Visitors to the Adirondacks will feel this infectious spirit on the ski trails described in this book.

As wild and innovative as their ski routes sound, the Ski to Diers insist that they're not doing anything new. Robbie Frenette, a master Adirondack boat builder and veteran Ski to Dier who hails from an old family of Adirondack skiers, emphasized that the Ski to Die Club is simply the modern torchbearer for an old tradition. "There's a long history of skiing in the Adirondacks," he explained. "Jackrabbit Johannsen was skiing Mount Marcy and the other High Peaks way back in the 1920s." Indeed, some of Jackrabbit's wilder descents of remote Adirondack peaks went unrepeated until the Ski to Die Club took up his mantle in the 1970s.

Frenette insisted, "We're just continuing what Jackrabbit started."

45 JACKRABBIT TRAIL

The Jackrabbit Trail from Lake Placid to Saranac Lake showcases the 35-mile-long route that connects the towns of Paul Smiths, Saranac Lake, Lake Placid, and Keene. This scenic tour includes woods, ponds, and mountains, with a nice mix of uphill, flat, and downhill skiing.

Distance: 5.5 miles, Whiteface Inn to McKenzie Pond Road, one way
Elevation: *Start*: 1,970 feet, Whiteface Inn Road; *Highest point*: 2,600 feet, McKenzie Pass; *Finish*: 1,600 feet, McKenzie Pond Road; *Vertical drop*: 1,000 feet, McKenzie Pass to McKenzie Pond Road
Maps: *Lake Placid and Saranac Lake Winter Trails Map* (Green Goat Maps), *Adirondack Park: Saranac/Paul Smiths* (Trails Illustrated)
Difficulty: Moderate
Gear: Cross-country, Nordic backcountry/telemark, AT
Fee: No fee is charged for skiing from Whiteface Inn Road to McKenzie Pond Road provided you stay on the marked Jackrabbit Trail.
Additional Information: For information about the Jackrabbit Trail, including trail conditions, contact the Barkeater Trails Alliance, 518-523-1365, BETAtrails.org

HOW TO GET THERE

Lake Place trailhead: Driving west from Lake Placid on NY 86, turn right on Whiteface Inn Lane (see signs for the inn). Go 1.3 miles, and directly opposite the entrance to the Whiteface Club, see the red plastic Jackrabbit Trail blazes on the trees (*GPS coordinates*: 44° 18.708′ N, 74° 00.440′ W). Parking is at the trailheads on either end of this tour.

McKenzie Pond Road trailhead (to leave a car or to start): From NY 86 just past Ray Brook, turn right on McKenzie Pond Road and drive 1.4 miles. A white sign for the Jackrabbit Trail is beside the road on the right (*GPS coordinates*: 44° 18.878′ N, 74° 06.115′ W).

THE TOUR

In 1985, a small, dedicated group of skiing dreamers came up with a bold idea: they would create a long-distance, town-to-town cross-country ski trail in the heart of the Adirondacks. The schemers—foremost among them were Tony Goodwin, then the trail manager at the Olympic cross-country skiing venue at Mount Van Hoevenberg, and Mark Ippolito, a local physician's assistant and avid skier—imagined a trail that would extend from Tupper Lake to Keene. They drew their inspiration from Scandinavia and northern Europe, where skiing between towns is an honored pastime, and from Vermont, where the Catamount Trail was just getting established. They formed the Adirondack Ski Touring Council (ASTC), and named their scheme the Jackrabbit Trail, after the legendary Herman "Jackrabbit" Smith-Johannsen (see "The Adirondacks: A Ski History" on page 257 for more

JACKRABBIT TRAIL

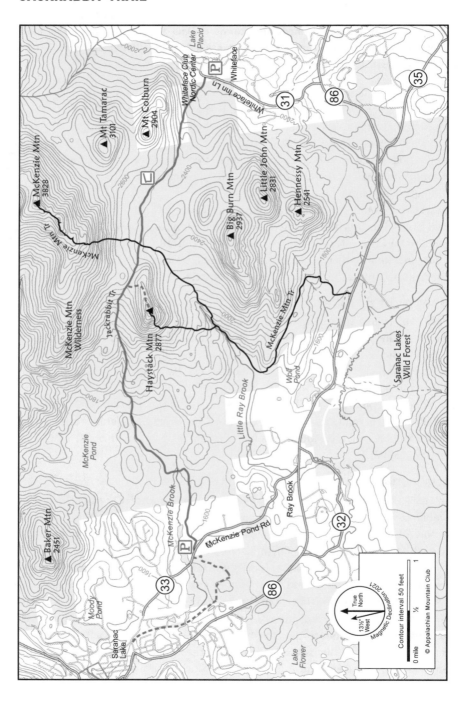

on Johannsen). In 2014, the ASTC became part of the Barkeater Trails Alliance (BETA), which now manages the Jackrabbit Trail.

Goodwin says, "The idea for the Jackrabbit Trail was not entirely original. A 1933 map of Lake Placid not only showed ski trails connecting Keene and Saranac Lake, it also made downtown Lake Placid the center of a vast network that would have qualified it as a cross-country ski center long before that term was coined." Goodwin and Ippolito set about scouting a route and cajoling numerous local landowners to allow a trail through their lands. The pair was helped by the discovery of a provision in state law that said that landowners who permit recreation on their property have "no duty to keep those premises safe." As permissions began flowing in, there remained just one detail to attend to: creating the trail.

The daunting task of establishing some 35 miles of trails through the North Woods was made easier by the decision to use existing trails and logging roads wherever possible. Not that this let the trail builders off the hook—many old byways suffered from decades of neglect. Facing the task of restoring a particularly bad section of Old Mountain Road in Keene (by then an eroded footpath), the trailblazers turned to an unusual source of help: prisoners from the Moriah Shock Incarceration Correctional Facility in Mineville. The resulting spectacle included having the guards, inmates, and Jackrabbit Trail volunteers all working side-by-side hefting 500-pound boulders, building bridges, and clearing brush. As a result of these efforts, Old Mountain Road is now skiable with only 6 inches of snow instead of 2 feet.

The Jackrabbit Trail is now a thriving reality. The trail includes ungroomed backcountry sections as well as groomed trails through four local cross-country ski centers (no fee is required for skiers provided they are passing through on the Jackrabbit Trail, which is marked with red plastic blazes). Part of the charm of the Jackrabbit Trail is that it starts, ends, and travels through the towns of Lake Placid, Keene, and Saranac Lake. You can stop for a drink or a meal along the way, or you can opt for the more ascetic pleasure of using the trail to head for the hills where no one will disturb you.

One of the best backcountry sections of the Jackrabbit Trail is the tour from Lake Placid to Saranac Lake. This tour travels through wilderness lands and includes a fun, 1.5-mile moderate downhill on which to make turns. Most people ski the trail from east to west since this maximizes the downhill skiing. You can start at the backcountry trailhead just across the road from the Whiteface Inn.

A trail sign marks the trailhead on Whiteface Inn Road (see earlier directions), and the broad logging road-cum-trail into the woods is obvious. About 200 feet in on the trail there is a trail register and a small gray sign that informs you, "McKenzie Pond Rd. 5.5 miles, Saranac Lake 7 miles." Proceed up the gentle logging road. In the 1930s, the Civilian Conservation Corps (CCC) upgraded this logging road to be a fire trail. It was intended as a way of getting firefighters into this remote area if needed. Thanks to their meticulous road-building efforts, this trail has survived the ravages of time and been reincarnated as a fine ski trail.

Skiers heading out on the Jackrabbit Trail over MacKenzie Pass to Saranac Lake. *Photo by Josh Wilson*

The trail continues uphill, rising slowly along the flanks of McKenzie Mountain, which lies to the north. The Jackrabbit Trail soon transitions from private to state land, noted by signs. The trail levels out and you ski along a beautiful plateau. The trail is lined by tall birches, then spruces and firs, which frame the path and transform it into a stately corridor through the wilds. You soon pass a lean-to and then arrive at a trail junction. A sign says that it is 2.1 miles to the summit of Haystack Mountain. Haystack Mountain is a worthy destination, but you can get there more quickly another way: continue up the Jackrabbit Trail to where it levels out and stop before heading downhill. This height-of-land is McKenzie Pass. If you choose not to leave a car at the other end of this tour, a good option is to ski to this pass then return to your starting point.

Haystack Mountain (one of eleven peaks in the Adirondacks named Haystack) lies uphill through the woods to the south (left). It is a 20-minute detour to bushwhack up through open woods to the summit. The summit is a ledge that boasts beautiful views of the Adirondacks from Giant Mountain to the Seward Range, including most of the High Peaks. This side trip and vista is a worthwhile bonus on this tour. The ski back down to McKenzie Pass is brushy and not memorable (this detour is for the views, not the turns), but it takes only a few minutes to backtrack.

From McKenzie Pass, the Jackrabbit Trail heads downhill for a fun 1.5-mile cruise. The trail is wide enough to make turns but gentle enough that you can go straight without picking up too much speed. The descent ends at a trail junction, where you can turn right for a short detour to McKenzie Pond. There are beautiful views across the pond. This section of the Jackrabbit Trail exits through an impressive pine forest then briefly follows a power line before arriving at McKenzie Pond Road, where you can pick up your car.

You have a final option to extend this tour another 2 miles into Saranac Lake and finish right at a local eating or drinking establishment. To do this, cross McKenzie Pond Road and continue on the Jackrabbit Trail, which is partly an old snowmobile trail here. The trail eventually turns to follow an old railroad bed. Just before crossing a 30-foot-long trestle, turn left and head into the town of Saranac Lake, where you will find restaurants and bars. Bon appétit!

OTHER OPTIONS

The Jackrabbit Trail can be skied as day trips ranging from 6 to 9 miles. One of the prettier sections of the Jackrabbit Trail goes from Cascade Cross-Country Ski Center to Keene, ending with a 3-mile descent down Old Mountain Road. It features beaver dams, ice cliffs, a pond, beautiful views, and a nice descent. Consult the Jackrabbit Trail map and website for details and directions to this and other tours.

46 JOHNS BROOK VALLEY HUT SKIING

The Johns Brook Valley lies in the heart of the Adirondack High Peaks. Camp Peggy O'Brien and Grace Camp offer the option of hut-based ski tours. There are numerous adventure skiing opportunities in the High Peaks near the huts.

Distance: 3.5 miles, Garden parking area to Grace Camp and Camp Peggy O'Brien, one way
Elevation: *Start/Finish*: 1,523 feet, Garden parking lot; *Highest point*: 2,362 feet, Camp Peggy O'Brien; *Vertical drop*: 839 feet
Maps: *Adirondack Park: Lake Placid/High Peaks* (Trails Illustrated), *High Peaks Adirondack Trail Map* (ADK)
Difficulty: Moderate (skiing to huts)
Gear: AT, telemark, snowboard
Additional Information: Reservations to stay at Camp Peggy O'Brien (accommodates 12 people) and Grace Camp (6 people) can be made up to one year in advance by calling the Adirondack Mountain Club at 518-523-3441, adk.org

HOW TO GET THERE

From NY 73 in the center of Keene Valley, see the "Trail to the High Peaks" sign next to the Ausable Inn and turn onto Adirondack Street. At 0.6 miles, the road turns right, crossing Johns Brook on an iron bridge. Continue uphill following signs to the Garden. The pavement ends just below the Garden parking area, and the road is poorly maintained in winter. Good snow tires may be required to park. The trail to Johns Brook Lodge and Camp Peggy O'Brien departs from the west end of the Garden parking lot (*GPS coordinates*: 44° 11.342′ N, 73° 48.956′ W).

HISTORY

The Johns Brook Valley is located in the heart of the High Peaks, the tallest mountains in New York State. The rushing Johns Brook is surrounded by the dramatic ice-plastered summits of Gothics and Wolfjaws, long snow-filled streambeds, and the skiable summits of Mounts Haystack and Marcy. This is first-class backcountry ski terrain.

The High Peaks offers some of the best hut-based skiing in the Northeast. Camp Peggy O'Brien and Grace Camp, located in the Johns Brook Valley and operated by the Adirondack Mountain Club (ADK), are the only private backcountry cabins in New York's Adirondack High Peaks Wilderness Area. Nearby Johns Brook Lodge (JBL), a beautiful ADK wilderness lodge built in 1925, is closed in winter.

Camp Peggy O'Brien was built by the ADK in 1989. The hut was named for Peggy O'Brien, a former ADK vice president who was chair of the Johns Brook Lodge Committee for eleven years. Grace Camp was purchased in 1929 to house volunteers. It burned down and was replaced in 1968 and was renovated in the early 1990s.

JOHNS BROOK VALLEY HUT SKIING

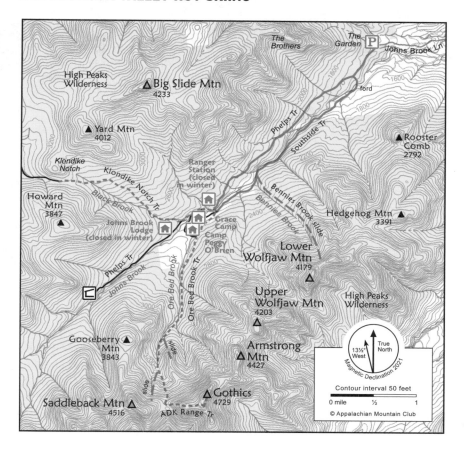

The 3.5-mile trip into the Johns Brook Valley and the two wilderness cabins meanders through a classic northern hardwood forest. This route was originally plied by loggers at the turn of the last century. It led to what was once a bustling lumber camp that served as the base of operations for logging the surrounding peaks. The axmen took timber from as high as 3,800 feet on nearby Big Slide Mountain, hauling out huge loads by horse team. After the loggers left, they were replaced by a hermit named Mel Hathaway, who occupied the abandoned logging camp until 1926. The logging camp has since been replaced by a ranger cabin and Johns Brook Lodge, which sleeps 28 people in the summer.

THE TOURS

From the Garden, the yellow-blazed trail known as the Phelps Trail (a.k.a. the Johns Brook Trail) climbs moderately. At a half-mile, you come to a junction with the Southside Trail, an alternate but equidistant route to JBL and a good option

Skiing Bennie's Brook Slide in the Johns Brook Valley. *Photo by Josh Wilson*

for the return leg of your trip (see later). Continue on the Phelps Trail as it gently climbs, with plenty of small turns and twists. There are a number of brook crossings en route. Numerous hikers and snowshoers travel this trail, so it is typically hard packed and can be icy. At 1.3 miles, the route passes the Deer Brook lean-to and then crosses Deer Brook on a single-log bridge. Unless you have the balance of a figure skater, it's best to take off your skis for the crossing.

Continue on rolling terrain and take in the views of Upper and Lower Wolfjaw mountains and the neighboring peaks that start to become visible on your left. The Phelps Trail finally turns a hard left and drops quickly to the ranger outpost (closed in winter) at 3.1 miles. Turn right, staying on the Phelps Trail, and shortly after passing the junction with Slide Mountain Brook Trail, turn left to cross an airy open-sided bridge over Johns Brook. After crossing Johns Brook, turn right and arrive a few minutes later at Grace Camp. Continue 0.25 miles and thread through a dark stand of conifers to arrive at the discreetly located Camp Peggy O'Brien, which stays hidden until you are practically on its front porch. There, nestled among the fir trees, is a handsome wood home with a steeply pitched green roof, wood porch, and handmade ski rack.

Inside both cabins, there is a propane stove, heater, and lights. It is a novelty to encounter such easy living in the heart of a winter wilderness. The camps are also equipped with a full set of cooking and eating utensils, and sleeping is on bunk beds with mattresses. Besides your usual day pack of clothing and equipment for backcountry skiing, bring a lightweight sleeping bag and food. Use this luxury as your cue to *pack light*. That's part of the pleasure of a hut tour.

To return to the Garden, the most enjoyable ski route is the Southside Trail. The trail is used primarily by skiers so it does not get as hard packed as the Phelps Trail. The Southside Trail has red ADK blazes for about half its length. At the midway point, you arrive in an open stand of hardwoods on a hillside, and the blazes stop. There are privately owned camps here, and the owners periodically snowmobile into this clearing, so be aware. Ski uphill a short distance until you see the Jeep road/snowmobile trail entering from the left (north). Follow this trail as it descends on woods roads. Keep your eyes peeled at 2.8 miles for a sign pointing the way back to the Garden. Bear left at the sign, cross the (hopefully frozen) Johns Brook, and follow the Southside Trail as it climbs out of a small but steep ravine and rejoins the Phelps Trail. If you miss the brook crossing, you will end up about a half-mile below the Garden and will have to walk back up the road.

There are numerous skiing options in the Johns Brook Valley. These can be accomplished as day trips from the Garden or from a base at Camp Peggy O'Brien or Grace Camp. Following are some of the best tours.

Gothics Slides and Ore Bed Brook
Difficulty: Most difficult

For adventurous Adirondack skiers, the ultimate descents are on the steep slides that lie throughout the range and in the streambeds that form natural passageways through the mountains. The slides can be difficult to reach, may involve technical mountaineering challenges, and often require intimate knowledge of the terrain.

Gothics (4,729 feet) offers skiers the opportunity to ski two nontechnical lower-angle slides and a streambed, all of which are easily accessible from Grace Camp and Camp Peggy O'Brien. Gothics is a majestic mountain with a triple summit and huge ice-plastered rock faces. The mountain got its name because its appearance "suggested Gothic architecture to Frederick Perkins and Old Mountain Phelps [an Adirondack guide]," recounts the book *Adirondack Trails: High Peaks Region* (the ADK guidebook notes that the mountain also may have been named earlier by a minister from Lake Placid).

From the huts, ski up Woodsfall Trail and turn right at the junction with Ore Bed Brook Trail. The trail climbs steadily, and at 2.3 miles, it crosses a large slide. This 500-foot slide offers beautiful views of Saddleback Mountain, the rock cliffs on Gooseberry Mountain, and the sweeping face of Gothics. You can ski this lower-angle slide and then continue down by skiing in Ore Bed Brook. The brook is a spacious corridor in which you can enjoy negotiating its natural rollovers and drops.

You can also continue farther up Ore Bed Brook Trail until you reach another longer and somewhat steeper slide that runs parallel to the trail. You can ski this slide, which also empties into the wide-open Ore Bed Brook drainage. The brook and the trail both lead back to Camp Peggy O'Brien.

This is an enjoyable introduction to Adirondack slide skiing. Gothics also has steeper and more demanding slides that involve technical ski mountaineering that are not described here. If you are an expert skier who is new to the Adirondacks, consider hiring a guide if you want to explore the steepest, wildest side of these mountains.

Note that on any open slope of 30 degrees or steeper, *you must assess the avalanche hazard before venturing onto it and back off if conditions are unstable.* Avalanche hazard is a very real threat on the exposed Adirondack slides.

For more on avalanches, see "Avalanche Awareness" on page xxxiii.

Bennies Brook Slide
Difficulty: Most difficult

Bennies Brook Slide is one of the more popular and easily accessible slides to ski in the Johns Brook Valley. The Y-shaped slide is about a mile long and reaches up toward the summit of Lower Wolfjaw Mountain (4,179 feet). When skiing down, the slide empties into Bennies Brook, where there are more turns, making for a long, continuous descent. The vertical drop is about 1,100 feet. From the ranger cabin (closed in winter) near Grace Camp and Camp Peggy O'Brien, ski across a short wooden bridge onto the Southside Trail. Cross a bridge over another major drainage (this is Wolfjaw Brook) and continue a short distance until you reach the next major drainage. This is Bennies Brook. You can ski up Bennies Brook or alongside it on the climber's left, whichever is easier going; there is no formal trail, although the woods are fairly open and there are likely to be ski tracks. Continue up the drainage until you finally break out onto the slide, where the climbing is straightforward. Bennies Brook Slide is steepest at the top (about 25 degrees), then relaxes to about 18 degrees—about the pitch of an intermediate ski run at a ski area. Avalanche awareness caveats apply here, especially on the steeper sections of the slide.

Klondike Notch
Difficulty: Moderate

This is a ski tour to a scenic pass. The red-blazed Klondike Notch Trail departs from JBL and follows the left bank of Black Brook, climbing steeply at times. At 1.3 miles, it passes a junction with the trail to Big Slide Mountain, but remain on the Klondike Notch Trail until you reach Klondike Notch, a saddle between Howard and Yard mountains, at 1.7 miles. This is an 866-vertical-foot climb from JBL. From the notch, you can ski back to the hut or continue skiing to Adirondak Loj, which is 7.3 miles from JBL. You can ski back to JBL from Klondike Notch as you like, either on the trail or through the trees.

47 WRIGHT PEAK SKI TRAIL

A ski tour on Wright Peak in the Adirondack High Peaks offers panoramic views from the summit and an exciting descent of the historic Wright Peak Ski Trail.

Distance: 1 mile, Wright Peak Ski Trail; 7 miles, ADK High Peaks Information Center to Wright Peak summit and ski trail, round trip
Elevation: *Start/Finish*: 2,179 feet (ADK High Peaks Information Center), 3,100 feet (bottom of Wright Peak Ski Trail); *Highest point*: 4,580 feet, Wright Peak summit; *Vertical drop*: 2,401 feet, Wright Peak summit to ADK High Peaks Information Center
Maps: *Adirondack Park: Lake Placid/High Peaks* (Trails Illustrated), *High Peaks Adirondack Trail Map* (ADK) These maps show Wright Peak and its hiking trail but not Wright Peak Ski Trail.
Difficulty: More difficult+
Gear: AT, telemark, snowboard
Fee: There is a fee for parking at the Adirondack Mountain Club (ADK) High Peaks Information Center.
Additional Information: ADK High Peaks Information Center, 518-523-3441, adk.org

HOW TO GET THERE

From Lake Placid, drive east on NY 73 about 3 miles. Turn on Adirondak Loj Road and proceed south approximately 5 miles to the end of the road. Park at the ADK High Peaks Information Center (*GPS coordinates*: 44° 10.890′ N, 73° 57.950′ W). Maps and supplies are available at the information center.

HISTORY

Wright Peak is perched in the heart of the Adirondack High Peaks. The ski tour, from its scenic open summit and the descent of the historic Wright Peak Ski Trail, is an Adirondack classic. It offers all the best elements of a great tour: an enjoyable climb, panoramic summit views, and a ski trail roomy enough to make many turns.

Named for Silas Wright, New York's fourteenth governor and a U.S. senator, Wright Peak is the northernmost summit of the 8-mile-long MacIntyre Range, whose most prominent summit is Algonquin Peak, the second-highest mountain in New York.

The Wright Peak Ski Trail is a by-product of the unique and peculiar politics of Adirondack State Park. In 1894, New York State citizens voted to add a provision to the state constitution proclaiming that the 2.5-million-acre Adirondack Forest Preserve would remain "forever wild." This clause was interpreted to mean that no trail exceeding 10 feet in width could be cut.

Enter Hal Burton. It was the 1930s, and Burton, an avid skier, newspaperman, and later a veteran of the U.S. Army Tenth Mountain Division, was eager to have

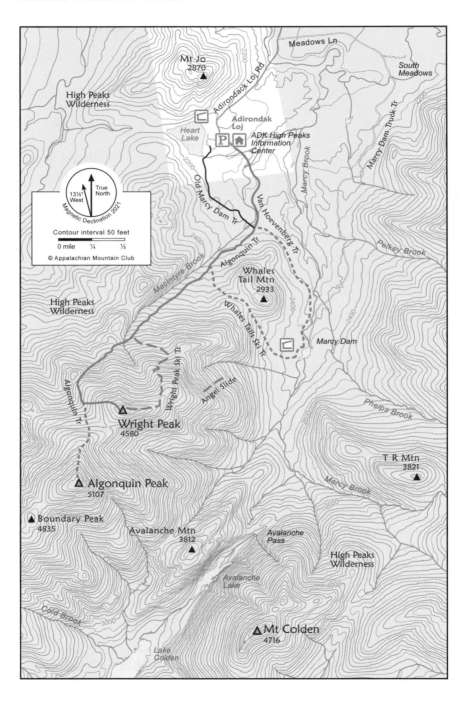

a good down-mountain ski run someplace within the Adirondacks. He and his friends watched enviously as the Civilian Conservation Corps built exciting ski trails throughout New England, while Adirondack skiers were forced to negotiate narrow, unforgiving hiking trails. Burton decided that Wright Peak would make an excellent location for a ski trail. It was easily accessible and possessed a good gradient for skiing. Burton managed to persuade New York State Conservation Commissioner Lithgow Osborne that he could build a "self-concealing" trail, and Osborne defended the concept at numerous public hearings.

At one hearing, a conservationist sniped at Osborne, "I gather you propose to approve this trail. When will construction begin?"

"The rangers," Osborne replied, "are already halfway up the mountain."

That was almost as far as the Wright Peak Ski Trail got. In October 1938, forest fires swept through the Catskills and all available rangers from the Adirondacks were transferred south to fight the fires. The rangers had just begun cutting the Wright Peak Ski Trail when they were forced to abandon the project. But Hal Burton was determined. He recounted later in the *Lake Placid News*, "I happened to have saved $400 for the down payment on a new car. Believe it or not, cars were cheap in those days, and so was the pay for woodcutters. The $400 went for the hire of guides from the Ausable Club. The new car had to wait a year, but the trail was completed."

The Wright Peak Ski Trail opened for skiing in December 1938. The trail was designed by legendary Dartmouth ski coach Otto Schniebs and New York State ski trail designer Bob St. Louis (who was later killed in World War II). Schniebs wanted a wide trail for speed, but St. Louis scaled it down. They followed old logging roads most of the way. Burton skied the run and was satisfied that his investment paid off. He wrote, "What a trail! Fairly narrow, to be sure, but it is still one of the most beautiful down-mountain runs in the East—frosted with rime on the upper reaches, brightened by sun on the lower, with the best and most reliable snow in the Lake Placid area."

Unfortunately, the Wright Peak Ski Trail was nearly done in by its many admirers. Within a few years, Burton skied the trail and "found only congestion—one skier every five minutes." He declared to the director of lands and forests, "This is intolerable." Burton's solution to the backcountry traffic jam was to propose building a new ski area in the Adirondacks. The seeds were thus sowed for the creation of Whiteface Ski Area.

Getting permission to build a ski area in the Adirondacks was a Herculean task: any relaxation of the "forever wild" status of the Adirondacks requires the approval of the majority of the state's voters and two successive legislatures, something that has rarely been accomplished. In 1940, New York State voters approved by a narrow 10,000-vote margin the construction of ski trails on Whiteface Mountain. The subsequent decline of backcountry ski trails was swift. The Wright Peak Ski Trail was maintained until about the early 1960s, but Whiteface and other lift-served slopes stole its thunder. The trail faded into obscurity.

A skier rounds a turn on the Wright Peak Ski Trail.

With the resurgence of backcountry skiing in the 1980s, Adirondack skiers were eagerly exploring any new terrain that held the potential for good skiing. Like the earlier generation, young Adirondack skiers chafed under the restrictions of the "forever wild" rule. Then Mark Ippolito, a local physician assistant with boundless energy for ski-related projects (see tour 45, Jackrabbit Trail, page 263, for another of his endeavors), discovered the Wright Peak Ski Trail on old maps. The law allowed for old trails to be restored, so Ippolito got permission from state park officials to take a crew of volunteers and cut their way up what they believed was the Wright Peak Ski Trail in spring 1987. Tony Goodwin, the executive director of the Adirondack Ski Touring Council, finished the job in 1989. But no sooner had the saws stopped than an outcry ensued. Angry conservationists insisted that the "new old trail" was wider than 10 feet and that it did not follow the original route. As proof, they noted that some of the trees that had been cut were older than the original trail. The trailblazers diplomatically assured the critics that a few large trees had to be removed for safety reasons, and the controversy died down.

The "new" Wright Peak Ski Trail was never recut all the way to the summit out of concern that summer hikers would start using the trail and trample fragile alpine vegetation. As a result, the top of the trail remains intentionally obscure. That has succeeded in warding off hikers, but it also has stymied many a skier hoping to drop into the trail from the top. To be certain you find the trail, your best bet is to climb it from the bottom, where it departs from Algonquin Trail.

THE TOUR

To reach the Wright Peak Ski Trail, leave the ADK High Peaks Information Center and take the blue-blazed Van Hoevenberg Trail 0.9 miles to the Algonquin Trail junction, then follow the yellow-blazed trail to Algonquin and Wright Peak. You soon cross a junction with the Whales Tail Ski Trail, which was cut in 1937 and leads up and over a saddle between Whales Tail Mountain and Wright Peak then drops to Marcy Dam. The Whales Tail Ski Trail is an enjoyable and more moderate ski, but it needs at least a foot of snow to be skiable, and it is prone to melting early because of its southern exposure.

The hiking trail up Wright and Algonquin climbs gradually, then crosses MacIntyre Brook at around 3,000 feet and ascends more steeply. The trail snakes briefly through a dense conifer forest and then emerges into a stunning grove of birch trees. The green forest gives way to a white-on-white world. The bottom of the Wright Peak Ski Trail intersects the hiking trail at 3,100 feet, noted by a trail sign. Most skiers climb the ski trail from here to the summit.

For those who enjoy a treasure hunt and want to ski the trail from the top, continue upward on the Algonquin hiking trail, soon crossing an old abandoned trail at an arrow. A few hundred yards farther is a camping area and then a prominent waterfall that crosses the trail and empties into a major drainage.

After 3.1 miles, you reach a junction: the yellow-blazed trail heads to Algonquin Peak (5,107 feet) in 0.8 miles, and the blue-blazed spur trail leads to the summit of Wright Peak in 0.4 miles. Follow the blue-blazed trail to climb steeply toward the Wright Peak summit, soon reaching timberline. It is best to suit up for the summit before stepping out onto the rocky ridge. You have to remove skis and climb over the rocks to reach the actual summit. Be warned that the summit can be plastered in rime ice and footing can be treacherous. Expect the full force of the weather on the exposed summit, and don't attempt it if visibility is poor or conditions are deteriorating.

From the summit of Wright Peak there are fantastic views of the enormous slides on Mount Colden, the snow-plastered dome of Algonquin Peak, and Mount Marcy. Your 360-degree panorama also includes Whiteface Mountain and Heart Lake to the north.

After savoring this scenery, it is time to find the top of the Wright Peak Ski Trail. From the summit, walk along the rocky ridge about 50 feet directly toward Mount Marcy, then stop and look down toward Heart Lake (that's the lake to the north in the shape of—you guessed it—a heart). You will see a prominent rock about 100 feet down with a geologically rare right-angle corner on it. It's as if Heart Lake and the rock are pointing at each other. Walk down off the summit ridge to this rock. Just above the rock, turn right, scramble over a small ridge, and see a narrow chute that heads downhill. Ski this chute about 80 feet until it ends, then look for where a 6- to 8-foot-wide trail breaks right. This is the top of the Wright Peak Ski Trail. Follow this trail as it contours west (toward Marcy) then begins gently descending.

The Wright Peak Ski Trail has benefited in recent years from the efforts of volunteers who have maintained the trail. From the top, the trail opens gradually and maintains a double fall line. It repeatedly traverses then drops, with the downhill sections getting progressively longer and wider. The trail widens to about 15 feet, and the skiing becomes steadily better. The Wright Peak Ski Trail then enters the huge birch glade visible from the hiking trail. This is a scenic and skiing highlight, as the fall-line shots get longer through this gorgeous forest. The ski trail snaps back and forth numerous times throughout its downhill journey, like a snake scrambling for cover.

After about a mile, you reach the yellow-blazed Algonquin hiking trail that you climbed. As you continue swinging turns down the hiking trail, you may have the sense that you are still on the ski trail. That's because you are—the original Wright Peak Ski Trail continued all the way to the junction with the Whales Tale Ski Trail. In 1974, Algonquin Trail was relocated to this lower section of the Wright Peak Ski Trail. The result is that there is plenty of room for turns on the footpath. Beware of several stream crossings as you head lower. In low snow, the hiking trail is rocky, and you must take extra care on the descent. Below the junction with the Whales Tale Ski Trail, Algonquin Trail rolls gently up and down. Continue to retrace your route back to the Van Hoevenberg Trail and finally to the High Peaks Information Center parking area.

The Wright Peak Ski Trail captures the spirit of the best 1930s-era trails. It rolls with the terrain, twisting and turning all the way down, continually surprising you. The hiking trail offers a rousing finish to the ski trail. You do not need to be an expert skier for this route—a good snowplow and the ability to stop when needed will see you through. The highlights are the dramatic alpine terrain and vistas on the summit and the powder you can enjoy all the way down.

48 AVALANCHE PASS AND LAKE COLDEN

This ski tour through Avalanche Pass to the dramatic high-alpine world of rock, ice, and snow on Avalanche Lake and Lake Colden features unrivaled scenery and fun downhill skiing.

Distance: 10.6 miles, ADK High Peaks Information Center to Lake Colden, round trip

Elevation: *Start/Finish*: 2,179 feet, ADK High Peaks Information Center; *Highest point*: 2,764 feet, Lake Colden; *Vertical drop*: 585 feet

Maps: *Adirondack Park: Lake Placid/High Peaks* (Trails Illustrated), *High Peaks Adirondack Trail Map* (ADK)

Difficulty: More difficult

Gear: AT, telemark, snowboard

Fee: A parking fee is required to park at the Adirondack Mountain Club (ADK) High Peaks Information Center

Additional Information: ADK High Peaks Information Center, 518-523-3441, adk.org

HOW TO GET THERE

From Lake Placid, drive east on NY 73 about 3 miles. Turn south on Adirondak Loj Road and proceed approximately 5 miles to the end of the road. Park at the ADK High Peaks Information Center (*GPS coordinates*: 44° 10.890' N, 73° 57.950' W). Maps and supplies are available at the information center. Alternatively, see directions to ski via the Marcy Dam Truck Trail, page 281.

THE TOUR

Skiing through Avalanche Pass to Lake Colden is one of the most spectacular ski tours in the eastern United States. This tour offers a combination climb and descent on a historic ski trail and a journey through a landscape of incredible grandeur. The highlight of the tour is skiing across Avalanche Lake, a narrow half-mile-long passageway hemmed by cliffs that rise directly out of the ice.

The ski tour into Avalanche Pass has long been a favorite among winter visitors to the Adirondacks. Jim Goodwin, a longtime Adirondack guide who began hiking and skiing in the High Peaks in the 1920s, recalled that by 1930, the ski in to Avalanche Pass "was very popular and just as beautiful as it is today. I skied that a number of times in those days, and I never remember a time when the track wasn't broken." He said that the trail "was fairly rugged. Intermediate skiers could handle it all right. Usually they'd fall one or two times." The 1939 Federal Writers' Project guidebook *Skiing in the East* described the tour as "a fine trip for intermediate skiers."

The ski tour into Avalanche Pass goes through Marcy Dam, the busy backcountry crossroads of the High Peaks. There are two routes into Marcy Dam. The most direct route (2.3 miles) is to take the Van Hoevenberg Trail from the Adirondack Moun-

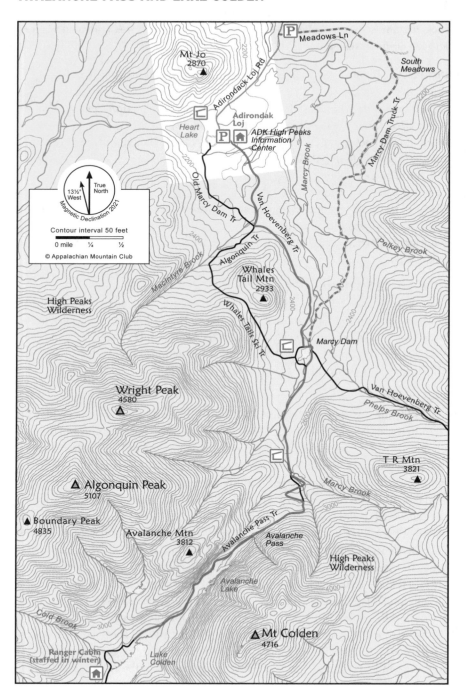

tain Club (ADK) High Peaks Information Center (next to Adirondak Loj) to Marcy Dam. This trail is heavily used by hikers, snowshoers, and climbers and is often icy.

Another ski route follows Marcy Dam Truck Trail from South Meadows. It is a longer route to Marcy Dam (3.6 miles), but this graded truck trail can be skied with just a couple of inches of snow, making it skiable early and late in the season, and the broad path is a fast ski. To reach Marcy Dam Truck Trail, take Adirondak Loj Road 3.7 miles to the junction with Meadows Lane. There are plowed parking spaces on Meadows Lane. Ski on unplowed Meadows Lane for 1 mile (you may be able to drive this section if there is little snow) then bear right at a gate and follow Marcy Dam Truck Trail to Marcy Dam.

Once at Marcy Dam, you are forced to a halt by the vista in front of you. To the west lies Wright Peak. You peer directly at Angel Slide, the twin landslides on the east face of Wright Peak that occurred during Hurricane Floyd in fall 1999. The broad slide on the left was the scene of a tragic avalanche accident in February 2000 in which one skier was killed and another was badly injured. This continues to be a dangerous playground. In February 2010, two skiers were partially buried in an avalanche while climbing Angel Slide; they were fortunate to escape with only minor injuries. You also have views here of Avalanche Pass, the height-of-land between Mount Colden and Avalanche Mountain. It is 2.2 miles to Avalanche Pass from here.

From the register at Marcy Dam, follow the blue-blazed Van Hoevenberg Trail to Mount Marcy, passing lean-tos where you can camp. After about 100 yards, bear right on the trail to Avalanche Pass, which is marked with yellow plastic disks. The trail is flat at first then rises gently for 1.1 miles, reaching the Avalanche Lean-to. From the lean-to, the hiking and ski trails diverge. Skiers should follow the ski trail—it is smoother and wider, and you get to preview what you will ski down. Snowshoers must stay on the hiking trail.

The next stretch to Avalanche Lake is unfairly dubbed "misery mile." Although it climbs steadily, the angle is quite reasonable and climbing skins are not needed. The ski trail crisscrosses the hiking trail a number of times. If you decide to walk rather than ski, please take the hiking trail, which is often firmly packed. Post-holing the ski trail ruins the experience for other skiers.

There is no mistaking where you are when you reach Avalanche Pass—the pass lives up to its name. In fall 1999, following high winds and heavy rain from Hurricane Floyd, a massive landslide swept down the slopes above and buried Avalanche Pass in 50 feet of debris. It took rangers days to hack through the tangle of trees and boulders to reopen the trail. Peering up from the pass, you now will see a 1,000-foot-long and several-hundred-foot-wide landslide ripped into the mountain. Skiing and climbing are prohibited on this slide because of the risk of triggering an avalanche onto unsuspecting hikers below.

Avalanche Pass offers a graphic display of how active the Adirondack environment is, as landslides and even earthquakes occur here with some regularity. Seeing

The stunning vistas of rock and ice are a highlight of the ski tour over Avalanche Pass.

the massive trees picked up and tossed down the mountain like Lincoln Logs leaves you with a renewed respect for the awesome forces of nature.

The short descent from Avalanche Pass to Avalanche Lake offers an introduction to classic Adirondack trail skiing. It swoops downhill then breezes around big boulders and icefalls before abruptly depositing you onto Avalanche Lake. Take care to avoid hikers and skiers who may be around a blind corner.

Avalanche Lake is a place where nature's drama is acted out in bold strokes. The view from the frozen windswept lake is of an utterly wild landscape. Black rock walls of Mount Colden (4,716 feet) and Avalanche Mountain (3,812 feet) soar up on both sides, dwarfing all who pass here. Mount Colden is raked with slides, and curtains of ice pour down onto the lake. Wind funnels through here, forcing you to move along briskly and protect yourself. You may see ice climbers on the famous Trap Dike, a slot formed on the side of Mount Colden. This is a landscape unmatched in the region for its accessibility and drama. It is a magnificent natural art gallery that will leave you awestruck.

There is more beauty to come on this ski tour. Ski straight across Avalanche Lake to its southwest end and reenter the woods. At 0.3 miles from the lake, you come to a trail junction. The sign indicates that the trail to Algonquin Peak and Lake Colden goes to the right, and a trail around the east side of Lake Colden goes left. Ignore the sign and simply ski straight ahead on flat ground, following an old phone line. You emerge onto Lake Colden in a few minutes.

From Lake Colden, there are spectacular views of the slides on Mount Colden. You also have sweeping views of the interior mountains, including a beautiful vantage point from which to view the white dome of Algonquin Peak and the Bear Claw Slide on its south face. A ranger outpost halfway down the west shore of Lake Colden is normally staffed in winter.

Returning to Avalanche Pass, you are ready to begin a classic Adirondack ski descent. From the top of the pass, the trail heads downhill like a roller coaster, complete with swooping downhills, banked turns, and forgiving runouts where you need them. Be careful to remain on the ski trail, which is cut wide for skiing, and not the hiking trail, which is post-holed and narrow. The ski trail has many long, flat sections where you can slow down. That is the beauty of this descent: it never gets too pushy, and a well-placed snowplow should suffice to check your speed.

This is Eastern trail skiing at its best. You turn where the trail turns and cruise where it relaxes. The skiing is fun and fast, but the intensity level on this trail is several notches below the Mount Marcy descent, which is more relentless. Consider the Avalanche Pass descent your bachelor's degree in Eastern trail skiing. It is good preparation for the master class that awaits you on Mount Marcy.

Passing the Avalanche lean-to, it is a steady downhill cruise all the way to Marcy Dam. You could consider camping at one of the Marcy Dam lean-tos. This would allow you to ski Avalanche Pass one day, camp in the heart of the High Peaks, and ski Mount Marcy the next day. This Adirondack "grand slam" will give you a full appreciation for what this great range has to offer.

49 MOUNT MARCY

The ski tour to the summit of Mount Marcy, New York's highest peak, is one of the great backcountry ski adventures in the East, featuring panoramic views and legendary trail skiing.

Distance: 14.4 miles, ADK High Peaks Information Center to Mount Marcy summit, round trip

Elevation: *Start/Finish*: 2,179 feet, ADK High Peaks Information Center; *Highest point*: 5,337 feet, Mount Marcy summit; *Vertical drop*: 3,162 feet

Maps: *Adirondack Park: Lake Placid/High Peaks* (Trails Illustrated), *High Peaks Adirondack Trail Map* (ADK)

Difficulty: Most difficult

Gear: AT, telemark, snowboard

Fee: There is a fee to park at the Adirondack Mountain Club High Peaks Information Center

Additional Information: ADK High Peaks Information Center, 518-523-3441, adk.org

HOW TO GET THERE

From Lake Placid, drive east on NY 73 about 3 miles. Turn on Adirondak Loj Road and proceed 5 miles to the end of the road. Park at the Adirondack Mountain Club (ADK) High Peaks Information Center (*GPS coordinates*: 44° 10.890′ N, 73° 57.950′ W). Maps and supplies are available at the information center, which is open daily from 8 A.M. to 5 P.M.

HISTORY

Skiing New York's highest peak showcases one of the best trail skiing descents in the East. The dome-capped, 5,337-foot Mount Marcy has lured backcountry skiers for a century.

The main attractions on Mount Marcy are the sweeping summit views and the 7.2-mile turn-packed descent. You follow the serpentine Van Hoevenberg Trail as it snakes, jogs, drops, and rolls down the mountain. The trail has a personality and a sense of humor, continually surprising you around each bend. Ski Mount Marcy once and you will be addicted to the thrill.

Mount Marcy has had a singular pull on mountaineers and skiers for the past two centuries. The first recorded ascent of the mountain was on August 5, 1837, by a party led by Ebenezer Emmons, a chemistry professor at Williams College who headed a section of the Geological Survey of New York. Emmons named the peak in honor of Governor William Learned Marcy. The mountain also bears the Seneca name *Tahawus*, which supposedly means "cloud splitter," although some sources insist that local Native Americans did not use this name.

MOUNT MARCY

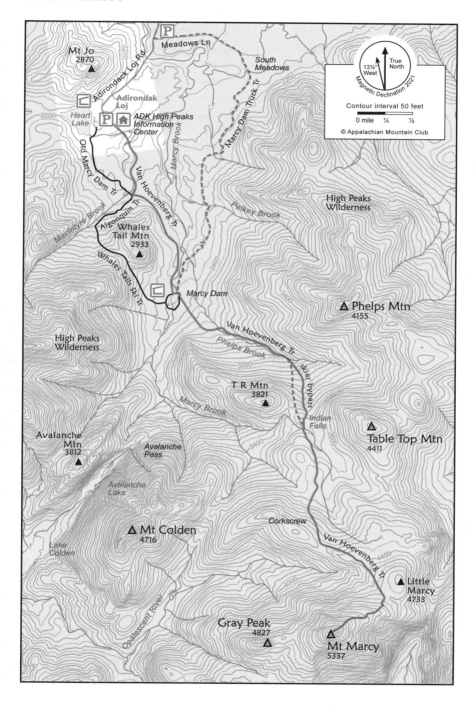

Mt Jo
2870 ▲

Meadows Ln

South
Meadows

Adirondack Loj Rd

Adirondak
Loj

Heart
Lake

ADK High Peaks
Information
Center

High Peaks
Wilderness

Old Marcy Dam Tr

Van Hoevenberg Tr

Marcy Brook

Pelkey Brook

MacIntyre Brook

Algonquin Tr

Whales
Tail Mtn
2933 ▲

Whales Tails Ski Tr

Marcy Dam

△ Phelps Mtn
4155

High Peaks
Wilderness

Van Hoevenberg Tr

Phelps Brook

skier bypass

T R Mtn
3821 ▲

Marcy Brook

Avalanche
Mtn
3812 ▲

Avalanche
Pass

Indian
Falls

△ Table Top Mtn
4411

Avalanche
Lake

△ Mt Colden
4716

Corkscrew

Van Hoevenberg Tr

Lake
Colden

▲ Little
Marcy
4733

Opalescent River

Gray Peak
4827
△

△ Mt Marcy
5337

**True
North**

**13½°
West**

Magnetic Declination 2021

Contour interval 50 feet

0 mile   ¼   ½

© Appalachian Mountain Club

The first recorded ski descent of Mount Marcy was made by John S. Apperson, Jean Canivet, and a third man in 1911. There are some claims of a ski ascent of Mount Marcy by Apperson or Irving Langmuir as early as 1908, but these are dubious. Apperson worked for General Electric in Schenectady, New York. He is responsible for several other notable first descents in the Adirondacks, which he explored for much of his life (see "The Adirondacks: A Ski History" on page 257).

The most influential skier to set foot on Mount Marcy and its environs was unquestionably Herman "Jackrabbit" Smith-Johannsen. Born in Norway in 1875, he arrived in the Adirondacks in 1915 and settled in at the Lake Placid Club, where he frequently guided winter trips into the mountains. Johannsen was famous for undertaking marathon ski tours. Following the 1932 Winter Olympics in Lake Placid, he took advantage of having the world's best skiers around by leading a group of them on one of his "pleasure tours": he skied from Adirondak Loj to Indian Pass, down to Tahawus, and back to Lake Colden—an itinerary that hikers take up to four days to cover. At Lake Colden, the 56-year-old tour guide then asked whether his guests would like to bag Mount Marcy, too. When no one declined, he started up the 2,600-foot ascent. They skied back to the Loj by moonlight.

The trails up Mount Marcy were crude in the early days, and winter ascents were expeditions. On one trip, Jackrabbit brought a group of five men from Schenectady to ski into Avalanche Pass. After spending the night, the men fought their way up the snow-choked Opalescent and Feldspar brooks to reach Lake Tear of the Clouds. Jackrabbit's daughter Alice Johannsen captured the spirit of those early Marcy journeys in her wonderful biography, *The Legendary Jackrabbit Johannsen*: "A thousand feet above them loomed the bold top of Marcy, snow covered and trackless. . . . When they finally set out again, it was with the sensation that they were real explorers, as they zigzagged their way out above the timberline, between patches of ice and snow, to the very top."

Skiing on Marcy improved slowly. In late summer 1935, a group of Adirondack skiers hiked up the Van Hoevenberg Trail in the rain and marked 127 trees for removal. Strict conservation rules forbade Adirondack trails from being significantly changed, but the skiers pressed their case. "Cutting these trees would go far toward preventing broken bones among the skiers who were then fast multiplying," reported *The Ski Bulletin*.

"Conservationists raised hell," recalled Hal Burton, who was on the scouting trip. But the skiers prevailed, and the trail was widened. At last, Adirondack skiers had a feasible ski route to the summit of Mount Marcy.

This merely made skiing on Mount Marcy possible, not easy. In January 1937, *The Ski Bulletin* reported, "The Van Hoevenberg trail up Mount Marcy from Heart Lake is not a good downhill ski trail. . . . It is, however, a very good trail to ski."

P.F. Loope from the *Schenectady Gazette* offered sage advice for skiing Mount Marcy that still applies: "At all places it is necessary to hold to a speed at which the skier can stop on short notice, for unless one knows every inch of the trail, a spill at high speed may mean plunging into a stump or stone buried under light snow." Nevertheless, he concluded, "For one interested in rugged winter mountain scenery this trip is among the best available."

The ski tour up Mount Marcy has long been one of the more popular winter outings in the Adirondacks. As big and demanding as this mountain is, it has the friendly feel of a "people's mountain." I have met older women out for a pleasant ski tour here, alongside young bucks on a mission to prove themselves. People climb the mountain with everything from snowshoes to snowboards, old wooden skis to AT and telemark skis. That is the spirit of Adirondack skiing: going for a stroll in the mountains, whatever your conveyance, is an honored pastime. What is important is that you go, not how you go.

THE TOUR

The Mount Marcy tour starts from the ADK High Peaks Information Center (HPIC). The most direct route (2.3 miles to Marcy Dam) is to take the Van Hoevenberg Trail from the HPIC. The section of trail to Marcy Dam, named for Adirondak Loj builder Henry Van Hoevenberg, is heavily used by hikers, snowshoers, and climbers. Another option that is less crowded but a mile longer is to ski in on the Marcy Dam Truck Trail (see directions in tour 48, Avalanche Pass, on page 279).

From Marcy Dam, pass the trail register and follow the blue-blazed Van Hoevenberg Trail up Mount Marcy. The trail climbs gradually until reaching a bridge across Phelps Brook at 3.5 miles from the HPIC. This is traditionally where you stop to put on climbing skins. After crossing the bridge, the trail climbs steeply for a short distance until a four-way junction. Snowshoers must take the narrow footpath to the right, but skiers proceed straight ahead on a skier-only trail (a short skier/snowshoer trail is also to the left). At 4.5 miles, the ski trail arrives at Indian Falls, where it merges once again with the hiking trail. There are dramatic views here of Algonquin Peak with its prominent slides, as well as the neighboring summits of Boundary Peak, Iroquois Peak, and Wright Peak.

The Van Hoevenberg Trail moderates from here, climbing more gradually through a fir and spruce forest. Signs warn that the trail is for skis or snowshoes only, and enforcement of this rule has made a considerable difference in keeping the ski surface in good shape. At 5.3 miles, you arrive at the Corkscrew, the steepest half-mile of the trail. A 6.2 miles, you reach a junction with the Hopkins Trail to Keene Valley, and at 6.5 miles, you come to the former lean-to site (since removed) known as the Plateau. From here, the Marcy summit cone looks immense. Like a giant vanilla ice cream scoop scraping against the sky, Marcy appears to offer unlimited ways to descend.

Continue climbing through steep scrubby vegetation, passing the junction with the Phelps Trail at 6.8 miles. You are now at the base of the summit cone. The final half-mile is above treeline and exposed to the full force of the weather. In foggy or snowy conditions, the summit area is extremely disorienting. You should assess the weather conditions and the energy levels of the members of your group before proceeding. Be especially careful to protect any exposed skin from wind and wear goggles for eye and face protection. Suit up in storm gear before leaving the last trees.

You probably will not be able to see any trail markings or cairns, so good visibility is crucial up here. Climb to the summit, zigzagging up wherever you find good snow that is out of the wind.

From the summit of Mount Marcy, the views are limitless. Mounts Haystack and Skylight appear as huge white domes that beckon climbers and skiers. The Green Mountains of Vermont are silhouetted in the distance, and you peer out on miles of roadless forest and summits. The world appears vast. It seems incongruous that you are standing on the roof of New York, one of the most populous states in the nation.

There was once a stone hut on the summit of Mount Marcy that was popular with skiers. The structure was built in 1928 and was designed and paid for by the chair of the Adirondack Mountain Club. Jim Goodwin, an Adirondack guide who began skiing in the High Peaks in the 1930s, told me that the hut "got a lot of action, especially for spring skiing." He recalled, "People would stay in the hut and ski down to timberline and back. It really was attractive skiing, and colorful as well." But conservationists viewed the hut as a violation of the sacred "forever wild" laws that govern the Adirondacks. The matter was settled sometime during the 1940s, when the hut was struck by lightning and partially destroyed. In the 1950s, rangers finished what nature started, completely dismantling the structure. There is no trace of the famous stone hut today.

The descent of Mount Marcy is where the mountain offers up a rich multicourse offering of treats. The summit cone brims with secret shots and hidden ravines where you can search for powder on your way down. You can retrace your climbing tracks (recommended if visibility is waning) and swing down through a beautiful steep bowl. The north face (to skier's left of the trail) offers a number of long lines, but you must take care to traverse back to the right at the bottom in order to rejoin the Van Hoevenberg Trail.

Once back at treeline on the Van Hoevenberg Trail, hang on for a high-speed, heel-snapping descent through Romper Room. This narrow, winding section through scrub trees delivers you back to the saddle between Mount Marcy and Little Marcy. Several long stretches of fast trail skiing soon bring you to the Plateau. From here, climb and descend on rolling terrain, then hang on as the trail drops again. This is the Corkscrew, a 10-foot-wide section of trail that spirals back and forth down the fall line. It ends with a hard right turn and a good runout where you can dump speed.

The Van Hoevenberg Trail continues descending steadily until Indian Falls. Below the falls, you reap the benefit of trail work. What used to be a narrow mile-long pipeline is now a fun skier-only trail that snaps and plunges but has enough room to link turns. This passes the four-way trail junction, rejoining the hiking trail, and charges downhill until ending at a right-angle turn onto the bridge over Phelps Brook. If you are really on it, you can ski across the bridge at full throttle; otherwise, prepare to hit the brakes, and cross the brook under control. The next mile to Marcy Dam is fast, fun cruising where you can stand on your skis and enjoy the ride (but stay alert for open drainages). Of course, standing on your skis may be all you are able to do at this point, having long since wrung the last turns from your tired legs. From Marcy Dam, the Van Hoevenberg Trail is a flat-to-rolling ski back to your car.

There is a rollicking drop-and-roll rhythm to skiing the Van Hoevenberg Trail, with frequent runouts that appear magically—and just when you need them. The trail is moderately steep and averages between 6 and 10 feet wide. It calls for quick turns. In good conditions, less experienced skiers can manage much of the trail with a solid snowplow. The final 2 miles on flatter ground add a nice cross-country finish to the tour.

Ski conditions on the Van Hoevenberg Trail improve with increased traffic. The more skiers, snowshoers, and snowboards that pass through, the better groomed the trail becomes and the easier it is to ski. Of course, a powder run is nice, too, but breaking trail uphill for 7 miles is no picnic. Some of the finest skiing and riding on Mount Marcy is in April, when warm weather and spring corn snow make both the climb and descent eminently enjoyable.

On top of New York: skiing the snowy summit cone of Mount Marcy.

The thrill of a Mount Marcy ski tour lies in its variety: skiers and riders empty their bag of tricks negotiating the mountain. Mount Marcy calls on the full range of ski skills, from skating the flats, to climbing uphill, to negotiating an exposed summit, to linking quick turns and skiing powder, crud, or whatever surprises the mountain has in store.

This is a full-day commitment that requires an early start and good preparation. Expect full winter conditions on the summit and be willing to abort your climb if conditions—either the weather or the energy of your group—deteriorate. The exposed Mount Marcy summit can be an unforgiving place for the unprepared, but it is an unforgettable highlight for the skier who finally lays claim to this prize.

As you contemplate a climb of Mount Marcy today, savor the wisdom of one of its earliest ski pioneers. As Jackrabbit Johannsen mused:

> All my life I have been anxious to see what lies on the other side of the hill, and at the same time, I have never failed to enjoy the scenery along the way. With all my senses "tuned in"—sight and hearing, taste and smell and touch—I was able to reap full benefit from each experience. So, I say, set your goals high, and stick to them, but approach them step by step so that at any given time your expectations are not impossibly out of reach. Climb your mountain slowly, one step at a time, following a well-planned route. And when at last you stand upon the summit, you can look beyond, to the farthest horizon!

5 MASSACHUSETTS

50 THUNDERBOLT SKI TRAIL, MOUNT GREYLOCK

The Thunderbolt Ski Trail was one of the most famous ski race courses in the country in the 1930s and 1940s. The trail has been restored to its original condition by local volunteers, making it once again among the finest down-mountain backcountry ski trails.

Distance: 6 miles, Thiel Road parking area to Mount Greylock summit, ascending via Bellows Pipe and descending Thunderbolt, round trip
Elevation: *Start/Finish*: 1,250 feet, Thiel Road parking; *Highest point*: 3,492 feet (Mount Greylock summit), 3,100 feet (top of Thunderbolt); *Vertical drop*: 2,242 feet, Mount Greylock summit to Thiel Farm
Maps: *AMC Massachusetts Trail Map 1: Northern Berkshires* (AMC); Download map at thunderboltskirunners.org
Difficulty: Most difficult
Gear: AT, telemark, snowboard
Additional Information: For current trail conditions, history, photos, and information about the Thunderbolt Ski Museum: thunderboltskirunners.org.

HOW TO GET THERE

From the McKinley Monument on MA 8 in the center of Adams, drive west up Maple Street to the end. Turn left onto West Road and drive 0.4 miles, then turn right on Gould Road at a sign for Greylock Glen. At the top of the hill where Gould Road turns left, keep driving straight on Thiel Road for about 300 feet until you reach concrete barriers. You can park here (*GPS coordinates*: 42° 37.667′ N, 73° 08.260′ W) and ski 0.4 miles on the road to the Thunderbolt trailhead.

THUNDERBOLT SKI TRAIL, MOUNT GREYLOCK

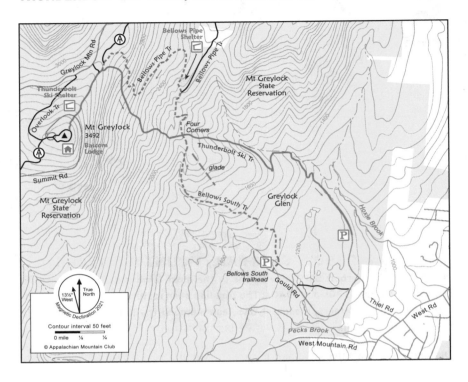

Skiers can also take a left onto Gould Road and park at the smaller Bellows South trailhead (*GPS coordinates*: 42° 37.633′ N, 73° 08.718′ W). From there, take Bellows South Trail to the Thunderbolt. The trail junction is known as Four Corners, where there is a kiosk.

HISTORY

The Thunderbolt.

The intimidating name brings a smile to the face of older skiers. It is described in awestruck terms in a 1939 guidebook to Eastern skiing as "one of the steepest and most difficult expert trails in the East." When the Thunderbolt was cut in 1934, it was an audacious proposition: a ski trail that started near the summit of the highest mountain in Massachusetts then plunged straight over the edge and hurtled 2,000 vertical feet through twists, narrows, and drops to the valley floor some 2 miles away.

Mount Greylock (elevation 3,492 feet) was first skied in 1908 by Irving Langmuir, from Schenectady, New York. Though he is perhaps better known as the winner of the 1932 Nobel Prize for chemistry, Langmuir was one of the first and most prolific ski mountaineers in North America in the early 1900s. His ski of Mount

Greylock was undoubtedly a rugged expedition because there were no ski trails on the mountain at that time.

Charlie Parker, a former caretaker of the AMC Bascom Lodge and an avid skier, designed the Thunderbolt Ski Trail. The Civilian Conservation Corps (CCC) provided the muscle to turn Parker's idea for a race trail on Mount Greylock into reality. Company 107 of the CCC, based in Savoy, Massachusetts, began building the ski trail in August 1934. Three months later, national downhill ski champion Joseph Duncan visited the mountain and viewed the run. He promptly declared the Thunderbolt "undoubtedly the most thrilling wooded ski run in the country," according to the excellent documentary film, *Purple Mountain Majesty: A History of the Thunderbolt Ski Trail*. The ski trail was named after an exciting roller coaster ride in Revere Beach, outside Boston.

The Thunderbolt quickly attracted a loyal following among New England skiers. It was one of a small number of Class A ski racing trails in the Northeast and was the scene of numerous national and regional championship races (among the other Class A trails were the Nose Dive at Stowe, the Wildcat Trail on Wildcat Mountain in New Hampshire, Whiteface Ski Trail in the Adirondacks, and the Richard Taft Trail on Cannon Mountain). Class A trails had to be 1 to 1.5 miles long with a vertical drop of 2,000 feet and at least one section with a gradient of 30 to 35 degrees. Top racers could earn a coveted rating with a good run here; skiing the Thunderbolt in less than 3 minutes made one an "A" racer, between 3 and 4 minutes qualified one as a "B" racer, and a "C" rating went to those who could schuss it in 4 to 6 minutes. The first race on the trail was held on February 16, 1935, and was won by legendary Dartmouth skier Dick Durrance in 2 minutes, 49 seconds. The course record on the Thunderbolt is 2 minutes, 8 seconds, set by Per Klippgen at the 1948 Eastern Championships.

The Thunderbolt was much more than a ski trail. Built in the wake of the Great Depression, the trail formed the hub of a bustling skiing subculture. Ski races became festive community events for the depressed mill town of Adams. Local ski clubs made the pilgrimage to Greylock every weekend, including the Mount Greylock Ski Club, the Thunderbolt Ski Club, and the Ski Runners of Adams, as well as local college teams from Williams and Amherst. A typical weekend in the 1930s would find about 40 skiers on the Thunderbolt, with more on weekends preceding a big race. Skiers sidestepped up the trail, packing the snow on the big turns to keep them from getting scraped off and "filling the bathtubs" of skiers who fell. The first race on the Thunderbolt drew a crowd of 3,500 spectators, and subsequent races drew as many as 6,000 people who arrived on the ski trains that came from New York and Boston. Spectators lined the trail and often took part in the trail packing.

The Thunderbolt spawned a ski craze in Adams. As more townspeople were drawn to take part in the social and athletic goings-on on the east side of Mount Greylock, a local furniture store began selling skis. As recounted in *Purple Mountain Majesty*, a pair of Groswold wood skis cost $22.50, more than double the weekly paycheck of local mill workers. The furniture store owner let customers pay in $1 installments.

Some historic highlights on the Thunderbolt included the 1938 Eastern Amateur Downhill race, which featured an appearance by a top German ski team sent by Adolf Hitler. The Germans won handily, defeating local ski hero Rudy Konieczny. Konieczny would meet the Germans again as a soldier in the U.S. Army Tenth Mountain Division fighting in Italy in 1945, where he was killed in combat. Rudy's Thunderbolt buddies still speak in awe of the graceful and talented young man who inspired and challenged a generation of Adams skiers. In June 1999, just after the 100th anniversary of the creation of the Greylock Reservation and with renewed local interest in the Thunderbolt Ski Trail, the friends and family of Rudy Konieczny restored and rededicated the Thunderbolt Ski Shelter in his memory. This beautiful stone warming hut for skiers just below the Mount Greylock summit was originally built in 1940 by the CCC.

The original Thunderbolt racecourse started from the summit of Mount Greylock and traveled down what is now the Appalachian Trail for 0.4 miles. It then banked east onto the current top of the Thunderbolt. Running parallel to the Thunderbolt is the Bellows Pipe Trail (sometimes referred to as the Bellows Pipeline), which was considered an intermediate ski run and is the preferred uphill route (see below). On days when the Thunderbolt was too icy, officials detoured racers onto the upper portion of the Bellows Pipe.

Skiers and riders of today can test their talents on the Thunderbolt and get a humbling taste of what inspired skiers nearly a century ago. Don't expect a geriatric meander—this trail is for skiers who like a lot of vertical drop in a short distance. It is an exhilarating steep run that keeps you swooping through turns throughout its entire length.

THE TOUR

Ski up Thiel Road past the concrete barriers, pass a sign for the Thunderbolt Ski Trail, and head uphill on an 8-foot-wide trail. The access trail follows a small brook (Hoxie Brook) on the right. Eventually you come to a fork in the trail. A sign here directs you to the left for the Bellows Pipe Trail and right for the Thunderbolt. Bear right and follow the trail as it bends around to the left. Keep climbing this access trail, and when Hoxie Brook breaks off to the north, the trail you are on widens. This is the Thunderbolt Ski Trail.

The ski trail climbs steeply and comes to a four-way junction known as Four Corners. There is a kiosk here. The preferred route to ascend the Thunderbolt is to turn right (north) here and skin up the Bellows Pipe Trail. In 0.3 miles, bear left to stay on the Bellows Pipe as it heads up the mountain (do not follow the trail straight, which leads to North Adams). You soon pass the Bellows Pipe lean-to and continue uphill at a moderate grade with excellent views of Adams below. The trail begins to switchback as you climb higher, finally connecting with the Appalachian Trail

(AT). Turn left and reach the Thunderbolt in a few minutes, and it is another 0.4 miles to the summit. Just before the summit, you reach the Thunderbolt Ski Shelter. Step inside, light a fire, relax, and eat some food. The excitement is about to begin.

The summit of Mount Greylock is not exactly wilderness—it has a large war memorial tower, Bascom Lodge, and a paved road. Bascom Lodge is a beautiful stone and wood structure that was built by the CCC in the 1930s; it is now operated in a public-private partnership and is open for lodging and dining from May through October.

Bill Linscott, 1942 state champion on the Thunderbolt, recalled that races began with a bang. Racers pushed off from the summit, quickly crossed Rockwell Road, and then dropped down and headed for the junction where the Thunderbolt bears east. "You would come off that road and be in the air for 50 feet—and that was if you weren't trying to get air. If you jumped, you'd go a lot further," he told me.

Dropping into the Thunderbolt from the summit is still dramatic. A nondescript spur leaves the AT, and just 50 yards beyond, the whole side of the mountain falls away, revealing unobstructed views of the Berkshire Mountains and the southern peaks of the Green Mountains. Lying before you is the impressive beginning of the Thunderbolt.

The legions of skiers who skied the Thunderbolt had names for every turn and dip on it—that was part of its cachet. The start of the trail at the AT was called the Big Bend, because it was the first major turn after bombing down from the summit. This 35-degree pitch is one of the steepest parts of the trail. The trail bends to the right, but the slope banks to the left—you have to defy gravity to hang on around this turn. The trail then narrows and takes a southerly traverse, and you come to the Steps—three ledge steps that are often icy.

The trail then accelerates toward the Needle's Eye. This is the crux of the Thunderbolt. The trail narrows to about 15 feet here and turns to the right, although the slope banks downhill into the woods. There is no room to make turns—you must simply schuss it. "If a skier came down and hit the Needle's Eye full tilt and didn't make the turn, he was in deep trouble," mused Linscott, who died in 2001. Just beyond the Needle's Eye is the Big Schuss, probably the steepest drop on the trail. It is about 200 yards long and up to 60 feet wide. At one time, a rope tow was operated on the Big Schuss.

The lower section of the Thunderbolt bears right after the Big Schuss. From here to the finish line, ski racers still had to contend with the Bumps—named for the eight to ten large bumps that had to be negotiated—head into the S-turn, and ski the Last Drop, the final steep pitch, before crossing the brook to the finish line. The original finish line has been abandoned by modern skiers (faint remnants of the bridge over the brook can be seen in the woods to the left). "If you didn't stop in time, you went for a swim in the river," recounted Thunderbolt veteran Greeny Guertin.

The Thunderbolt strikes again: a skier charges down the Thunderbolt Ski Trail on Mount Greylock.

To Linscott, who was 16 years old when he won the championship, the memory of skiing the Thunderbolt was fresh. "By the time you hit the S-turn, your legs are gone and your wobbly knees are bumping up and down. . . . You were awfully glad to see the finish line when it came. Most skiers could just about stand up at the end."

World War II marked the end of the Thunderbolt's heyday. Many of the young people who flocked to the mountain went off to fight in the war. They returned to tackle new adventures, raising families and finding jobs. The lure of lift-served downhill ski areas further dampened interest in the venerable old trail. A proposal in the 1970s to create a commercial ski area on the east side of Mount Greylock died, but not before lights were installed and trails were cut; the remains of these can still be seen in the ski glade off the Bellows South trail. The Thunderbolt started to grow in, and by the early 1980s, ski traffic on Mount Greylock was reduced to a trickle. It looked as though the Thunderbolt was destined for the scrap bin of ski history.

When I first skied the Thunderbolt in 1987 while researching *Classic Backcountry Skiing*, the first edition of this guidebook, the trail was brushy and narrow, a shadow of its former self. A local ranger tried to dissuade me from even trying to find it. She warned, "It hasn't been skied in years. It's dangerous."

In the 1990s, something remarkable occurred in Adams: the Thunderbolt was resurrected. A high school teacher and skier in Adams, Blair Mahar, assigned his class to interview local residents about the old ski trail. Suddenly, kids heard their parents and grandparents come alive with stories. The class assignment evolved into the remarkable 1999 documentary movie, *Purple Mountain Majesty*. The film went on to win awards. The documentary, combined with the growing popularity of backcountry skiing and snowboarding, sparked a revival of interest in skiing the 'Bolt.

But first, the trail had to be brought back to life. The Thunderbolt Ski Runners, a local ski club, was reborn, and a new generation of devotees went to work maintaining the trail, clearing underbrush, and restoring it to its original width. They hung beautiful signs on the trees facing both uphill and downhill to identify sections of the trail. They have installed new bridges, meticulously maintained the trail, and restored its width to between 20 and 40 feet wide. The Thunderbolt is now the only one of the original New England Class A race trails that still exists as a down-mountain ski trail without a chairlift.

The Thunderbolt revival needed one more thing to be complete. In March 2010, the town of Adams and the Thunderbolt Ski Runners held a 75th-anniversary race on the Thunderbolt, commemorating the first downhill ski race on the trail. The winning downhill time in the 2010 race was 3 minutes, 1 second—12 seconds behind Dick Durrance's winning time in 1935 and 53 seconds slower than Thunderbolt course record-holder Per Klippgen's time in 1948. Modern equipment and technique are still no match for the guts, passion, and style of the ski pioneers.

Today's Thunderbolt skiers have done more than restore a ski trail. They have created a living museum on Mount Greylock, bringing history to life and re-creating the vibrant community that thrived around the trail. There is also a Thunderbolt museum in Adams that tells the history of the trail.

Rich Adamczyk, a member of the Thunderbolt Ski Runners and one of those who now maintains the trail, recounted as we climbed the mountain, "My grandmother told me about days when she would come with hundreds of people to watch the race. I have a picture of snowboarding it with my father in 1993 when I was 13." He skis the Thunderbolt four to five times a week. "It's always a great time. The skiing is good, it's got a strong history, it's in my backyard, and it connects me to a lot of people locally."

Today, the Thunderbolt is once again a playground for skiers and riders. The limiting factor for skiing it is the fickle snow conditions in western Massachusetts. The best advice for getting a good run on the Thunderbolt is to go when it snows. You will be well rewarded for seizing the moment: a powder day on the Thunderbolt is still as good as skiing gets.

As you descend this epic run today, allow your mind to drift. Picture yourself shadowing a 1930s racer down the Thunderbolt. The skier, clad in wool knickers, is bearing down the mountain on his long wooden boards. His baggy clothes flap hysterically in the wind. Friends cheer as his skis chatter through the Needle's Eye. He rockets down the Big Schuss, launches over the Bumps, and banks through the S-turn. You follow, hanging on as you hurtle through history.

The sidelines of Thunderbolt Trail are quiet again. Only the sound of your skis or snowboard slicing through fresh powder breaks the silence of the woods now. The legends of this run are tucked beneath its snowy mantle. But as you descend this great mountain, you can still feel the same trepidation and reverence that earlier skiers felt for this old trail.

The Thunderbolt is still electrifying.

POSTSCRIPT: SAVING WINTER

Skiers are canaries in the coal mine for climate change. If you care about back-country skiing, you need to care about stopping climate change. The habitat of backcountry skiers is under threat.

The future of skiing is at stake. Winters are shorter. The snowpack is diminish-ing. Each year breaks records as the hottest ever. A study sponsored by Protect Our Winters (protectourwinters.org), a climate action group, projects that the average number of days with snow cover in New England will decline by 50 to 75 percent, depending on greenhouse gas emissions. Other studies project that most ski areas in southern New England will be out of business by 2040, and there will not be skiing in New England by the end of the century.

Concerned? I certainly am.

We cannot take skiing for granted. As skiers, we should pursue our passion both on and off the mountains. We have powered a movement for community-supported skiing. We need to harness that same passion to stop climate change.

The work is global, but it begins locally: our communities and our states must commit to being carbon neutral. We have to immediately transition away from fossil fuels to renewable energy. We must protect public lands. We have to work for climate justice, ensuring that vulnerable and low-income people benefit from and participate in the transition to a carbon-neutral future.

Stopping climate change can feel overwhelming. But we get there one step, one turn, at a time.

We are stronger together. Join climate action groups such as Protect Our Winters and 350.org. Or form a group in your community to take action locally.

As skiers, we have to be part of the climate change solution. Our snowy future depends on us.

— *David Goodman*

LEAVE NO TRACE

The Appalachian Mountain Club (AMC) has a lengthy history with Leave No Trace (LNT) and champions its principles. With the sheer number of people in the outdoors these days and encroaching pressures on open space everywhere, we all must make an effort to minimize our impact on the land. AMC offers LNT master educator classes in partnership with the Leave No Trace Center for Outdoor Ethics to train those who will help train others.

The LNT program in the United States was created in the 1980s as a cooperative effort between the U.S. Forest Service, the National Park Service, and the Bureau of Land Management. Its purpose was to develop hiking and camping principles that promoted a new wilderness land ethic. In the early '90s, the U.S. Forest Service partnered with the National Outdoor Leadership School to develop a science-based curriculum for training public land managers, outdoor professionals, and outdoor recreationists. Today, the seven LNT principles are widely accepted as the seven commandments of any serious and educated hiker or backpacker. They are easy to understand and, with some guidance, quite simple to put into practice.

It is important to note that in many locations, public land agencies have used some of the seven LNT principles to establish rules and regulations for outdoor users. This means that not practicing some of these principles results in infractions with concrete consequences, such as a fine or expulsion from a public land area.

LNT principles also must be included in a common-sense approach to risk management. During a critical incident, any actions taken to mitigate the situation should prioritize the following elements, in this order:

- Safety of the individual (that is, yourself and others)
- Safety of the equipment
- Safety of the environment

If you keep this in mind, you will be able to respond to an emergency without feeling bad about the impact your action might have on the environment. For instance, in a situation in which someone in your party has broken through ice and is soaked, it would be appropriate to set up camp near the site of the incident, even if it is near a water source, and to build a large fire to dry the wet clothing while actively warming the person. You might be breaking a few LNT principles, but this situation calls for you to prioritize the unfortunate companion.

THE SEVEN LNT PRINCIPLES

Below, you will find the seven LNT winter use principles adopted by the Leave No Trace Center for Outdoor Ethics, which manages and promotes LNT in North America. Visit lnt.org to learn more.

PLAN AHEAD AND PREPARE

- Know the area and what to expect; *always* check avalanche and weather reports prior to departure. Consult maps and local authorities about high-danger areas, safety information, and regulations for the area you plan to visit.
- Prepare for extreme weather, hazards, and emergencies.
- Monitor snow conditions frequently. Carry and use an avalanche beacon, probe, and shovel.
- Educate yourself by taking a winter backcountry travel course.
- Visit the backcountry in small groups, but never alone. Leave your itinerary with family or friends.
- Repackage food into reusable containers.
- Use a map and compass to eliminate the need for tree markings, rock cairns, or flagging.

TRAVEL AND CAMP ON DURABLE SURFACES

On the trail

- Stay on deep snow cover whenever possible; in muddy spring conditions, stay on snow or walk in the middle of the trail to avoid creating new trails and damaging trailside plants.
- Travel and camp away from avalanche paths, cornices, steep slopes, and unstable snow.

At camp

- Choose a site on durable surfaces—snow, rock, or mineral soil—not tundra or other fragile vegetation.
- Camp at a safe, stable site out of view of heavily traveled routes and trails.
- Keep pollutants out of water sources by camping at least 200 feet (70 adult steps) from recognizable lakes and streams—consult your map.

DISPOSE OF WASTE PROPERLY

- Pack It In, Pack It Out. Pack out everything you bring with you. Burying trash and litter in the snow or ground is unacceptable.
- Pick up all food scraps, wax shavings, and pieces of litter. Pack out all trash, yours and others.

- Pack out solid human waste. In lieu of packing it out, cover and disguise human waste deep in snow away from travel routes and at least 200 feet (70 adult steps) from water sources.
- Use toilet paper or wipes sparingly. Pack them out.
- If necessary, use small amounts of biodegradable soap for dishes. Strain dishwater into a sump hole.
- Inspect your campsite for trash and evidence of your stay. Dismantle all snow shelters, igloos, or wind breaks. Naturalize the area before you leave.

LEAVE WHAT YOU FIND
- Leave all plants, rocks, animals, and historical or cultural artifacts as you find them.
- Let nature's sounds prevail. Keep loud voices and noises to a minimum.

MINIMIZE CAMPFIRE IMPACTS
- Campfires cause lasting impacts in the backcountry. Always carry a lightweight camp stove for cooking.
- Use dead downed wood if you can find it. Put out all fires completely. Widely scatter cool ashes.
- Do not cut or break limbs off live, dead, or downed trees.

RESPECT WILDLIFE
- Winter is an especially vulnerable time for animals. Observe wildlife from a distance. Do not follow or approach them.
- Never feed wildlife or leave food behind to be eaten.
- Protect wildlife and your food by storing rations and trash securely.

BE CONSIDERATE OF OTHER VISITORS
- Be respectful of other users. Share the trail and be courteous.
- Yield to downhill and faster traffic. Prepare for blind corners.
- When stopped, move off the trail.
- Separate ski and snowshoe tracks where possible. Avoid hiking on ski or snowshoe tracks.
- Learn and follow local regulations regarding pets. Control dogs. Pack out or bury all dog feces.

AMC provides LNT training courses throughout the year, and it might be wise to take one of these formal training workshops if you are an avid hiker or backpacker, or if you intend to lead others into the backcountry. Find a course near you at outdoors.org/activities.

INDEX

A

Acadia National Park, 123–129
   map of, 124–125
Adamczyk, Rich, 297
Adams, Mount, 98–102
Adirondack Mountain Club High Peaks
  Information Center (HPIC), 273, 279, 284
Adirondack Mountains (New York)
   Avalanche Pass and Lake Colden,
    279–283
   Jackrabbit Trail, 263–267
   Johns Brook Valley, 268–272
   Mount Marcy, 284–290
   ski history in, 257–262
   Wright Peak Ski Trail, 273–278
Adirondack Ski Touring Council (ASTC), 263
Airplane Gully (Great Gulf), 83
Alexandria Trail (Mt. Cardigan), 1–6
Algonquin Peak, 277
Allen, Jack, 213
Al Merrill Loop (Mt. Moosilaukee), 13
American Eider Schussboomers, 261
American Inferno races, 46–49
Ammonoosuc Ravine (Mt. Washington),
  92–97
   map of, 93
Antone Mountain (Merck Forest), 250–251
Apperson, John, 46, 258–259, 282
Approach Trail (Baxter State Park), 152–153
Ascutney, Mt., 164–166
Ascutney Outdoors Center, 164
Austin, Peggy Johannsen, 259
avalanche awareness, xxxiii–xxxvi
   in Baxter State park, 157
   in Tuckerman Ravine, 54
Avalanche Brook Trail, 67–70
Avalanche Lake, 279–282
Avalanche Pass, 279–283

B

backcountry attitude, xxxii–xxxiii
backcountry repair, xxix–xxx
backcountry shelters
   in Baxter State Park, 155
   on Mount Greylock, 294
   in New Hampshire, 44, 53, 76
   in Vermont, 161, 171, 231
   See also huts and lodges
backcountry skiing, history of, 7, 9, xvii–xxiii
   Adirondack region, 257–262
   on Mount Greylock, 292–294, 297
   on Katahdin, 148–150
   in Tuckerman Ravine, 45–50
Baldface Mountain, 33–35
   map of, 34
Bald Hill (Camel's Hump), 186–188
Baldwin, Jeff, 225
Barnett, Steve, xxiii
Bartlett Mountain, 237–241
Battell, Joseph, 177
Baxter, Percival P., 148
Baxter Park Traverse, 155–157
Baxter State Park, 146–157
   avalanche awareness in, 157
   map of, 147
   ski routes in, 152–157
   winter regulations, 150–152
Bennies Brook Slide (Johns Brook Valley),
  272
Big Jay Mountain, 242–246
bindings, xxviii
Black Mountain Ski Trail, 19–22, 130–133
Blood, C.W., 205
Bolton Backcountry Trails, 189–190
Bolton–Trapp Trail, 193, 198–204
Bolton Valley Sports Center, 200–201
Booth, John, 258

boots, xxvii
Braintree Mountain Forest, 169–172
Brandon Gap, 173–176
Brautigam, Dave, 184
Bright, Alex, 9
Bruce Trail (Mt. Mansfield), 211–216, 225
Bryant, Edward, 189
Bryant Camp, 202
Burt, Craig Sr., 213, 218, 220
Burt, Henry M., 95
Burton, Hal, 213, 273, 275, 286
Burton, Jake, xxiii
Burt Ravine (Mt. Washington), 92–97
Burt Trail (Mt. Mansfield), 222

C

Cadillac Mountain (Acadia N.P.), 129
Camel's Hump, 177–188
    Bald Hill, 186–188
    Honey Hollow Trail, 182–185
    Monroe Trail, 178–181
Camel's Hump Nordic Center, 188
Camel's Hump Skiers' Association, 184
camping. *See* backcountry shelters; huts and
    lodges
Camp Peggy O'Brien, 268–271
Cannon Mountain, 14–18
Cardigan, Mount, 1–6
Carleton, John, 46
Carriage Road (Mt. Moosilauke), 9, 11–13
Catamount Trail (CT), 159–163, 182–185
Cathedral route (Tuckerman Ravine), 64
Center Headwall (Tuckerman Ravine), 61–62
Champney Falls Trail (Mount Chocorua),
    118–121
Chimney Couloir (Baxter State Park), 153
Chimney Pond (Baxter State Park), 153
Chittenden Brook Hut, 176, 254
Chocorua, Mount, 118–121
The Chute (Tuckerman Ravine), 61
Civilian Conservation Corps (CCC),
    xxviii–xx
climate change, 299
climbing skins, xxviii–xxix
Cog Railway (Mt. Washington), 94–95
Coleman, Abner, xxi
Comey, Arthur, 148–150
Connie's Way (Pinkham Notch), 116
Coppermine Trail (Cannon Mountain), 15, 16

Crescent Ridge, 39–42
    map of, 41
crevasses, 55

D

Dana Place Trail (Wildcat Mountain), 27
Dartmouth Outing Club (DOC), 7, xxii
Dewey Mountain (Mt. Mansfield), 231–232
difficulty, explained, xxiv–xxv
Dodge, Brooks, 82
Dodge, Joseph Brooks Jr., 46, 49–50
Dodge's Drop (Tuckerman Ravine), 64–65
Dorr Mountain (Acadia N.P.), 129
Double Barrel (Oakes Gulf), 89–90
Doublehead Ski Trail, 28–31
Dover Town Forest, 248–249
Duchess route (Tuckerman Ravine), 65–66
Duke's Trail (Mt. Cardigan), 1–6
Duncan, Joseph, 293
Durrance, Dick, 48–49, 213, 293
Dutch Hill Ski Area, 247–248

E

Eastern Amateur Downhill race, 294
Emmons, Ebenezer, 284
Ethan Pond Trail (Pemigewasset Wilderness),
    106–107

F

Feffer, Tad, 150
Field, Darby, 82
Firescrew Mountain, 1–6
first aid, xxxi–xxxii
Flagstaff Lake Hut, 144–145
Fowler, William, 46
Franconia Inn cross-country ski trail
    network, 16, 18
Freeman, Zac, 169–170
Frenette, Robbie, 261–262
Fridtjof Nansen Ski Club, xxvii
frostbite, xxxi–xxxii

G

Gardiner's Lane (Bolton Backcountry), 190
Getchell, Dave, 150
glade zones, 32
    Bald Hill, 186–188
    Braintree Mountain Forest, 169–172
    Brandon Gap, 173–176

Maple Villa, 36–38
Merrymeeting Glade (Black Mountain), 133
RASTA and, 167–168
Sterling Valley, 233–236
Willoughby State Forest, 239–240
Goodrich, Nat, 205
Goodwin, Jim, 261, 265, 279
Goodwin, Tony, 263, 276
Gorman Chairback Lodge, 136–137, 140
Gothics Slides (Johns Brook Valley), 271–272
Grace Camp, 268–272
Grand Falls Hut, 141, 145
Granite Backcountry Alliance (GBA), 32
Great Basin (Katahdin), 154–155
Great Gulf (Mt. Washington), 80–86
map of, 81
Greeley Ponds, 108–110
Greylock, Mount, 291–298
ski history of, 292–294, 293
Grout Pond Recreation Area, 163
Gulf Hagas, 140
Gulf of Slides (Mt. Washington), 71–75
map of, 72

H
Hamlin Ridge Trail (Baxter State Park), 154–155
Hannah, Sel, 16, 49
Harris, Fred, 45
Hathaway, Mel, 265
Headwall route (Tuckerman Ravine), 57
Hell's Highway (Mt. Moosilauke), 9–10
Hermit Lake camping area, 44, 53
Higgins, John, 225
Hillman, Henry, 9, 49
Hillman's Highway (Tuckerman Ravine), 49, 63–64
Holden, Glen, 194
Honey Hollow Trail (Camel's Hump), 182–185
Hooke, David, 9
Hor, Mount, 237–241
Houston Trail (Mt. Mansfield), 225
100-Mile Wilderness, 134–140
map of, 135
huts and lodges
in Adirondack Mountains, 268–271
Maine Huts and Trails, 141–145

in Maine's 100-Mile Wilderness, 134–140
in New Hampshire, 1–4, 53, 103–107, 114
in Vermont, 173–176, 198–200, 202, 214, 231, 254
hypothermia, xxxi

I
icefall, 55
Ippolito, Mark, 263, 265, 276

J
Jackrabbit Trail, 263–267
Jackson Ski Touring Foundation (JSTF), 23–27
Jay Peak Resort, 244
Jay State Forest, 244
Jenkinson, Rick, 38
Jewell Trail (Mt. Washington), 80, 83, 86
Joe Dodge Lodge, 53, 114
Johannsen, Alice, 259, 286
Johannsen, Herman Smith "Jackrabbit," 258–260, 286, 290
John Sherburne Ski Trail. *See* Sherburne Ski Trail
Johns Brook Lodge (JBL), 268–269
Johns Brook Valley, 268–272
map of, 269

K
Katahdin, 148–155
map of, 147
ski history of, 148–150
Katahdin Woods and Waters National Monument, 136
Kendall, Paul, 169, 172
Kimball Ski Trail (Mt. Cardigan), 1–6
King, Thomas Starr, 98
King Ravine (Mt. Adams), 98–102
Klippgen, Per, 293
Klondike Notch (Johns Brook Valley), 272
Konieczny, Rudy, 294

L
Lake Colden, 279–283
Lake Willoughby ski tours, 237–241
Lane, Gardiner, 193–194
Langmuir, Irving, 258–259, 286, 292–293
Laughlin, James, 143
Leave No Trace principles, 301–303

Left Gully (Tuckerman Ravine), 60
Leuchtenberg, Dmitri von, 3, 15
Lincoln Woods Trail (Pemigewasset
  Wilderness), 118
Linscott, Bill, 296–296
The Lip (Tuckerman Ravine), 57, 60
Little Headwall (Tuckerman Ravine), 66
Little Lyford Lodge, 136–137, 140
Little River State Park, 192–197
Lobster Claw (Tuckerman Ravine), 63
locator map, iv–v
lodges. *See* huts and lodges
Long Pond Trail, 140
Loope, P.F., 286–287
Lord, Charlie, 206, 213, xix
Lower Snowfields (Tuckerman Ravine), 66

M
Mahar, Blair, 297
Maine, 123–157
Maine Huts and Trails tour, 141–145
  map of, 142
Maine Woods Initiative, 136
Main Gully (Oakes Gulf), 89–90
Mount Mansfield region, 205–232
  Bruce Trail, 211–216
  Nebraska Notch/Dewey Mountain, 228–232
  Ranch Valley Grand Tour, 216–217
  Skytop Trail, 218–222
  Steeple Trail, 223–227
  Teardrop Trail, 206–210
Maple Villa glade zone, 36–38
Marcy, Mount, 258, 284–290
Marcy Dam, 279–283, 287
Marsh, Sylvester, 94–95
Massachusetts, 291–298
Matt, Toni, 48–49
McCusker, Angus, 167–168
Medawisla Wilderness Lodge, 136–137, 139
Merck Forest, 250–251
Merrill, Al, xxii
Merrill, Perry, 206, xxviii
Merrymeeting Glade (Black Mountain), 133
Mitterskill Ski Area, 16
moderate difficulty ski tours
  in Maine, 123–129, 134–140, 141–145,
    152–153, 155–157
  in New Hampshire, 103–107, 108–110,
    111–113, 114–122

in New York, 263–267, 268–272
in Vermont, 159–163, 218–222, 247–253
Monadnock State park, 121–122
Monroe, Will S., 178
Monroe Brook (Oakes Gulf), 91
Monroe Trail (Camel's Hump), 178–181
Moosalamoo National Recreation Area,
  252–253
Moosilauke, Mount, 7–13
  map of, 8
more difficult ski tours
  in New Hampshire, 4–6, 7–13, 19–22,
    23–27, 28–31, 36–38, 39–42, 67–70,
    76–79
  in New York, 273–278, 279–283
  in Vermont, 164–166, 169–172, 173–176,
    182–185, 192–197, 193, 198–204,
    218–222, 223–227, 228–232, 233–236,
    237–241, 247–249
most difficult ski tours
  in Maine, 130–133
  in Massachusetts, 287–294
  in New Hampshire, 4–6, 14–18, 33–35,
    71–75
  in New York, 271–272, 284–290
  in Vermont, 173–176, 178–181, 186–188,
    206–210, 211–216, 223–227, 237–241,
    242–246
mountaineering judgment, xxxii–xxxiii
mountaineering skills, xxx–xxxiii

N
Nansen, Fridtjof, 258
navigation, xxx–xxxi
Nebraska Notch (Mt. Mansfield), 228–232
New England Ski Museum, 17
New Hampshire, 1–122
New York, 257–290
Noble, Frasier, xxi
North Basin (Baxter State Park), 153–154
Norton, J.R., 177

O
Oakes Gulf (Mt. Washington), 87–91
  map of, 88
Old Camp Trail (Mt. Mansfield), 221, 226
Old Jackson Road (Pinkham Notch), 116
O'Leary, Ed, 193
Olmstead, Frederick Law, 126

Ore Bed Brook Trail (Johns Brook Valley), 271
Osborne, Lithgow, 271
Overland Trail (Mt. Mansfield), 216
overnight accomodations. *See* backcountry shelters; huts and lodges

P

packs, xxix
Paradise Pass (Bolton Backcountry), 190
Parker, Charlie, 293
Peckett, Katharine, xvii, 3, 14–15
Pemetic Mountain (Acadia N.P.), 129
Pemi East Side Trail (Pemigewasset Wilderness), 118 Pemigewasset River tours, 116–118
Pemigewasset Wilderness, 106–107, 116–118
Pemi Traverse, 107
Perkins, Frederick, 271
Phelps Trail (Johns Brook Valley), 269–271
Phillips, Hollis, 13, 48
Phillips, Leonard, 13
Pinkham Notch ski tours, 114–116
Pinkham Notch Visitor Center, 44, 67, 71, 76, 114–116
Pipeline Gully (Great Gulf), 83
Poplar Falls Hut, 144–145
Pote, Winston, 82, 114
Presidential Range, ski trips in, 43–102. *See also* Washington, Mount
Proctor, Charles, 3, 9, 46
Prospect Farm trails (Wildcat Mountain), 26–27
Protect Our Winters, 299

Q

Quimby, Roxanne, 136

R

Ranch Camp (Mt. Mansfield), 213–214, 225
Ranch Valley Grand Tour (Mt. Mansfield), 216–217, 227
Randolph Mountain, 39–42
Ray, Tyler, 32, 41, 168
Richard Taft Trail (Cannon Mountain), 9
Ricker Basin, 193, 195
Right Gully (Tuckerman Ravine), 62–63
Rikert Ski Touring Center, 252
Rives, Sharon, 169

Rochester/Randolph Area Sports Trails Alliance (RASTA), 167–168
Rumford Whitecap Mountain, 130–133
Russell Pond (Baxter State Park), 155

S

Saddle Trail (Baxter State Park), 149, 153–154
St. Louis, Bob, 275
Sargent Mountain (Acadia N.P.), 126–127
Sawyer Pond, 111–113
Schniebs, Otto, 7, 9, 10, 275
Sherburne Ski Trail (Mt. Washington), 76–79
Shoal Pond Trail (Pemigewasset Wilderness), 106–107
Short Line Trail (Mt. Adams), 98–102
Sise, Al, 9, 46
ski equipment, xxvi–xxx
    different ski types, xxvi–xxvii
    evolution of, xxii–xxiii
ski mountaineering-level trails
    in Baxter State Park, 153–155
    Burt and Ammonoosuc Ravines, 92–97
    Great Gulf, 80–86
    King Ravine, 98–102
    Oakes Gulf, 87–91
    Tuckerman Ravine, 56–66
ski poles, xxviii
Ski to Die Club, 261–262, xxiii
Skytop Trail (Mt. Mansfield), 218–222
slope steepness, xxvi
Sluice (Tuckerman Ravine), 62
Smith, Geoff, 261
Snapper Trail (Mt. Moosilauke), 10, 12, xxi
snowboarding, xxiii, xxv–xxvii
snowmobiles, xxvi
South Basin (Baxter State Park), 153
Southeast and East Snowfields (Tuckerman Ravine), 60
splitboards, xxiii, xxv–xxvi
Spruce Goose Ski Trail (Pemigewasset Wilderness), 103–104
Square Ledge Ski Trail (Pinkham Notch), 114, 116
Steeple Trail (Mt. Mansfield), 223–227
Sterling Valley, 233–236
Stirling, Eric, 140
Stowe Mountain Resort ski area, 205, 211, 218, 223

Stowe View Chutes (Bolton Backcountry), 190
Stratton Pond (Vermont), 159–162
Sugar Hill Reservoir, 252–253

T

Taber Gully (Baxter State Park), 154
Taft Trail (Cannon Mountain), 15–16
Taylor Lodge, 231
Teardrop Trail (Mt. Mansfield), 206–210
Thoreau, Henry David, 146, 148
Thunderbolt Ski Runners, 293
Thunderbolt Ski Trail (Mt. Greylock), 291–298
tour ratings, xxiv
Von Trapp, Johannes, 200, 220
Trapp Family Lodge, 198–204, 218, 223
Tucker Brook Trail (Cannon Mountain), 15–18, xxi
Tuckerman Ravine, 44–66
    dharma of, 51–52
    first descents in, 49–50
    frequently asked questions, 52–54
    history of skiing in, 45–50
    maps of, 45, 58–59
    mountain hazards, 54–56
    ski and snowboard routes in, 56–66

U

Underhill, Robert, 149
Underhill Trail (Mt. Mansfield), 216–217, 220, 222
Upper Nanamocomuck Ski Trail, 111

V

Van Hoevenberg Trail (Mt. Marcy), 260, 281, 284–290
Vermont, 159–252

W

Warren, Larry, 143–144
Washington, Mount, 43
    Avalanche Brook Trail, 67–70
    Burt and Ammonoosuc Ravines, 92–97
    Great Gulf trails, 80–86
    Gulf of Slides trails, 71–75
    history of skiing on, xxvii–xxviii
    maps of, 45, 58–59, 68, 72, 77, 81, 88, 93
    Oakes Gulf, 87–91
    Sherburne Ski Trail, 76–79
    Tuckerman Ravine, 44–66
Waste, Connie, 116
Waterman, Guy and Laura, 82, 149
Wells, Ed, 10
West Branch Pond Camps, 137, 139–140
Whiteface Ski Area, 261
Whiteface Ski Trail (Little Whiteface Mountain), 260
Wildcat Valley Trail, 23–27
Williamson, Marcia, 151
Willoughby State Forest, 237–241
Wilson, Joe Pete, xxii
winter camping, xxxii. *See also* backcountry shelters; huts and lodges
Winter Olympics (1932), 259, 286
Woods, Henry, 9
Woodward Mountain Trail, 192–197
Wright Peak Ski Trail, 260, 273–278

Y

Young Catamounts, 194

Z

Zealand Falls Hut tours, 103–107
    map of, 104
Zealand Notch (Pemigewasset Wilderness), 106–107

ABOUT THE AUTHOR

Photo by Ed Ziedins

David Goodman is a bestselling author, broadcaster, skier, investigative journalist, musician, and mountaineer. He writes about a diverse mix of topics, from the outdoors to world politics. His work has appeared in *Outside*, *Mother Jones*, the *New York Times*, *Ski*, *Powder*, *Backcountry*, the *Los Angeles Times*, and other national publications. He also hosts a weekly radio show and podcast, The Vermont Conversation.

Goodman is a three-time winner of the Harold S. Hirsch Award for Excellence in Ski Writing, the highest award of the North American Ski Journalists Association—twice for magazine writing and once for *Classic Backcountry Skiing: A Guide to the Best Ski Tours in New England* (AMC Books, 1989). He is also a recipient of the International Ski History Association's Ullr Award for his writing on ski history. Goodman is the author of twelve books, including four *New York Times* bestsellers that he co-authored with his sister, journalist Amy Goodman: *The Exception to the Rulers*, *Static*, *Standing Up to the Madness*, and *Democracy Now!*

David Goodman is a graduate of Harvard University. He has worked as a mountaineering instructor for Outward Bound. Goodman's travels have taken him to five continents. But his favorite place to explore is still in his backyard, the mountains of the Northeast. He has two children, Ariel and Jasper. He and his wife, Sue Minter, live in Waterbury Center, Vermont. See dgoodman.net for his other writing.

AMC BOOKS UPDATES

AMC Books strives to keep our guidebooks as up-to-date as possible to help you plan safe and enjoyable adventures. If we learn after publishing a book that relevant trails have been relocated or route or contact information has changed, we will post the updated information online. Before you hit the trail, visit outdoors.org/books -maps and click the "Book Updates" tab.

While hiking, if you notice discrepancies with the trip descriptions or maps, or if you find any other errors in this book, please let us know by submitting them to amcbookupdates@outdoors.org or to Books Editor, c/o AMC, 10 City Square, Boston, MA 02129. We will verify all submissions and post key updates each month. AMC Books is dedicated to being a recognized leader in outdoor publishing. Thank you for your participation.

Essential Guide to Winter Recreation

Andrew Vietze

This accessible guide walks readers through planning outdoor winter adventures of all kinds, with practical advice emphasizing preparation, safety, outdoor stewardship, and fun. Whether snowshoeing, skiing, camping, or more, this comprehensive guide includes information on when to go, how to stay warm and dry, how to navigate, where to make camp, how to read the weather, what to eat to stay energized, and other handy skills that will boost cold-weather mastery for beginners and advanced adventurers alike.

$21.95 • 978-1-62842-051-7 • ebook available

White Mountain Winter Recreation Map & Guide

AMC Books

Featuring more than 30 trails maintained for winter skiing and recreation in the Pinkham Notch, Tuckerman Ravine, and Kancamagus areas, this map and guide includes trip descriptions, trailhead access and parking locations, seasonal road closures, safety and avalanche awareness tips, and detailed ski and hiking trails. Waterproof and tear-resistant for years of use on the slopes, this full-color, topographic map is the ultimate guide to backcountry winter recreation in the White Mountains.

$9.95 • 978-1-62842-117-0

Southern New Hampshire Trail Guide, 5th Edition

Compiled and edited by Ken MacGray with Steven D. Smith

This comprehensive trail guide covers New Hampshire hiking trails south of the White Mountain National Forest, including the state's beloved Lakes Region and Seacoast. Every trail description provides turn-by-turn directions, making route finding straightforward and reliable, while suggested hikes feature icons showing kid-friendly trips, scenic views, and more. Whether you're a first-time hiker or an experienced backpacker, this trail guide is a must-have.

$23.95 • 978-1-62842-115-6 • ebook available

Outdoor Adventures Acadia National Park

Jerry and Marcy Monkman

Now with an enhanced focus on recreation, *Outdoor Adventures: Acadia National Park* (formerly *Discover Acadia National Park*) spotlights 50 hiking, biking, and paddling trips for all ability levels. Covering the popular Mount Desert Island, as well as the hidden gems of Isle au Haut and Schoodic Peninsula, this is the definitive guide to enjoying the best of New England's only national park.

$22.95 • 978-1-62842-057-9